EGYPT and SINAI

Eternal Battleground

GREGORY BLAXLAND

EGYPT and SINAI

Eternal Battleground

FUNK & WAGNALLS

NEW YORK

Published by Funk & Wagnalls,
A Division of Reader's Digest Books, Inc.,
by arrangement with Frederick Muller

PRINTED IN THE UNITED STATES OF AMERICA

"And they shall draw their swords against Egypt, and fill the land with the slain."

Book of Ezekiel. xxx. 11.

CONTENTS

	Acknowledgements	*Page* 10
1	The Invaders' Prey (525 B.C.–A.D. 1798)	13
2	The Coming of the French (1798–1800)	21
3	The Coming of the British (1800–11)	29
4	Aly's Empire (1811–49)	44
5	Mastheads through the Desert (1849–74)	52
6	Pride and Consequence (1875–82)	58
7	The Subduing of Arabi (1882)	67
8	The Victors Humbled (1882–5)	86
9	Prestige Restored (1885–1914)	100
10	Through Two Wars (1914–45)	118
11	Withdrawal (1945–7)	140
12	Defeat (1947–50)	148
13	Explosion (1949–52)	160
14	Revolution (1952–3)	173
15	Evacuation (1953–6)	181
16	Outrage (1956)	197
17	Plans Frustrated (1956)	205
18	Ultimatum (1956)	221
19	The Agonized Approach (1956)	233
20	The Soldiers' Return (1956)	249
21	Military Might-Have-Beens	268
22	Farewell Again (1956)	278
23	Balance Sheet (1957–65)	288
	Appendix: Sources	305
	Index	319

Illustrations

between pages

Murad Bey	72–3
Lieutenant-General Sir Ralph Abercromby	72–3
Mohammed Aly	72–3
Ismail Pasha	72–3
Vicompte Ferdinand de Lesseps	72–3
Arabi Pasha	72–3
Lieutenant-General Sir Garnet Wolseley	72–3
Tewfik Pasha	152–3
Evelyn Baring, first Earl of Cromer	152–3
Abbas Hilmi	152–3
Saad Zaghlul	152–3
Field-Marshal Earl Kitchener of Khartoum	152–3
Field-Marshal Viscount Allenby	152–3
King Farouk I	152–3
Miles Wedderburn Lampson, first Baron of Killearn	152–3
Mustafa El Nahas Pasha	232–3
Lieutenant-General Sir George Erskine	232–3
Gamal Abdel Nasser, acclaimed on his return to Cairo after announcing the seizure of the Suez Canal Company	232–3
Sir Anthony Eden leaving No. 10 Downing Street after issuing his ultimatum in October 1956	232–3
General Hakim Amer	232–3
The Allied British and French commanders at Gamil airfield in November 1956	232–3

MAPS

page

Lower Egypt and the Sinai	12
Alexandria and Rosetta	30
Upper Egypt and the Northern Sudan	88
Port Said	250

ACKNOWLEDGEMENTS

I ATTEMPT IN this book to bring the Suez crisis of 1956 into relationship with previous struggles for dominion over Egypt. It was an idea long entertained, but I doubt whether it would have reached fulfilment if I had not met Mr. J. R. Tillard and obtained from him facts and thoughts on the Suez crisis hitherto unrevealed or disregarded. It was under the stimulus of our exchanges that I embarked on this book.

My own experience of Egypt is limited to a month in military transit shortly after the Second World War. However, one need never lack information on the affairs of the country, and the 103 published works that I consulted (apart from newspapers) form only a fraction of the whole. The appendix, headed "Sources", shows the range of the material used, and my thanks go to those who so industriously produced it, the librarians at the Ministry of Defence (Central and Army), the Foreign Office, the Kent County Library, the Canterbury Library, the Folkestone Library, and most of all those at the Institution of Royal Engineers, Chatham, where although not a member of the Royal Corps I received most painstaking aid.

I also had discussion or correspondence with sixty people who were closely concerned either with the British occupation of Egypt or with the troops' return to do battle, over which Whitehall keeps the cloak of secrecy so zealously fastened that the investigator is forced to rely almost entirely on unofficial sources.

I owe a very special debt to two men who not only put their immense knowledge of Egyptian affairs at my disposal but were also kind enough to correct and criticize my drafts. One of them, whose life's work was spent in Egypt or the Sudan, must remain anonymous. The other was closely involved as a soldier in all the British Army's dealings with Egypt in the post-war years: Brigadier J. H. S. Lacey, C.B.E., formerly of the Royal Engineers.

Many others went to great trouble in providing me with information and views, and again some of them prefer to hide behind anonymity. It would be invidious to pick out a few, and I wish here merely to express my gratitude to them all. In the appendix I have indicated what help I received chapter by chapter, naming my principal informants (unless they asked otherwise) and pointing to the contributions made.

Publishers to whom I am indebted for permission to quote extracts are: Cassell (Sydney A. Moseley's *With Kitchener in Cairo*, Winston Churchill's *The Second World War, Vol I.* and Sir Anthony Eden's *Full Circle*), Chapman and Hall (Ferdinand de Lesseps's *Recollections of Forty Years*), Chatto and Windus (Elizabeth Monroe's *Britain's Moment in the Middle East*), Eyre and Spottiswoode (Winston Churchill's *The River War*), Hamish Hamilton (J. Christopher Herold's *Bonaparte in Egypt*), Hodder and Stoughton and the Executors of the late Lady Cecil (Lord Edward Cecil's *The Leisure of an Egyptian Official* and Glubb Pasha's *A Soldier With the Arabs*), Hogarth Press and Dov Joseph (Dov Joseph's *The Faithful City*), Hutchinson (Terence Robertson's *Crisis—The Inside Story of The Suez Conspiracy*), Macmillan (Hon. J. W. Fortescue's *History of the British Army* and John Morley's *Life of Gladstone*), John Murray (Gordon Waterfield's *Layard of Nineveh* and Sir Philip Magnus's *Kitchener—Portrait of an Imperialist*), Oxford University Press (P. G. Elgood's *Egypt and The Army*), and Her Majesty's Stationery Office (Colonel J. F. Maurice's *Military History of the Campaign of* 1882). I also thank the Royal United Service Institution and General Sir Gordon MacMillan for permission to quote from the latter's article, *The Evacuation of Palestine*.

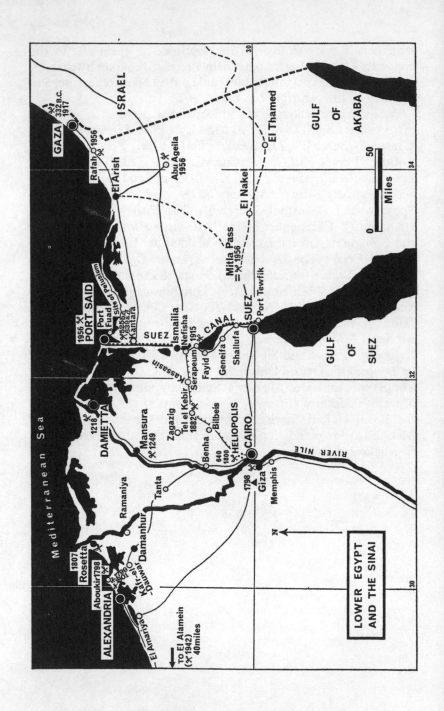

LOWER EGYPT AND THE SINAI

Mediterranean Sea

ISRAEL

GULF OF AKABA

GAZA
332 B.C.
1917
Rafah 1956
El Arish
Abu Ageila 1956
El Thamed
El Nakel
Mitla Pass 1956

PORT SAID 1956
Port Fuad
Site of Pelusium
1850
1859
Kantara
SUEZ
Ismailia
Nefisha 1915
SUEZ CANAL
Port Tewfik
SUEZ

Serapeum
Kassasin
Fayid
Geneifa
Shallufa

GULF OF SUEZ

DAMIETTA
1218

Mansura
1249

Zagazig
Tel el Kebir 1882
Bilbeis

Benha
640 1800
HELIOPOLIS
CAIRO

RIVER NILE

1798
Giza
Memphis

Ramaniya
Tanta

Damanhur

Rosetta 1807
Aboukir 1798
Kafr el Dauwar
1799 1801

N

ALEXANDRIA
El Amariya

TO El Alamein (1942) 40 miles

50
Miles
0

CHAPTER ONE

The Invaders' Prey

(525 B.C.–A.D. 1798)

IT WAS A friendly and informal parting. Dressed in his workaday khaki drill, Brigadier John Lacey said a smiling good-bye to his three companions and stepped into a launch off the quay of the former Navy House, Port Said. Thus departed the last commander of British Troops in Egypt, watched only by a chubby little Egyptian colonel of police and by two Englishmen, the consul and a shipping agent. The launch chugged out to a ship moored in the mouth of the Suez Canal, the chartered tank landing ship, *Evan Gibb*, inelegant but strangely imposing in the fleeting orange glow radiated by the sun as it climbed the roof line of Port Fuad. Preceded by an army table, on which Britain's last foothold in Egypt had been signed away, the Brigadier climbed aboard to join the seventy-eight officers and men already embarked, the remnant of an army that had been in occupation for seventy-four years. There were neither cheers nor jeers as their ship steamed into the Mediterranean. The inhabitants of Port Said yawned, stretched or went on sleeping, unaware that the day that dawned, June 13, 1956, was the one for which they had clamoured so long.

Not until 8 a.m. did the ascent of the green and white flag of Egypt up the staff of Navy House bring the joyous message home to the people. The town was in an uproar of delight. The British had gone, and to hasten them on their way the Egyptian press thundered their valedictory insults. "Egypt has ended her suffering", rejoiced Cairo's oldest paper, *Al Ahram*. Others preferred to dwell more on the discomfiture of the erstwhile tormentors with

13

such offerings as, "With their tails between their legs, the cur dogs slink away."

Britain might have expected congratulation. The withdrawal had been completed five days ahead of the dateline stipulated in the agreement signed twenty months previously, and furthermore it was undeniable that, thanks to the aid and guidance supplied by Britain, the country which her soldiers left in 1956 was infinitely more prosperous than the one they had invaded in 1882. Experience showed that gratitude could never be expected for such favours; even so, this vulgar gloating over the departure of a well-meaning mentor, if no longer a friend, was not easy to digest with dignity. Official reaction amounted to no more than a sigh of pained resignation. The less inhibited, such as leader writers of the *Daily Express*, could give full vent to their indignation, though the many thousands with knowledge of Egypt, gained in the Forces, were content to let it pass with, "What else d'you expect from those Gyppos?"

What few people realized, few even among the Egyptians, was that there was deeper cause for emotional outburst than the ending of a military occupation only seventy-four years old. For the first time since 525 B.C. no flag or banner flew in Egypt displaying the authority of a foreign overlord.

525 B.C. was the year of the conquest by Cambyses, the Persian, and it brought to an end the brief dynasty of the Saite Pharaohs, who had sought to revive some of the glories of Ancient Egypt which even then were obscured by the dust of some two thousand years of conquest and decay. It was a thousand years since the Pharaohs of the eighteenth dynasty had embarked on military adventures which gained them brief tenure of an empire from Ethiopia to the Euphrates, perhaps 850 since Moses had brought the tribe of Israel on its remarkable march of escape through the Sinai desert, and about a hundred since the first attempt had been started to connect the Nile and the Red Sea by canal. The Chaldeans, under Nebuchadnezzar, had recently established military ascendancy over Syria and Egypt, drawing from the vindictive Ezekiel the gloating cry, "O son of man wail for the multitude of Egypt", and once Cambyses had defeated them the road to Egypt lay open. He reduced the coastal fortress of Pelusium (near the site of Port Said), and advanced up the limb of the Nile which used to debouch there. Apparently without opposition, he occupied the capital, Memphis, on the western bank by the Great Pyramid.

The Persians were harsh rulers and found easy victims in the indolent peasants of the Nile who throughout the twenty-six dynasties of the Pharaohs had been so intimately acquainted with the feel of the lash. The enervating climate by the river and the abundant fertility of the soil it waters combined to deprive them of any spirit of adventure and they asked no more than to haul up their bucket of water and cultivate their plot. Hopelessly un-military, they were yet hardy and stoical people, and it was their pride through the ages that the taxes demanded by greedy con-querors, lured to their land by its riches and ancient glories, must be eked from them by force of the whip, across back, head, or soles of the feet according to the whim of the extortioner. And every so often they have turned and surprised their rulers with violent acts of defiance, for they are as volatile as they are shiftless, friendly at heart but consumed with hatred of authority. The Persians soon found this out.

It was a happy day for the Egyptians when in the autumn of 332 B.C. Alexander the Great and his Macedonian soldiers bat-tered down the great wall of Gaza and slew all its Persian and Syrian defenders as the culminating act of a two-month siege. This completed Alexander's victories over the Persians and he had as easy a passage into Egypt as Cambyses, taking the same route accompanied by his fleet—and indeed there was no other feasible access, except by a more westerly branch of the Nile. Nor, for that matter, was there any part of Egypt worth possessing other than the delta of the river and its thin, rich strip, almost a thousand miles long, which constitute a mere three or four per cent of an otherwise barren land.

Alexander brought a brief phase of enlightened despotism, showed tolerance for the religion of the people, and founded and richly ornamented the great port which bears his name and which he made his capital, bringing brisk trade from the adjacent shores of Africa, Asia and Europe. But the Ptolemies, who inherited this part of his empire, quickly reverted to tyranny and misrule, indul-ging in orgies of display at the expense of the people. In the second century B.C. the Romans intruded to save the tottering Ptolemy dynasty from Syrian aggression and Egypt virtually became their vassal. Cleopatra, having gained her throne with aid from Caesar, held the Romans off from full possession of her land by the lure of her body, and this led to schism within the Roman Empire and to the annihilation of the fleet of Antony, her lover, after she had

16

withdrawn her ships when the Battle of Actium reached its crisis. Again the invaders, advancing leisurely along the coastline from Syria, met scarcely any resistance in Egypt. When Octavian's legions stood before Alexandria the Egyptian forces deserted to them, and the Romans entered the city and found Antony and Cleopatra dead.

The year was 30 B.C. and it was the start for Egypt of 670 years under Roman rule. Harsh demands were made on her granaries to feed the Imperial legions, but for the most part it was a period of unwonted good order under the influence of which trade prospered, notably at Alexandria, and the immigrant population of Greeks, Jews, Lebanese and Italians grew in size. The people were initially allowed freedom at least in their religion and became staunch Christians. Their faith brought them harsh persecution in the third century A.D. and later, after the Byzantine remnant of the Roman Empire had embraced Christianity, they were denounced and outlawed as heretics for sticking to their Coptic belief in the single nature of God. After a sudden invasion by the Persians and their subsequent ejection, the faltering hand of Byzantium fell yet more harshly on the heretics, and in her misery under European domination Egypt was ready, as the slave she was in the intercontinental market, to be claimed by the East.

The Arabs came in 639, seven years after the death of the Prophet Mohammed, when four thousand cameleers under Amr Ibn El As swept in by the familiar invasion route from Syria on the crest of their new-found religious fervour. Pelusium, crumbling away without her river outlet, which had dried up, fell after a month's siege. Amr then took the desert route through the site of Tel-el-Kebir, his force swollen by many Bedouin. Tough resistance was encountered at the fortress of Babylon, near the site of Cairo, which did not fall until Good Friday, 641, when with the aid of six thousand reinforcements Amr's men at last scaled its massive walls, having previously enticed the Romans to battle at Heliopolis and defeated them there. Alexandria followed, capitulating on the arrival of the Moslem fanatics although garrisoned by fifty thousand Byzantine troops, backed by a fleet in the harbour. A surprise counter-attack regained the city three years later, but only briefly, and by 646 the millennium (all but) of Greek or Roman rule was past recall.

The warlike Moslems at first kept themselves apart from the people and made no attempt to impose their religion on the faithful Copts. But the simplicity of Islam appealed to the Egyptians, and the Moslems gradually gained conversions, encouraged by an edict from the Caliph which allowed them to acquire land and wives outside Mecca. Persecution of Christians by discriminatory taxation quickened the flow, until at last the Copts became the minority group they are today, preponderating only in remote districts of Upper Egypt and in clerical and financial posts in the cities, aptitude for which did not earn them popularity. Yet the Arabs, though they left their mark on the population more deeply than any of their predecessors, were poor rulers, becoming ever more rapacious, and their neglect brought famine and dire poverty to a habitually oppressed people. "Milk till the udder is dry", commanded one Caliph, giving unusually candid expression to the conqueror's eternally predatory instinct.

The next invasion came from the West, launched by the heretic descendants of Fatima, daughter of Mohammed, whose empire expanded right cross Africa, from the Atlantic to Libya. Their first two attempts to invade Egypt were repulsed with heavy loss, but in 969 their ambitious general, Gohar, marched in almost unopposed and rapidly took possession of all Egypt. The country acquired new stature, new influence. Gohar built himself a new capital, the city of Cairo, established the Fatimid Caliphate in great splendour, and made it the centre of an empire which again extended to the Euphrates but withered and rotted in the course of the next two hundred years.

In 1097 Jerusalem fell to the Christian counter offensive and the Crusaders established their kingdom. As the power of the Fatimids declined, a strange struggle for possession of Egypt developed between the Christian King Amalric of Jerusalem and the Kurdish general, Shirkuh, whose mercenaries were known as Saracens, being in the pay of Syria. Both were in turn invited to the aid of the Fatimid ruler Shawar against the other, and at one stage, in 1168, Amalric occupied Cairo, while Shirkuh held Alexandria. Amalric withdrew, hoping to lure Shirkuh back towards Syria, but was himself outsmarted, shut out of Cairo and forced by Shirkuh's men to make swift retreat. Having saved the Fatimid dynasty, Shirkuh promptly contrived its overthrow. He died almost as promptly and was succeeded by his nephew Saladin, who proclaimed himself Sultan of Egypt. This was the chivalrous scourge of the Crusaders who, in 1187, recaptured Jerusalem for Islam with his Saracens.

The Crusaders twice sought to regain the Holy City by the devious method of invading Egypt. The first attempt, made in 1218, would have succeeded if they had been content to remain in Damietta, which they captured after a ferocious battle. So highly did the Saracens value this port that they offered Jerusalem in exchange, but in a surge of confidence the Crusaders decided to advance on Cairo. They were stranded by the Saracens' flooding of the Nile and forced to capitulate.

The second attempt was made by King Louis IX of France—the good St. Louis—who brought a great army to Cyprus, including an English contingent under the Earl of Salisbury, cousin of King Henry III. In May 1249, 1,800 ships are said to have set sail for Egypt, and although only seven hundred of them reached Damietta the sight was sufficient to put the Saracen garrison to flight. The remainder of the fleet, blown to Syria, did not arrive until October, and only then did Louis decide that the advance on Cairo should begin. Great difficulty was encountered in crossing a tributary of the Nile near Mansura, but a ford was eventually found. Once on the far bank the Count of Artois insulted the Earl of Salisbury, with the result that they both flung their men precipitately into battle, before King Louis had made the crossing. The Saracens were ready for them. The Earl was killed in a mad urge to display his valour, the Count was drowned trying to escape, and the King arrived just in time to salve what he could from the wreck of defeat. His lines both of advance and retreat were barred, and after a few months' vain probing he was forced by hunger to surrender. It was a bad time to be captured, for Egypt was falling under the heel of crueller tyrants who extorted a large ransom before Louis and his fellow captives could be released from the misery of their imprisonment. It is perhaps not so surprising that 716 years should pass before the French and English again felt inclined to combine in an attempt on Egypt.

A string of murders, as complex as macabre, brought an end to the rule of Saladin's descendants in this year 1250. Its perpetrators were the soldier slaves they imported, the Mamelukes, those redoubtable men-at-arms from Turkestan and the Caucasus who could gain freedom by promotion and with it the right to grow a beard. It was the start of a long period of gangster rule which nonetheless brought lustre to Egypt in its earlier years. The mighty Beybars, who seized power in 1260, was a man of wide achievement. He won glory as a soldier by halting the advance of the

Mongols who had swept into Asia Minor under the impetus of the late Jengis Khan's inspiration; he made Cairo a holy city of Islam by retrieving the acknowledged Abbasid Caliph from the clutches of the Mongols; he brought prosperity for his country by the canals and irrigation dykes he constructed; and he won cultural fame by the remarkable beauty of the mosques and palaces he had built. Inevitably the lustre eroded under the proud and selfish successors of this brilliant despot.

The arrogance of the Mamelukes led to their submission to the Ottoman Turks, the tribe that had been pushed westwards by the conquests of Jengis Khan and expanded into Europe, capturing Constantinople in 1453. Ghuri, the old Mameluke Sultan who had no use for any such modern device as cannon, provoked the anger of the Turkish Sultan, Selim, and did battle with him near Aleppo, whither Beybars had extended Mameluke rule. Outflanked and outmanœuvred, the Mamelukes crumpled before the Turkish guns and disintegrated in a shemozzle of charging and bolting horses, with Ghuri trampled to death beneath them. Having allowed the Mamelukes time to divide between themselves in dispute of the succession, Selim entered Egypt in 1517 and laid siege to Cairo. The defenders were soon intimidated into submission and Ghuri's successor Tuman was executed with sadistic ceremony. Selim purchased the title of Caliph from its degenerate holder and moved the treasures and teachers of the Caliphate to Constantinople. Egypt had become part of the Ottoman Empire, but Selim wisely made no attempt to hold the Mamelukes permanently in thrall and demanded only that annual tribute be paid to his viceroy, the Pasha.

The country was divided into twenty-four districts, each under a Mameluke bey who was a master in the art of extortion from a people seemingly bled white already. The only other arts they practised, and with passionate zeal, were combat and display. They combined the two in dazzling symphony. Dressed in gorgeous robes and turbans, which glittered with jewels and gold embroideries, they rode magnificent Arab stallions and would gallop into battle discharging musket and several pairs of jewel-handled pistols (which would be tossed aside for the foot-soldiers, mere bearers, to pick up and reload), hurling javelins, and finally wielding their scimitars, all in the course of a single charge. Decapitation at a single blow was the basic attainment aspired to by the fledgeling, and the expert aimed at dual decapitation by slashing with a dazzling scimitar in each hand while gripping the reins with his knees. It was not to be expected that the practitioners of such skills should feel anything but contempt towards the Egyptian peasants —"that pack of women", as Shirkuh, the first mercenary invader, had called them—or have any thought for their welfare. The peasants groaned under the oppression imposed on them by their own military incapacity, and in their despair surrendered to sloth.

The country fell into a horrifying state of lawlessness and decay. The canals lay dry, the desert regained conquests of irrigation, and the roads were so infested by Bedouin bandits that the Mamelukes found a profitable side business in providing escorts for travellers. Wild dogs and villains roamed the streets of the cities and no European dared go out at night, other than the semi-criminal, parasitic type already well established in business. The British Government thought the outlook so bleak that in 1796 they withdrew their Consul. Two particularly rascally tyrants held Egypt by the throat: Murad Bey, the mighty man-at-arms, with wide blond beard and flashing eye, and the more elderly, less imposing but no less crafty Ibrahim Bey. For a time they had defied the authority of Turkey and thrown out the Pasha, but they had been sufficiently brought to heel to re-admit him and he lived in the Citadel, a sort of captive tax-collector.

It was this destitute land that sparked fresh ambitions in the restless mind of General Bonaparte. By the end of 1797 he had completed the conquests that took him across Italy as far as the Ionian Islands. He was 28 years old. He had reached the land of Alexander; he, Bonaparte, would be just as great.

CHAPTER TWO

The Coming of the French

(1798–1800)

THE NEW TASK assigned Bonaparte was the invasion of England. He reported to the Directorate of the Republic that it was no longer feasible; Egypt offered a brighter prospect. It so happened that a similar recommendation had been made by the new Foreign Secretary, Talleyrand. His proposal, made a week before Bonaparte's, was based on a plan prepared as far back as 1777. Its purpose was to make Egypt a French colony, in compensation for those she had lost in the Seven Years War. France had special influence in the Middle East. Pressure by Louis XIV had squeezed the Capitulations out of the Ottoman Sultan, conferring privileges on foreign nationals in his Empire, and France had since then been tacitly recognized as the mother protectress of Christian churches. Enmity with Britain made it desirable to strengthen her influence and to spread it eastwards in support of the rebel, Tippoo Sahib, in India. The Directorate presented their grand design on April 12, 1798. Bonaparte was to seize Malta and Egypt, disrupt British influence in the East, drive a canal through the Isthmus of Suez (a project for long considered and periodically attempted), improve the lot of the Egyptian people, and at the same time maintain good relations with the Turkish Government, the Sublime Porte.

An expedition of four hundred ships, fifty-five thousand troops and a civilian army of scientists, doctors, biologists, sociologists, archaeologists and engineers assembled with amazing speed. They left Toulon on May 19, duly conquered Malta, and arrived off Alexandria on July 1, where their appearance caused the despatch of a message to Murad Bey in Cairo: "My Lord, the fleet which has just appeared is immense. One can see neither its beginning nor its end. For the love of God and of his Prophet, send us fighting men." Fighting men had in fact been there only two days earlier. Admiral Nelson's squadron had sailed in and at once sailed off to Crete in urgent quest: a week previously his ships had overtaken the French during a foggy night and sailed almost through them without knowing it.

Constant sea-sickness had so emaciated Bonaparte's soldiers that even standing was an effort. On the night of his arrival he landed them at the fishing village of Marabout, eight miles to the west of Alexandria, and led them towards the city at dawn next morning, unsupported by artillery, unfed and with no water. Parched and exhausted, they struggled through the sand, enveloped the city and fell upon its walls in face of a bombardment of a few cannon-balls, many bullets and quite as many rocks. After a brief, sharp struggle, in which two divisional generals were wounded, they were inside, fighting savagely through narrow, squalid streets and falling with demented fury on anything that might hold water. "I can assure you that it was thirst which inspired our soldiers in the capture of Alexandria", wrote a lieutenant who took part.

Just before noon Bonaparte received a delegation at Pompey's Pillar, outside the city walls, and accepted the surrender of the decayed and bedraggled city, shrivelled in population to a mere ten thousand. Having exhibited his sense of justice by ordering a French soldier to be shot on the spot for the offence of taking a dagger from "a peaceful Arab", he handed copies of his proclamation to his dazed submissives. It said in effect that he came as the servant of Allah and friend of the Ottoman Sultan with the sole purpose of liberating the people of Egypt from "that gang of slaves, purchased in Georgia and the Caucasus, [which] has tyrannized over the most beautiful region of the world".

The march on Cairo began on the evening of the following day, July 3, long before unloading was complete. Four divisions were to march due south, joining the Nile sixty miles distant, while a fifth was to march along the coast to capture Rosetta, at the river's mouth. Bonaparte, as usual, was in a hurry, his haste aggravated by fear of the flooding of the Nile, due in August. He had wrongly assumed that there would be water in the canals and had not bothered to provide his troops with canteens or to modify their normal marching dress of thick serge coat, breeches, gaiters and heavy equipment. His neglect caused hundreds of them to die, some merely from thirst, others by balls from their own muskets, the sole means of escape from torment, others at the hands of marauding Bedouin who eagerly followed the withering columns. The remainder formed hollow square and somehow staggered on, "crying", as Lieutenant Desvernois recorded, "and asking what wrong they have done to be led like this into the desert to die". Gradually the wells became less scarce, the mirages less frequent. When the troops reached the Nile, after six days' marching, they broke ranks and threw themselves into it.

The first battle against the Mamelukes, fought at Shubra Kit on July 13, was indecisive. Bonaparte advanced his divisions at dawn and halted them in square to await the assault. He had, by some magic power of communication, steeled his troops for battle, and their fire was further roused by the strains of the Marseillaise, which he ordered the bands to play. The appearance of the enemy amazed these sophisticated soldiers skilled in the modern science of war. In the words of Desvernois: "In the background, the desert under the blue sky; before us, the beautiful Arabian horses, richly harnessed, snorting, neighing, prancing gracefully and lightly under their martial riders, who are covered with dazzling arms, inlaid with gold and precious stones. Their costumes are brilliantly colourful; their turbans are surmounted by aigret feathers, and some wear gilded helmets. They are armed with sabres, lances, maces, spears, rifles, battle axes, and daggers, and each has three pairs of pistols. . . . This spectacle produced a vivid impression on our soldiers by its novelty and richness. From that moment on their thoughts were set on booty."

The Mamelukes were equally amazed. For three hours they did nothing but circle the extraordinary bristling squares. They then tried a few disjointed charges, but did not persevere in face of the deadly grapeshot and musket fire which the squares emitted, and soon withdrew in bewilderment. Their supporting flotilla of seven gunboats, manned by Greeks, was very much more successful. The French flotilla, with a number of eminent civilian passengers on board, was blown far ahead of the army. Three of its five ships were soon knocked out, and they all might have been destroyed if a lucky round had not hit the magazine of the Mamelukes' flagship and sent her sky high. The result was panicked flight on land and sea.

Along rutted camel-tracks, the French continued their march up the Nile's west bank, much oppressed by heat-stroke, lameness and diarrhoea. The Mamelukes waited for them outside Cairo. Murad (whose summer palace was on that side) was on the west bank of the Nile with several thousand horsemen and many thousand foot-soldiers, or attendants, including a force of Albanian Turks; Ibrahim (whose palace was on that side) was on the Cairo bank with a rather smaller force; connecting them were the ships of the flotilla. The French, twenty-five thousand strong, began their approach before daylight on July 21 and made a wide right hook so that their axis was at right angles to the river. To their right rose the magic forms of the Pyramids, clearly visible above the haze, though nine miles distant. Ahead was the glittering line of Murad's cavalry, their backs to the river and their right resting on the fortified village of Embaba, held by the Turks and some conscripted ruffians. Beyond stood the curvaceous outline of Cairo, mystic and strange. "Soldiers, forty centuries look down on you," Bonaparte said he told his men. Whether or not his message reached them, the setting surely inspired a sense of destiny in these hitherto jaded soldiers, however fierce the midday sun.

Bonaparte advanced his five divisons in echelon from the right, that is in graduated formation, the right leading, with the object of cutting Murad's horsemen off from his infantry. The issue hinged on the ability of Desaix's division, the right-hand spearhead, to withstand the Mameluke assault. It was made with devastating speed—there was no probing this time—but the division just managed to form square, and though the Mamelukes threw their horses at them with reckless fury, sometimes turning and pulling them over backwards on to the infantry, they could achieve no more than a few dents, made by dead horses, in exchange for fearful losses. Many times the pattern was repeated, until at last Bonaparte's left-hand divisions were able to reduce the village of Embaba without fear of cavalry intervention, while Ibrahim's men blinked helplessly into sand clouds blown across the river. There was a headlong flight into the fast-flowing Nile, drowning being preferred to a fate at the hands of the demon Frenchmen, but Murad escaped southward with some two thousand Mamelukes, having first made a mighty blaze of his fleet, which added fantasy to the scene deep into the night.

The French were left to reap at leisure the richest harvest of booty ever found on a battlefield, for not only did the Mamelukes carry into battle their armouries of bejewelled weapons but thousands of gold pieces too. The Bedouin also reaped a rich harvest, plundering the fugitives who throughout the night streamed eastwards, taking all the wealth they could carry out of Cairo which itself was in the grip of voracious marauders. Glory formed a small fraction of the gains won at the Battle of the Pyramids.

The French entered Cairo next night, greeted only by the ululations of the women who, like the remainder of its 300,000 inhabitants, hid behind barred doors. Bonaparte reported, "It would be difficult to find a richer land and a more wretched, ignorant and brutish people." Still, he set about improving their lot by setting up his Institute of scientists and scholars, and he sought to prove his mandate from Allah by appointing a divan, or council, of the priest sheikhs of Al Azhar and was only with difficulty persuaded not to wear turban and caftan to preside over them. Thankful though they were not to be plundered by these strange foreigners, the Cairenes were unimpressed by their advances.

Meanwhile, on August 1, Britain had made armed intervention in the affairs of Egypt, and in a brilliant, spectacular manner. Watched by a handful of appreciative Bedouin and by eight thousand gaping French sailors, Admiral Nelson's squadron of fourteen battleships appeared over the horizon and with the aid of a strong following wind swept down on the French fleet, at anchor in Aboukir Bay, like hounds in full cry, each ship vying with her neighbour to be first in at the kill. Admiral Brueys thought his line of thirteen battleships was protected by shoals on the landward side, but without hesitation the British closed on either side and by advantageous positioning brought their guns to bear with deadly effect. The French fought to the last far into the night, the climax coming when Brueys' flagship, already a flaming furnace, blew up with a frightening explosion which stunned all guns into a ten minutes' silence. Next day two French battleships and two frigates slunk away, leaving the battered but still floating British ships with what remained of the others; 1,700 Frenchmen had been killed against 218 British. "The Battle of the Nile" Nelson named this victory, vying with Bonaparte and his Pyramids in grandiloquence. It was fought about midway between the river mouth and Alexandria.

The main effects of this victory, apart from the boost it gave to the morale of the British people, were to strengthen Turkey's opposition to the French seizure of her possession and to persuade the Directorate that their Army of Egypt must work out its own salvation. Ruffin, the French chargé d'affaires at Constantinople, had tried so hard to convince the Turks of France's good intentions. On September 2, he was most hospitably received by a group of Ministers, told that the French presence in Egypt, the "navel of Islam", could no longer be tolerated, and was ceremoniously escorted to the most inhospitable Seven Towers prison. War was declared a fortnight later.

Bonaparte did not appear in the least perturbed. He continued to express his devotion to Allah and the Egyptian people, even after the October rising, when the Cairene mob used the pretext of rage against the grasping infidel to indulge in an orgy of murder and looting, and such was the resistance that Bonaparte was forced to bombard and storm the Mosque Al Azhar in a two-day battle which inevitably ended with its desecration by French troops. By a judicious combination of public clemency and private executions he succeeded in restoring discipline and morale in the city. Yet the Egyptians, with the perversity of masochists, still evinced a preference for the tyranny of the beys to the liberalism of the French. Murad meanwhile was taking Desaix on a thrilling but abortive chase all the way to Aswan and back to the Pyramids, while Ibrahim had taken refuge in Syria. Facing up at last to the reality of war with Turkey, Bonaparte set off to invade Syria early next year, 1799.

This adventure was not a success. Stubborn resistance was encountered at Jaffa, on the collapse of which Bonaparte had his 2,500 prisoners systematically shot over the Easter week-end, sending a message meanwhile to Ahmed Pasha, governor of Acre, his next objective: "Since God gives me victory, I wish to follow his example and be merciful and compassionate, not only towards the people but also towards its rulers." Mercy was a joke word for Ahmed. He preferred to be known as Djezzar, or Butcher, a title proudly won for his services in eliminating the rivals of a former employer, the late Aly Bey of Egypt. He had good reason to chuckle, for though the walls of Acre had stood unrepaired since Saladin defended them against Richard Coeur de Lion, he had a strong garrison and an invaluable asset in the support of two English battleships commanded by the dashing and eccentric Sir Sidney Smith. Bonaparte's siege artillery, coming up by sea, was sent to the bottom; his soldiers, harshly diminished by plague, were hurled up the ramparts and hurled down again; and for the first time in his career his resolve had to give way to the tenacity of enemy soldiers who were as eager to evade the fate of their colleagues at Jaffa as to placate the avid Butcher, insatiable in his demands for French heads to be laid at his feet. After nearly two months' pounding, Bonaparte withdrew his stricken, ragged army and returned to Cairo to stage a victory march which fooled no one.

The Turks now tried their hand at invasion. They landed in Aboukir Bay on July 15, with Smith in close support, reduced Fort Aboukir, 15 miles from Alexandria, and prepared defensive positions around it, hoping that Murad and his Mamelukes might turn up to join them. Bonaparte himself was about to fall on Murad back at the Pyramids. Dropping this project, he concentrated a force of ten thouand at Aboukir with lightning speed, and at dawn on July 25 the Turks, superior in numbers though they were, were being fast driven from their three defence lines by an inspired infantry and cavalry assault. They took to the sea, though few could swim. Yet fewer reached the ships. Among them was a lieutenant from the Macedonian seaport of Kavalla who was to achieve as much for Egypt as that former Macedonian, Alexander. His name was Mohammed Aly, and, held by the seat of his pantaloons, he was pulled out of the water, so it was said, by a British sailor.

Bonaparte returned to Cairo to celebrate the Feast of the Prophet. A few days later, on August 18, he slipped quietly away with a few trusted staff officers and the civilian chief of the Institute. Before dawn on August 23 he sailed in a frigate from near Alexandria and slid homewards through the British blockade. It was not that he regarded the Army of Egypt as doomed, but merely that there was more scope for his ambition elsewhere.

Without confrontation he bequeathed his command to General Kléber, together with long instructions. A fine soldierly figure, forthright and demonstrative, Kléber was furious. He could see no future for the Army of Egypt and opened peace negotiations with Turkey. The Turks were encouraged to advance from Syria and invest the port of El Arish, where the French garrison, choosing to mutiny rather than resist, threw out ropes to help the Turks up the ramparts, a service for which they were all massacred. Undeterred, Kléber continued to negotiate and on January 28, 1800, terms were agreed between himself, the Grand Vizier of Turkey, and Sir Sidney Smith, self-appointed envoy extraordinary for the British, under which the French were guaranteed a safe passage back to France. But instead of the congratulations which he expected, Smith received chilling rebuff from his superior, Admiral Lord Keith; the British Government could countenance no agreement. A letter was sent to Kléber demanding unconditional surrender. Kléber made reply to his troops: "Soldiers, the only answer to such insolence is victory: prepare yourselves for battle."

The Turks were now at Bilbeis, on the Delta's edge, some thirty miles from Cairo. They sauntered on almost to Heliopolis where, on the evening of March 20, Kléber's men fell on them just as the Grand Vizier decided that they had had sufficient exertion for one day. Outflanked from the direction of the river, they were forced into headlong and chaotic flight right out of Egypt. With them, hard pressed to keep up, went a British officer, the first apparently to see battle on Egyptian soil. He belonged to the British military mission and his name was Captain Thomas Lacey, a kinsman of Brigadier Lacey, whose departure brought the British occupation to an end, and like him an officer of the Royal Engineers.

Not all the Turks took flight. As the Grand Vizier hastened away from his elated, over-confident pursuers, his son slipped round the battlefied with a strong force of cavalry and seized Cairo. There was a month's horror, of murder, chaos, siege, bombardment and assault, before the ravaged city was regained by the French. By now, far too late, the British Government had agreed to accept the evacuation terms after all.

CHAPTER THREE

The Coming of the British

(1800–11)

ALTHOUGH HENRY DUNDAS, Minister for War in Pitt's Tory
Government, appreciated the strategic importance of Egypt, it was
not until the autumn of 1800 that he was able to convince his
colleagues of the need to eject the French by force. The instructions for the invasion, so far from conveying concept of grand
design, made Lieutenant-General Sir Ralph Abercromby, Commander-in-Chief in the Mediterranean, sigh. The war experiences
of this scholarly and humane old Scot, 67 years old, had added
cynicism to his native wariness but had not diminished his loyalty.
Twice he had held command in disastrous expeditions to Europe,
both of which ended in evacuation, and twice again, in the West
Indies and in Ireland, he had been driven to submit his resignation
by the inadequacies of the troops assigned to him. Since taking up
command at Gibraltar, he had received a stream of haphazard
instructions for tasks as impractical as they were disjointed. Now
he had to conquer Egypt with fifteen thousand men, with vague
prospect of aid from the Turks and from a small force from India.

The Government had no political designs on Egypt. The
soldiers' task was merely to remove the French and restore the
status quo, and so easy did it appear from London that it was anticipated that it would be accomplished before the following summer, when Abercromby could release most of his troops, maintaining a small garrison in Alexandria to prevent the return of the
French. "There are risks in a British warfare unknown in any
service," Abercromby caustically told Dundas in a letter pointing

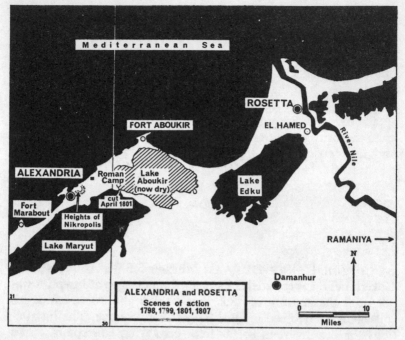

Mediterranean Sea

ROSETTA

FORT ABOUKIR

EL HAMED

River Nile

ALEXANDRIA Roman Lake
Camp Aboukir
(now dry) Lake
Edku

cut
April 1801

Fort
Marabout

Heights of
Nikropolis

RAMANIYA →

N

Lake Maryut

Damanhur

ALEXANDRIA and ROSETTA
Scenes of action
1798, 1799, 1801, 1807

0   10

Miles

to problems of transport and supply hitherto unconsidered. He
was unaware of the greatest risk. By optimistic interpretation of
pessimistic reports, captured from the French at sea, the War
Office fell ten thousand short of reality in their estimate of the
French strength.

The expedition got under way two months behind schedule,
staged at Malta, which had been captured by the British the previous year, and disembarked at Marmorice, on the Turkish coast
off Rhodes, in January, 1801. There they were to train, equip and
join up with a Turkish expeditionary force. The latter failed to
materialize and further depressing news came from Major-General
John Moore, who, sent for liaison with the Grand Vizier's army
at Jaffa, reported it to be in a sorry state of sickness, indiscipline
and disorder. Abercromby gritted his teeth and set sail for Egypt
on February 22. "I never went on any service entertaining greater
doubts of success, at the same time with more determination to
conquer difficulties," he wrote to the War Office.

His difficulties had in fact been eased by a Moslem fanatic who
had stabbed General Kléber to death during the previous summer.
General Menou his successor, was the one French general who

was bent on colonizing Egypt. A nobleman by birth, paunchy and pasty in appearance, and touchy and vain by nature, he had adopted the Moslem faith, married the daughter of an Egyptian bath-house keeper in Rosetta, and was now engaged on a series of ambitious reforms, including vast demolitions to build boulevards in Cairo, much to the rage of the people. He had been warned of Abercromby's approach, but was too engrossed in civil matters to take military precautions. Further warning came on March 2, when the British ships appeared in Aboukir Bay. Citizen-General Abdullah Menou merely made proclamation to the people, assuring them that God "by whom armies are guided . . . always goes before the French troops and destroys their enemies" and that the English, "the oppressors of mankind . . . shall be tumbled headlong into the sea". And for the benefit of doubters, he swore by God and his Prophet that if anyone excited commotion "his head shall that instant be taken off".

Nautical considerations led Abercromby to Aboukir Bay, scene of glory for the Royal Navy. His ships lay at anchor far out at sea and there they were forced to wait by heavy seas which churned up their passengers mercilessly. Having made a night-time reconnaissance in a cutter, he chose to land just inside the bay, close to the fort and the promontory it stood on. It was an obvious place, bound to be strongly defended, but further eastwards the narrow coastline between the sea and sea-lake tapered to the merest strip, from which deployment would be difficult, while west of the bay the approach would be harder for the rowboats. The indefatigible Sidney Smith made a reconnaissance of the 400-yard channel which, yet further eastwards, connected lake and sea; he landed at its neck and brought back a captive French corporal, an Arab and a jackass. He recommended that the boats should pass through this channel by night and be landed on the shores of the lake, between Aboukir and Alexandria, thus taking the enemy in rear. But Abercromby preferred the more British method, direct in approach, painstaking in planning, stately in tempo.

At last the storm abated and in the early hours of March 8 the transports disgorged their landing craft five miles out at sea. The assault force formed up. In the first line there were fifty-eight flat-boats containing men of ten battalions, packed tight fifty to a boat, each man carrying three days' rations. Behind came three lines of cutters and launches with more infantry and fourteen field-guns. Supporting them were two gunboats and a bombship on each flank. Dawn broke as the sailors rowed, and the full force of the sun beat down on them long before they came within range of the fifteen guns pointed at them from fort and sand-dunes. Their ball, grape and langridge, when at last they opened, were well directed and their targets were soon drenched by plumes of water. Many boats were pierced and at least one, carrying Coldstreamers, went to the bottom with a direct hit through the midst of its passengers. The French infantry, 1,600 in all, opened up with their muskets, but still the boats came on. "Huzza!" cheered the sailors as they tugged on their oars. "Huzza!" responded the soaked and dry-mouthed redcoats.

Because of the curve of the bay the boats struck shore in succession from the right, and the first troops to tread Egyptian sand were those on the extreme right, the flank companies of the 40th, since merged into the Lancashire Regiment (Prince of Wales's Volunteers), the 23rd (Royal Welch Fusiliers), and the 28th (Gloucestershires), led by John Moore from the first boat ashore. The French ran down to greet them with the bayonet. The British burst from the close confinement of their boats with such verve that their assailants fled, and with the indomitable Moore still at their head they clambered on hands and knees up the massive, almost perpendicular sand-dune which was their objective. So amazed were the French to see them on the summit that they did not stay to fight. As more boatloads came in, harder hit in passage than those on the right, the French cavalry charged across the beach and there was more than one moment of crisis before the horses and their proud riders wavered, sprawled and flopped in front of the hastily formed squares of Scotsmen, guardsmen, men of the Line and Corsican Rangers, one of the four regiments of European expatriates in Abercromby's force. Resistance collapsed as the long line of boats touched down ever further leftwards and discharged its impetuous redcoats. Soon the full breadth of the isthmus, all sand-dunes and date-palms, was in British hands, except for the fort which was surrounded and stifled.

The British had arrived, at a cost of 652 dead and wounded in the shallows and on the beaches. They had given a magnificent display of courage which would not have been needed if they had gone in elsewhere. For it transpired that the French commander had concentrated almost his entire strength at Aboukir, and until the arrival next morning of some 3,500 men from the south, Alexandria lay open.

Desperately anxious about supply problems, particularly that of water, Abercromby sat fast for the next three days while his ships, hampered by bad weather, completed unloading. He had no idea of the enemy strength and suffered the further handicap of weak eyesight. Probing forward, he advanced some four miles against light opposition on March 12 and next morning captured an important feature, site of a Roman camp, after some stalwart work by his two advanced guard regiments, the 90th (Cameronians) and 92nd (Gordon) Highlanders. But in the afternoon he suffered heavy losses in an attempt to exploit his success towards the heights of Nicopolis, in front of Alexandria; the day cost a further 1,300 men. On March 18 the surrender of Fort Aboukir freed more men for the advance, but next day Menou arrived from Cairo, marching his infantry and artillery across the parched basin of Lake Maryut, which was divided from the sea-lake of Aboukir by a causeway, held at its extremity by the British since March 13. Fortunately for the British, Menou left behind in Cairo as many men as he brought, showing himself a poor pupil of Bonaparte. Nonetheless with over ten thousand he at least equalled the strength of the British, whose sick-list was formidable, and in the pre-dawn hours of March 21 he hurled his men against their positions in true Napoleonic style.

This was the start of the first set battle fought by two European armies for possession of Egypt, and it proved a furious affair. The redoubts and ruins of the Roman Camp formed a salient on the right of the British line, and it was to cut its neck that the main French effort was directed. They attacked with all the fury of men never defeated in open battle in eight years' campaigning. The musket fire they met gave them a new experience. Moore's battalions, holding the salient, held fast, and in the foremost redoubt the 28th (Gloucestershires) won such glory, in withstanding assault from front, flanks and rear, that they were awarded a second, rearwards-facing cap badge. An onslaught on the British centre fared no better, though the 3rd (Scots) Guards suffered heavy losses before it was repulsed. In desperation Menou then hurled his cavalry against the Roman Camp position. Caught in the open, the Black Watch and the Minorca Regiment were almost overwhelmed, and for a few anxious minutes Abercromby himself was in the grasp of the French hussars. But the Highlanders rallied and retrieved their Commander-in-Chief and the horses, floundering in the loose sand, were felled in their hundreds by the fire

3

from the redoubts. Some of Moore's battalions had run out of ammunition and were reduced to hurling stones when the French disentangled what they could from the writhing carnage and withdrew, leaving on a few acres of sand over a thousand dead, three divisional generals among them, to be buried by their foes, together with six hundred wounded to be removed and tended. The British themselves lost 243 dead and 1,250 wounded.

Abercromby had been slashed across the chest by a sabre and had a musket ball, fired from long range, lodged in his thigh. He paced up and down in a forward position, watching the French retire, until he sank to the ground. He was carried away on a litter, worrying about the return of the soldier's blanket beneath his head. "God bless your honour," called his weary, hardened men. Gangrene set in and a week later the old man died.

For eleven days, until the arrival of Menou and his thousands, the British had had a great chance of grabbing Alexandria. They had let it slip, and now there was deadlock, with both sides in equal strength holding strong positions divided by a plain. They were similar in another respect too: Major-General Sir John Hutchinson, the new commander of the British, was just as unpopular with his officers and men as Menou. His appearance repelled and his manner offended—such a change from Abercromby, except that he also had bad eyesight. He was no fool, however, and no coward, and he quickly took advantage of little expected bounty in the form of four thousand good Turkish troops who on March 25 arrived at Aboukir Bay under command of the High Admiral, the handsome, black-bearded Capitan Pasha. Among them, now second-in-command of a contingent of Albanians, was the same Mohammed Aly who had been driven seawards from Aboukir in the summer of 1799.

Hutchinson sent the Turks and a small British detachment eastwards, and without much difficulty they captured the port of Rosetta as a preliminary to an advance up the Nile. Now, to secure the flank of his force before Alexandria and thus make more men available for this new thrust, and at the same time cut Menou off from reinforcement and supply, he consented to a measure he had formerly opposed, the cutting of the canal-causeway between the sea-lake of Aboukir, and the dry one, Maryut. "The army was in rapture," wrote Lt.-Col. Sir Robert Wilson, a cavalryman who was there. "Never did working party labour with more zeal." And when the final fascine was removed, on the evening of

April 13: "Joy was universal. The water rushed in with a fall of six feet, and the pride and peculiar care of Egypt, the consolidation of ages, was in a few hours destroyed by the devastating hand of man."

The army's rapture at this confinement by flood, of both their enemies and themselves, turned to dismay when Hutchinson, having advanced to Ramaniya and driven away an irresolute force of Frenchmen, announced his intention of marching on Cairo. His senior officers came near to mutiny and were quelled only by a stern rebuke from Moore, wounded in the great battle and still laid up, whose support they sought. The 40-mile march from Rosetta had brought tribulation enough. To continue for a further hundred in ever increasing heat, merely to meet at the end of it an enemy larger in size and impregnably entrenched, seemed the idea of a lunatic, specially as Alexandria, not Cairo, was the primary objective. Hutchinson was aware of the risks. He also realized that only by advancing on Cairo could he co-ordinate and sustain the effort of his allies. For not only did he have the Capitan Pasha's force with him, but a very much greater Turkish host was advancing from Syria to join him: that extraordinary compound of splendour and filth, of the military and the political, the Grand Vizier's Army.

A dignified old man with one eye and a silver beard "of extraordinary length and beauty", the Prime Minister (for that is what the Vizier was) had with him his foreign secretary, the Reis Effendi, Ibrahim Bey with a few Mamelukes, and a number of brigand-like chieftains, whose followers flocked, rather than marched, around them in their thousands. Having captured Damietta, this army was advancing up the eastern branch of the Nile, which joins the western one just to the north of Cairo, constantly reinforced by any Bedouin band eager for plunder, until its numbers reached around twenty-five thousand fighting men, with as many camp followers, camels, donkeys, goats and sheep. Covetousness for the riches of Cairo was the one thing that held the horde together. The French found it a strong agency, for a force sent to scatter the invaders was enveloped by cavalry and bustled into retreat. On May 24 Hutchinson crossed the Nile and its various tributaries and was ceremoniously received by the Grand Vizier in a pavilion of silk and gold splendour. To celebrate the junction a grand tournament followed.

Five days later an equally notable junction was effected. Taking great care to avoid the Capitan and his Turks, Osman Bey joined the British with 1,200 mounted Mamelukes. Osman was the successor to Murad, who had died of plague in April after sending Hutchinson a letter assuring him of his support: "It is on the English faith alone that I can depend." (He had also taken the precaution of offering his services to Menou, but Menou had haughtily declined.) The British were much impressed by the Mamelukes, whose discipline and martial bearing contrasted so shraply with those of the Turks. With these much admired cavaliers on their right, the Capitan's stout soldiers alongside them and the derided rabble of the Grand Vizier converging from the left, the redcoats trudged on, tattered and sweat-soaked, across the chocolate, richly cropped soil of the Delta, their rate of progress restricted by problems of supply. They did not plunder the hovel-villages, as the French had done, but merely gaped at the squalor of the peasants, "their nakedness scarcely covered, their persons all over dirt and filth, and their disgusting eyes almost eaten up by swarms of flies", as Captain Walsh described it. The British had eye trouble too, being badly afflicted by a form of ophthalmia, attributed to the heavy night dew, which in some cases caused permanent blindness. This and dysentery took an ever increasing toll.

Meanwhile, Dundas's plan for a combined invasion from India was in painful labour. Suez was found to be practically inaccessible by sail during the spring, and only a half-regiment was landed there, which joined Hutchinson's force after a most harrowing march through the desert. The main force, under Major-General David Baird, gradually assembled at Cosseir, further down the Red Sea coast, until at last it reached a strength of over five thousand, rather more than half of whom were British, the remainder Indian. A hundred miles of desert lay between them and the nearest point of the Nile, at Kena. The march began on June 19, staggered because of a shortage of camels, and was completed over a month later, with the loss of only three men. It was an epic as much of organization as of endurance, but as they were still 400 miles from Cairo they could be of little aid to Hutchinson, except to swell the sense of doom, by rumour of their coming, which already had the French garrison in its grasp.

North of Cairo the variegated armies closed in unimpeded, and on June 16 the Mamelukes entered the village of Embaba, scene of their disaster nearly three years earlier. Since leavnig Ramaniya the British had spent thirty-seven days on a journey which had taken Bonaparte eleven, with two battles thrown in. No doubt unimpressed by such progress, the French commander, General Belliard, sent a blunt refusal to Hutchinson's first offer of surrender terms and startled the British with a cannonaded *feu de joie*, the strange cause of which transpired to be the reported capture of Ireland. But the French, though strong in numbers and fortification, were sorely stricken not only by plague but by an even more insidious complaint, homesickness. There was no point in defending a place they longed to be out of, bringing terrible suffering down on themselves and on a people who loathed them quite enough already. A truce was sought. Dressed in splendour, delegates of all the combatants came to Giza, on the Nile's west bank, and just as they had done at El Arish some eighteen months previously, the French agreed to leave Egypt in exchange for a free return to France with their arms, accessories, loot and all the baggage they could carry.

So long did the preparations for their departure last that it was not until the night of July 10 that the first British troops—the 89th (Royal Irish Fusiliers)—entered the Citadel, that inhospitable, dun-coloured compound of battlements rising from the south-east corner of the city. Next day musket fire and screams announced the entry of the Turks into the city. The Vizier nonetheless restrained them from excesses and they indulged instead in a form of protection racket, guarding shops in exchange for a share of the profits. As for the British in Cairo, according to Wilson, they "expected little, yet did not reduce their ideas low enough". They had, however, made good use of the time on their hands by viewing and scaling the Pyramids, an experience by which "their minds aggrandized with honest pride and honourable reflections".

The return down the Nile was a remarkable spectacle. First came the Turks, motley and sprawling and sorry to have no French heads for proud display on their bayonets; next the British, four thousand strong, in fine order under Moore, who had returned from hospital and been left in charge while Hutchinson, a sick man, stayed in Cairo to restore, as best he could, the authority of the Mamelukes; next the French with eight thousand unruly soldiers on the march and another five thousand sick, riding with civilians, treasure, baggage and the revered coffin of General Kléber aboard a colourful fleet of three hundred vessels; behind them came the British cavalry, warding off the Mamelukes who brought up the rear. After only a fortnight on the march the head of the throng reached Rosetta on July 31, where the French peacefully embarked on British ships, having first put up for auction, without great response, the dark ladies who had faithfully done duty for absent wives. Death by strangulation was the usual award for such service to the infidel.

Enraged by Belliard's defection, Menou declared that he would defend Alexandria to the last. "I know how to die, but not how to capitulate," he wrote to Bonaparte. He was expecting ships to fight their way through with strong reinforcements. The navy failed him after a half-hearted effort, and with no prospect of relief Menou found that he did know how to capitulate after all. Granted the same service as Belliard, he concluded terms on September 2 and a few days later was removed, surly and querulous to the end, in a British ship, leaving Madame Menou to return to her parent's bath-house.

Just before the French departed, Baird arrived at Rosetta with his Anglo-Indian force after a rapid voyage down the Nile with a brief visit to Cairo interposed. His journey of some 650 miles across Egypt and a further 2,000 by sea was perhaps the longest unnecessary one ever made, but with quicker decision by the British Cabinet the entire expedition would not have been necessary either. Still, it had won for British arms a much-needed victory, which in view of the strength available to the French seems almost miraculous.

Ousted by force, France now turned to diplomatic means to dispute British influence in Egypt, a policy she was doggedly to pursue for the next hundred years. The first thing to be secured (with aid from Russia) was the evacuation of the British troops, and this was agreed under the Peace of Amiens, signed in March 1802. The British were slow to go. The military championed the cause of the Mamelukes. They had seen for themselves the brutish inefficiency of the Turks and the hatred they inspired, and had even seen the Turks attempt, with partial success, to murder the leading beys while they were aboard the Capitan Pasha's launch on their way to dine with the British admiral at Alexandria. The politicians' main concern was to retain the alliance of the Turks, Egypt's rightful owners. The two aims seemed incompatible, but eventually it was agreed that the Mamelukes should withdraw to the province of Aswan in exchange for a guarantee of Turkish protection. The British troops therefore left Alexandria in March 1803, taking with them many pieces of ancient sculpture which, as national as opposed to private property, they had removed from the French Institute of Egypt before its departure. They also took Elfi Bey, to do propaganda work for the Mamelukes in London, and left behind a liberal supply of arms for them and a staunch advocate in the crippled staff officer, Major Missett, who became the first British agent in Cairo since 1796. Soon he was openly encouraging revolt against the Turks.

It was the Turks' own Albanian soldiers, however, who upset the balance of power in Cairo. They mutinied, drove out the Turkish Pasha to Damietta, and made a tenuous alliance with the Mamelukes. The British Ambassador in Constantinople thereupon sent a certain Major Hayes in an attempt to re-establish the authority of the Pasha, and for a time the two British majors, both serving officers, were busily striving for rival causes. Now the Machiavellian genius of Mohammed Aly revealed itself, and the simple ambitions of the majors were pounded to pulp.

Aly succeeded to the command of the Albanian contingent when his chief was murdered soon after his *coup d'état*. He first co-operated with the Mamelukes to defeat and capture the Pasha at Damietta. Next, he divided the beys among themselves, helped one, Bardisi, to drive the other, Elfi—just returned from London—into the desert. He then compelled Bardisi to tax the people of Cairo in order to pay the Albanian soldiers, as a result of which the Cairenes rose up and with aid from the Albanians (now paid) drove Bardisi into the desert. Having graciously welcomed a new Pasha back to Cairo, Aly again incited revolt and had him deposed by acclaim of the people in favour of himself. At once he acknowledged dutiful submission to the Sublime Porte, and was at length sourly acknowledged in return. Such is a brief account of a two-year saga of murder, battle, rioting, pillage and famine, each of which presented opportunity seized with cold precision, and with aid from the people of Cairo, by the unerring hand of the sturdy little Macedonian Turk, Mohammed Aly, founder of a dynasty, founder of Modern Egypt.

War had long since reopened between Britain and France; it was declared, ironically enough, in March 1803, just as the British troops were sailing out of Alexandria. Emperor Napoleon, as he now was, saw Egypt as a lure for the dispersal of British forces and was for ever putting out rumours that the French were going to reoccupy it, a task in which he was energetically assisted by Monsieur de Lesseps, the French agent in Cairo. Britain fell for the bait when Turkey was driven into alliance with France by Russian encroachment. Towards the close of 1806 Lord Grenville's coalition Government of All-the-Talents instructed their Commander-in-Chief in the Mediterranean to send a small force merely to capture Alexandria "for the purpose of preventing the French from regaining a footing in that country and of enabling H.M. Forces there to afford countenance and protection to such of the parties in that country as may be best disposed to maintain at all times a friendly intercourse with Great Britain". How this most delicate task was to be achieved by sitting at Alexandria was not explained. The British Consul, the excitable Major Missett, was the prime instigator. Convinced that Aly was on the side of the French (a view not shared by the French Consul), he had for long been bombarding the War Office with requests for troops to combine in a rising with the Mamelukes.

Command of the expedition fell to the unfortunate Major-General Alexander Mackenzie Fraser, a brave officer, recalled from the reserve, who had no pretensions to high command. With a force of little more than six thousand, composed mainly of four British infantry battalions and three of European expatriates, together with seven hundred women and children, he sailed from Sicily and on March 17, 1807, arrived off Alexandria at half strength, the remainder having been held up by storm. Missett, who accompanied the expedition, knew the city was lightly held by troops of the Sultan, now officially at war with Britain, and he urged haste to anticipate the arrival of Mohammed Aly's men. Fraser chose Bonaparte's route and landed his men near Marabout, but heavy seas enforced a night of isolation for the first ashore and hampered operations next morning. In the evening three battalions set off for Alexandria. They brushed aside an outpost but were halted at the Pompey Gate by barricades and musket fire. Fraser enveloped the city and pushed eastwards as far as Aboukir, barring the approach from Rosetta. On March 20 the remainder of his ships arrived at Aboukir and Alexandria surrendered.

Fraser might have thought that he had accomplished his mission, but now Missett, hoodwinked perhaps by Alexandrine merchants or else with ideas of sparking off his Mameluke rising, insisted that Alexandria would quickly starve unless Rosetta and Ramaniya were also captured. He ignored the fact that the French had held out for almost six months without command of the sea—and Fraser, having no veteran of that campaign on his staff, was unable to remind him. He agreed half-heartedly and took half-hearted measures. Instead of going to Rosetta himself with a worthwhile force, he sent two battalions under two major-generals, Wauchope in command, Meade as second-in-command.

The troops had no difficulty in capturing the high ground overlooking Rosetta and there they spent the night of March 30. Next day they advanced on the jumble of solid, flat-topped houses, minarets and palm-trees that comprised the town. Although depleted by an ambush by the banks of the Nile, the 31st (Queen's Royal Surreys) forced a breach through the mud wall and broke in with a cheer, driving a few Turks up the main avenue and side alleys. The French renegade battalion, Les Chasseurs Britanniques, were less successful on their left, but rallied by Wauchope they too broke in, leaving Meade severely wounded behind them.

The battle seemed won. The troops relaxed and took their ease, though how far inside they got was never clearly established. Fire suddenly opened on them, from rooftops and windows, front and behind. Wauchope was shot dead: retreat was ordered by urgent bugle call. Meade, lying wounded outside the town, with no reserve and very little information, ordered a complete evacuation. Back came the soldiers, steadily repulsing infantry and cavalry charges which succeeded only in finishing off the stragglers. 467 were lost, killed, wounded or missing.

The news of this unexpected victory had an electrifying effect in Cairo where, with revolt brewing, many of the Albanian troops were making arrangements for flight to Syria. Now there was wild enthusiasm to crush and drive out the infidel. Missett obligingly browbeat Fraser into making another attempt on Rosetta, pointing to reports of a rising by the Mamelukes and of a victory which, as he might have guessed, proved fictitious. Three battalions set off this time, with a combined light infantry regiment and some cavalry and artillery, command of which was entrusted to Brigadier-General William Stewart, there being a shortage of major-generals.

Having secured a strong right flankguard position at El Hamed, Stewart's men closed on Rosetta on April 8, but the defenders were now very much more active and it soon became apparent that there could be little chance of a successful breach. They waited hopefully for promised aid from the Mamelukes, but no Mameluke turned up. Stewart tried intimidation by bombardment, though he had only eight guns, but this too had little effect. For ten days the futile siege continued, redeemed only by a dashing raid across the Nile which wiped out a Turkish battery.

Meanwhile, ominous reports kept coming in of heavy boat movement down the Nile, and on April 20 the Turkish cavalry appeared in strength and inflicted serious loss on the El Hamed garrison. Stewart sent reinforcements during the night, but was himself almost captured by a cavalry host which had swept round El Hamed into the plain. In the morning he ordered a full withdrawal and himself extricated the besieging force with splendid steadiness in face of constant assault, both by cavalry masses and infantry from the town. He had to order the destruction of his heavy guns, which were spiked by the bayonets of his rearguard regiment, the 35th (Royal Sussex), but he got all his sick and wounded away on camels, staunchly escorted by the 78th (Seaforth) Highlanders. The flank force was less fortunate. Albanian infantry and Turkish cavalry fell on it from both sides, and in the end not one man got away out of its 800-strong hotchpotch of units. The prisoners were forced to carry the heads of their dead comrades to Cairo, where they were displayed on poles in Ezbekia Square.

Mohammed Aly's conduct after this resounding victory again showed him to be no ordinary Turk. Instead of laying siege to Fraser's depleted force, he made overtures, sending first an envoy and then an officer prisoner; for despite Britain's military failings, which had saved his collapse from power, he retained deep respect for her sea power and its potential for blockade. The officer told how kindly the prioners were being looked after and carried a proposal from Aly, to the effect that he would deny any foreign army entry into Egypt and if the British cared to withdraw he would release the prisoners he had taken. It was so easy to negotiate with such a very reasonable man, and when a new Tory Government replaced the one of All-the-Talents, terms for evacuation were speedily agreed. The British pulled out of Alexandria on September 19, with nearly all ex-prisoners and a dejected, but not starving, Major Missett on board. Aly, whose behaviour Fraser described as "truly noble", had been at pains to scour the slave houses to retrieve British captives (for there had been an auction), but he retained a few men, mainly Highlanders, who volunteered to serve in his own army. Some rose to high rank, and their influence may still be observed in the red hair and freckles of some Egyptians. Aly was now firm in his mastery of Egypt. But the Mamelukes remained, and though they were no longer quite the fellows they were—their best leaders were dead and their numbers were declining, cut as they were from their source of supply in the Caucasus—they could still make a scourge of themselves alike to government and countryside. Aly spent a year or two subtly engaged in reducing their powers, lulling their suspicions, and bringing the more defiant to heel by military measures. Then he invited them all to a great parade in Cairo, on March 1, 1811, to celebrate the appointment of his son to a pashalik. It was a chance of display such as no Mameluke could resist. They duly paraded at the Citadel and marched off behind the Albanian contingent, down the steps and narrow pathway, cut through the rock, which leads to the Bab-el-Azab gate. Once through this gate, the Albanians shut it fast and opened fire on the poor unsuspecting Mamelukes. There were other Turks waiting for them at the far end of the passage. There could be, and was, no escape—except for one who is said to have put his horse at the rampart wall and landed in the moat far below, leaving hoof-prints for perpetual display to tourists. It was the end of the Mamelukes.

CHAPTER FOUR

Aly's Empire

(1811-49)

THIS PARADE WHICH assembled so merrily at the Citadel had real enough purpose besides the elimination of the Mamelukes. It was to be the send-off of a great crusade. For Jedda, of which Aly's son Tussun had been appointed Pasha, was the nearest port to Mecca and for years this region of the Hejaz had been in the cruel grasp of the heretical Wahabis who denied all pilgrims access to their holy shrine. The Pashas of Syria and Baghdad had both failed to regain the most treasured possession of their Ottoman Sultan, Caliph of Islam, "Shadow of God upon Earth". Now the Pasha of Cairo had his chance, and in presenting it the Sultan no doubt also saw good opportunity for draining the energies of those fearsome Albanian troops. Aly was quite willing to take the risk.

The first attempt failed ignominiously. The second succeeded in taking Mecca early in 1813. The Wahabis rallied, and for a year Aly led his army himself, suffering reverse at first, but eventually crushing the enemy in a bloody battle at Biselah. He returned to Cairo, leaving Tussun in command, and another Wahabi revival followed. Now, towards the end of 1815, Tussun died and his brother Ibrahim was sent to take command. This stocky ball of energy, with blue eyes and ginger beard, soon showed that he had inherited genius from his father, if of a harsher, less subtle, brand. He resolved to assail the Wahabis in their remote desert stronghold of Darayyah, where they had always been quite safe. Having assiduously inspired hatred of them among the local Bedouin, he set out with a train of thirty thousand camels and with six thousand ruffian mercenaries, Turk, Albanian, Greek, Moor and Armenian, who never before had had such demands made on their discipline and endurance. A gruelling march was followed by a desperate three months' siege, which ended with the fall of Darayyah in September 1818, and with it the capture and public humiliation of the Wahabi leaders. Thus was the Sultan-Caliph's authority restored, to the glory of Egypt, shining knight of the Ottoman Empire.

Mohammed Aly's ambitious eye now turned southward, where the Sudan, or Land of the Black, offered prospect of further glory and of gain in the form of gold and slaves, either of which might be convertible to much-needed soldiers. The expedition was entrusted to his third son Ismail and set sail up the Nile in July 1820, a sprawling, many-coloured array, billowing with medieval flamboyance. There were Turks in their gold-braided jackets, pantaloons and red slippers, each soldier accompanied by a slave and a donkey, Greeks in their Evzone kilts and long stockings, Kurds in breastplates and conical headwear, Bedouin with their chieftains in ceremonial chain-mail and helmet, and a bedraggled throng of camp-followers in variegated galabiyas. No one had more than the vaguest notion what to expect or even who ruled the territories, 800 miles deep, which they intended to conquer. No opposition was encountered until November, when the force reached Korti, 300 miles beyond Wadi Halfa, and was assailed by Shaiqiya tribesmen. The latter found fanaticism a poor substitute for firearms and learnt the same lesson a month later. On this second occasion Ismail captured the virgin who led the tribesmen from the back of a gorgeously attired camel. He returned her washed and perfumed, her virginity intact, and so amazed the Shaiqiyas that they made peace at once.

Unfortunately Ismail did not maintain this early standard of humanity. The march continued, virtually unopposed, all through the following year, until in January 1822 the soldiers halted, with the Abyssinian mountains rising before them. Behind them effete dynasties lay in shreds, their peoples murdered or sent captive to Cairo, their homes plundered. Revenge fell on Ismail on his way back. He had insulted the chieftain of Shendy on the outward trip and now when he returned in October he made savage demands for slaves and booty and slapped the face of the chieftain when told they could not be met. That night Ismail held a banquet, and the natives set fire to his house, roasting him inside it. Their triumph was short-lived, for Aly's son-in-law was also in the Sudan, with an army in Kordofan. He duly wrought terrible retribution.

Aly's conquest of the Sudan had profound effect on the history of Egypt. He sent Turkish officials to administer it and they established their headquarters in a little fishing village named Khartoum at the fork of the junction between the Blue and White Niles. It was the birth of a colony which Egypt was to treasure with all the passion of a jealous and irresponsible mother.

The negative results of the campaign had even greater, and very much more immediate, effect on the Egyptian people. For it did not bring what Aly wanted. The gold just failed to materialize, and as for the slaves, they died in their thousands from exhaustion or from other complaints even more trivial. One could never build an army with such men, and the need for soldiers was never greater, for malaria and dysentery had taken a fearful toll of the mercenaries, and such was the trouble they caused wherever they were stationed that it hardly seemed worth buying replacements, even if the money were available. Aly therefore took a step that must have caused sardonic laughter to echo through the vaulted tombs of the pharaohs, kings, caliphs and beys who had ruled Egypt before him. He ordered the conscription of the peasantry, the fellahin.

The method used was the simple one of the provision by each district of a given quota. Some were therefore able to gain exemption by a bribe to the district mudir, raised in size by a little beating; others were obliged to have recourse to flight, hiding or self-mutilation. To establish the whereabouts of fugitives, recruiting parties gave the womenfolk liberal doses of the bastinado or else strung them up by their hair to put that extra touch of pepper into their hidings, while women who helped men to blind themselves or remove their teeth were executed and their bodies displayed. The peasants clung to their freedom with the same dogged courage as they did to their money. But it was a hopeless struggle, and in their thousands they came into the camps, usually chained in pairs, some missing an eye, some a finger. Once there, they were far more amenable to discipline than the mercenaries, and under the able direction of the Frenchman Colonel Sève, or Suleiman Pasha, some thirty thousand peasants were soon beaten into military shape. It seems doubtful, however, whether any of them rose even to the rank of sergeant and certainly the officers were foreign, Turk, Albanian or rascally European.

This new national army, Egypt's first ever, soon got the chance to show its mettle under the leadership of the redoubtable Ibrahim. The Greeks were in revolt against their Turkish overlords and to incite the intervention of Egyptian arms the Sultan made Aly Pasha of Morea, the southernmost province of the Grecian peninsula. Aly duly sent a force to claim his domain, consisting partly of mercenary veterans, partly of peasant conscripts. A landing was made in January 1825, and in May Ibrahim defeated the Greeks at Navarino, a victory in bright contrast to the efforts of the Turks themselves. Next year he came to the Turks' aid and helped them capture first Missolonghi and then Athens. The rebels were no match for the well-trained Egyptian soldiers and their brilliant commander.

Now the European powers brought pressure on the Sultan. The Greeks, eager enough to indulge in atrocities though they were, had the sympathy of all romantics at a time when romanticism was at its height, and it grew all the more fiery at news that Greek prisoners, women and children included, were suffering the routine fate of sale in the Cairo slave markets. Even more important, from a practical viewpoint, was the fact that Greek sailors had turned to piracy and were causing havoc on the trading routes. Confronted by a combined demand for an armistice from Britain, Russia and France, the Sultan procrastinated, hoping to play one off against the other. In this he failed, and at length an allied fleet, British and Russian, destroyed the Turkish and Egyptian one at Navarino. Cut off from supply, Ibrahim's army remained in Greece for a further nine months until its return, hungry and wretched, under a convention signed by Aly and the British Admiral Codrington on August 6, 1828.

Aly had been made the cat's paw of the bungling, obstinate diplomacy of the Sultan, and he was furious. More than anything else he coveted the friendship of Britain—A "lasting league of commerce and amity" was how he put it to the British Consul-General, Salt. He suggested that, with the military weakness of Turkey so blatantly revealed, Britain would do far better to rely on a strong and independent Egypt as bulwark against the menace that has always dictated British policy in the Eastern Mediterranean, Russian infiltration. "With the English for my friends I can do anything," he plaintively burst out in a moment of obvious candour. But English foreign policy was no willowy thing to be blown this way and that; the Turks stood directly between Russia and the Mediterranean, and their friendship could not be forfeited.

As if to prove his point Aly waged war against the enfeebled Empire for which he had so dexterously wielded the sword. For his services in Greece he had been promised (but not awarded) the pashaliks of Syria and he now moved in to take occupation, using as a further excuse the recovery of six thousand fellahin, fugitives from his recruiting gangs, who had taken refuge in that country. With an army of seven thousand infantrymen and eight thousand cameleers, Ibrahim crossed the frontier in November 1831 and in December laid siege to Acre. It again proved a tough nut to crack, but Ibrahim had more patience than Bonaparte and quite as much determination, and at the end of May 1832 his men finally stormed into the city after a desperate assault, in which he personally struck down any officer who lagged behind.

From now on his progress was swift and dramatic. In the course of the summer months he entered Damascus, routed the Turks at Homs, entered Aleppo, routed the Turks at the Beylan Pass, and bit deep into Turkish territory proper. Aly now ordered a halt, but in December the Grand Vizier himself brought an army, only to be routed and captured at Konia, where Ibrahim fell on the very much larger Ottoman force under cover of fog. Admittedly the Turks were at low ebb, their fighting prowess enfeebled by the massacre of the Jannisaries which the Sultan had ordered a few years earlier for much the same reasons as Aly's for that of his Mamelukes. Even so, there could have been no victory, however masterful the commander, without the fortitude displayed by the peasant conscripts under their mercenary officers. Over 100,000 of them had now been forced into service, either with the navy or army, and they were finding it to be a case of "once a soldier always a soldier, in Ibrahim Pasha's army".

Ibrahim was now in full cry for Constantinople, with the route wide open to his invincible troops, but again came orders to halt. For the thing that Aly most feared had happened: the Turks had called on their old enemies, the Russians, for assistance, and Britain was insisting that Aly's men must stop before the Czar's were secure across the Bosphorus. Aly complied. He was granted leasehold right of all his possessions, including the province of Adana along Turkey's southern shore, with annual tribute payable to the Sultan.

Aly's empire within an empire now extended 2,000 miles, from the Euphrates in the north to the Abyssinian frontier in the south, and almost as far at its longest stretch from east to west, an area not much smaller than the whole of Europe. He ruled the key centres of the Moslem faith, Mecca, Damascus and Cairo, and most of Arabia. Yet the main prize still eluded him. Nominally, at any rate, Egypt was still part of the Ottoman Empire, and on Aly's death all his pashaliks, Cairo included, would be in the gift of the Sultan to bestow as he pleased. Again he made overtures to the British promising an army of 150,000 to stem the Russians if only Britain would support his declaration of independence. Palmerston was now Foreign Secretary, and he promptly cut Aly down to pasha size. His Britannic Majesty's Government, it was made quite clear, was not in the habit of sanctioning rebellion against an honoured ally.

But another Government, just as interested in the affairs of Egypt, did not feel bound by such scruples. Aly turned to France, and the French tried to negotiate with the Porte on his behalf. The attempt evoked no more than a display of Turkish obstinacy, but it encouraged Aly to act. In May 1838 he announced his intention of declaring his independence and of withholding tribute owed to the Sultan. The French expressed their dismay as strongly as the British, and the Porte ponderously deliberated on how to deal with such insubordination. And while they did so there was further friction between Britain and Egypt. Wanting a coaling station for her steamers, Britain seized the port of Aden early in 1839, under the noses of Egyptian soldiers active in the Yemen. Surely the British "would be persuaded that Aden formed part of the Yemen", Aly protested in vain.

Instigated by Russia though discouraged by Britain, the Sultan resolved to attack the rebel, relying on the effect of Prussian training to restore the prestige of his arms. But once again the mighty Ibrahim humiliated him, routing General von Moltke's army of Turks and capturing all their guns and baggage at the Battle of Nazib in June 1839. A week later the Capitan Pasha, hearing that he was going to lose his command anyway, brought the Turkish fleet to Alexandria and handed it over to Aly.

There followed a period of prolonged and anxious diplomacy between the capitals of Europe. As a result, Russia was constrained to accept co-operation with Britain, as an alternative to war, and in July 1840 Aly was presented with a combined ultimatum, demanding the return of the Turkish fleet and the withdrawal of his troops to the frontier of Southern Syria—or of Egypt itself if he did not accept within ten days—in exchange for the inheritance

4

of his pashalik of Egypt by his heirs. France was the odd power out, and with promise of aid from her Aly bided his time, giving vague assent to withdrawal but holding on to the Turkish fleet. The Sultan pronounced him deposed from all his pashaliks and withdrew all consul-generals in Egypt. Aly calmly waited for the wrath to descend. He took measures to defend his country, concentrating troops at Damanhur, south of Alexandria, but he also made sure that foreigners were afforded protection and freedom of travel. It was with Lord Palmerston, not the English, that he was at war, said the wise old Pasha.

The French failed him, and to enforce the ultimatum an allied force was landed near Beirut in September, consisting of 5,000 Turks, 1,500 Royal Marines and 200 Austrians, under a dashing old sailor, Commodore Sir Charles Napier. They found Ibrahim's famous army a poor shadow of its former self, disheartened by its isolation, weakened by blockade, and scattered by the need to suppress risings brought on by their harsh conscription of the people. Tyre and Sidon fell to assault, and Napier, who had a taste for the land battle and was proud of the honorary rank of major-general conferred on him by the Portuguese for services in the Peninsula War, then marched inland with his Turks, leaving the Royal Marines behind. He met Ibrahim himself in the mountains and decisively defeated him. This led to the fall of Beirut. On November 4 Acre fell after only one day's bombardment, so suddenly had morale collapsed.

The British part of the combined fleet then slipped away from its Russian, Austrian and Turkish allies and made for Alexandria. Aly gave the wily Napier entry into the harbour and on November 27 signed a convention with him. Under the terms finally agreed Aly was left with Egypt, by payment of annual tribute, and with the Sudan by right of occupation; he was to reduce his army to eighteen thousand men and build no more ships for his navy; in exchange he secured his dynasty for his family under the Turkish rules of succession by the oldest member. It was the end of an imperial venture, less disastrous than most.

From now on Aly was in increasing amity with the allies he most desired. He had been remarkably tolerant of Britain's interference and had retained perspective even in the darkest days of crisis, as this remark to a representative of a new steamline company, the P. and O., reveals: "It is very bad policy on the part of your Government to fight with me; this is your high road to India, and I shall always promote it." The advent of the steamer immeasurably increased the value of this high road, since Suez was so hard to approach by sail, and with British aid a transit service was established, by steamboat to Cairo, where travellers could stay at Mr. Shepheard's new hotel, and by stage coach to Suez, at a cost of £15. It gained great popularity with residents in India and soon three thousand people were using the route each year. The tourist had arrived and glorious new vistas of opportunity presented themselves to many agile minds, Egyptian, Armenian and Greek.

The French meanwhile pressed for their long-cherished project of a canal through the Suez Isthmus: Bonaparte's engineers had reported a discrepancy in the water levels on either side, but this had been disproved by subsequent French studies, much to the joy of an imaginative diplomat brought up in their consulate in Cairo, Ferdinand de Lesseps. The French still had great influence in Egypt, and it was to be seen personally in the army, dockyards, arsenals, banks and hospitals, but they had proved ineffective allies and in any case had less to offer than the great trading nation, Britain. Britain, having developed the overland route, opposed the construction of the canal and Aly readily accepted her advice. He had stronger reason than a desire to please the British; the canal, he was sure, would deprive Egypt of all chance of full independence.

Aly died in 1849, sadly demented in his final year yet at 80 having long survived his exact contemporary, Napoleon Bonaparte. As shrewd as charming, ruthless of purpose but less cruel than most Turks, he had used his versatile genius to perform marvels for Egypt. Order had been built out of chaos, and security with it, and—greatest achievement of all—trade had been increased literally ten-fold. Nowhere was this more apparent than in Alexandria, which had risen in population from 15,000 to 150,000 and contained a polyglot host of traders revelling in the immunity, both from arrest and taxation, that was provided under the old Turkish Capitulations and could be obtained, by the purchase of a pass, from any venal consulate. Even the peasants were better off. Aly, the great one-man band, took a keen interest in the cultivation both of corn and cotton and threw his great energy into ambitious irrigation projects. He also made some provision for the education of the peasants and gave them a better chance of justice, though the lengths to be travelled in this direction are aptly illustrated by a decree he brought out making it illegal, on pain of death, for a village sheikh to beat anyone to death *unless provoked*.

CHAPTER FIVE

Mastheads through the Desert

(1849-74)

IBRAHIM HAD DIED just before his father, and the pashalik fell to Abbas, son of the oppressor (until his roasting) of the Sudan, Ismail. Abbas was a cruel reactionary—riding horses and flogging women were his chief interests—and under him Egypt slid back into the tyranny and lethargy of her darker years. Foreigners were snubbed and cheated, and only the British gained advantage, in the form of a concession for the Cairo—Alexandria railway. In 1854 Abbas was strangled by some Mameluke slaves he had unwisely imported as his bodyguard, and the whole of Egypt rejoiced.

But the loudest whoop of joy came not from Egypt, but from a farm in France. Having risen to high rank in the French diplomatic corps, Ferdinand de Lesseps had been in retirement since 1849, when disagreement with the military commander of an expedition to Rome, sent to restore the authority of the Pope, led to his resignation as special envoy. De Lesseps had been brought up in Egypt, where his father was French Consul, and from boyhood he had been fired with enthusiasm for the singularly French project of carving a canal through the Suez Isthmus. Enthusiasm turned to obsession, which chafed with the agony of frustration when first Aly and then Abbas refused to countenance the endeavour. Now Abbas was dead, and in his place came Said, son of Aly himself, a large naïve, clownish young man who had been educated in Paris and there infused with all the ambitions of a go-ahead reformer. De Lesseps had helped to tutor Said in Egypt and, much to the joy of Aly, got rid of some of his fat by making him take exercise. They had become good friends. De Lesseps caught the first ship for Egypt, where he received a warm welcome from his former pupil.

In a very short time he drew up a draft concession for the construction of the canal by an independent company. This he presented to Said, who is reputed to have signed it without reading it, merely saying, "I accept your plan. Consider the matter settled. You may rely on me." He made a bad deal for Egypt. Not only did he agree to part with, in return for 15 per cent of the net profits, two strips of land, one for the canal itself, the other, potentially rich in produce, for a fresh-water canal from the Nile (to supply the workers), but he also undertook to provide forced labour. De Lesseps busily set about forming his company. Palmerston told him with remarkable candour that the scheme would upset Britain's commercial and maritime advantages and he must therefore oppose it, and the French, being then allied to Britain in a war against Russia, were disinclined to give him official encouragement either. De Lesseps therefore put his shares up for sale to private individuals. He sold plenty in France, especially to ladies of fashion but drew blank in Britain, Russia, Austria and the United States. However, he put the outstanding shares to the account of the Pasha and gaily went ahead, undeterred by the witholding of the Sultan's permission and the chilling disapproval of the British Government.

Work began on April 25, 1859, and being a great showman, de Lesseps himself wielded the first pickaxe to fall on the hovel-strewn strip of sand-dunes, isolated by an inland lake, from which there were to arise such glories as the great store of Simon Artz. The enlargement of de Lesseps' first scratching was entrusted to twenty thousand conscript peasants, animated by the time-honoured stimulant of the hippopotomus-hide lash, the courbash. Britain's protests gained strength, but Said was as determined as de Lesseps. "My name will be immortalized," he defiantly declared, with ironic accuracy, when warned by the British Consul that he might be deposed if he persisted in the venture. By October 16, 1862, the excavations had reached Lake Timsah and this time de Lesseps assumed the role of works foreman, having assembled a distinguished gathering which included high dignitaries of the Moslem and Catholic faiths. He addressed them: "In the name of His Highness Mohammed Said, I command that the waters of the Mediterranean enter Lake Timsah by the grace of God!"

Said, gross and torpid, was in the grip of an incurable disease. He died in January 1863 and was succeeded by another young man in his early thirties, his nephew Ismail, son of Ibrahim. He was an ugly fellow, short, ungainly, squint-eyed, his face covered by unseemly tufts of red hair, but he had acquired remarkable charm of manner during his tours of the capitals of Europe, which, coupled with inherited shrewdness, proved a useful aid to the advancement of his grandiose ambition. He was eager enough to let the digging continue, but Palmerston, in his second term as Prime Minister, had decided that it must stop. In the cause of humanity and justice, he curtly informed the Turkish Sultan that he must withhold his sanction so long as slave labour was employed and Egypt was denied the strip of land that was being made so productive by the freshwater canal. The Sultan reacted with typically shambling evasion, and the work was finally brought to an end by a British threat to stop it by force.

The French were indignant, and naturally enough it was to them that de Lesseps turned for a solution of his problems. The Emperor Napoleon did not fail him. A commission was appointed which summarily fixed a payment of £3,360,000 to be made by Ismail to release him from his obligations under the offending clauses. This was accepted as readily as the original concession, and there could be no barrier now to the famous project which had such greater appeal to Aly's descendants than it had done to the old patriarch himself. Nor was there any attempt at obstruction by the British Government, for Palmerston had died in the autumn of 1865 and been succeeded by Earl Russell, a truer and more flexible Liberal. The Sultan duly issued his firman. The work steamed ahead, with great activity by powerful dredgers, rock-busters and a motley army of labourers drawn together by the lure of a wage of over a shilling a day. C. M. Doughty tells of the ditcher who had travelled 700 miles and worked under a European woman: "and the wifeman, he said, with pistols in her belt, was a stern overseer of her work-folk. There was a Babel of nations, a concourse of men of every hard and doubtful fortune". De Lesseps assiduously provided both for their religious and medical supervision. The death-rate during these last four years of construction came to no more than 1·5 per year out of every thousand, according to the chief medical officer's statistics.

For Ismail the dredgers scooped up glory and prestige. In 1866 he won from the Sultan, in exchange for the doubling of his annual tribute, the title of Khedive, followed by the right of succession by his direct male descendants, as opposed to the senior of the family as a whole. In 1868 he toured Europe, bringing news of progress to heads of states and pressing them to attend the opening ceremonies themselves; for he had keener sense of exhibitionism even than de Lesseps himself. The British people, a number of whom had always been enthusiastic despite Governmental discouragement, now looked forward to the day almost as eagerly as the French, and when, in March 1869, the sluices were ceremoniously thrown open to let the Mediterranean and Red Sea waters rush into the Bitter Lake (which was lower than sea level) the Prince and Princess of Wales were the most honoured spectator-guests of the Khedive. But at the final ceremony, planned for November 17, 1869, pride of place was reserved for France, in the gracious person of the Empress Eugénie. Austria sent her Emperor, Prussia her Crown Prince, and Russia a Grand Duke, brother of the Czar. Her Britannic Majesty was represented by a certain Mr. H. G. Elliot, Ambassador to the Sublime Porte. The Porte had no representative at all, so independent had Ismail become; nor for that matter had the United States.

Money meant nothing to Ismail, and he let it flow as freely as the waters of his canal in staging "the greatest festival Egypt had seen since the days of the Ptolemies". He spent three days receiving his guests outside Port Said in his yacht *Mahroussa*, while ashore three splendid pavilions had been constructed where guests were entertained in a style that no westerner could match. Arab chieftains came from miles around and their tents added further colour to the scene, forming a dazzling complement to the myriad flags that fluttered from the masts of the fifty men-o'-war, of all nations, lying outside the harbour. Bands played, guns barked their salutes, and on the evening of November 16 the rites of Moslem, Jewish and Christian Churches were celebrated and the canal was blessed by their high priests. Meanwhile the courbash was cutting the flesh of slaves in Cairo, where a great road to the Pyramids was in its last stage of preparation for the distinguished guests who were to go on to the capital and hear, among other things, a special opera composed for the occasion by Verdi.

The opening itself began at 8 a.m. next morning, when a fleet of sixty-seven guest vessels headed southward from Port Said while a flotilla of Egyptian warships passed through the entrance next Suez from the Red Sea. Roving Bedouin were treated to the amazing spectacle of mastheads and funnel-tops gliding through the desert, and those who climbed the bank to watch must have marvelled at the miracle that brought this great array of ships, with their strange, illustrious passengers, through their land. It was beyond them to realize the consequence of the miracle, that the great nations that showed such interest in Egypt would keep close and jealous watch on her affairs. "We are all Europeans now," boasted Ismail, unable as yet to perceive the irony of his words.

Leading the variegated convoy from Port Said was the French Imperial yacht, *L'Aigle*, carrying the Empress and the man of the moment, de Lesseps. The atmosphere inside was tense, almost febrile, as witness de Lesseps himself: "Within the cabin sat the Empress Eugénie, a prey to the most grievous emotions: every moment she thought she saw the *Aigle* stop, the honours of the French flag compromised, our labours lost. Overcome by her feelings she left the company, and we overheard her sobs—sobs which do her honour—for it was French patriotism flowing from her heart."

French honour was vindicated, but tribulation lay ahead both for France and the Canal Company. Within a year the Emperor Napoleon was a prisoner of the Prussians, the Empress a fugitive from her own countrymen, and Paris besieged: events which were to have their influence on the history of Egypt. As for the Canal Company, it proved no money spinner in its early days and was soon in serious financial difficulties. With France in ruins, de Lesseps appealed for aid from the British Government, but though he had been honoured by the Queen and made a Freeman of London, he was now denied even an interview by Lord Granville, Foreign Secretary to Gladstone. De Lesseps, very cross, threatened to stop the passage of British ships and succeeded in exasperating a number of their captains with the delays he imposed for alleged technicalities.

Ismail, however, had better luck with the British a few years later. He longed to be rid of the shares that had been foisted on his predecessor, Said, for want of an alternative buyer, and in December 1874 he let it be known to the British Government that they might be obtainable through the French banker who held first option. Disraeli was now Prime Minister. He had opposed the building of the canal almost as strongly as Palmerston—"a most futile attempt", he had called the project in 1858—but now that it was built he realized its importance as gateway to India, and India had a very special place in his romantic heart. Here was his chance to gain control of the gateway, or at any rate to deny it to the French. After a heated Cabinet meeting, the purchase of the shares was confirmed at £4,000,000, which was £320,000 more than the option offered the Frenchman. Rothschild readily advanced the cash.

Disraeli made the most of his purchase, hailing it as a great coup for the British Empire. "You have it, madam," he joyfully wrote to the Queen. "The entire interest of the Khedive is now yours." (But not "The Canal is yours", as has sometimes been stated.) The Queen was thrilled. "How jolly!" wrote her grandson, Prince Willy of Germany, the Kaiser-to-be. "England has bought the Suez Canal." In fact the shares amounted to rather less than half the total ordinary ones, and as no single shareholder was entitled to more than ten votes, the influence Britain had bought at such cost was limited indeed. The only concession made by the company was to allow three British members on to its predominantly French board, thus increasing its size from 21 to 24. "It is an act of folly," growled Gladstone from his country retreat (for Parliament was in recess); he had always regarded the canal as entirely a commercial venture, neither to be impeded nor aided by the Government. He was as wrong as he was right, for in fifty years' time the Government's holdings were paying, against all expectations, an annual dividend of around £1,500,000.

CHAPTER SIX

Pride and Consequence

(1875-82)

THE FOUR MILLION Ismail had gained was a pittance compared to what he already owed. Egypt had to have everything which a modern state could desire: roads, railways, telegraph lines, factories, schools. It was immaterial whether the economy could afford such luxuries or the people put them to advantageous use; so long as foreign firms were prepared to provide the services, and foreign banks the capital, modernization must go ahead. Finding that contracts could be wrung from the Khedive's Government on terms that amounted almost to robbery, the foreigners swarmed in with gold-rush zeal. In twenty years the number of European residents rose from six to a hundred thousand. The begging business boomed as never before, hoarse, guttural chants of "Baksheesh" greeting the foreigner wherever he went.

There was just as great a boom in the building trade. Cairo was transformed. Edwin de Leon, a former consul-general, described his dismay on returning after a few years' absence. The old fortess-like aspect was gone. Instead of massive walls, the city was now skirted by palatial garden suburbs and entered, not through a gate, but along wide boulevards. Worst of all was the view of Ezbekia Square from Shepheard's Hotel. Gone was the rambling garden wilderness in which Cairenes had delighted to linger, listening to story-tellers or watching dancing-girls. In its place were a copy of Paris's Rue de Rivoli, its shops and houses "square, formal, uniform, hideous-looking imitations of the ugliest architecture in the world", and a prim little garden, where dull Europeans promenaded to the strains of an Egyptian military band. The dress of these dull Europeans was also being copied (except for the head-wear) by officials, businessmen, cabbies and even the ladies of the harem. The pride and glory of the city and its people had been sacrificed, so de Leon thought, on the altar of Ismail's ambition.

He was now inextricably enmeshed in the web he had woven, bound ever tighter by the contractors and racketeers who had struck such harsh bargains with him and whose interests were well protected by the mixed courts (on which the Egyptian judge was in a minority) that had been appointed to settle disputes between foreigners and had power to make awards against the Khedive him-self. The full plight of his finances was revealed in April 1876, when he was obliged to suspend payment on treasury bills. The national debt stood at over £100,000,000. For the next three years Ismail wriggled desperately in its clutch, yielding independence in the process but doing little to curb his lavish private expenditure which he charged to the public account. A Commission of the Public Debt failed to unravel the tangle, and in 1878 the British and French Governments intervened to secure a full inquiry.

As a result of its findings Ismail bowed to the principle of ministerial responsibility and entrusted power to a strangely alien government under the former exile Nubar Pasha, an Armenian Christian, with a Briton, Rivers Wilson, as Minister of Finance, and a Frenchman, de Blignières, as Minister of Public Works. Ismail soon broke it up with tactics favoured by his grandfather, Aly, during his rise to power. He stirred up a public demonstration against Nubar, rescued him from its grasp, and relieved him of office in the cause of security. He then got rid of Wilson and de Blignières by similar means. The British and French Governments meekly stood by—until Bismarck, hearing that Ismail was about to repudiate a substantial debt, told them bluntly that if they did not intervene he would do so himself. There could be no brisker spur. After an unsuccessful attempt by the British and French consuls to persuade Ismail to resign, the Sultan was prevailed upon to issue a firman of deposition. Ismail went quietly and with dignity. On June 27, 1789, he sailed from Alexandria for Naples in his royal yacht, *Mahroussa*, with a wailing, black-draped harem and a rich store of treasure on board. Thus departed the grand-father of King Farouk.

His successor, Tewfik, had an unenviable inheritance. The son of Ismail and a harem slave, he was a not bad-looking man of 27, intelligent and pleasantly mannered, but ill equipped by temperament and experience and control the conflicting forces competing for power in Egypt. On the one hand were the hungry creditors, represented by an International Commission of Liquidation, and to see that its demands were met two Controllers were appointed, one French and one British. They had dictators' powers over all matters financial, but had nothing to back their authority nearer than the ships of their fleets roving the Mediterranean. Chafing against the strait-jacket they imposed, and equally determined to clip the power of the Khedive, were the National Constitutionalists, a league of intellectuals, mainly Turkish in origin, who sought a more democratic form of government, based on the Western pattern, though adapted to suit Eastern conditions. Their ambitions fell far short of enforcing the will of the people with whom they did not even share the affinity of a common language.

Yet the worm was beginning to pierce the surface; the little-considered will of the people was at last astir. Ismail had roused the pride of Egyptians by showing off their achievements to the world and had in turn nettled that pride by flooding the country with foreign overlords. As in the days of Bonaparte's occupation, the spread of immodest Western customs gave offence to devout Moslem minds, and offence was soon turned to hatred of all foreigners in minds less devout. Under the leadership of El Afghani, an inspired young idealist exiled from Constantinople, an earnest call for a revival in the faith of Islam went out from the Al Azhar Mosque and lit flames in many breasts, usually more nationalist than religious. Nowhere did they burn so brightly as in the officer ranks of the peasant army. The army had been a great plaything of Ismail's and had at one time reached a strength of seventy thousand, but now it was being reduced even below the eighteen thousand stipulated in 1840. The men had no objection to discharge, but not so the officers, and of course the ones most certain of being retained were the mercenaries of the old officer corps, the men from Turkey and the Circassia, the region of the Caucasus, who regarded and treated the native Egyptian officers as very inferior material.

Among those who smarted under the domination of these arrogant foreigners was Colonel Ahmed Arabi, son of a village sheikh. He had made a meteoric rise to that rank in the early days of his conscripted service, but twenty years of frustration and humiliation had followed. He was a tall, well-built man, with high forehead, beaked nose and dashing moustache. But there was nothing dashing about his manner. He was grave and passionately sincere, prone to melancholy and constantly worried, yet he could inspire his peasant soldiers, not with the flamboyant truculence of a rabble rouser, but with the slow, pastoral quality of his speech and with quotations from the Koran, in which he was well versed. Arabi was instrumental in forming a secret officers' society, which blossomed openly into the Egyptian Nationalist Party, the pioneer of the "Egypt for the Egyptians" movement.

Hearing that they were going to be dismissed from the Army, Arabi and another colonel bravely approached the Prime Minister, laid before him complaints about the soldiers' pay and rations, and demanded the dismissal of the War Minister, a much disliked Circassian named Osman Rizky. A few days later they were asked to report to the War Office at Kasr-el-Nil Palace, which later was to be turned into barracks so well known to British troops. There they were arrested and at once arraigned before a court martial, but no sooner had their summary trial started than the men of the colonels' two regiments stormed into the Palace, frisked all its occupants, including the War Minister himself, and carried off the ex-prisoners with bands playing through cheering crowds. The Khedive meekly bowed to this great wave of nationalist fervour and after summoning the two colonels told them that Osman Rizky was dismissed. They for their part apologized for their behaviour and swore their allegiance to him.

This was in February 1881, and the following September Arabi again turned to mutiny to achieve political ends, parading his men in Abdin Palace and demanding that the Khedive dismiss his Prime Minister, the pro-British Riaz Pasha. Again the Khedive gave way and the Constitutionalist, Sherif Pasha, came to power, amid great rejoicing by the people. Soon there was dispute between the Khedive's new Ministers and the two Controllers, and the French and British Governments were becoming very worried indeed.

The Dual Control was never quite the harmonious partnership that the title implies. Britain was disinclined to interfere, except to redress an obvious wrong; France, still in the throes of the inferiority complex wrought by defeat in war, was eager to make her influence felt. Britain was under the Liberal Government of Gladstone, who had been helped back to power by the unpopularity of Disraeli's venture into Zululand and was determined to avoid any similar military involvement; France, on the other hand, gloried in the recent annexation of Tunisia and had a new Prime Minister who was the very emblem of the nation's pride, Gambetta, the great resistance leader in the Franco-Prussian War.

Gambetta was determined to deal firmly with these hotheads who were challenging the authority of the Dual Control, and the British, for want of alternative ideas, acquiesced in the despatch of the combined note which he drafted, Lord Granville, Gladstone's Foreign Secretary, merely adding a rider claiming freedom of action "if action should be be found necessary". The note, delivered on January 6, 1882, was virtually an ultimatum that any attempt at change would bring retribution. "The British and French Governments," ran the most telling passage, "consider the maintenance of His Highness the Khedive on the throne, on the terms laid down in the Sultan's firman and officially recognized by the two Governments, as alone able to guarantee, for the present and future, the good order and development of general prosperity in Egypt in which France and Britain are equally interested. The two Governments, being closely associated in their resolve to guard, by their united efforts, against all causes of complication, internal or external, which might menace the order of things established in Egypt . . . feel certain that His Highness will derive from this assurance the confidence and strength which he requires to direct the destinies of Egypt and his people."

The note caused dismay in Cairo, not least among the British representatives at the Consulate and the Dual Control. Many saw it as a warning that Egypt was to be swallowed up as Tunisia had been, and instead of easing tension it greatly increased it. The National Constitutionalists gave way to the Army men and in February the Minister of War, Mahmoud Sami, became Prime Minister, with Arabi taking over his post in charge of the Army. At once fresh battalions were raised, pay rates increased, officers promoted with scant qualification, and Circassians exiled after a strange court martial. Meanwhile the two Controllers were passively relegated to the role of spectator. Arabi himself was losing control of his nationalist steed, and the one man willing to halt him with a jolt was now out of office; for the fiery Gambetta had been succeeded by the circumspect de Freycinet and French foreign policy was in process of a turnabout, obsessed with sorry memories of Napoleonic misadventures. Britain turned her hopes to a Turkish intervention, but the Porte had not yet decided whether to support Arabi or to oppose him. Nor, for that matter, had the Khedive Tewfik. He was prevailed upon to dismiss Arabi on May 27 but had him reinstated next day after threats from the Army and pleas from religious leaders fearful of massacre. Meanwhile, British and French battleships arrived at Alexandria, more to bring comfort to a panicking population than with any belligerent intention.

On the evening of June 11 the mob broke loose in Alexandria, hounded Europeans through the streets, and slaughtered some fifty of them, with yells of "Oh, Moslems, kill them!" It was the riff-raff's way of expressing the mood of defiance that gripped the country, and if any plans were made for concerted action they almost certainly had no higher inspiration.

Arabi, who had no reason to welcome the outrage, sent his soldiers in to restore order, refugees embarked in their thousands under the alert eyes of the allied fleet, and the statesmen of Europe ponderously assembled at Constantinople to discuss means of dealing with this strange phenomenon, a national rising by the Egyptian people. Turkey boycotted the conference, insisting with characteristic lack of realism that it was a problem concerning her alone which she already had in hand; in fact the Sultan, still smarting under the impudence of the Anglo-French note, was involved in "tortuous and occult devices", a peep of which was afforded by his conferment on Arabi of the Order of Medjidie First Class. However, the Sultan did consent to issue an order suspending work on the fortifications of Alexandria, which menaced the security of the allied fleet, and for a while the work was stopped.

When it began again Gladstone's Government, influenced perhaps by the rising indignation at the truculence of the upstart Egyptian, decided that the time had come to use the cane. Admiral Sir Beauchamp Seymour, the massive, bushy-bearded commander of the British fleet—"Swell of the Ocean" he was irreverently called, though a jersey was his favourite dress—was ordered to stop the construction work, if necessary by force. The French were invited to co-operate but decided instead to retire. Seymour delivered his ultimatum and was assured that all work had stopped. Electric-powered searchlights—new marvels of invention—revealed this assurance as the mockery it was; "Perfidy!" screamed the Egyptians when the powerful rays caught them at their midnight labours.

Seymour carried out his task of destruction on July 11, having given prior warning to clear the harbour of foreign shipping. He used eight iron-clad battleships, mighty in armament, forest-like in the intricate rigging of their superstructures. It was a splendid chance to try out the Navy's newest and greatest guns on land emplacements and Seymour made the most of his opportunity. The bombardment began at 7 a.m. and went on until 5.30 p.m., with occasional pauses to allow the smoke to clear. The batteries were methodically demolished, except for those at Fort Marabout, which were silenced by an impudent, unsponsored assault by Commander Lord Charles Beresford in his gunboat *Condor*. Highest concentrations were directed against the guns around Ras-el-Tin Palace, seawards of the harbour, where over a hundred were destroyed and a great blaze was started. "The Egyptians," to quote Seymour's despatch, "fought with determined bravery, replying to the hot fire poured into their forts from our heavy guns until they must have been quite decimated." They succeeded in killing five British sailors and wounding a further twenty-seven and are believed themselves to have lost over a thousand killed or wounded. Next day Seymour sent parties in to examine his battered targets, and not being fully satisfied with the results added a few more rounds, some of which destroyed a beautiful old mosque at Fort Pharos.

There had been terrible scenes in Alexandria. The 11th was a day of flight, demolition and death, for many shells overshot their targets and wrought great destruction, most of all in the Arab quarter. On the 12th, Arabi's soldiers joined the fugitives, leaving the city in the clutch of hooligan hordes, many of them released from prison, who revelled in a chance of loot, murder and arson beyond their wildest dreams. Offices, shops and well-to-do houses were ransacked and turned into a mighty blaze, while "Christian dogs" skeltered for their lives and those that could jumped into rowboats and found refuge with the fleet.

Gladstone had specifically forbidden a landing through curious inhibitions against offending the powers assembled in conference. However, the call of chaos was a shrill one, and on the morning of the 13th Seymour sent ashore a strong force of marines to take possession of the pitted hulk of Ras-el-Tin Palace, followed that evening by a provost force to restore order in the city. Beresford, its commander, "found a pandemonium of hell and its devils" and set about rounding up the thugs lurking the rubble and bringing them before a court of impressed Egyptians for the instant discharge of justice. Just before he started this task, a forlorn party of Egyptian cavalry rode into Ras-el-Tin with white handkerchiefs on their sabres. Behind them, in a coach, was the Khedive Tewfik, come from Ramleh to seek protection from his own mutinous troops who were, so he understood, out to murder him.

This greatly clarified the issue for the British Government, since they could now revert to the simple aim, proclaimed with such force at Gambetta's instigation, of "the maintenance of His Highness on the throne". Gladstone made a last despairing attempt to persuade the Turks to intervene, uninhibited by the thunderous denunciation he had made, when in opposition, of their savagery as colonists. The Sultan prevaricated as usual. The powers of Europe, still in sedate conference at Constantinople, turned to Britain; they accepted the need for the bombardment but were much alarmed by its consequence, for lawlessness had spread across Egypt and the lives, property and financial interests of all Europeans were in grave peril. On July 22 Gladstone obtained, by a vote of 275 to 19, the Commons' authority for the despatch of a force to Egypt "to suppress a military revolt in that country". It was still hoped that the French might co-operate, if only in defence of the Suez Canal, but on July 29 a motion in the French Chamber to that effect was defeated by 416 votes to 75 and de Freycinet's Government fell. Georges Clemenceau, his successor as Prime Minister, thought only of revenge against Germany and regarded any commitment outside Europe as a wasteful diversion.

Thus the vagaries of France's politics, still lurching in the hangover of national defeat, left it to her rival to occupy the country on whose internal affairs she (France) had exerted the greater influence, and it fell solely to Britain's Liberal Government to reassert the authority of an autocratic, semi-alien ruler over the nationalist aspirations of his people. It was not done without cost. The bombardment of Alexandria made controversy flare in Britain, and though those who raised protest were more vociferous than numerous, they included Gladstone's Radical friend, "dear old John Bright", who resigned from the Cabinet. It "turns a white day into a black one," wrote Gladstone to Granville when he received the resignation on the day following the bombardment. He defended himself by blaming all on Arabi. It was he who "by fraud and falsehood" had forced the fleet to use its guns in self-defence, he who with "seemingly wanton wickedness" had incited the conflagration and pillage that followed, he who had defied the authority of "the Khedive, the Sultan, the notables, and the best men in the country".

"We should not fully discharge our duty, if we did not endeavour to convert the present inferior state of Egypt from anarchy and conflict to peace and order," he told the House on July 22, and in this same speech, "It has been charitably believed, even in this country, that the military party was the popular party, and was struggling for the liberties of Egypt. There is not the smallest rag or shred of evidence to support that contention." He had persuaded himself, in other words, that the peasant soldiers were akin to Mamelukes. It was a feat of mental acrobatics demanded by the Liberal conscience.

CHAPTER SEVEN

The Subduing of Arabi

(1882)

NO SECRETARY OF State for War ever made himself as unpopular as Gladstone's man, H. C. E. Childers. Under a former Liberal Government infantry regiments were formed into pairs, sharing a depot and alternate tours at home and abroad but retaining their separate identities. Now Childers had the effrontery to carry these reforms of Mr. Cardwell to their logical conclusion. In 1881 the paired regiments (that is all except twenty-seven which already had two battalions) were amalgamated and the revered numerical titles of all regiments of the Line gave way to new county ones. Thus such famous regiments as the 43rd and the 52nd found themselves converted overnight into the 1st and 2nd Battalions of the Oxford-shire and Buckinghamshire Light Infantry, and there was wide-spread rage against the "astounding impudence of a Mr. Childers", as a retired officer termed it, on seeing his beloved 35th Foot turned into the 1st Royal Sussex. How the soldier would face up to the test of battle when such pillage was made of his loyalties was the question asked by the old and bold.

Most formidable of all opponents of reform was His Royal High-ness The Commander-in-Chief, the Duke of Cambridge, better known as Royal George, a man with passionate pride in the Army and all its fine traditions, which he could defend with the weight of twenty-five years' tenure of his post. But Childers had an ally just as powerful, just as influential, in his Adjutant-General, Sir Garnet Wolseley, "the very model of a modern major-general", hero of the people for his victories in the Empire's far-flung wars, infuriator of clubland with his reforming zeal and professionalism. He was the Montgomery of his era and similar in many ways, being an ex-infantryman from an unfashionable regiment, slight of build, sharp of feature, penetrating of eye, irritatingly aware of his own ability and unfailingly proved right. There was joy, and no surprise when his name was announced as the commander of this expedition to Egypt, the largest and most important ever despatched in peacetime.

Wolseley had turned his brain to the problem long before Seymour's guns had bombarded Alexandria, before even the June massacre. Whilst the rapid seizure of the Suez Canal appeared essential to his crisp mind, so did the capture of Cairo, for it was from there that fresh water flowed to the canal stations. New irrigation ditches encumbered the traditional invasion route by the Nile and he chose instead the shorter approach from Ismailia, affording as it did the combined lifeline of canal and railway. Just as important was Ismailia's central position which made it the ideal concentration point for the troops which would have to converge from west and east if the necessary force of two infantry divisions and a cavalry brigade (subsequently enlarged) was to be formed.

All this is revealed in a memo to the Commander-in-Chief, dated July 3, which is remarkable for its clarity of purpose and attention to detail. He was much concerned about the provision of rolling-stock and asked for "5 locomotives, with large separate tenders, 5 brake-wagons, with ample supply of tools for repairs; also at least 10 miles of steel rails, with bowl sleepers, bolts, nuts, fish-plates, keys, points and crossings in proportion . . . This will enable us to cut down our transport very much, specially as it may be expected that the Egyptian army would make its stand somewhere in the neighbourhood of Tel-el-Kebir.

"If the action comes off there," he concluded, "no serious fighting may be anticipated until Cairo is reached; indeed, although it is possible that some attempt might be made to hold that city, if the Egyptian army is well defeated in the field, any further resistance would be insignificant."

Preparations went fast ahead. Troops were alerted and commodities ranging from mules to fire-wood were ordered from far and wide. It was now that the Liberals realized that the Tories' acquisition of Cyprus was not quite the "mad undertaking" that Gladstone had described it in the House. Disraeli had won the right to occupy this island in exchange for services rendered to

Turkey at the Congress of Berlin in 1878. Its appeal for him lay in its romantic past; he had acquired for his Queen the Isle of Venus, gem of all colonial collections. Lord Salisbury, his Foreign Secretary, who had done the spade-work, was more concerned with its practical value. He saw the need for a base, or *place d'armes*, from which aid could be given against the menace of Russian expansion. He appreciated the need for speed. "How utterly impossible," he wrote about Malta to his Ambassador at Constantinople, "efficient and prompt military aid is from a port which is four days' sail from the scene of action." The Turks were impressed by the argument and the deal was made. Now the Liberal Government showed their appreciation of it by sending to Cyprus an infantry brigade. It was to be prepared to seize the Suez Canal within 24 hours of receiving orders.

In the event this brigade went, not to the Canal, but to Alexandria. It was a move forced on Wolseley that he turned to good account. Seymour's marines and seamen were doing their best to restore order in Alexandria, but it had quickly become apparent that the task called for a very much larger force. The 1st Battalion, The South Staffordshire Regiment, were the first soldiers to arrive. They had reached Cyprus on July 13, re-embarked on the 15th, and on the 17th marched down the gangplanks into the dust and wreckage of Alexandria harbour. The rest of the brigade followed over the next two days, and thus the British gained a foothold before the war—or rather, police operation—officially began, for it was not until the 22nd that the Commons voted in favour of intervention and the Khedive formally declared Arabi a rebel.

Wolseley was quick to see the value of this foothold he had involuntarily gained. "Keep Arabi thoroughly alarmed", the brigade commander was instructed: a task made all the easier by the planners in London who had, with rare cunning, for long been naming Alexandria as the base for proposed operations. The soldiers stopped rounding up looters, vagabonds and criminals deliberately let out of jail, and set out to harry the Egyptian army. They found it entrenched at Kafr-el-Dauwar, some fifteen miles south-east of Alexandria, covering a five-mile gap between the lakes of Maryut and Idku. It was in the best possible position to contain a thrust from Alexandria, while there was another strong force around Aboukir, threatening the flank of any such thrust.

Arabi could if he wished have made himself dictator of Egypt, but despite the picture painted by the British press he was no megalomaniac and preferred to place himself under a National Council which assembled at Cairo, taking the place of the Khedive's ministers who, headed by Sherif, the Constitutionalist, fled to join him at Alexandria. A Jehad, or Holy War, conferring Islam's warrant to kill, was declared: death to the infidel! Certainly in four towns they savagely met it. Further to goad the fervour of the people, messengers rode forth with a proclamation from Arabi announcing the sinking of the British fleet; the Admiral was slain and the sea was full of corpses, but it was admitted that a few British soldiers had temporarily entered Alexandria, where they were torturing their captives. A slight adjustment to this report was made when the Egyptians gained real success in the capture of a midshipman. Astronomic promotion was in store for him. After being kindly received by Arabi, he was taken to Cairo, where he heard a tremendous clamour as his closed carriage was driven through the streets in the early hours of the morning. The people had been told that Admiral Seymour himself was inside it.

A system of short service, employed over the years, made a liberal supply of reservists available, and the Egyptian Army rapidly rose to a strength of over sixty thousand trained men. There can be no telling how much coercion was needed to herd the reservists in from the Nile villages, but certainly there was enthusiasm enough in Cairo. Provision of uniform for such a force seemed an almost insoluble problem, yet by frantic endeavour every man was equipped with red tarboush and blue tassel, loose white cotton tunic, wide drill trousers and gaiters. There was a good supply of Remington rifles available, provided by Americans who had also been training the army. The Chief of Staff was a former officer of the Confederate Army, General Stone, who wisely remained in the background when rebellion broke out. Guns came from Germany, made by Krupps, and there were nearly three hundred all told. It was indeed a force to be reckoned with—if only the flame lit by Ibrahim still burned.

With pride and majesty Wolseley's men departed for the fray, some twenty thousand from Britain and the Mediterranean stations and a further seven thousand from India, with others to follow. Before "a mighty and sympathizing throng of Londoners", the first ship from Britain sailed from the Royal Albert Docks, Woolwich, at noon on Sunday, July 30, a mere eight days after the great decision had been approved by Parliament. On board was the Duke of Connaught, "darling, precious Arthur", the 32-year-old son of the Queen, who had been entrusted with command of the 1st Guards Brigade; with him was his divisional commander Lieutenant-General Sir George Willis—"a very nice quiet old fellow", according to one of his brigadiers—and the 1st Battalion, The Scots Guards. Bands played, handkerchiefs fluttered, and cheers echoed and re-echoed from bank to bank as the red-clad soldiers set off down the great river. They were bound, it seemed so certain, for fresh fields of glory on which to enrich the proud name of Britain and her Empress Queen.

The Queen herself was at Osborne, on the Isle of Wight, receiving homage from Wolseley before his departure two days later. He had intended to travel by train across Europe, but had suffered complications after a sharp chill and on doctor's orders took the sea voyage instead.

Meanwhile excitement was mounting in Alexandria. Reinforcements for the British steamed steadily in from Mediterranean stations, and the Khedive, who had declined the offer of evacuation, fully recovered his composure, gaining the admiration of a British major-general for his light-hearted attitude towards Arabi, whom he described as "the destroyer before the Prophet prophesied". Such foreigners as remained had also regained their jauntiness, especially the cosmopolitan flotsam, Italian, Levantine, Maltese, Greek, who were finding increasing amusement in insolence to the British. Jaunty too, and almost as insolent, were the corps of journalists of all nationalities, most of whom were hoping to witness the humiliation of British arms. They found the opening manœuvres encouraging. The British probed the enemy lines in some strength, supported by an armoured train, but fell back (as they intended) before fire which was massive in volume and negligible in effect. The correspondents reported "aimless skirmishing" and made many censorious comments. They were galling to the commanders and disturbing to the British public, but they had the desired effect of strengthening Arabi in his conviction that the main effort was to be made from Alexandria.

Already, on August 2, British marines had landed at Suez and occupied the town without challenge. That they aroused singularly little suspicion was due largely to the fortuitous presumption of de Lesseps, who had hurried from France to Egypt at the first sign of crisis. Hearing that Arabi intended to block the canal, he had rushed to assure him that the British would never venture to invade territory which belonged personally to him, de Lesseps.

On August 16 Wolseley reached Alexandria, where there was now great military activity, with the whole of the 2nd Division deployed for battle, the 1st fast disembarking to join them, and the Household Cavalry—a combined regiment of Life Guards and Blues—adding dignity and importance to the proceedings. The Commander-in-Chief issued a few sharp instructions about rolling-stock and went earnestly into conference with Admiral Seymour. Much to their later indignation, his divisional commanders were kept in the dark as to his real intention and had no inkling that the orders they received for a combined sea and land assault on Arabi's positions were a ruse. On the 18th those men of the 1st Division already ashore were re-embarked. Next day they steamed into Aboukir Bay; the sailors stripped their warships for action and the soldiers gazed anxiously at the bristling shore defences they were to assault that night. The scene of former glories, so it seemed, was an irresistible lure for the High Command.

But when darkness fell, the ships slipped away to the north-east, and as they did so ripples of activity silently electrified the calm of the night from one end of the canal to the other. At Port Said marines crept ashore from the sea and the canal, stifled sentries, burst into barracks, and gained control of the town while most of its citizens slept. At Ismailia the marines also landed without detection, and after a short, sharp fight for the lock gates they entered the attractive little French-style town and drove the Egyptians out of Nefisha railway station with some shells from their warships. Old de Lesseps was awakened and in his anguish tried to throw himself on the bayonets of the marines, only to be restrained in the best police force tradition: "Now, now, sir, we don't want no bloodshed here." From Suez the Seaforth High-landers, spearhead of the troops from India, swept northwards to seize the fresh-water lock at Shuluf, on which Suez was dependent. Meanwhile, a frigate sailed up the canal from Port Said, taking possession of barges and dredgers, cutting cable lines and im-pounding all ships in passage in the *gares*, or passing bays, to clear the route for Wolseley and his transports.

Thus the canal fell without blemish into British hands during the course of a brisk night's work, the co-ordination of which was much aided by their right of free passage which they had subse-quently violated. Sanction for the deed was obtained from the Khedive. Nonetheless, the French were stung to deliver sharp protest, and though de Lesseps regained some of his composure he

Murad Bey, the Mameluke war-lord defeated at the Pyramids

Lieutenant-General Sir Ralph Abercromby, posthumous conqueror of the French

Mohammed Aly, Pasha
of Egypt and founder
of a dynasty

Ismail Pasha, Mohammed Aly's
spendtnrift grandson and, until
exiled, Egypt's first Khedive

Vicompte Ferdinand de Lesseps, builder of the Suez Canal
and hence of Egypt's destiny

Arabi Pasha, Egypt's first patriot, after his defeat and imprisonment

Lieutenant-General Sir Garnet Wolseley, victorious in Egypt, later thwarted on the Nile

gave vent to his wrath by ordering all the canal workers to stay at home. But the greatest fury raged in the breast of Arabi. He had been so eager to wreck this alien-controlled waterway, which presented such menace to the security and independence of Egypt, and had approved detailed plans for its destruction, which had been prepared, predictably enough, by a Russian. Instead of following his instinct and letting the obstruction work go ahead, he had heeded to the word of an infidel and now had to pay the price.

Next day Wolseley's twenty-one transport ships entered the canal through Port Said, the soldiers marshalled on deck for church parade, for it was Sunday, August 20. Their entry was delayed by a gesture to the French by which a mail ship, caught in the canal, was allowed to proceed, and two British steamers impudently sneaked in behind her. The grounding of various ships—for no pilots were available—caused further delay, and it was not until 9 a.m. on the 21st, fifteen hours behind schedule, that Wolseley reached Ismailia. By dusk half his ships stood off the harbour, the Grenadiers still being stranded in the canal, with behind them all the cavalry, hospital units and artillery.

Ismailia is on the shore of Lake Timsah and the ships were moored outside the single pier, across which their cargoes had to be discharged by lighter, one at a time. It was a slow and laborious business, but this had been foreseen by Wolseley, who had cut his fighting troops to the minimum to speed the build-up of his administrative tail. Much is made by Colonel Maurice, the official historian, of the calculated risk he ran thereby. Even so, two thousand marines and seven infantry battalions preceded the supporting and administrative units. It was high, if unconscious, tribute to Arabi that risk should be envisaged in the protective power of such a force, even if a high proportion had to be employed on stevedore duties.

The first stratagem of the enemy was revealed by an alarming drop in the level of the fresh-water canal which, running from Cairo past the village of Tel-el-Kebir (which is 35 miles from Ismailia and a further 52 from Cairo), was to be the line of Wolseley's advance. He was forced to take the offensive sooner than he intended. At dawn on August 24 the Household Cavalry rode the six miles to Magfar and went pounding into action (for the first time since Waterloo) to hack down the few defenders of a dam which had been industriously built there, blocking the water. To support them came a force of Mounted Infantry, Royal Marines, the 2nd York and Lancasters, and the only two guns yet unloaded, and as they took up position thousands of Egyptian soldiers, brought up by train, advanced towards them, blackening the haze over the desert horizon. Wolseley, typically, was on the spot to meet the crisis. He ordered his meagre force to stand fast and sent for reinforcements, five miles away. Soon afterwards, a shell screamed into the position, killing a horse a few yards behind him.

It was a great chance for the Egyptians, outnumbering the British as they did by around eight to one in guns and infantry. But their infantry lacked daring and were kept their distance by the steady fire of the York and Lancasters and the sharp-shooting mounted infantry, while the timely arrival of two Gatling machine-guns, manned by sailors, soon deterred their attempts to turn the flanks. Their gunners, however, fired with zest and accuracy and would have done much damage but for the soft sand and some inept fuse-setting; they did at least force the cavalry and mounted infantry to pull back. The two British guns were fought with magnificent spirit, though they had to be pulled out of the sand after every shot, a fearful exertion under the broiling sun. Heat was in fact the deadliest enemy. The soldiers had pith helmets, veils and sun-glasses, but were otherwise dressed for home service, in red or blue tunic and thick serge trousers. The desert seemed like a furnace to the men come straight from England, and many reeled and collapsed, especially in the ranks of the battalions that toiled through the soft sand in answer to Wolseley's call for reinforcements, which were not in the end needed. There were forty-two casualties from heat-stroke against thirteen from enemy fire; it was the most gruelling day of the campaign for those engaged.

Wolseley pushed on next day, anxious to end further damming of the canal. The Egyptians did not wait to fight but quickly withdrew to their trains; a wide right hook by the Cavalry Brigade interrupted their departure and deprived them of seven guns and seventy-five railway carriages. On the following day, August 26, the all-important lock at Kasassin was captured. Wolseley could now afford to halt—and indeed he had to, for his supply line was strained to the utmost and his troops were getting little more than biscuits. There was a transport crisis. Ration carts needed double teams of horses to lug them across the roadless desert, and arrangements for the provision of pack animals had sadly miscarried, largely through the duplicity of the Turks, who were still trying to back both runners. An attempt to obtain camels in the Sinai desert had ended in "the cruel and foul murder by lawless Arabs" of the distinguished professor and two officers who had bravely posed as Arabs to make the attempt. The railway line was Wolseley's main hope, but here too his requirements had not been met and it was some time before he could get anything more than a disjointed, mule-propelled service going.

He was now only nine miles from his chosen battlefield of Tel-el-Kebir—"if," as he wrote to Lieutenant-General Sir Edward Hamley, still at Alexandria with his 2nd Division, "Arabi will only in kindness stay to fight me there". The Egyptians gave promise of such an intention by launching a strong attack on the Kassassin position late in the afternoon of the 28th, after some lengthy grimacing. They were held, at some cost, by the 2nd Brigade under Major-General Gerald Graham, who sent a message to the Cavalry Brigade Commander, Major-General Drury Lowe, asking for a flank attack. The officer bearing the message got lost and by the time he found Lowe he was in such an overwrought state he blurted out that Graham could only just hold his own. Lowe responded loyally, despite the fact that he had just withdrawn his regiments after a tiring day on call. Consequently the Egyptians were set upon in moonlight by some weary, yet dauntless, squadrons of the Household Cavalry and the 7th Dragoon Guards. They brought down some horses and riders with their guns and rifles, then ran or plunged flat on the ground. The Householders careered over them and imagined that they had overrun some gun lines (which it transpired they had not) before trotting back to camp.

The correspondents made much of this spirited charge, and thrilling pictures were drawn for their papers of Egyptian gunners being hacked down by the Horse Guards as they fought their guns to the last. But it was a long time before they had anything else to report. They quickly lost patience, and as the days passed the demand for action turned to scathing censure of "delay" and "sloth." Even *Punch* showed its impatience with a cartoon captioned "Veni, Vidi—", showing Wolseley busying himself with maps and despatches. Wolseley described the correspondents as "those modern curses of armies", but they could never divert him from his purpose, however hard they might unwittingly try. And his purpose was clear: to fell Arabi at a single blow delivered with all his might. Not until all his men, weapons and vehicles had been squeezed through the narrow pipeline of Ismailia's pier and all his rolling-stock assembled would he be ready to do that. It was a drawback of the shortest route to Cairo that it had the weakest spring-board.

Arabi, for his part, was still uncertain, as he afterwards admitted, from which direction the attack would come. The British continued to be very active before Alexandria, despite the steady transfer of the 2nd Division to Ismailia, and quite probably Arabi expected thrusts of equal strength from both fronts, for he did not appreciate the principle of concentration, and had his own forces dispersed in five different localities, too far apart to support each other. Yet he was very sensitive to the threat to Tel-el-Kebir, having formerly been its commandant, and he moved his headquarters there in time personally to direct the attack on the 28th. This he hailed as a great victory, showing characteristic inventive genius which his successors have strived to emulate. Four thousand of the British had been slain, ran his bulletin, at a cost to the Egyptians of a mule and a camel. The world was working just retribution on the aggressor. France had captured Cyprus and Russia India, and Britain, tottering to her fall, was vainly imploring Turkey to aid her.

It may be that Arabi half believed the truth of his own communiqué, for the British showed no inclination to come after him and now came reports from Bedouin that they were pulling back. Arabi gleefully sent practically his entire force—eighteen infantry battalions, with strong artillery and cavalry support—into battle, forming two massive prongs which assailed the British, with considerable gusto, soon after dawn on September 9. They stove in the outpost positions, but flopped rapidly when sustained rifle and artillery fire rained down on them from positions behind. So far from withdrawing, the British were there in strength, and now their cavalry appeared, threatening the flanks of either prong. Panic seized the disillusioned Egyptians. They shed their boots and ran, pursued by the formidable combination of Graham's infantry and Lowe's cavalry. With Arabi's forces in complete disorder, the road to Tel-el-Kebir lay open. But Wolseley was not to be drawn. To the chagrin of his men and the scorn of the press, he ordered a retirement to the original position in front of Kassassin. Arabi had declared that he would burn Cairo to the ground rather than yield it to the British, and Wolseley was not going to tempt him to do so by jostling him prematurely into retreat before he (Wolseley) had the momentum to seize the city at a single bound.

The opportunity to rush the defences of Tel-el-Kebir was therefore allowed to go begging.

There was considerable risk in this policy, for though the Egyptian was an irresolute attacker there could be no telling how sturdily he might defend, and on the bare and jagged hill in front of Tel-el-Kebir he had very strong defences indeed. The work put into this position, stretching northwards from the canal and its adjacent railway line, was prodigious. For almost four miles, zigzagging twice as far, there was a continuous ditch, 6 ft. deep and 10 ft. wide in many (though not all) places, from which the gravelly sand had been scooped back to form earthworks for the defenders. The attackers were thus faced with a sheer 6 ft. drop followed by a graduated climb of some 10 ft. at the top of which they would find rifles aimed at them point-blank along the breastworks. Further defences had been built in rear by the sweating, still toiling, labour force, and there was a chain of strongpoints with guns and extra fortifications. To man his positions Arabi had twenty battalions of infantry, of which ten occupied his main defences, one an advanced position right of centre, six isolated positions on the right in the flat cultivated strip, one and a half miles wide, south of the canal, and only three, with 1,700 cavalry, reserve positions in rear. His strength, according to his own estimate, was 22,500 men and sixty guns, with an incalculable horde of Bedouin in support. Prisoners had given Wolseley fair assessment of this force.

Arabi had three days in which to recuperate from his disastrous offensive—a last, neglected chance to concentrate his divisions—before the last of Wolseley's men toiled into the camps around Kassassin to complete a many-coloured array of seventeen battalions of infantry, eight regiments of cavalry and eleven batteries of artillery, bringing the strength to 17,400 troops and 61 guns. The men of the new county regiments were battle-stained and stubbly of beard, having borne the brunt of the fighting so far and proved themselves as staunch as ever under their new identities. Bivouacked alongside them by the canal, each displaying their individuality in their dress and musical calls, were guardsmen, riflemen, marines, sailors, gunners, sappers, dragoons and hussars; Highlanders and Irishmen; and to European eyes the most colourful of all, the turbaned warriors of Major-General Sir Herbert Macpherson's Indian force, Jats, Sikhs, Dogras, Mahrattas, Baluchis, enlisted for the most part in the armies of Bengal and Madras. The spring was at last fully wound for release.

At dawn on September 12, with the last of his troops still marching up, Wolseley for the first time divulged his plan to his generals, having brought them up in darkness to an outpost hill ahead of the main position. They watched Arabi's sentries ride out for the daylight vigil from the big, honeycombed hill. "Note the time!" spoke Wolseley. He would attack before they set out next day.

The main assault was to be delivered to the right of centre, with the 2nd Division on the left and the 1st on the right, each with a brigade of four battalions all forward and a weaker brigade in reserve. A naval officer, versed in the art of navigation by the stars, was to direct the advance of the left-hand brigade, a sapper officer that of the right-hand one. There was to be a gap between the divisions, in which the artillery was to march, well placed to bring fire to bear wherever it was most required. Lowe's cavalry, raised to divisional strength by the addition of three lancer regiments of the Bengal Cavalry, was to operate further to the right and sweep round the enemy's flank, while the Indian infantry was to advance on the left of the canal, echeloned behind the others so that the inhabitants of the villages in the cultivated belt would not have time to spread the alarm. The Naval Brigade was to support them with their Gatlings and a 40-pounder gun, brought up along the adjacent railway line. At nightfall the troops were to march to a forward concentration area, 6,600 yds. from the enemy lines, where they were to deploy into battle formation. The advance from here was to begin at 1.30 a.m. at a speed of one mile an hour, calculated to bring the troops on their objective as the first streak of dawn brightened the sky.

Such was the plan for what was to become a classic example of the surprise dawn attack, but at the time of its unfolding it struck more than one of Wolseley's subordinates as ambitious to the point of folly. There were no such aids as luminous compasses and watches in those days, and the men's experience of night operations extended no further than the few night marches they had made during the current campaign, with the object of avoiding the heat of day. So much could go wrong when nerves got jumpy on a pitch-black night—and there would be no moon to help them. Wolseley knew the risks as well as anyone. He realized too that his reputation was at stake not only as field commander but as advocate of reform, for there were many ears eager for evidence with which to condemn the new-fangled county system and short engagements. Yet he had faith in his men, and to make sure that they did not betray it he ordered that no rifle should be loaded.

This proved a wise precaution, for there were scares enough as the troops set off in their battle formations, twinkling stars above them, crisp sand beneath them, and their neighbours just visible at their sides. A whispered warning, "Bedouin ahead!" (which apparently were staff officers riding behind) brought the centre of the Highland Brigade, the left-hand spearhead, to a halt, and the wings, unheeding, formed confused horseshoe, facing each other in alarm. The right-hand brigade, under the stalwart Graham, also got badly entangled and three different formations were successively ordered, half-battalion columns, line and company columns. These contortions took time—longer than they imagined, so it seemed, when to their horror the commanders saw the sky brighten, with their hilltop objective still far away. Darkness returned just as rapidly; it was the passing of a comet, so it transpired.

When at last, just before five, the sky began permanently to brighten behind them, it gave the Highlanders (but not Graham's men, who were about half a mile behind) a grimly clear outline of the redoubts which, with two higher features to left and right, rose before them 300 yds. ahead—they had needed every minute of the hour allotted for each mile. Three shots rang out, followed by a shell which failed to explode. The Highlanders strode on in silence, whipping their bayonets on their rifles without a pause. A mighty flash gave the whole hillside a halo as streams of bullets and shells zimmed over the kilted men, dropping a few in rear. Through the din came the sound of bugles: "Charge!" The Highlanders broke silence with a lusty roar, swept forward in two continuous uneven waves, and plunged down the 6-ft. drop into the defence ditch.

For about half an hour Egypt faced up to the fury of Scotland. There was no foothold in the soft sand of the defence ditch. Men clambered, panted, heaved each other and swore, and as quickly as they were hoisted up they dropped down groaning or mute. Officers grabbed hold of whatever men they saw, regardless of regiment, and with the swirl of the pipes to inspire them forced dents in the defences by weight of guts, butts and bayonets. But the entrenchments were in depth and no sooner had one fallen than resolute tarboushed faces, mere dark splotches in the half-light, would appear behind the next. The steadiness of these simple, untutored troops won the admiration of their opposing brigade commander, the veteran Major-General Sir Archibald Alison, who at one stage was seen fighting a lone battle, firing his pistol with the one hand that had survived his many campaigns. "At every reverting angle," he wrote, "at every battery and redoubt, they rallied and renewed the fight. Five or six times we closed on them with the bayonet, and I saw these poor men fighting hard when their officers were flying before us." (The officers had already become a standing joke among the British.)

The centre, the objectives of the Camerons and the Gordons, was carried with less loss of time than of life, but the flanking features, with their extra fortifications and gun emplacements, stubbornly held out. The 2nd Highland Light Infantry, attacking the left one, came to grips with black-faced Nubians, from the Sudan frontier, and at one point were driven back. There was chaos on the hillside, with the officers frantically rallying their men, and Hamley, the divisional commander, personally collecting reinforcements and urging them into the breach. The 1st Black Watch were also much belaboured in their assault on the right-hand strongpoint.

A quarter of an hour behind the Highlanders and half a mile beyond their right, Graham's men made their charge. Despite the clearer light and longer warning, the resistance here was less effective, and the battalions of this brigade—the Royal Marine Light Infantry, the 1st Royal Irish Fusiliers (who had marched from Ismailia with scarcely a pause), the 2nd York and Lancasters, and the 2nd Royal Irish—having advanced almost unscathed under "what appeared to be an overwhelming fire of musketry and artillery" (as Graham described it), fell on their objective with fine cohesion and, to the accompaniment of murderous yells from the Irish, stormed across a shallower defence ditch from which they quickly drove the Egyptians, who nonetheless fell back fighting.

With aid from the 3rd 60th, the Black Watch had meanwhile stormed their strongpoint. "Make way for the guns!" came the cry, and up galloped the gunners, hauled their guns across the defence ditch, and trained them on that other strongpoint which was causing the H.L.I. such turmoil. As they opened up, dust clouds became visible far beyond the hill. Led by the Bengal Cavalry, the Cavalry Division had made their outflanking movement and were enveloping the enemy's left rear. They signalled panic to the Egyptians. Arabi hurriedly finished dressing and emerged from his tent to see his men streaming down the hill towards him, hastened along by Highlanders, Irishmen and the Duke of Connaught's guardsmen, released at last from divisional reserve. He is said to have made a brief attempt to restore order out of the utter confusion, but was then persuaded by his servant to flee. Those of his cavalry, reserve battalions, and Bedouin irregulars who had not forestalled him briskly followed his lead.

Some troops still fought, such as various groups of gunners, the Nubians grappling with the H.L.I., and the occupants of an advanced post, finally blasted out by gunfire, which the 2nd Division had been lucky to by-pass during the night advance. The rest tore madly past the tents of the camps, leaped on to waiting trains, or stormed across the stone canal bridge, barging each other over, to flatten the crops in the field beyond. Two trains pulled out, festooned with white tunics half attached to owners scrambling for a hold, but the third was stopped by the gunners on the Black Watch's hill—having at last seen the Nubians overwhelmed, they took advantage of the first peep of sunlight behind them to show their marksmanship. Beyond rose a dust cloud, made by the fleet and handy steeds of the Egyptian cavaliers fleeing from the Bengal lancers, who soon swept round to the railway line. As they did so the Bengal Infantry, advancing south of the canal, closed in on Tel-el-Kebir village, in company with Lieutenant-Colonel Stockwell's Seaforth Highlanders, and cut off the fugitives streaming over the bridge. It was all over soon after six o'clock, and by quarter past nine, thanks to the marvel of telegraphy, Wolseley had received congratulation from his Queen. The nut had taken some cracking, but had an empty inside.

Nearly two thousand Egyptians lay dead on the bare hill and its surrounds, while over five hundred lay writhing and crying for water to ease the agony of their wounds. Betrayed by their own officers, who had proved such feeble and cowardly substitutes for the Circassians they had been so keen to drive away, they were caught once again in the talons of the foreign eagles which seemed doomed eternally to prey upon their land. It was left to their enemies to write their epitaph, men such as Alison and Wolseley's trusted staff officer, William Butler, who with a poet's instinct wrote: "No word should soldier utter against them; let that be left to the money-changers. They died the good death. Dust to dust. They did not desert the desert, and Egypt will not forget them." But no individuals could be picked out for immortality to rank with Lieutenant Brooks of the Gordons and Private Donald Cameron of the Camerons, who both gained posthumous glory as

6

the first to top the redoubt. These were among 57 of the British force killed in the battle, out of a total of 469 casualties, of which 231 were from the Highland Brigade. There had been a further 279 casualties since the advance from Ismailia began.

There was important work still to be done. Drury Lowe was ordered to push on with his cavalry, along the line of the canal, and reach Cairo before Arabi set fire to it, while Macpherson's Indians were to switch from left flank to right and seize the important railway junction of Zagazig, 25 miles distant, thus disrupting any troop concentration that might be attempted. There was no token of resistance. Macpherson's one squadron of Bengal lancers gave up hounding down stragglers and began to race each other for Zagazig, overtaking streams of Egyptian soldiers, most of them armed. Two officers and six troopers drew clear, clattered into the station, and caught three heavily laden trains in the act of departure, with others filling up. One pulled out, and its driver was shot by an officer galloping alongside. The train crashed into another, and blocked the line. Meanwhile, the sight of the fearsome Indians had put the occupants of all trains to flight, soldiers though they were meant to be. Soon after 4 p.m. Macpherson telegraphed Cairo from the station to forward news of Arabi's total defeat. At 9 p.m. he received obsequious reply from "The Commission named by the Egyptian Nation": "The whole Egyptian nation present their gratitude at the manner your Government have employed in support of His Highness Tewfik Pasha, our Khedive. . . . We are leaving immediately to lay before him the submission of the army." It might have been possible to have rushed a brigade through to Cairo—the line was open from Tel-el-Kebir and was double track from Zagazig—but Wolseley was relying on horsepower for that task, and he was not the man to change his mind.

The Cavalry Division had made less dramatic progress. The Indian Brigade gave ecstatic pursuit for twenty miles and by noon were in Belbeis, where they almost caught Arabi, but the guns were held up by soft sand and canal intersections, and Lowe ordered a halt. Swayed by the bolder spirits of his subordinates, who knew nothing of the message Macpherson had received at Zagazig, he agreed to leave the guns behind and at 4.30 next morning a force set out in high jingle, consisting of two and a half regiments of the inexhaustible Bengal Cavalry, the 4th Dragoon Guards, and the Mounted Infantry. There were 32 miles to go by the direct canal route, but with a detour added to avoid a swamp the troops rode rather further. They were greeted as liberators, ever more joyously the nearer they drew to Cairo. The sun was well on the decline when the silhouette of the famous domes and minarets at last appeared on the horizon. Though no smoke was to be seen rising, Lowe was still anxious. He had a ridiculously small force with which to enforce the surrender of the 15-20,000 fresh troops that were known to be in and around the city. He therefore kept his force in the background, hoping that it would be thought larger than it was, and sent on his staff officer, the intrepid Lieutenant-Colonel Herbert Stewart, with fifty troops, dragoons and Bengal lancers, to demand the surrender of Abbassia Barracks, which stands a few miles outside the city on its north-west corner.

It was a bold piece of bluff, which was not in fact needed. The Egyptians had made their preparations, even to the extent of issuing white flags to the troopers, armed with which a squadron rode out to meet the conquerors. All was meek submission. The Governor of Cairo, the chief of police, and the officer in command of the Citadel came to Abbassia in answer to Stewart's summons, gave assurances of their co-operation, and asked only that the troops should be kept outside the city that night. Arabi, in tears of shame, had taken refuge in the house of the chief of police, all fight extinguished despite the reinforcements he could have called on.

Stewart demanded the evacuation of the Citadel and arrangements for its hand-over were agreed. After dark, 84 men of the 4th Dragoon Guards and 54 mounted infantrymen, under Captain Watson of the Royal Engineers, rode round the outskirts of the city, stifled by dust clouds from garbage heaps, awed by the grandeur of the tombs of the Caliphs, haunted by eyes that gazed blankly from every cranny, until the Citadel's gaunt jumble of turrets and buttresses towered above them. Watson was admitted through the Bab-el-Wezir gate, but found to his alarm and aggravation that the place was alive with Egyptian soldiers. There were five thousand of them inside. Typically there had been a hitch— but no change of attitude. Watched by Watson and a couple of his men, the Egyptians trudged with their rifles dutifully, endlessly, out through the city entrance, down the passage which had once been drenched with Mameluke blood. It was well past midnight before the British were installed, exhausted by 48 hours of almost non-stop activity. Their slumber was soon disturbed by a fearful jangle which shook the very foundations. The prisoners in the dungeon had just realized that they had new masters and were furiously trying to free their chains to escape death at the hand of the infidel. They were calmed with much difficulty.

Arabi came to Abbassia Barracks during the night and, abject in apology, surrendered himself to Drury Lowe. He disclaimed any intention of ever fighting the British, for whom he had the greatest respect—"irreconcilable war exists between the Egyptians and the English," he had proclaimed eight weeks previously—but the war had been forced on him, and being a soldier when fighting began he went on fighting. Now that was all over, the Egyptians and British were brothers again, and he trusted himself to British honour as a soldier who had been defeated. Lowe curtly replied that he raised matters which did not concern him; his orders were merely to take him prisoner.

Next morning, the 15th—one day ahead of the date he had predicted—Wolseley himself reached Cairo by train, accompanied by the Duke of Connaught and some Scots Guardsmen. Officials bowed down before him, business went on as usual, with little outward sign of joy or grief, and twenty thousand ex-soldiers, disbanded by decree of the Khedive, started the journey homewards, having dumped their arms in huge piles at Abbassia and Kasr-el-Nil barracks. It was the copy-book ending to the copy-book campaign. Yet not all the far-flung detachments of Arabi's army submitted quite so sheepishly. At Tanta the one-armed Alison found himself, despite the governor's professed capitulation, in the midst of some armed and most belligerent soldiers, infantrymen, cavalrymen, and always the most resolute of Arabi's men, gunners. An ugly situation was saved by the audacity and swagger of three companies of Gordon Highlanders who marched imperturbably through the masses in the town square and cowed some three thousand troops into surrendering their arms.

On the 25th the Khedive returned to his capital, driving from the station in triumphal state, with Connaught at his side and Wolseley facing him, along streets ceremonially lined by British soldiers. This was followed a few days later by a grand victory parade in front of Abdin Palace, at which the Khedive and his ministers wore glittering decorations bestowed on them by Queen Victoria, and Admiral Seymour sported the Sash of Osmania, awarded by a grateful Sultan. It was like the end of a fairy-story, with everyone seemingly in raptures of delight, though what the Egyptians really thought of it all is nowhere recorded.

Arabi had no friend left in Egypt who dared stand up for him:

death to the traitor, not the infidel, was now the cry. But he had friends in liberal England and the Liberal Government heeded to their liberal pleas. The British, who had toppled him, might have completed the task by spiriting him quietly away. But they had acted, theoretically, with the sole object of restoring the authority of the Khedive and they could not slight that authority now—not openly, at any rate. After some wrangling between the two Governments, the Khedive dutifully agreed to exercise his prerogative of mercy if Arabi should plead guilty, before an Egyptian court, to the charge of rebellion. The barrister who came from England to defend him, commissioned by the Egyptian Prisoners' Defence Fund, somewhat regretfully advised him to enter such a plea. He was tried, sentenced to death, and committed instead to perpetual exile, by gracious mercy of the Khedive, all in the course of an hour. On Boxing Day he sailed in a special ship for Ceylon, with his family and six associates, having impressed many different people by his quiet dignity in adversity. The Turkish Egyptians were disgusted. They saw the reprieve as a demoralizing surrender to sentiment, undermining the authority they held, and the Prime Minister, Riaz Pasha, who had held that office when Arabi first wielded the powerful weapon of mutiny, resigned his post in protest.

As for Arabi, he was eventually given a pardon, again under British instigation. He returned to Egypt in 1901 and until his death in 1911, aged about 71, he lived quietly in a village fifteen miles south of Cairo, concerned only with the well-being of his family. His return caused scarcely a stir, and people seldom took notice of him, except for the occasional urchin who would cheekily raise the old cry, "God give you the victory, O Arabi!" Arabi had always been an earnest and conscientious Moslem, but the help of God, however often invoked, could not make good his military deficiencies, and instead of victory came total defeat. "O Arabi, you have brought the English to Egypt!" was the parting shot from an Egyptian officer at a ceremony intended to humiliate him after his trial. It makes an unkind epitaph, but that is precisely, and perhaps inevitably, what Egypt's first patriot achieved. And the sad part is, from the Egyptian viewpoint, that Arabi would not have been ashamed of this epitaph. The trust which he and his counsellors had placed in British liberalism at the moment of their defeat had been fully vindicated, and after his return from exile he showed himself out of sympathy with nationalist agitation for the departure of the British.

CHAPTER EIGHT

The Victors Humbled

(1882-5)

GLADSTONE REALLY DID mean to leave Egypt. He had sent his troops in to restore the *status quo*, and the *status quo* had been restored, even to the continuation of the annual tribute to the Turkish Sultan. Anxious to placate the powers of Europe, which had been so willing to leave the dirty work to Britain and were so jealously suspicious of her intentions now that the job was done, Lord Granville, the Foreign Secretary, sent them a circular assuring them that the British would withdraw "as soon as the state of the country and the organization of proper means for the maintenance of the Khedive's authority will permit of it". This was in January 1883, and as a mark of their sincerity the Government began to pull out their troops. This caused almost as much alarm among the powers as if the British had threatened to annex the country: with the British gone, who would stand security for the recovery of their debts? The inheritance from his father still hung like a stinking albatross round Tewfik's neck.

Yet his debts were not the only rotting carcase infesting his realm. The Sudan, that treasured symbol of imperial prestige, was in the furore of revolt, led by an earnest and (initially) highly devout dervish, or holy man, named Mohammed Ahmed. Just as Arabi's original aim had been to cleanse the army of foreign matter, so Ahmed's had been to purify the religion of Islam from pollution by the sinful, grasping aliens, Turco-Egyptian, who ruled the land and often made a nice profit on the side from illicit slave-trading. The intrusion of foreigners gave the concept of a holy war as strong appeal in the Sudan as in Egypt, and thanks to the fiercer spirit of the people and the incompetence of the Egyptian security forces, it had a much better chance of success.

The ease with which Ahmed struck down the troops sent to round him up made manifest his miraculous powers; in fact all he had to do was to strike at night when the Egyptians, sentryless and trouserless, slept. His claim was proved. This man must indeed be the Mahdi, the promised one sent by Allah to complete the conquests of the Prophet! Offered the option of a four-fifths share of the booty or a certain place in paradise if they fell in the attempt, the crude black natives flocked to his crude black standard in ecstasy of ardour. By the end of 1881 he controlled almost the whole of Kordofan, to the south-west of Khartoum, and though some garrisons put up obstinate resistance, he had made further gains by the time Arabi's revolt was ended, especially in the acquisition of rifles and guns.

Tewfik could not let this war of independence rage unchallenged. He could expect no aid from the British Government; this was made abundantly clear by Gladstone, savage and merciless though the followers of the Mahdi were increasingly showing themselves to be. But certain Britons were prepared privately to offer their services, and one such, a retired officer of the Indian Army, was made Commander-in-Chief of the Sudan: General Hicks Pasha. To erase the stain on Egyptian honour thousands of Arabi's vanquished soldiers were pressed back into service and herded in chain-gangs down to Khartoum. Hicks was persuaded to invade Kordofan with a force of ten thousand of these wretches, aided by a small staff of Europeans. He seemed to be impelled by the death wish; "I am like Jesus Christ in the middle of the Jews," he said before he set out. He lunged into the interior and was soon led astray by treacherous guides. The men began to die of thirst as they toiled blindly through the scrub in a dense, unwieldy mass, with six thousand ailing camels in their midst. Water was close at hand, but none knew where. Then, on November 3, 1883, the mass was ripped to shreds by murderous fire from all around them. Next day Hicks led the survivors onwards, only to be hacked down, defiant to the end, by a fresh onslaught. His entire force was gobbled up without trace—not quite literally, perhaps, but very few escaped slaughter.

The fate of Hicks's expedition persuaded the British Government that the policy of non-interference in Egyptian affairs was all

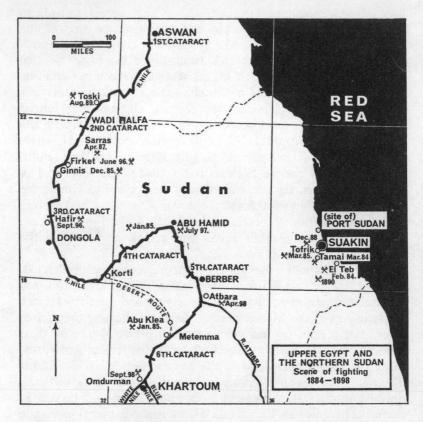

very well—provided the Egyptians did not make fools of themselves and thus jeopardize their chance of financial recovery. It was decided that the Egyptian Government must be advised to give up the Sudan and that from now onwards any such advice, proffered in Egypt's best interests, must be accepted. The delicate task of enforcement fell to the strong yet tactful personality of the new Agent and Consul-General, Major Sir Evelyn Baring, who had been an original member of the Dual Control (which to the anger of the French was not restored) and had returned to Egypt in September after a three years' absence. He exerted pressure by dropping hints that in the last resort he would take over government himself. The Khedive submitted, accepted the resignation of one government determined to stay in the Sudan, and appointed one willing to get out.

Withdrawal from Khartoum, with its large Egyptian population, presented a tricky problem. The British Government suggested Major-General Charles Gordon. Baring did not want him, nor did the new Prime Minister, Nubar Pasha; the one because he thought his flighty and independent nature unfitted for the task, the other, carrying even greater weight of argument, because of the inflammatory effect of the intrusion of a Christian in the Mahdi's holy war. But London pressed hard, and the offer was eventually accepted. Gordon was a great hero of the people at a time when hero-worship was no sin; "one of our national treasures", he was described in the House of Lords. Led by the *Pall Mall Gazette*, the press were clamouring for his despatch, and Gladstone's Government, little realizing the hazards, were willing enough to respond to the demands.

Gordon knew the Sudan well, having served as its Governor-General under Khedive Ismail. He had gone there to crush the slave trade and had eventually resigned in disgust at the obstruction and corruption he encountered in fighting a practice which Ismail vehemently condemned in public but patronized in private. Slight, curly-haired, and boyish for his 51 years, "Chinese Gordon", as he was called for his inspired leadership of Chinese peasants in a cruel civil war, radiated the shining virtues of the true crusader, fulfilling both imperialistic and liberal concepts of Britain's mission in the world. Right was his only guide, compromise a word he despised, and God's the one authority he respected. He was as convinced as the Mahdi himself that an honourable bullet through the heart purchased an express ticket to paradise.

After a quick round of calls in Cairo and a three-week journey up the Nile, Gordon arrived in Khartoum on February 18, 1884. He received a tumultuous welcome. Khartoum, so it seemed to the British public, had been saved from the hand of darkness and would never be surrendered now. Then came an extraordinary request. Gordon wanted to hand over authority to Zobeir Pasha, a man blemished by the indelible stain of involvement in the slave trade! Baring strongly backed the proposal; Zobeir had tremendous influence in the Sudan and was the only Moslem capable of rallying opinion against the Mahdi; better the one-time slave dealer than the blood-stained fanatic. But the Government, knowing their public, said no, nor would they consent to the despatch of any troops to Gordon, Egyptian, British or Indian Moslem, nor concede to any of his wilder requests, which came streaming from

Khartoum at a stunning rate, ranging from an incursion deep into Equatorial Africa, to an appeal for a Turkish expeditionary force, or the resignation of his commission.

Nonetheless, the Government did get themselves drawn into military involvement. Osman Digna, a fiery slave-trading emir, raised the Mahdi's flag in the Eastern Sudan, threatening Suakin, the old port of Sudan, and the route thence to Berber, on the Nile. To subdue him, a force of 3,500 Egyptians advanced from Suakin and on February 5, 1884, reached the village of El Teb, 40 miles down the coast. It was led by a British cavalryman, General Baker Pasha, and consisted entirely of the Gendarmerie, since the Egyptian Army, re-forming under British officers, was not considered ready for action. A thousand Arabs attacked and in Baker's words, "the Egyptian troops threw down their arms and ran . . . allowing themselves to be killed without the slightest resistance". Baker brought 1,500 survivors, mostly unarmed, back to Suakin, leaving his enemies to carve up the corpses of most of his European officers and joyfully distribute his guns and rifles.

Britain could not ignore the very real threat to Suakin and troops were despatched—strictly for its defence. But their commander, Sir Gerald Graham, big, bold and resolute, obtained permission to sally forth, on plea of relieving an Egyptian garrison, which in fact fell just as he moved off. With six infantry battalions, two cavalry regiments, and gunners of the Royal Navy and Royal Artillery, most of them veterans of Tel-el-Kebir, he fought two battles, at El Teb on February 29 and at Tamai on March 19. It was the first time the British encountered these ferocious Dervishes, as the Mahdi's followers were called, and it was an amazing experience for them both. Osman Digna's men were the half-naked fuzzy-wuzzies of the eastern tribes of the Sudan, led by shaven-headed emirs in the patched robe of the warrior, the gibba. Mere wounds did not halt these men, though they might bring them to the ground. They had to be killed to be stopped, and at the two battles around three thousand were slain before the remainder made off. There were no prisoners.

It was no walk-over for the British. Shot and spear cut gashes in their gasping, steaming squares, and at Tamai there was fearful confusion when the left-hand square was rashly ordered to charge a ravine, from which swarms of Dervishes rushed into the gaps that opened between the attackers and wrought swift slaughter with their swords. "Discipline was forgotten," chided Graham in an order of the day; but the troops had good cause to chide their commander, especially the Black Watch, who had been criticized for caution at El Teb and were consequently over-impetuous when the mad order came to charge the Tamai ravine. 109 of the British were killed in this battle, out of a total of 410 casualties between the two.

Graham was now chafing to advance to Berber and bring aid to his old friend and brother officer of the Royal Engineers, Charlie Gordon. Baring backed his proposal to the hilt, but the Government turned it down, "having regard to the dangers of the climate of the Soudan at this time of year, as well as the extraordinary risk from a military point of view". Berber was 280 miles from Suakin, of which only the last hundred were real desert. The administrative problems were immense, but a glance at the War Office files of 1801 would have shown that General Baird had brought five thousand men across the desert in the month of July. Probably a more potent factor in the governmental reckoning was the protests of the humanitarians, appalled by Graham's annihilation of these primitive natives. Yet in allowing Graham to advance to battle Gladstone had been swayed by the appeals of the Anti-Slavery Society. There could be no satisfying these fervent people in England who were so passionately concerned about African affairs.

Meanwhile the Mahdi was tightening his grip on Khartoum as the unexploited brandishing of British arms sent further waves of nationalism throbbing across the Sudan. Gordon, in one of his interminable wires to Baring, might contemptuously talk of "the trumpery nature of this revolt, which 500 determined men could put down". Such an opinion, if he really held it, was no doubt based on the impact of his arrival at Khartoum; but every day's inactivity brought strength to the Mahdi, both physical and moral. By the end of May Berber fell to his tribesmen, and Gordon's river lifeline relied solely on its width. It was apparent now to all but the British Government that a relief force must be sent. True, Gordon had six thousand Sudanese troops with him and could extricate himself. But he had been sent to evacuate the Egyptian population and would never himself abandon the city until every man, woman and child had been got safely away. The British people knew their hero. Their rage mounted. Huge protest meetings were held, drawing chauvinist and humanitarian alike. Gladstone was hissed wherever he appeared in public, but this formidable old man who had yielded so often to the voice of the people turned a cold, sullen ear, refusing to be drawn into the type of military involvement which he so much hated just to satisfy the people's whim and indulge their hero's craving for the theatrical. He was aware, as he was later to admit, that the despatch of Gordon had been a great mistake, but that was a poor reason for making another, even greater mistake.

In the end he had to relent. The Opposition harried him tirelessly, and at last one of his own men turned against him. Lord Hartington, his War Minister, threatened to resign. Faced with the break-up of his Government, Gladstone gave way, and on August 5 sanction for an expedition was given by the House—should it be proved necessary! The Cabinet grudgingly decided that some form of expedition was required, but right up to the middle of September they entertained the hope that it might not have to make the long, long journey to Khartoum.

The spur that drove the normally placid Hartington to action came from the heel of his Adjutant-General, Lord Wolseley of Cairo, as he had now become, friend and ardent admirer of Gordon. For many months he had been engaged in heated controversy with Lieutenant-General Sir Frederick Stephenson, Commander-in-Chief in Egypt, as to the best line of advance. Stephenson and his colleagues in Egypt, both naval and military, did not think the line of the Nile, 1,650 miles from Cairo to Khartoum, was feasible or even navigable in its little-known, rock-strewn reaches above Wadi Halfa. They recommended the route from Suakin, 280 miles across country to Berber with a further 220 to Khartoum; it was estimated that a railway line could be built in three months, and the work was ordered, but cancelled when Berber fell. But even on foot it was a journey that the late Hicks Pasha had accomplished in little more than four weeks.

Wolseley recoiled in horror from the thought of marching the men across the sweltering desert, with each man needing about two camels' load of water and food for the journey, carried along a route infested by Osman Digna's fiery swarms. He had waged river warfare in Canada and was sure that boats could be built to carry the men into battle in shade and comfort, with their rations and accoutrements with them, through all the miles and hazards of the Nile. Avoidance of battle with Osman was a strong factor with an unwarlike Cabinet, and after spending another seventeen days on communication and deliberation, they opted for Wolseley's plan.

Rather than impose on Stephenson a plan he rejected, they once again appointed Wolseley to command.

It was difficult to strike a happy balance between the conflicting claims of strength and speed, and it was Wolseley's inclination to err on the side of strength; not for him the lightning, lightweight punch. Eight battalions of infantry were earmarked, most of them already in Egypt, one regiment of cavalry, and a camel corps of four regiments specially formed, and hurriedly trained, for the task—the Cavalry, Guards, Rifles, and Mounted Infantry (Royal Sussex and Essex Regiments) provided the officers and men. Flatboats were built with desperate speed by private firms, while voyageurs came from Canada to navigate the whirlpools, porters from West Africa (where they had impressed Wolseley on a previous campaign) and tons of tinned meat from Chicago, the Army's first introduction to bully beef. Another innovation was that the men were allowed to discard their scarlet tunics in favour of grey ones, though the infantry took their reds with them for morale purposes in battle.

A forward springboard was formed at Wadi Halfa, on the Sudan frontier, where huge dumps of stores accumulated and Egypt made her contribution in the supply of porters and lines of communication troops. The carriage of the boats beyond the 2nd Cataract called for a prodigious effort, but their arrival was erratic, because the steamers bringing them ran out of coal, causing delay which Wolseley estimated at as much as three weeks. Not until November did the endless column begin its journey from its forward base along the muddy, swirling river and its jagged, glaring banks, unknown as yet to British troops.

For the infantry the journey started as a pleasure cruise past the glories of Ancient Egypt and ended in hardship. They had a train ride to Assiut, a ten-day trip by barge or Cook's steamer to Aswan, a train ride round the 1st Cataract, another steamer trip to Wadi Halfa, and another train ride round the 2nd Cataract. Here the flatboats were waiting for them and now the toil began. Each boat had room for twelve men, reserve ammunition, rations for a hundred days, twelve oars, an awning and two sails, but conditions were seldom suitable for sailing and for most of the way the troops had to row themselves against a strong, sometimes impetuous current, aided by a voyageur along the most difficult stretches. There were many barriers, especially in the early stages, and the men seemed to be for ever hauling on their tracklines or carrying their boats on their shoulders, a fearful exertion in heat which once attained 140° F. Hands were rubbed raw and there was much envy of the cameleers—"that band of patricians" as Ian Hamilton, an anguished boatman, described them—as they rode nonchalantly by. After six weeks' labour, in mid-December, the head of the far-flung regatta reached Korti, where a halt was called for a rest. They had come 420 miles from Wadi Halfa but had a further 520 to go.

Gordon was now a lone white man among his downcast black soldiers and his "hens", the Egyptian officers and officials, for whom he had even greater contempt than for his own governmental chiefs in Cairo and London. He had sent his staff officer, Colonel J. D. H. Stewart, down-river in September with the French and British consuls, in order to hasten relief; their steamer had got stuck on a rock and they had been murdered by a treacherous sheikh. The one contact left was a spy service run by a lone British officer, Major Herbert Kitchener of the Royal Engineers, operating from Dongola. Through him Gordon heard of Wolseley's approach with an army "strong enough to wipe Mohammed Ahmed and all his followers off the face of the earth" (Wolseley's words), but he had no means of following its progress. Daily he peered through his telescope, down the empty river or round the line of his defence wall, where his sentries flopped ever more lethargically, often dropping asleep—"pieces of wood" an eyewitness, Bordeini Bey, described them. Women cried for bread, but dogs and date-palm fibre were all that remained to be eaten. The dead lay unburied—no one had the energy—but though the Dervishes kept firing with guns and rifles they still dared not assault. The hair of Gordon's head had turned white, but he still held it high. "Go, tell the people Gordon fears nothing," he proclaimed. It was true.

On December 30 Wolseley strove to make up lost time by sending his Camel Corps, with detachments of sailors and the 19th Hussars, across the 176 miles of desert and scrub which lay between the great loop, 400 miles long, which took the river past Berber. There was an urgent need of remounts—the inexperience of the cameleers showed itself in the sad state of their beasts—but none had arrived, and consequently a supply shuttle service had to be run, enforcing a further nine days' delay. (It would have been quicker, as the Royal Irish were to prove when sent forward in support, to have dismounted the troops and used all camels as pack transport.) However, the column had a most vigorous commander in Major-General Sir Herbert Stewart, he who had received the surrender of Cairo. He hustled his men on to such effect that by the evening of January 16 they were hard by the wells of Abu Klea, 24 miles from the Nile, almost speechless from thirst, their way barred by Dervishes who sniped at them all night and feverishly beat their tom-toms. Warned of Stewart's approach by the preliminary dumping, the Mahdi had concentrated ten thousand of his most trusty warriors who had wisely bided their time while the two thousand men of the Camel Corps toiled into their net.

Next morning Stewart left behind most of his camels and his sick, guarded by a detachment five hundred strong, and slowly advanced in square formation, his men dismounted, their faces bronze and bearded, making sharp contrast to their grey helmets and tunics. They entered a narrow valley, fired on from both sides. Suddenly a mighty black-and-white phalanx arose from a ravine 500 yds. distant. Led by mounted, white-bearded emirs, the Dervishes came on in three seething prongs, waving swords, spears, and scrolls from the Koran, and chanting prayers to Allah. There was a ferocious and desperate struggle. The new Gardner machine-gun, manned by the poor sailors, jammed, and the soldiers, with no magazines to help them, could not flick their cartridges fast enough into the breeches of their rifles to fell the hordes. A wedge was driven into the square, in which attackers and defenders were jammed so tight that it was hard to wield bayonet or sword, and many grappled with hands, fists and boots. But the camels, squatting passively with their ammunition packs as if nothing unusual was happening, formed a bulwark, and the tide at last ebbed and receded. The British waded out of the carnage and re-formed square with a cheer, their glazed eyes brightening at sight of the wells of Abu Klea which stood undefended before them. Seventy-four of them lay dead amid the 1,100 Dervish corpses counted by an industrious staff officer, and a further ninety-four were wounded.

Dense scrub now added to the tribulations of Stewart's men, and not until the morning of January 19 did they enter wider spaces and get a distant view of the palm-trees by the Nile. The Dervishes had regrouped and were waiting for them, relying as much on their rifles as their swords. With what Winston Churchill described as "the stubborn grandeur of the British soldier", a smaller square, barely nine hundred strong, carved their way through, frequently halting to pick up wounded brought down by persistent and well concealed fire and once to repulse a massed charge which had not quite the fanatical fury of the one at Abu Klea. They reached the great river, their exhaustion forgotten, at that brief moment of sundown magic when the glaring rocks turn to purple and the muddy brown water to silver. Behind them lay Stewart, mortally wounded by a bullet early in the day.

The Dervish marksman who hit this bold and energetic leader might in retrospect claim Gordon too. For on the morning of the 21st four thinly armoured steamers—Gordon's "penny steamers" —arrived from Khartoum to collect relief for the anguished garrison, 120 miles away. Yet Colonel Sir Charles Wilson, who took over, was so concerned about security that he spent three days in strengthening his Nileside position and the armour of the boats before setting off upriver with two of the steamers. On board he had twenty men of the Royal Sussex, red tunics in their packs ready for the march into Khartoum, and some two hundred Sudanese troops who had come with the steamers.

On the following day, January 25, 1885, news reached the Mahdi of the defeat of his warriors at Abu Klea. The Austrian, Rudolf Slatin, governor of an invaded province and now a manacled prisoner in the Mahdi's camp, has vividly described the wailing that broke out. Overwhelmed by defeatism, the Mahdi decided to withdraw from Khartoum, but was persuaded by a lone councillor that Allah would surely countenance a last, swift attempt. At first light next morning the Dervishes swarmed through a gap between the ebbing Nile and the defence wall. There was no resistance from Gordon's half-dead troops. Gordon waited without flinching on the steps of his Palace, dressed for parade, his sword in its scabbard, his revolver in its holster. Spears were plunged into him ecstatically. His body was sliced up and his head was carried before the Mahdi, who gloatingly sent it round for Slatin to see. An orgy of slaughter smote the inhabitants of Khartoum, with the most eager hounding reserved for those who had the olive skin of Turk or Egyptian. The lives only of attractive girls were safe. The Mahdi had developed some highly unspiritual habits in between his prayers to Allah.

Wilson's steamers arrived on the evening of the 28th, sixty hours after the onslaught, having been badly delayed by buffeting in the last cataract. Hostile gunfire and jeers from the banks told their story, but Wilson bravely struggled on to make sure that no Egyptian flag flew. On the way back his steamers ran aground, and he had to send an officer off in a small boat to slip past Dervish positions and deliver the miserable tidings, coupled with an urgent call for help. Help was brought, after a saga of repair work under gunfire, by that dashing sailor, Captain Lord Charles Beresford, who had accompanied Stewart's column on a donkey, and as his makeshift gunboat chugged, hissed and fizzled on its journey southward news of the disaster jerked northward just as painfully, across the desert to Korti and along the hundred miles of riverline over which the infantry of this force "strong enough to wipe Mohammed Ahmed and all his followers off the face of the earth" was dispersed.

None felt more wretched than the Commander-in-Chief, Lord Wolseley. He had met his Arnhem, but it was a more personal and more tragic defeat than the one incurred by the inheritor of his talents. He had failed the man he most admired, and now his hair too turned grey and his heart was torn by a compound of grief, fury at the Government for their fatal vacillations, and anguish in the tantalus of might-have-beens. There were so many ifs. If Herbert Stewart had not been killed—a rather tenuous if, this one, but the prompt return of the steamers *might* have got troops to Gordon on the night before the onslaught, and their arrival *might* have deterred the Mahdi from attacking—if the coal had not run out, if more camels had been made available . . .

But the basic flaw lay in the plan itself. After all the governmental procrastination, the boat ride up the Nile was a luxury which could not be afforded, especially for so large a force as eight battalions, none of which in the event got near enough to strike even a distant blow. Kitchener was well placed at Dongola to assess the strength of the Madhi's forces. A telegram from him to Baring, dated August 31, estimated that Gordon could hold out until the middle of November. "I do not think a large expedition would be necessary from here," he said. "A flying column to Khartoum composed of cavalry and artillery and some infantry on camels or on foot—altogether about 4,000—could, I believe, relieve Khartoum in less than the time required." Such a column, which events proved adequate for the task, could have been rapidly assembled from material already in Egypt. Wolseley's preference for greater bulk and refinement, boats built in England and a camel corps *d'élite* drawn from the smartest regiments on home service, inevitably added two months to the departure of the expedition, and perhaps not realizing Gordon's peril until too late, he did not

7

aim at reaching him until January 31. His plan was pursued with tireless vigour, especially the assembly of the boats, and it provided him with a most neatly balanced force, administratively as much as tactically. But it was the one occasion when his sense of balance let him down, since the striking of it took so long.

No one in England blamed the commander or the men who had striven so hard. A groan of anguish rumbled across the country and then found more piercing expression in hysterical abuse of the Prime Minister, while the Queen, having ordered a national day of mourning and despatched him an august rebuke, took to her bed. Egypt had even greater cause both for grief and indignation. Britain had lost a hero; Egypt had lost her empire, with thousands of her people killed, while others were left to their fate in doomed garrisons which in two cases were not overwhelmed, after courageous resistance, until the end of a further six months. The British Government had proved themselves meddlesome and profligate taskmasters. They had insisted on the evacuation in the first place, had forced on the reluctant Egyptians a man of their own choice, and had obstinately rejected his own proposal for his replacement by the one Egyptian subject whose influence might stem the revolt. They had inflamed the passions of the rebels by giving battle and then withdrawing, and when finally they did decide to intervene, their troops arrived too late.

Gladstone's reaction to the catastrophe was to play the jingo: Gordon must be avenged, the whole of the Sudan subdued! There was little that Wolseley could do. His Camel Corps were worn out and he brought them back to Korti, hard beset by a host of jubilant Dervishes. His infantry pushed on up the river towards Abu Hamid and won a small battle in which their commander, Major-General Earle, was foolishly killed. Graham meanwhile returned to Suakin, where a force of thirteen thousand British and Indian soldiers was rapidly assembled. Again Osman Digna gave battle and again he was twice defeated, but the second was a desperate affair, in which a mixed brigade, violently assailed while they were cutting brushwood for their perimeter fence, or zeriba, suffered 253 casualties and lost nine hundred camels before driving off these audacious tribesmen, over a thousand of whom were turned into corpses. Gladstone was made to realize that he had committed himself to a long and costly campaign. He seized the first opportunity to transfer his new-found imperial zeal elsewhere. It was presented most conveniently by the Russians, who, in the course of frontier negotiations with the Afghanistans, seized a disputed village on the last day of March. Gladstone dramatically pointed to the threat to India, called for a vast note of credit for defence measures, and brought thunderous denunciation on the Czar's bewildered Government.

Thus was the spotlight switched from the Sudan, and the troops quietly drifted back down the river all the way to Wadi Halfa, handing the Land of the Black over to total darkness. But there could be no leaving Egypt now. Gladstone's bungled policy had brought about the one thing it had been aimed at avoiding: so long as the Mahdi held the Sudan in tyranny, honour demanded that the British troops in Egypt must remain.

CHAPTER NINE

Prestige Restored

(1885-1914)

THE MAHDI DID not long survive his triumph over Gordon and the British. He died of typhus fever in June of that year, 1885, after nominating Abdullah as his successor, or Khalifa. None but the most ruthless of tyrants could have ridden the tempest that raged across the Sudan in dispute of the succession. Abdullah was such a man. He quickly struck down jealous rivals and directed the fervour of warring tribes to his own expansionist ambitions. One army met disaster on the Abyssinian frontier, later to be avenged; another, of no great strength, was entrusted with the invasion of Egypt. It advanced up the Nile and on December 30 was utterly routed at Ginnis, 100 miles south of Wadi Halfa.

This battle marks the start of a new comradeship in arms. Five battalions of British infantry took part, and one from the Egyptian Army, supported by a British cavalry regiment, Egyptian gunners and a combined camel corps. Stephenson himself took command, and after enveloping the enemy camp under cover of darkness he won the day with trifling loss. The Egyptians fought with credit, much to the delight of their British officers.

There had been no great rush for secondment to the Egyptian Army when it had been re-formed soon after the British arrived in Cairo. No one envied its Sirdar, Major-General Sir Evelyn Wood, his task of turning the remnant of the derided rebel army, that puffed-up bullfrog which had subsided at a single prick, into a cohesive fighting force. Financial stringency, which initially restricted its size to eight battalions, imposed its own frustrations, but it at least made discrimination possible in the selection of the Egyptian officers who had to form the bulk of the officer corps. Every British soldier knew the joke about the Egyptian officers: each knew that he himself would run but hoped his neighbour would stay to fight. Twenty-six British officers and ten N.C.O.s were persuaded to serve with these objects of contempt. They were drawn by the lure of challenge, by the prospect of wider responsibility and better pay, and they had skins hard enough to withstand the jibes which the wearing of the tarboush inevitably drew, for the officers had to identify themselves with their men. They did not regret their daring. The hard and stoical peasant conscripts— for the fellah would never volunteer—responded wonderfully well to their new treatment. They got regular pay and regular leave, were properly fed and no longer beaten for such offences as falling sick, and when their period of engagement was ended they returned to their villages free, fit and smiling, a phenomenon unknown since the peasant army was first raised. Furthermore, they were quick to learn and most amenable to discipline. Pride bloomed in the breasts of their British officers, and sharp retort fell on the head of any of their colleagues in British service who made fun of the Egyptian soldier.

The army expanded. During 1884 volunteers were enlisted from the negroid tribes in that part of the Sudan still in Egyptian hands, and they were formed into new battalions under British and their own native officers. The blacks were very different material, capricious, delicate, idle, childish, prone to panic and insubordination, yet capable of doglike devotion and valour. Though they needed most patient training they had warrior instinct which could never be sown in the fellahin, and the six battalions that were raised shouldered the heaviest burden of all troops both in the defence against and reconquest of their fevered country.

By May 1886 the Egyptian Army had taken over responsibility for defence of the all-important Nile approach at Wadi Halfa, with British troops acting as longstop back at Aswan. The Egyptians showed their prowess by trouncing a small Dervish force at Sarras, south of Wadi Halfa, in April 1887, but a much more searching test was in store in August 1889, when the Khalifa, having defeated the Abyssinians and subdued various attempts at subversion, sent northwards a motley army of some 13,700 fighting men and camp followers, under the brave and skilful Wad-al-

Nejumi, the one Dervish leader who remained true to the principle of ascetic devotion to Allah.

Nejumi attempted an ambitious turning movement round the west flank of the Wadi Halfa position but was thwarted both by his own supply problems and the tactical skill of Colonel Josceline Wodehouse, using the river axis, and of Major-General Sir Francis Grenfell, Wood's successor as Sirdar of the Egyptian Army, who struck southward from Toski. Egyptian guns and rifles wrought deadly destruction from well-chosen positions and were just as effectively employed in the attack. The Dervishes were routed, with 1,200 killed and 4,000 taken prisoner, at a loss to the Egyptians of 165 casualties, and it was all done before any British reinforcements came into battle, except for a handful of cavalry. Starving camp followers, mostly women and children, littered the desert. Nejumi himself was killed after twice being wounded and his body was defended to the last by a faithful band. His five-year-old son lay dead beside him, while his baby boy was brought in from the battlefield by his nurse.

Around Suakin the Egyptians were just as successful. Osman Digna continued to terrorize the neighbourhood, despite the opposition of certain tribes which rallied against him under the instigation of Colonel Kitchener, Governor of Suakin, whose efforts were checked by a severe wound in the jaw. In the winter of 1888 Osman laid siege to Suakin in earnest, and both Egyptian and British troops were brought in. They attacked on December 20, smashed into the Dervish defences, and forced the siege to be raised. Two years later the Egyptians were permitted to venture further and they advanced to Tokar, near El Teb. Here, close to the scene of that early humiliation when the Egyptians ran without defending themselves, they dauntlessly withstood the fury of Osman Digna's hordes and routed them completely. The Egyptian losses were a mere 58 killed and wounded. They had shown themselves, under British leadership, worthy defenders of their soil.

Irish issues had meanwhile thrown party politics in Britain into convulsions. They were the direct cause of Gladstone's defeat in the House in June 1885, of his return to power, with added strength, at the winter election, and of his defeat again the following summer. This second election brought Lord Salisbury to power with a solid Unionist majority. There was no change of policy over Egypt. Indeed, Lord Salisbury showed himself just as eager to withdraw as Gladstone and he described the British occupation as an "intolerable hamper" on relations with France, Russia and Turkey. He reached agreement with Turkey for an eventual evacuation, subject to Britain's right to return in an emergency. France and Russia, bitterly jealous of Britain, objected to the return clause and prevailed upon the Turks to withhold ratification. Unable to find terms of withdrawal acceptable to all, the powers concentrated instead on safeguarding navigation through the Suez Canal. After three years' heated debate a Convention was signed at Constantinople in 1888, by eight European powers and Turkey, under which they defined the international status of the Canal, guaranteed not to disturb its free use by any nation in time of peace or war, and made Egypt responsible for its defence, under Turkish tutelage. Britain stipulated, however, that the Convention should not come into force while her occupation, which of course was temporary, lasted.

Thus Britain's management of Egyptian affairs haphazardly continued. The power of Lord Cromer, as Sir Evelyn Baring became, waxed strong. He nursed the country's economy back to health with the care and patience of a matron, restraining as best he could the appetites of the foreign creditors that still circled, vulture-like, over the Egyptian carcase. Half the national income had to be allotted to the international *Caisse de la Dette*, which administered the repayment of debts, but at least some of it could now be levied from foreigners under a concession which made them liable to taxation. Cromer also overhauled the administration, bringing in British officials to redress "the utter incapacity of the ruling class", whilst managing to afford the Khedive and his Ministers every semblance of free decision.

Not until Tewfik died suddenly in 1892 was Cromer obliged to intrude more obviously. His successor, the 18-year-old Abbas Hilmi, proved to be a rash, self-willed young man, very eager to assert his authority. First he tried to form a ministry without consulting Cromer, and he then seriously upset the British officers in his Army by publicly criticizing it. Cromer promptly put him in his place, and as Hilmi had no great claims to the loyalty either of the ruling class or the people, he was confined to an existence of sulky isolation.

In July 1895 Salisbury returned to power after three years in opposition. Fresh ideas had for some time been revolving round his patrician head as he rode his tricycle about his Hatfield estate—

ideas about the Nile and its importance to British interests and of the need for a continuous sphere of influence, stretching from the Mediterranean to the East African coast, which would safeguard for all time the short route to India. Indications of French ambitions for a counter belt of influence, running from west to east, gave some urgency to Salisbury's leisurely-conceived designs, and that winter advantage was taken of a plea from the Italians for a diversion against Dervish pressure on Eritrea, following their defeat at Adowa at the hands of the Abyssinians. The Egyptian Army was to be let loose, charged with the invasion of Dongola, the province to the south of Wadi Halfa.

The cost of the expedition was to be borne by a grant from the accumulated reserve, approved by the *Caisse de la Dette* by a vote of four to two. France and Russia were the two dissenters, and France was not prepared to let the matter stand at that. But she could not prevent the despatch of the expedition. The Reserve was called up, and for the first time the peasant conscripts rejoined the colours without constraint by lash or chain.

For four years now Major-General Sir Herbert Kitchener had been Sirdar of the Egyptian Army, a harsh and sombre personality, popular with no one, yet respected with grudging awe by his British officers and revered by the native troops he understood so well. Deftly, he concentrated his forces and set them off for Dongola, at divisional strength, on March 18, 1896. British aid was limited. A battery of Maxim machine-guns and a reserve battalion accompanied the column, and to free more Egyptian troops an Indian contingent was despatched for the defence of Suakin, where they languished miserably, tormented by inactivity and disease.

The Dervishes made no stand near the frontier but waited passively, three thousand strong, at their fortified camp at Firket, on the Nile's east bank, while Kitchener laid a railway line to Akasha, 86 miles inside the Sudan. He advanced unmolested and on June 7 struck a devastating blow. It was delivered at dawn, after a long and difficult night approach through a narrow defile between the river and a mighty boulder. Ten battalions went simultaneously into the attack, five Egyptian and five Sudanese, organized in there brigades, each under a British major. The Dervishes fought back stubbornly when they saw what was upon them. They fired their ill-kept Remington rifles from their mud walls and loop-holed huts, but they were outnumbered, outgunned and outflanked, and the British-led battalions kept coming at them, the Egyptians with commendable resolution, the Sudanese with dash. An hour's fighting, ferocious at times, was sufficient. The Dervish commander lay dead with eight hundred of his men, and 1,100 were taken prisoner, many of them wounded, while the remaining thousand fled, pursued by the mounted troops who had made a wide left hook which halted short of the river. The Egyptians lost twenty killed and eighty-four wounded (including one British officer). Their three-to-one superiority somewhat dimmed the lustre of this victory, but no troops could have gained it with greater economy or despatch.

Cholera and sand-storms now drained the joy from Kitchener's soldiers and rain-storms washed away most of his railway line. However, four gunboats and two other steamers were hauled up the cataract by two thousand manpower—though one other, the newest and biggest, brought up by components, exploded a cylinder on its launching and cast Kitchener into the blackest gloom.

The gunboats proved their worth when the Dervishes were next encountered in mid-September. They were in position at Hafir, thirty miles north of Dongola town, holding extensive entrenchments along the Nile's west bank, where they had slipped to evade the Egyptian troops advancing along the opposite bank. Guns, Maxims and rifles belched lead and flame from the iron-clad tugboats, making shattering union with every weapon the soldiers could bring to bear from the far bank. The Dervishes were blown out of their trenches or flopped like rotten apples from the trees they had climbed for better fire effect, but they went on firing with great spirit, hitting the boats more often than damaging them, and only showed sign of anxiety when the gunboats steamed past their position, under cover of artillery fire, towards Dongola. Now they withdrew back to their capital, hotly engaged by Lieutenant David Beatty and his native crew in the *Abu Klea*. They came out to give battle when the Egyptians arrived on September 22, but did no more than grimace before withdrawing again, far away this time, back to the extremities of the forlorn advance which Wolseley's men had made. The province of Dongola, birthplace of the Mahdi, had been retaken: the task of the Egyptian Army was accomplished, with little loss and great efficiency.

Victory celebrations in Cairo were soon submerged beneath the humiliation that the legacy of Khedive Ismail could still inflict. The French had sued the Egyptian Government before the international mixed courts of Egypt on the grounds that the cost of the expedition, £E500,000, did not constitute "extraordinary expenditure" and should never have been authorized by the *Caisse de la Dette*. In the fullness of time a tribunal deliberated the issue, and being composed mainly of Francophil judges, gave judgement in favour of France, which the Court of Appeal confirmed. Wretched Egypt, forced to repay money drawn from her own hard-earned income and already spent on her own legitimate endeavours, sanction for which had been humbly begged and approved! But a fairy godmother was at hand to frustrate the machinations of the wicked uncle. "Her Majesty's Government will advance the sum required," wired Salisbury, and only two days later, amid great rejoicing, the money was conveyed in boxes of gold to the *Caisse de la Dette*. Never did Union Jack radiate such gladness as the one over the British Residency that day, and never were the brows of Frenchmen, seated in their many offices in Cairo, Alexandria and along the Canal, so dark.

Salisbury's swift response bears mark of the impact made by Kitchener during a swift visit to London a month before the final judgement was made. He had come to press the need for a continuation of the advance to Berber and for the financial aid entailed. His powers of persuasion prevailed.

Kitchener devoted the first six months of 1897 to his mighty project of building a desert railway from Wadi Halfa to Abu Hamid, and in July he sent a column, under the daring Major-General Archibald Hunter, to seize this latter place. With one Egyptian and three Sudanese battalions, Hunter marched 146 miles in nine days, with the climax an arduous night march and a dawn assault on the fortified village. The Dervishes greeted them with a punishing volley. Sixty men dropped, two dead British officers among them. But the Sudanese charged with a cheer, killed and drove out their fellow countrymen. Such was the shock of this thrust that amazing reports now arrived of the evacuation of Berber, 150 miles up the river. Off went the gunboats to confirm that this was true, and they soon steamed on to Metemma, another 100 miles on, where they found the Dervishes strongly entrenched, and treated them, almost with immunity, to a deluge of shells.

The brave and defiant occupants of these posts were the men of Mahmoud, a vain and ambitious young chieftain who had sped to Metemma to eliminate a garrison that had tired of the rule of the Khalifa. Kitchener had sent a column along the desert route to their relief, but like Stewart's camel riders twelve years earlier they had arrived too late. For the power of the Dervishes was by no means exhausted, though their land was ravaged by long years of famine and chaos and its population had dwindled to half its former size. The Khalifa roared defiance. He sounded his great war drum at Omdurman, his chieftains rallied to its stirring boom, and plans were made for a combined assault on the insolent invader.

Kitchener was fully conscious of the peril facing his force at Berber, 160 miles ahead of the railway line which was in the painful labour of its last few miles to Abu Hamid. It was a difficult position to consolidate, and neither the funds nor reinforcements were available to continue the advance and finish the job. He grew pessimistic, sultry, unbearably curt, while Cromer, worried grey about finance, wrote to Salisbury, "I tear my hair over the hurried decision of March, 1896" (when the invasion began). There was nearly three months' anxiety before the British Cabinet relented and agreed, in the closing days of 1897, to give further aid to Egypt, in the form of both money and men. Kitchener shed his gloom and indecision; Khartoum was the objective now.

Jealous dissension much diminished the striking power of the Dervishes and in the end only the indefatigable Osman Digna joined Mahmoud's forward army, bringing its combined strength to twelve thousand fighting men. The two leaders were scarcely on speaking terms and it was not until March 1898 that Osman agreed to co-operate in an advance down the river. Finding the Egyptians in strength at Fort Atbara, they tried a wide turning movement to their right which brought them to the dry river bed of the Atbara, 30 miles east of the Nile, where they were stranded by supply difficulties. Here they built a zeriba and waited, with characteristic lack of initiative, for the blow to fall.

With a brigade of four newly arrived British battalions, clad in khaki drill and armed with the new magazine-loaded Lee-Metford rifle, Kitchener now had fifteen battalions, twelve thousand bayonets strong, with plentiful artillery support. He advanced them by agile bounds, until as day broke on Good Friday, April 8, they lay in their battle formations, with the Dervish camp below them a few hundred yards away. Shells screamed into the Dervish entrenchments, rockets (fired by sailors) screeched and sighed, and machine-guns barked their harsh fury, until there was nothing to be seen of the objective except a dense dust-cloud. The infantry then advanced in a continuous crescent, almost a mile long, to the thump and swirl of drums, fifes, pipes and brass and the crackle of volleys from the high ground behind. Gaps were methodically cut through the fences, under cover of intense rifle fire, and the defenders were just as methodically pierced by bullet and bayonet as they fought at their mud breastworks or charged from their putrid huts, in which women and children lay screaming or dead. Only the Negroes surrendered; the Arabs died or ran. About a third made their escape, the ever artful Osman Digna among them, but Mahmoud was found hiding in a hut and was dragged out, dignified in his sullen contempt. Bound and chained, with a halter round his neck and a whip to keep him going, he took part in the victory march through Berber, much to the delight of the crowd, the pride of the Sudanese-Egyptian troops, and the grim satisfaction of their British comrades, whose morale was nurtured by the battle-cry, "Remember Gordon!" (though it was thirteen years since he died).

The tally of Dervishes dead at this battle amounted to two thousand in the zeriba and another five hundred around its exits. Casualties among the allies reflect the relative contributions made. 132 of the British were killed or wounded, of whom seven were serving with the Egyptian Army; 375 of the Sudanese; and 52 of the Egyptians, the majority of whom were artillerymen or cavalrymen, since their infantry was held in reserve.

Kitchener paused to build up his strength and allow the hottest months of summer to pass. Reinforcements, which included a second British infantry brigade, another Egyptian brigade, and the 21st Lancers, brought his strength to over twenty-five thousand, of which just under a third were British. This great force marched serenely up the west bank of the river, a cavalry screen ahead, camelry acting as flank guard, and twenty-four battalions of infantry on the march, British and Egyptian in parallel columns, with seven batteries of artillery and seven of Maxims, while on the east bank marched a supporting army of friendly tribes, motley and excited. On the river itself there was a massive fleet of transport vessels, headed by ten bristling gunboats. Two standard-bearers rode with Kitchener, one with the Union Jack, the other with the scarlet flag, with gold star and crescent, of Turkish Egypt, but it was the latter that predominated, dwarfing the British flag and flying alone in glory when he pitched tent for a halt, for the Sirdar was the Khedive's servant—and stern and tense he looked, knowing well how many officers in Her Majesty's service, far senior to himself, grudged him the honour of leading this mighty expedition.

Around midday on September 1 the infantry were within five miles of Omdurman, the capital the Dervishes had built themselves opposite Khartoum, which lay in ruins. Only now did news arrive of the presence of the enemy; it was brought to the Sirdar, with considerable awe, by a subaltern attached to the Lancers, Winston Churchill. The Khalifa had harangued his masses into action and had assembled some 52,000 (so it transpired) on the hills above Omdurman, whence they approached the Lancers in massive phalanxes, distinguishable from each other by the different colours of their banners. Kitchener fortified a position, in the shape of a splayed horseshoe, against the river's bank and awaited the assault, with every rifleman and gunner, on land and river, apprised of the range, and itching to fire. Half-left and half-right of his position, each at a distance of rather more than a mile, two substantial hills rose from the plain.

The Dervishes attacked in mass next morning, but not until the sun had been up for over an hour. They met inevitable, ludicrous, sickening slaughter. So shattering was the repulse that Kitchener feared a retirement to Omdurman and sent the Lancers off by the shortest route to cut it off, at the same time directing the infantry, the British on the left, towards the left-hand hill. Waiting behind this hill, in hope of just such a movement, was a horde of seventeen thousand under the Khalifa in person, while another horde almost as large lurked behind the other hill, now on the right rear of the allied army, having been lured by the Egyptian cavalry further from the battlefield than they intended. The great moment was at hand, the moment of fulfilment of the Mahdi's prophecy.

Two or three thousand of the Khalifa's men sneaked down a dry stream bed towards the river and popped up just as the 21st Lancers, making their first charge in battle, were upon them. There was a fury of thrust and slash before the Lancers struggled on, gashed and breathless, leaving twenty dead or dying men behind them. Dismounting, they had to resort to the rifle which proved a more effective weapon against such a stubborn foe.

The mass of the Khalifa's men swarmed round the other side of the hill and charged across the plain towards the brigade commanded by Lieutenant-Colonel Hector MacDonald, "Old Mac" the ranker. It consisted of one Egyptian and three Sudanese battalions, and with eighteen light guns in support had been pushed westwards to protect the right flank and was a mile clear of the brigade on its left. Three brigades, two Egyptian and one British, stormed to the top of the hill and with long-range volleys blunted and drew on themselves part of this great assault, while the other British brigade came running over from the left to fill the gap. The Dervishes fell fast but were still closing on MacDonald's men when the other horde, having returned from its abortive chase after the Egyptian cavalry, swept down on MacDonald's exposed right flank. Disaster seemed imminent—and would perhaps have been unavoidable if the attacks had been launched simultaneously—but with superb calm MacDonald redeployed from left to right, neatly switching his fire-power as the peril subsided on one flank and mounted on the other. His Sudanese troops reacted to the new threat smartly, but their fire was extravagantly wild, and it was due primarily to the steadiness of the Egyptians, infantry, gunners and cameleers brought up in support, and to the prowess of the Lincolnshires, who sprinted round the right flank to make deadly use of their Lee-Metfords, that this attack too was brought to a groaning, heaped-up halt. Thus the crisis was met by a combined effort from the three races that fought under Egypt's flag.

The Khalifa's huge black standard still boldly fluttered, but below it lay nothing but corpses, a particularly poignant handful among the thousands that littered the battlefield. Their comrades at last deserted them, pursued by the Lancers, with impetus weakened by their premature release. Kitchener letting himself go in the exuberance of victory, remarked that he appeared to have given them "a good dusting". His men had killed 9,700 Dervishes. Science had won vengeance over savagery, at a cost to its manipulators, in killed and wounded, of 181 British, of whom 71 belonged to the 21st Lancers and six to the Egyptian Army; 178 Egyptians; and 123 Sudanese. Of the total of 482 casualties, only 48 were killed. More than two hundred Dervishes died, in other words, for every man they killed themselves.

The Khalifa himself still lived. He had ridden from the field on his donkey when he saw the battle was lost and hastened to organize the defence of Omdurman. Finding the task impossible, he made brief communion at the Mahdi's once splendid tomb, now sadly holed by howitzer fire specially assigned the task, and made off into the scrub with Osman Digna, slippery to the last, and a few thousand faithfuls, there to roam belligerently until being hunted down and shot in battle fifteen months later.

There remained one task for Kitchener to carry out. Sealed orders, which he did not open until the battle was won, required him to journey upriver to prevent French infiltration into the southern wilds of the Sudan. The arrival of a Dervish steamer brought news that the French had already arrived; her captain had come to give the Khalifa information on a mysterious force of foreigners, 300 miles up the White Nile at Fashoda, and was obliged to give it to the Sirdar instead. Taking with him two Sudanese battalions, a detachment of the Cameron Highlanders and a battery of Egyptian artillery, Kitchener set off on September 10 and reached Fashoda after nine days' steaming. Sure enough, the Tricolour was flying over the mud fortress, protected by a force of 120 West African soldiers who had come all the way from the Atlantic coast and been over two years on the march. Their redoubtable commander, Major Marchand, came aboard Kitchener's gunboat and was received with courtesy and genuine admiration. Accepting the advice of Colonel Reginald Wingate, his Intelligence chief, Kitchener had donned his tarboush, in place of the sun-helmet he wore on the campaign, and all his boats flew the Egyptian flag.

He had come, he told Marchand after a convivial luncheon, to reclaim the lawful property of the Khedive—he did not add that the British had dispossessed the Khedive of his property but had changed their minds when they saw the danger of its being grabbed by the French. Marchand replied that he was there on the instructions of his Government and must remain there until further instructed—he did not add that he would have been devoured by the Dervishes if the British had not considerately intervened. It was agreed without rancour that the matter should be left for the two Governments to decide, and in the meantime Kitchener put his troops ashore near the French encampment and with elaborate ceremony hoisted the Egyptian flag. Being hopelessly outnumbered on the spot, and unprepared, though not unwilling, to go to the length of general war, the French Government had inevitably to give way. Back came their soldiers down the Nile, with all facilities provided just as they had been for the shorter journey nearly a hundred years before. There was wild joy in London, bitter resentment in Paris.

No sooner had the French left Fashoda than the Union Jack was run up alongside the Turco-Egyptian Star and Crescent, and indeed the two flags already flew side by side over Government

House, Khartoum. For Kitchener served other people besides the Khedive, people even more appreciative of what he had achieved. In London, Lord Kitchener of Khartoum, avenger of Gordon, received the most exuberant welcome that Queen Victoria's uninhibited subjects could give. The loudest cheers of all greeted his remarks at the Guildhall banquet given in his honour: "We have hoisted the British and Egyptian flags at Khartoum. Never, I hope, will they be hauled down again."

Khartoum would have meant nothing to the British people if Gordon had not been sent there, but so involved had they become in his fate that it occurred to no one that the British flag had not in fact been hauled down for the reason that it had not previously been flown. It seemed only natural that it should be flying there now, and pride demanded that it must remain. Anyway, the Egyptians had already shown themselves quite incapable of administering their colony, or province as they regarded it, and were further hampered by the absurd privileges which had to be extended to foreigners under the Ottoman Capitulations. A novel form of government by partnership was therefore instituted, a "condominium" under joint British and Egyptian rule, with the Turkish influence excluded even nominally. The Khedive would appoint the Governor-General, but the British Government would make the selection (the first of course being Kitchener) and the British would also control the sanction of foreign consulates, would in fact run the country, while the other partner drew a half-share in prestige. After all, the Sudan would never have been reconquered but for British leadership. Yet the Egyptians had paid the larger price, both in lives and cash. £800,000 was the total contribution by the British Government, while Egypt paid £1,613,213, a large part of which admittedly went on railway lines of lasting use. As Winston Churchill put it, "English history does not record any instance of so great a national satisfaction being more cheaply obtained."

The administration of this new condominium called for constant consultation at governmental level and gave further cause for the retention of British troops in Cairo, as token of the authority of the man to whose voice the Khedive was obliged to heed. The British had in fact made themselves indispensable. They had come as firefighters and stayed on as caretakers, and the longer they stayed the harder it became to imagine how the complacent Egyptians could ever manage without them. At last even the French recognized this, goaded by the growing menace of an expansionist Germany and the powers of conciliation of Salisbury's successor as Prime Minister, Arthur Balfour. Under the 1904 agreement the British Government declared "that they have no intention of altering the political status of Egypt" and the French "that they will not obstruct the action of Great Britain in that country by asking that a limit of time be fixed for the British occupation". France had given up the long struggle for domination, but her influence remained. French was still the language taught in schools, still the language of communication between Egyptians and Europeans, Britons included.

Britain also agreed to accept and enforce the Suez Canal Convention of 1888. Around the same time the Egyptian economy was freed from the powers of compulsory extortion exercised by the *Caisse de la Dette*. Great was the benefit derived from the maternal British presence, great and everlasting seemed its calming influence on the land.

The achievements of British guidance were there for all to see. Prosperity came from irrigation developments, such as the construction of the Aswan dam and repair of the barrage at the head of the Delta which Mohammed Aly had built as a defence against invading fleets. These works between them made perennial cultivation possible and enormously increased the output of crops, both of cereals and cotton—though at dire cost to the physique of the fellahin, which rotted under the impact of working in a perpetual swamp, spawning seat of hookworm and mosquito, agents of bilharzia and malaria. The population rose to eleven million, almost double that of 1882, and their houses, shops, roads and railways had grown at an even faster rate.

Greatest of all was the advance in the tourist trade. A trip to Egypt was well within the means of the middle-class Englishman in those prosperous days and they came in their shoals to gape at the Great Pyramid, appease the pestering swarms of vendors, and revel in the marbled magic of Cairo's hotels, where they would be waited on by great black men in flowing robes, who would emerge noiselessly from the shadows like slaves of the lamp. And trade came too from the thousands who came in with the slipstream of the British occupation, the officials, engineers, businessmen, the officers and their families, all so contented with the easy luxury of their exotic way of life and its busy social whirl.

Suddenly the British were jolted out of their hubris by a strange event. A party of officers of the Mounted Infantry, in the course of a long march in the summer of 1906, went to the Delta village of Denshawi to shoot pigeons. They had been invited, rather vaguely, by a sheikh, but either they had gone to the wrong place or the sheikh did not turn up. At any rate, they took up stands for the shoot, somewhat aggravated by the surly aspect of the villagers, who did not seem at all keen to have their pigeons shot. Surliness turned to open aggression. One of the officers was accosted and had his gun snatched from him, and no sooner was it in the hands of the peasants than it went off, wounding four of them. At this moment a fire mysteriously broke out on a threshing floor, whereupon the villagers got very rowdy and rough. Major Pine Coffin, the senior, sought to appease them by making his colleagues hand over their guns, but as the disarmed party returned to their gigs they were set upon, cuffed and clubbed. Two of them, Captains Bostock and Bull, slipped away and ran off towards camp to summon help. Bostock got there first, and quickly got some troops galloping to the rescue. They found Bull unconscious by the roadside; he was rushed to hospital but died of heat apoplexy, aggravated, so it was thought, by a blow on the head received during the fight. The others were rescued from their tormentors, bruised and dishevelled, but otherwise none the worse, except that Pine Coffin had a badly damaged arm.

Fifty-two of the villagers were arrested and tried before a special court, the President of which was an Egyptian, its members British. The sentences included four hangings and six floggings, both to be carried out at the scene of the crime, and two life imprisonments. The people of Egypt also passed judgement. The British were their enemies, as harsh and tyrannical as any Mameluke or Turk.

Cromer was in England at the time, but he allowed the sentences to stand; it was the only way, he thought, of teaching these silly people a lesson. He knew that, despite all the blessings conferred by the British, there was discontent in the land, evinced as it was by ardent nationalist agitation, which gained fresh momentum from the Anglo-French agreement and the realization it inspired that the British occupation had become permanent. But its depth had been concealed from him (if it was known) by the bland Turco-Egyptian administrators who provided him with his one, inaccurate mirror of public feeling. It was in any case not for him to tamper with the constitution; that was a matter for the Egyptians to decide among themselves. He was prepared to encourage democratic progress, provided it did not impede efficiency, which must always be the foremost goal. It was a goal he had aimed at with great success, which made it all the sadder that the closing year of his illustrious rule—for that is what it was in practice—should be marred by this revealing display of hate and vengeance, producer of such a lasting crop of bitterness. Efficiency, in fact, was the root cause of the bitterness, for its pursuit made Cromer bring in an ever-increasing number of British officials whose efforts, ironically, were directed at the extermination of oppression and corruption.

Cromer remained firm in his beliefs. In his valedictory address a year later he warned the fellahin "against allowing themselves to be duped and misled by their pseudo-representatives. . . . I shall urge that this wholly spurious and manufactured movement in favour of a rapid development of parliamentary institutions should be treated for what it is worth; and, gentlemen, let me add that it is worth very little." He made his departure from Cairo through silent and deserted streets.

There was now a Liberal Government in Britain, after ten years of Conservative rule, and Cromer's successor in Cairo, his former Financial Adviser, Sir Eldon Gorst, showed such liberal inclinations that the British residents were aghast. Instead of the mounted escort and stately coach, he drove through the streets in a two-seater car, dressed in open-necked shirt and joking with passersby—having first taken the precaution of securing the release of the prisoners of the Denshawi trial. Englishmen were replaced by Egyptians in the civil service, and the General Assembly was thrown open so that the people could hear the landlords and notables who were supposed to represent them hold forth in debate. The results were not encouraging. Efficiency deteriorated, and nationalist agitation, so far from being assuaged, roared all the louder at the smell of red meat. Students kept coming out in mass, and indeed a lop-sided educational system, unadjusted by the British, gave every encouragement for this folksy ritual, since those who did go to school usually stayed there until they were 18, with little prospect thereafter except of clerical employment, vacancies for which could be won from the Government through the blackmail of commotion in the streets.

The climax came, ironically, with the murder of Boutros Pasha, the first pure Egyptian ever to be appointed Prime Minister—but he was a Copt, a member of that mournful, undemonstrative sect possessed of the dignified pride of a minority people, and had further put his signature (as Foreign Secretary) to the degrading Sudan Condominium Convention and, worst of all, had been presiding judge at the Denshawi trial. Ownership of the Canal was the issue that caused his death. The Canal Company offered most generous terms for a forty-year extension of their concession, from 1968 to 2008, and Boutros's eagerness to accept earned him a bullet through the ribs after he had unwisely put the matter before the General Assembly. The murderer, a Moslem fanatic, was duly executed and hailed a great hero by the nationalist press. There was concern in London lest the British influence be swept away by the torrent that Gorst's liberalism unleashed.

Gorst conveniently died the following year, 1911, and the Liberal Government hastened to despatch the man best qualified to apply the strong hand that was obviously needed, Kitchener of Khartoum. Quiet returned abruptly. Kitchener, riding forth in splendour, was the Imperial type which the Egyptians expected, respected and could not but admire. He for his part had genuine affection for the soldiers he had commanded in battle and with all his mighty energy embarked on a series of land reforms and developments which enormously improved the lot of the peasant who, though no longer liable to tax extraction by torture, was still the metaphorical whipping boy of the country's economy. "Welcome to Lord Kitchener—the Friend of the Fellah", blazed the banners as he made his almost messianic progress on his tours of inspection.

Kitchener also widened parliament, both in composition and power, though within firm safeguards, but he throttled with a grasp of iron anything that might impede his own authority, such as the prerogative of the Khedive or the freedom of the press, and scarce a squeak came from the victims. He also undid the "Egyptianization" of the administration on which Gorst had been so keen. There was a great influx of Englishmen, none of whom endeared themselves to the Egyptian people as did their leader.

Lord Edward Cecil, Kitchener's former A.D.C. who was promoted to the post of Financial Adviser, has left a delightful sketch of the Anglicized Cairo of those days in his book *Leisure of an Egyptian Official*, which had not been written for publication and caused hurt to many Egyptians when it was published. He describes, with devastating wit, the banalities of the highly de-

manding social life—pan-European of course—and its various, un-
officially recognized layers of society, the smart military set and the
smug military set, the smart official set and the smug official set, the
smart professional set and the smug professional set, and so on.
He lightly describes the workings of government and the types to
be found on the interminable committees sitting under the aegis of
their British advisers, the jovial and venal Minister of State, shrewd
and ignorant, "the soul of selfish good nature", the melancholy
Copt, "proud in his contempt of the Moslem, servile in view of
his power to oppress him", the Egyptianized descendant of the
Napoleonic invasion, avid for prestige, and the cringeing Syrian
clerk, evoker of shameless bullying. And he describes the common
people, the shambling, shiftless, exasperating, captivating people.

Another book of this period, written by the journalist Sydney
Moseley and entitled *With Kitchener in Khartoum*, presents a
different, but not necessarily contradictory, picture. In one of his
chapters he tells Why The Englishman Is Disliked. "The Land of
Paradox," he found, "has become the City of British Snobs. Offi-
cialism is there in its element. Petty tyranny, narrow-mindedness,
tactlessness, and bumptiousness germinate and thrive." Though
contemptuous of the half-Turkish upper-class Egyptian, he
thought the friendship of the "growing Egyptian" well worth culti-
vating, but realized the barrier imposed by his servile manner.
"The cringeing and abjectness of the native have transformed
many responsible Britons in Egypt from masters tolerant towards
their inferiors into the kind of tyrant who recalls Egypt's darkest
hour."

This book not surprisingly also caused hurt, especially among
the longer-established advisers who, in many different departments,
had won the trust and affection of Egyptians by their devotion to
their interests and did not deserve to be included in such a general
bombardment. But it would not have been launched without provocation. The habit of occupation had made Egypt a colony in the
eyes of newly arrived Englishmen and their wives, most of all
those belonging to regiments come from India to complete a
foreign tour, and it was the custom in those days to keep the
natives in their place.

CHAPTER TEN

Through Two Wars

(1914-45)

STRATEGIC CONSIDERATIONS HAD so far played little part in the retention of British troops in Egypt, or for that matter in the appointment of the soldier, Kitchener, as British Agent. Turkey had always been regarded as the bulwark protecting Britain's short route to India, and though Turkey had her complaints against each of the three new allies, Britain, France and Russia, it was hoped, and indeed assumed, that she would remain neutral in a European conflict. Yet Turkey had for many years been wooed assiduously and lavishly. As early as 1889 the German Kaiser had paid a ceremonial visit on the Sultan, the first and only Christian monarch ever to do so, and he came again with even grander ceremony in 1898, the year of Omdurman. Tokens of friendship had followed in the form of guns, rolling-stock, railway lines and instructors, and just in case there was any doubt where the Kaiser's ambitions lay, the matter was explained in an authoritative book on German strategy by a certain Dr. Paul Rohrbach: "England can be attacked and mortally wounded by land from Europe only in one place—Egypt."

Britain herself may have given her old ally the final shove into the arms of her new lover by confiscating for her own use two battleships which were being built for Turkey in Tyneside dock-yards; one of them had been completed and her crew of Turks were about to embark. This was on July 31, 1914, and on August 2 Turkey signed a secret treaty with Germany but did not as yet make declaration of war.

In Egypt the outbreak of war caused greater commotion among the foreigners, concerned either about their country or their investments, than among the natives. It was the dead season in Cairo, and both nominal and actual rulers were away on holiday, Khedive Abbas Hilmi in Turkey, Consul-General Kitchener in England. They stayed away. The pro-Turk Hilmi had no inducement to return to what was in effect, if not yet in name, enemy-occupied territory, while Kitchener was needed for other duties at home. Hussein Rushdi Pasha, the Prime Minister of Egypt, was prevailed upon to issue a declaration of assistance to Britain, forbidding all trade with enemy nations and urging the people to aid the British in every way they could. Unwisely, he obtained no balancing promise or concession from Britain. The Legislative Assembly, whose function in the eyes of most members was to criticize and deride the Government, was prorogued for the duration. All this was accepted without protest. The people of Egypt had relapsed into that state of apathetic resignation with which they had endured the Mamelukes and the courbash.

The Turks meanwhile made brash troop concentrations and protested their neutrality. Not until October 29 did they do anything openly hostile, when their ships joined the Germans in bombarding Sebastopol. At the same time Turkey formally claimed Egypt to be an integral part of the Ottoman Empire and demanded full control. War was inevitable, though it was not declared until November 6. In the meantime martial law was declared in Egypt and Lieutenant-General Sir John Maxwell, commanding British troops, issued a proclamation which outlined the cause and effect of this step and made a rash undertaking that Britain would "bear the sole burden of the war without calling on Egypt for aid". Six weeks elapsed before the Government announced their decision as to the status of this supine portion of an enemy empire which by lucky chance, and with the acquiescence of the owner, they already occupied. The majority of the Cabinet favoured annexation, but they yielded to advice from the British Agency and declared a Protectorate, a word which had about it a touching and misleading suggestion of a voluntary appeal for aid by the weak to the strong. The first edict issued by the protectors was the deposition of Hilmi in favour of his uncle, Hussein Kamal, with the title of Sultan in place of Khedive. This was popular with the Egyptians in as much as they cared, for Kamal was a kindly and unpretentious old man, but in their haste to fill the vacuum the British had committed themselves to perpetuating a régime almost as unpopular as their own.

Already the Turks had crossed the frontier into the Sinai desert. The few British troops, with Egyptian artillery support, were complacently withdrawn. Though a Turkish army had successfully used this invasion route as recently as 1801, it was thought impossible that they should do so again; Lieutenant-Colonel Elgood observed that in military circles in Cairo "if it was suggested that Egypt should become an actual theatre of war, the remark would be received with an incredulous smile". Even so, troops were hurried in to reinforce the Lancastrian Territorial Division which had early relieved the Regulars—it would be a good chance, said Kitchener when he sent them, for the cotton weavers to see how the real thing is grown—and by the end of the year two Indian divisions and an untrained division of Australians and New Zealanders had arrived. The Indians took over defence duties while the others were entrusted with internal security, a task made more complicated by the plunderous and capricious tendencies of certain of the Australians. The Suez Canal, it was decided, should be the means rather than the object of the defence, and the Indians dug themselves positions all along it. Strategy was thus sacrificed to tactical convenience, for the main point in defending Egypt was to keep open the Canal.

Djemal Pasha, the Turkish commander, exuberantly styled himself "the Saviour of Egypt" and declared his objective Cairo, where he fondly imagined that the Egyptians, roused by the well-worn call for a Holy War, would hail him as their liberator. Without waiting for extra divisions which were slowly on their way, he marched across the desert, along the middle and firmest route, with twenty thousand infantrymen and ten batteries of artillery. After a feint attack against Kantara he attempted a crossing opposite Tussum, south of Ismailia, on the night of February 2, 1915. Pontoons, brought all the way from Constantinople, were successfully launched under cover of darkness; but the Indians were ready for them on the west bank, and those few Turks who did not meet death in midstream were quickly disposed of when they reached the far side. A fresh assault was made in daylight but broke against the defences of Serapeum, on the eastern bank, and the guns of French warships on the Bitter Lake. French seaplanes also played a valuable part.

The Turks gave up and at nightfall began the weary toil back across the desert, unpursued. They had lost some 1,500 men, the majority of them missing or prisoner, and in exchange had done no more than hold up shipping for a week. Kress von Kressenstein, the able German left in command at the front, showed that more could be achieved by small patrols operating from a desert base. By sniping and dropping mines into the canal, they caused very much more alarm than damage and so scared the Canal Company that for many months all ships were halted at night.

Well organized though the Turkish expedition was, it failed almost as much through psychological as tactical misappreciation. The Egyptians showed no urge whatever to welcome the Turkish invader, and indeed one or two detachments of their army ably co-operated in the task of repulse. Apathy still reigned, and only commercial interest was aroused when Sir Ian Hamilton's men assembled in their thousands at Alexandria and Port Said and set sail for war. Warmer emotions were aroused when they returned almost as numerously, prostrate and bandaged, after grievous encounters on the beaches of Gallipoli, and the Egyptians co-operated wholeheartedly in providing makeshift hospital accommodation and nursing aid. But as the wounded emerged into convalescence they gained popularity with few people except the purveyors of vice.

Not until the closing months of 1915, when the British, having been forced out of Gallipoli, gave more active attention to the Turkish threat to the Canal, were the Egyptian people made to realize how hollow were the promises relieving them of aid in the defence of their country. The Egyptian Expeditionary Force was formed, with headquarters at Ismailia, and its commander, the bustling and restless General Sir Archibald Murray, was made senior to, and soon superseded, Maxwell in Cairo, whose tact and understanding had made the administration of martial law barely noticeable to the people. A defence line was thrown out twelve miles eastwards of the Canal, demanding for its maintenance an extensive network of roads, pipelines and light railways. The Egyptian Government accepted the demand without complaint and provided the labour by calling up army reservists and by enrolling volunteers with the lure of good pay and short engagements. As Murray turned to the offensive and slogged across the desert, accompanied by all the paraphernalia needed to sustain an army operating far from its base, so did the demand increase, soon exceeding voluntary supply. In default of their promise, the

British military authorities advocated conscription. The Egyptian Government preferred to fall back on an older-established form of compulsion. Each province was allotted its quota of "volunteers", and the unfortunates who were dragged away were those unable to obtain exemption by bribe or favour.

A massive force was raised by these various means. The Egyptian Labour Corps rose to a strength of around 155,000 men, large contingents of whom served as far afield as France and Mesopotamia. Another 170,000 passed at various times through the ranks of the Camel Transport Corps, for which 72,000 camels were provided, mainly by arbitrary requisition. This latter corps won a great reputation for its unfailing delivery of supplies. It marched in close support of the fighting troops and when General Sir Edmund Allenby, having superseded Murray, penetrated deep into Palestine towards the end of 1917 the Egyptian camel men had to endure the unaccustomed rigours of winter as well as the hazards of the forward zone. 220 of them were killed in action, 1,400 wounded, and a further 4,000 died from exposure or disease. Such was the contribution of a race uninterested in the quarrel, exonerated from participation, and generally despised by the troops of the protecting power.

Curiously, the British Government sowed the seeds of another quarrel just as Allenby's first great success, the capture of Gaza, was announced on November 9, 1917. It was on this day, in hope of rallying support elsewhere, that the Balfour Declaration was issued, bestowing favour on the establishment in Palestine of a national home for the Jews. It attracted little attention and no Egyptian can at the time have imagined that it would have the remotest influence on his country's destiny.

As the war advanced, the military administration in Cairo grew in size, deteriorated in quality and became ever less considerate of the victims of their rulings. The Egyptian Government displayed atavistic addiction to tyranny in giving effect to the military's behests. Censorship was savagely applied, detentions were widespread, often made on political grounds, and requisitions, of men, animals and crops, fell most harshly on the poorest, while concessions to vested interests caused shortages and made prices soar. But when in May 1917 the military, sensing unrest, demanded the surrender of all privately owned arms, whether shotguns, swords or knuckledusters, the Egyptian Government demurred and made it clear, when obliged to issue the order, that they did so under military compulsion. It was a humiliating measure that greatly enraged the people, since weapons meant almost as much as wives to their owners. Apathy turned to simmering resentment, which was spiced by the pepper of jealousy when Feisal's Arabs eventually swept into Damascus, yelling their claims to an independent state. The British Government proclaimed their right to self-determination but made no mention of Egypt's rights. It was hardly a cause for wonder that the peace that came in November 1918 seemed a weird, distorted thing in Egypt. The voice of the people screamed raucously to be heard.

Fomented by the long years of sufferance, sufferance of the demands of wartime and of the snubs unthinkingly delivered by the occupying troops, frustration burst with a pop. Saad Zaghloul was the prime puller of the cork. This lanky, long-faced man was born of humble stock, but had gained advancement by wit and brainpower, made a good marriage and become Minister of Education under Cromer, whose patronage he enjoyed. Later he had been in opposition and had cultivated such power of demagogic oratory that his words could intoxicate. He had behaved responsibly during the war, but the moment it was over he demanded full independence, presenting himself before the British High Commissioner (as the Agent had become under the terms of the Protectorate) as head of the people's delegation, or Wafd, by which name his party was known.

The Commissioner was Sir Reginald Wingate, former Sirdar of the Egyptian Army and Governor-General of the Sudan, a man with 35 years' devoted service to Egypt. He recommended that Zaghloul should be heard in London together with the Prime Minister, Rushdi, who had his own less ambitious proposals for reform and was fully aware of the force of the nationalist movement. A curt refusal came back. The British Cabinet had more pressing matters on their hands and had in any case decided that in view of the strategic importance of Egypt Britain must not relax her control, whatever might be allowed to happen in other, more backward lands. Wingate received a rap for heeding to "native aspirations", delivered by Curzon, who was in charge of the Foreign Office during Balfour's absence at the Paris peace conference. Wingate persisted with his warnings, stressing the danger in the rising temper and pleading for a sop to nationalist ambitions. It was conceded that he should come home for consultation on the understanding that the Prime Minister (but not Zaghloul) should follow. An insulting telegram caused the latter to cancel his trip and resign office, with Wingate already in London. The gunpowder was charged. It was ignited by the arrest and deportation of Zaghloul, with three other eminent nationalists, for arousing disorder in defiance of the martial law.

No one had anticipated, not even Wingate, that a mad blood lust would rage across Egypt from Alexandria to Aswan. It started on March 10, 1919, the day after the arrests, with the predictable and semi-authorized ritual of student demonstrations in Cairo. They fast gathered size and momentum. Streetlights were shattered, tramcars overturned, shops stoned and pillaged, and the offices of Anglophil newspapers ransacked. Support for the movement, if not the violence, was widespread and spontaneous, and even doctors and lawyers gave their allegiance, refusing to undertake Government work. Then the fellahin joined in and, probably by no prearranged plan, the demonstration plunged into savage rebellion. First in the Delta, and then in Upper Egypt too, railway lines were torn up, stations burnt to the ground, and the houses of Europeans attacked by hysterical masses. Egyptian Army detachments hit back hard. Fourteen rioters were shot dead in an assault on the railway station at Tanta, thirteen in Cairo when a lorry-load of soldiers was attacked, fourteen in Alexandria, twelve in Damanhur, and in each instance some fifty others were wounded.

The rebels succeeded in cutting off Cairo from all communication except wireless and in laying siege to Europeans forced to congregate in single houses; at Assiut three thousand fellahin and Bedouin were held at bay with the aid of a hundred Punjabi soldiers, while at Minia a small, ill-armed party of Europeans survived a five-day siege, thanks to the loyalty of a company of Egyptian infantry and the courage of an Egyptian doctor. Many people were murdered by the peasants and their Bedouin allies, some Europeans but more often Syrian, Copt or a private enemy, and once a complete party of British soldiers fell into their hands. It consisted of three officers and five men who most unwisely boarded the night train from Luxor unarmed. They were assailed and brutally murdered in the course of two halts. Their bodies were mutilated and hung up for display, and at every station the train passed mobs were waiting to howl their appreciation. The brave boasted that they had (quite literally) drunk the blood of an Englishman.

For a week the British Army stood on the defensive, hoping that the Egyptian authorities would unravel the turmoil, unled though they were by any Ministry, since no one had taken Rushdi's place. Then Lieutenant-General Sir Edward Bulfin, Allenby's resolute and able lieutenant, arrived from Palestine and sent forth mobile columns, headed by armoured cars, to the relief of the beleaguered groups of Europeans. The rage of the volatile peasants subsided as rapidly as it had flared up, their defiance drained at sight of the conquerors of the Turk. Only Major-General Sir John Shea and his Londoners, striking deep into Upper Egypt, encountered any resistance, mainly from brigand bands.

On March 25 the awe-inspiring figure of Allenby—Field-Marshal Viscount Allenby he was soon to become—arrived in Cairo. He had been in Paris when the rebellion started, advising Lloyd George on the claims of the Arabs who, unlike the Egyptians, were permitted to present their case for an independent state before the Peace Conference. Lloyd George decided that Allenby was the man for Egypt and the unfortunate Wingate, still in England, was relieved of the High Commissioner's post. The Egyptians trembled in fear of the wrath to come; 85 people were put on trial for the train atrocity, of whom 51 were sentenced to death and 23 later reprieved. Yet in the cities in particular the unrest could still be seen smouldering in protest strikes by wide sections of the community, and in a sudden flare-up in Cairo British troops shot nine people dead before fury was quenched.

The British residents were well pleased with the appointment of Allenby as High Commissioner. This great soldier of such pugnacious demeanour appeared to them as the very man to cow the Egyptians back to their customary subservience. A shock was in store for them. On April 7, a mere fortnight after his arrival, Allenby announced that Zaghloul and his deported colleagues were free to return and go wherever they chose. The decision was seen, by one resident at any rate, as "a bombshell . . . nothing short of calamitous" and was denounced both in Egypt and Britain as "surrender to the forces of disorder". The frenzied reception accorded the repatriates and the prolongation of rioting and strikes provided Allenby's critics with ammunition. But the "Bull" had finished with waging war. Like other soldiers before him, including Wingate, he had sympathy for the aspirations of the Egyptian people and was determined that they should have the chance, unhampered by obstructing grievance, to work out their own destiny; and unlike Wingate, he had the backing of the Cabinet, who had been scared into swift retreat. This conciliatory gesture did at least persuade the pasha politicians to take up the reins of government which in their pique they had let go.

Putting faith in its anaesthetizing influence, the British Government appointed a commission under the wise Lord Milner, charged with examining means of restoring the autonomy of Egypt within the Protectorate. The Egyptians abominated the concept of titular protection, however much freedom they might enjoy within it, and when the Commission arrived, seven months after its appointment, it was boycotted, even though it widened its own terms of reference. However, it continued its deliberations in London, whither Zaghloul was induced to come. Some progress was made, but there could be no surmounting the barrier of mass intimidation which not only held the Sultan's Ministers in its sway but also its own Wafdist instigators. Zaghloul was given a most sympathetic hearing and could have won a favourable settlement if he had had the courage to accept compromise and its accompanying onus of restraining his people.

As it was, Egypt was held in thrall by a few murder gangs and by swarms of schoolboys who found that running amok in the streets was a much more stimulating pastime than sitting in a classroom. Sometimes their elders joined in, and in May 1921 thirty Egyptians and fourteen Europeans were killed in ferocious rioting in Alexandria, the handling of which Allenby left to the Egyptian authorities until too late. In December of that year tactless demands by the British Government brought negotiations to a close, with the result that the Prime Minister, Adly Pasha, resigned and no one could be persuaded to succeed him. In the same month Zaghloul was again deported, this time to the Seychelles. It was a humiliating step for Allenby, but there was no great disorder, partly because Zaghloul's puerile agitation had lost him support, partly because Allenby was in no mood for nonsense. The nationalists turned to occult terrorism. Isolated Britons were murdered in crowded streets and no one ever dared see it happen.

A man less determined than Allenby might have regarded the deadlock as final as it was depressing and governed indefinitely through the agency of the British under-secretaries of the Egyptian governmental departments. Allenby decided instead that he would himself have to obtain the concession which the Egyptian politicians had been unable to grasp. He returned to England, fought a Cabinet resolved to see him out of office rather than give way, and won one of the greatest victories of his career. On February 28,

1922, he returned to Egypt, bringing with him a Declaration of Independence. For a brief moment the whole of Egypt acclaimed him their hero.

In granting Egypt her independence, the British Government had laid down four "reserved points" to be settled by negotiation: security of communications with the Empire; the defence of Egypt; the protection of the rights of foreigners who still indulged in the privileges conferred by the Capitulations; and the Sudan. Thus the issues nearest the Egyptian heart remained unsolved and long years of barter lay ahead. In the meantime the Egyptians turned their attention to revising their constitution and this also involved much wrangling. Since the death of Kamal in 1917, yet another son of Ismail, Fuad, had been Sultan. He had enjoyed little influence and even less popularity, but now proclaimed King, he showed himself as crafty as he was ambitious. So prolonged was the tussle between moderates, nationalists and monarch that it was not until April 1923 that a Constitution, far too liberal for the King's liking, was approved. It was followed by the passing in July of an Act of Indemnity, under which the many British officials due to be discharged were granted compensation. Only now, under the terms of the Declaration, was martial law at last abolished.

The first election under the new Constitution brought the Wafd to power with a huge majority and in January 1924 Zaghloul became Prime Minister, having returned from exile only four months previously. He soon showed that agitation still appealed to him very much more than administration. The complete evacuation of the British, from both Egypt and the Sudan, was his one ambition, and to this end the Wafd stirred up trouble in the Sudan and blamed the British for fictitious atrocities. In this same month of January, Ramsay MacDonald was appointed Prime Minister of Britain. He had given Zaghloul high hope of sweeping concessions, but when Zaghloul visited him in September, MacDonald turned down, as he was bound to, his high-handed demands. On his return he raised some of his wildest men to high office and tuned up the Cairo mob to a fever pitch of rage. Then, on November 19, Sir Lee Stack was shot in his car by men dressed as students and armed with revolvers. He was taken to Allenby's house where he died next day. As Sirdar of the Egyptian Army and Governor-General of the Sudan, Stack was an obvious target for the nationalists' fire. He was also an admired friend of Allenby's.

Now at last, in the fury of trust betrayed, Allenby played the part so long expected of him. A few hours after the funeral he drove to the parliament buildings, dressed in lounge-suit and accompanied by a strong escort of the 16/5th Lancers, to the flourish of whose trumpets he entered the Cabinet office. He handed Zaghloul an ultimatum, with a copy in French, which still remained the language of communication in court and governmental circles. "His Majesty's Government," it said, "consider that this murder, which holds up Egypt as at present governed to the contempt of civilized peoples, is the natural outcome of a campaign of hostility to British rights." (In fact, approval of the ultimatum with a number of reservations, was in the process of being deciphered.) It laid down seven requirements, which included penance, a fine of £500,000, withdrawal from the Sudan of all Egyptian soldiers, and a concession to the Sudan (of rather doubtful relevance) over their use of Nile water. Zaghloul had already tendered his personal apologies; it is as certain that they were sincere as that his senior lieutenants were implicated in the plot. He accepted the fine, but could agree to no concession over that treasured symbol of Egyptian pride, the Sudan. But instead of fighting the issue he meekly resigned and gave way to a Government willing to comply with the British demands. A touch of the whip had once again done the trick —yet almost unnoticed, the terrorists achieved their object, though five of the actual assassins did not live to know it, thanks to brilliant detective work by the police. There were no more British Sirdars— even if the Inspector-General performed much the same function.

A sequel to Allenby's demands, before their final acceptance, taught the British Army a lesson which in later years was not remembered. Two battalions of Egyptian infantry refused to march out of their barracks in Khartoum, and at the same time Sudanese troops in another part of the town mutinied with them. The Sudanese were prevented from joining up with the Egyptians but they broke into the hospital, murdered the staff, and when attacked by the 2nd Leicesters killed an officer and an N.C.O. before they surrendered. A hard core of Egyptians, led by young officers, had meanwhile barricaded themselves in the officers' mess, where they were surrounded. The first assault by the 1st Argyll and Sutherland Highlanders was repulsed. A 4·5 in. gun was brought up and pounded the building at 100 yds. The Argylls attacked again and were again repulsed. The third time they were successful, and this incredible stand came to its inevitable end. Six of the Argylls were killed and seven wounded.

Some months later Allenby resigned in private protest against pointed interference with his staff by the Foreign Office, and he departed in June 1925, richly endowed with tribute from Egyptians, which evinced as much admiration for his firmness as for his sympathy. His place was taken by Lord Lloyd, a man with a strong sense of Imperial mission who saw himself as the Egyptian people's shield against the follies of their politicians and as protector of foreign interests, in defence of which he could claim wide powers under the reserved points of the Declaration. He moved in proconsular style and frequently the trumpet clarions rang out to announce the comings and goings of the High Commissioner.

The Egyptians responded to the firmer hand on the reins. Passions subsided and terrorism was dropped as an instrument of policy. Even Zaghloul, as President of the Chamber, showed unwonted restraint, as a result of which he was taunted as a British toady in newspapers controlled by the King, who had political toadies of his own. Zaghloul died in 1927 and was succeeded in the Wafd leadership by his former partner in exile, Mustapha Nahas, a lawyer who had been appointed judge at a young age and who had a most injudicial flair for demagogy. He too was of humble birth, but in fact he and his Wafd colleagues had as little sympathy for the common people as their abler rivals of the old Turkish school, who had no inhibitions about privately displaying their contempt for the feelings of the masses. A senior Wafd Minister aptly summed up the general feeling when asked by a British Embassy official in later years why the fellahin were perpetually oppressed. "They are very much happier that way—it is what they expect," was the revealing reply.

The British Foreign Office did not share Lloyd's scorn for the "broken idol", as he termed it, of Egyptian nationalism, and when the Labour Government returned to power in 1929 he was replaced by Sir Percy Lorraine. Nahas Pasha, appointed Prime Minister in 1930 for the second time, tried to reach agreement over the four disputed points, but he overplayed his hand and negotiations collapsed as predictably as resignations and rioting followed. There was then a period of political duelling between King and rival Ministers which first went in the King's favour and then swung against him.

In 1934 Lorraine was succeeded by Sir Miles Lampson, a man of the same commanding build as Cromer, Kitchener and Allenby. A fresh menace now gave cohesion to the Egyptians' ranks, the menace of encirclement by the Italian Fascist Empire, the devil worse than the one they knew so well, and in the autumn of 1935 they proposed fresh negotiations. They received rude rebuff. Sir Samuel Hoare, the British Foreign Secretary, having already nettled the Egyptians by criticizing the revision of their constitution which they had enacted, stated in a speech on December 5 that his Government were much too occupied with the international crisis to consider any question of a treaty with Egypt. The mobs were out in force. "Down with 'Oare! " was their cry.

Their wish was granted. Within a fortnight of his speech Hoare resigned because of the indignation over a compact he prepared with Pierre Laval, recognizing Italy's conquest of Abyssinia. In his place came Anthony Eden, Prince Charming of Baldwin's Government. Almost at once the Egyptians were publicly invited to London for negotiations.

King Fuad, autocratic and pro-Italian by tradition and instinct, caused some obstruction, but he was a sick man and died in April 1936, being succeeded by his 17-year-old son Farouk, who would have been due to go to the Royal Military Academy, Woolwich, the following term. Negotiations gathered speed and by August full agreement was reached. British troops, reduced to a fighting strength of ten thousand, would withdraw to the Suez Canal zone, together with the Royal Navy and Royal Air Force, where they would remain until the Egyptian Army was adjudged capable of defending it; a military mission would advise the Egyptian Army in place of the British officers serving with it; and most important of all, the British agreed to obtain international consent for the abolition of the Capitulations, a task they successfully achieved, thus for the first time in history giving Egyptians higher status in their own land than foreigners and flushing the polyglot parasites from the shelter of their consulates in pursuit of the prize of Egyptian nationality. The British also made concessions over the Sudan, though not enough to satisfy the Egyptians. It was to remain a condominium, "with the primary aim ... the welfare of the Sudanese", but Egyptian troops could be readmitted and the people immigrate without restraint. Thus there was redemption of Allenby's humbling, though in fact immigration to the land from which his precious Nile water flowed had no appeal to the Egyptian.

The treaty was signed with imposing ceremony in the Locarno room of the Foreign Office. Eden expressed his "keenest pleasure" and spoke of "the growing conviction in both countries that their interests are inseparably linked ... I have said this is the end of an epoch. I prefer to think of it as the beginning of a new stage." He also spoke glowingly of the achievements of Cromer. Wall-eyed Nahas Pasha, Egypt's Prime Minister, replied in French, with an accent for which he received patronizing compliments from *The Times*: "Today we offer to a world prey to disquieting convulsions the example of how much balance, reason, and hope can be secured by a sincere understanding achieved in a spirit of peace." He also spoke glowingly of the achievements of Zaghloul. The treaty was duly ratified, without division by the House of Commons, and by a massive vote in the Egyptian Parliament.

Nahas received a hero's welcome on his return, Eden had the unique distinction (for an Englishman) of being portrayed on an Egyptian postage stamp, and British troops in Egypt had the bizarre experience of being cheered. But as time wore on the Egyptian people became disillusioned with the achievements of Nahas and the intentions of the British. The occupation of the great cities still continued, for the simple reason that the Egyptians had agreed to build barracks and roads for the British by the Canal and it was not a requirement that they were able to fulfil with any speed. Unaware or unappreciative of such a commitment, the people felt they had been tricked and they chafed with frustration at the everlasting presence of the invading army, marching up and down in all the best barracks in Cairo. Admittedly an Egyptian policeman now took the place of the British sentry outside the imposing embassy building by the banks of the Nile, but somehow the Ambassador (as Lampson had become) did not seem to be conscious of the fact that he was no longer High Commissioner.

It was not that there was any arrogant strutting to inflame nationalist passions. The British were far too self-assured for that. They merely had the complacent air of owner occupants, officers, men, and most of all their wives, bred in them by years of obsequious submission by the clerical and shopkeeping classes who owed so much of their prosperity to them. All had the same easy air of permanence as the Nile itself. On an island in the river lay the British Eden of Gezira, with its smart residential district and its polo grounds, golf course, and playing fields owned by the famous military Sporting Club. Kitchener had started it, when Sirdar, merely as a polo ground for the Egyptian Army, but after he returned as Consul-General, to find the club expanded, he had its Egyptian members expelled for discussing politics on club premises. A few had since been readmitted and were regarded rather as pets, such as a certain scion of Eton and Balliol affectionately known as Is-it-was-it Bey. Without such qualifications there could be no scaling the Olympian heights on which British officer society dwelt.

Although most soldiers regarded the entire Egyptian race as a joke, the relationship between them was not such an unhappy one. For the highest and lowest layers of Egyptian society there was neither affection nor sympathy. The millionaire pashas luxuriating in their limousines, proud of the prestige displayed by an expansive paunch, were the objects of derision and sometimes the targets of boorish pranks, while the foetid, croaking beggars were too pervasive, persistent and light-fingered to evoke pity from anyone who had been in Egypt longer than a week. Yet in between these two extremes there were many people with endearing qualities, most of whom could enjoy a joke as much as the British, ranging from the tramcar driver to the swarming optimists gleefully clinging to his vehicle's tail, from the vendor in the market-place to the excitable but friendly peasant who produced his wares. The troops, in the cafés and bazaars they frequented, had closer contact with these people than their officers, and their aptitude for making friends did not desert them.

That this friendly relationship was mutual was nicely illustrated when feeling was running high in the autumn of 1935. A sergeant and three guardsmen of the 3rd Grenadiers, returning to Kasr-el-Nil Barracks from guard duty on the G.O.C.'s house on Gezira Island, found the bridge blocked by a full-scale riot. Stones were being hurled with great vigour, gas-standards dismantled and the gas ignited, and a dense mob was yelling, "Down with Hoare—Egypt for the Egyptians!" With arms sloped and bayonets fixed, the guard marched calmly on, to the soothing chant of the sergeant's "Left-right-left". Soon they were completely swallowed up, but instead of hurling things at them the Egyptians gave them room and the guardsmen retained their parade-ground precision without receiving a touch. Screams and jeers turned to cheers, and when the guard at last emerged triumphant into the sanctuary of their barracks the rioters paused to give them a round of hand-clapping before carrying on with their task of hurling missiles and abuse.

The Irish Guards, who followed the Grenadiers into Kasr-el-Nil in 1936, enjoyed a better climate and perhaps a greater capacity for appreciating the happy-go-lucky nature of so many of Cairo's million inhabitants. The bars seethed with "Micks", swapping jokes with all and sundry, and Kasr-el-Nil itself was in uproar of delight when some quaint, antiquated musicians, come to town for King Farouk's wedding celebrations, formed semicircle in front of the barracks and gave their rendering of *It's a Long Way to Tipperary*. Towards the Egyptian Army, however, the Irish entertained very different feelings. As one of them has written, "The ordinary people were our friends, we got on very well with them, but the Wog Army got our goat." It was the appalling pretentiousness of these puppet soldiers that so riled the guardsmen. A private war was waged, and any Egyptian soldier parading the streets with shirt hanging outside his trousers was liable to receive forceful correction.

At officer level, relations were friendly as far as co-operation on military matters went, but the British had acquired little respect for their Egyptian colleagues, and their favourite joke was that promotion in the Egyptian Army was decided solely on the size of the tummy. Nor did the Egyptian officers enjoy any great status in Egyptian society. Indeed, an army career had no appeal to the ordinary town-loving, luxury-loving Egyptian, and a commission was regarded more as a means of ascent up the lower rungs of the social ladder than as anything very estimable in itself. The ascent was accompanied by indignities. A retired officer of an infantry regiment has recalled with amazement (because it seemed quite normal behaviour) how he sat with his feet up in a railway carriage, displaying a subaltern's stars on his drill tunic, and not feeling in the mood for company, waved languidly at two fat Egyptian captains who entered, flicking his fingers at them with a "go-away" look on his face. Being accustomed to doing as they were bidden, the Egyptians went without protest.

Not all Egyptian officers were made of such flabby stuff, either in pride or body. In 1938 a newly commissioned infantry officer, tall and upright, joined a regiment at Mankabad, near Assiut. This man, Gamal Abdel Nasser, son of a postal clerk, had been fired from early boyhood with the ambition to erase the humiliation of his country, and here on this Nile garrison he found others dedicated to the same resolve. It was not only at the British occupation that they riled. They were just as keen to wipe out the influence of the Mohammed Aly dynasty and the squabbling, cynical, lever-pulling politicians. "We must fight imperialism, monarchy, and feudalism," the latter-day Arabi earnestly beseeched his apostles, "because we are opposed to injustice, oppression and slavery."

They formed their own revolutionary society, christened it the Free Society of Officers, and pledged themselves to work secretly and assiduously for the cause until the time was ripe to strike.

The approach of war made the revolutionaries' pulse quicken, but they had no chance to intervene. The Egyptian Government accepted without hesitation the obligation of co-operation to which they had bound themselves under the 1936 Treaty. Though they did not declare war themselves, they broke off diplomatic relations with Germany, locked up German nationals and declared martial law. The response was less enthusiastic when Italy hovered like a vulture eager to fall on the carcase which in June 1940 the British Empire appeared to be. King Farouk had Italian friends and a number of Italian hangers-on, and in the four years of his reign he made himself more popular with the people than any of his predecessors, having the advantage over them of being able to speak Arabic (and English too). In Aly Maher he had a Prime Minister who was willing enough to defy the British. But neither of them had reckoned with the dominant personality of Sir Miles Lampson. With all the authority of a Cromer, the British Ambassador (whose wife was half Italian) ordered the King to appoint a more amenable Prime Minister, and the King did as he was ordered. Except for the royal barber and one or two other household attendants, the Italian nationals were interned, and a number of fifth columnists, quickly losing their nerve, were rounded up.

One of the first military steps ordered by the British War Cabinet was the summary relief and removal of the three Egyptian battalions entrenched at Mersa Matruh as part of a carefully prepared plan of defence. Certain of their more fiery officers smarted under this scathing blow to their pride, but no fuss was made of the matter, outside the crypto-revolutionary clique. This was partly due to the tact of the Commander-in-Chief, Lieutenant-General Sir Archibald Wavell, who was as admirer and biographer of Allenby had sympathy with the Egyptian people and was fully aware of the urgent need to secure their co-operation. As the Italians drove into Egypt towards Mersa Matruh, Wavell promised Hassan Sabry the Prime Minister, that he would give him earliest news of their ejection. An angry telegram arrived from Wavell when Winston Churchill, anticipating a great victory, announced the recapture of Sidi Barrani before it was complete. Sabry was the first to receive the exciting news when it became accomplished fact. Wavell's troops sped on, far beyond Egypt's frontier.

The Egyptian people displayed as much emotion over the advance and repulse of the Italians as they had done in the case of the Turks. They were spectators, on the whole more anti-Fascist than anti-British, but reluctant to compromise themselves and eager to get the thing finished. Unfortunately there could be no quick release; their country was too valuable a prize to be lightly conceded by either side. Hitler had ordered, "The Suez Canal must be taken". His troops swept through Greece, and Rommel struck in the desert, meeting light, stunned resistance. A mighty pincer movement closed on Egypt, preceded by a propaganda and subversion offensive which had sparked off rebellion in Iraq. Wavell's resources were stretched to breaking point to meet the new threats from west to east.

To counter Nazi propaganda in the Arab countries, Anthony Eden, newly reinstated as Foreign Secretary, made a statement which in due course was to serve as the very complement needed to make the Balfour Declaration's propensity for conflict complete. It was made for much the same reason, pressure of external events, and it too seemed harmless enough at the time. Speaking at the Guild Hall on May 29, 1941, with the authority not only of his office but as a scholar in Oriental languages with expert knowledge of the Middle East, he said, "It seems to me both natural and right that the cultural and economic ties between the Arab countries, and the political ties too, should be strengthened. His Majesty's Government for their part will give their full support to any scheme that commands general approval." Though they were slow to germinate, the seeds of the Arab League had been sown.

Brisk military action in Syria and Iraq freed Egypt's eastern flank from immediate menace, and in the west Rommel's men were halted near the frontier. But the war had been brought much closer to Egypt and the bombs came down on the Suez Canal ports and on Alexandria—where 650 people were killed in the summer of 1941—while Cairo groped in an uneasy blackout. Mines presented as great a menace as bombs to shipping in the canal and to detect their fall at night netting was elaborately spread over the waterway and rolled back at daylight to let the ships pass. The Egyptian Army made a contribution here, in the menial role of observers, and they also rendered valuable service as anti-aircraft gunners, a role for which the best of their recruits (perhaps on British instigation) were picked. Thousands of civilians also played their part, finding good wages waiting for them in depots, workshops and hospitals. Meanwhile, lack of imported fertilizers and a reluctance to introduce rationing or to diminish the money-spinning cotton crop caused a food shortage which of course was blamed, without justification, on the demands of the occupying armies. Crisis was averted by timely co-operation between the British and Egyptian supply authorities.

As the tide of battle flowed and ebbed, it was observed in Cairo that the bronzed soldiers from the desert lost their relaxed self-assurance and became increasingly boisterous, urgent in their determination to make the most of a few precious days' leave. For the officers, scarves, pink shirts, cord trousers and suède boots marked them as fighting men in proud contrast to the immaculate khaki drill and fly whisks sported by members of Groppi's Horse, as the denizens of the two great headquarters, G.H.Q. and B.T.E., were facetiously termed from the eat-and-drink houses they frequented. The Edwardian interior of Shepheard's with its brass and mahogany bar, was the favourite haunt of the desert men, and any Egyptian officer daring to venture inside it, or for that matter into any of Cairo's smarter bars, was made to feel like a mouse in a lion's den.

Germany's sweeping advance through Russia and the recoil of Auchinleck's offensive set off sparks of defiance in Cairo, and the students came out chanting, "We are Rommel's soldiers". King Farouk caught their mood, it seems, and needing a new Prime Minister, he turned, on February 3, 1942, to his old collaborator, Aly Maher. Lampson told him to appoint Nahas, who had never wavered in opposing the Axis Powers, on the grounds that he commanded the widest backing. Farouk refused. Lampson thereupon took advantage of means not normally available to an Ambassador.

Next day an ultimatum was delivered and ignored. After dark, soldiers of a British infantry battalion took up position around the palings surrounding Abdin Palace. Two armoured cars then drew up on either side of the palace gate. They were there, on Lampson's insistence, to cow the palace guard, whose barrack was inside the grounds, and if necessary to escort Farouk to Suez, where a cruiser was waiting to take him out to sea. Lampson followed in his car, accompanied by Lieutenant-General R. G. W. H. Stone, newly appointed to the command of British Troops Egypt, and their two A.D.C.s. Behind them came a lorry, carrying a platoon from an officer cadet training battalion. Warning of their coming had been given and all were admitted without fuss. Leaving their soldiers to wait in the courtyard, Lampson and Stone were duly received by Farouk, who had with him his Chamberlain, Hassanein Pasha. Lampson presented an instrument of abdication and the King seemed willing enough to sign, complaining only of its scruffy appearance. Hassanein then whispered to him in Arabic, and the King naïvely enquired if he might have a second chance if he relented and made Nahas Prime Minister. Lampson agreed at once and the interview came to a harmonious end.

The event caused no greater stir in Cairo than any other ministerial change, until rumour enlarged the drama of the occasion and the size of the force employed. Nor did it have apparent effect on Farouk, who seemed relaxed and amiable when admitted to a British military hospital following a car accident some months later. But he had suffered deep humiliation and there can be little doubt it increased his cynicism and hastened his descent towards obesity and to preoccupation with the intricacies of lust.

Thus the Wafdist Nahas, who could hardly speak a word of English, became the hero of the British and the enemy of nationalist Egypt. He did not waver when Rommel flung back the Eighth Army and swept into Egypt, sending the smoke of burning documents billowing from the incinerators at the British Embassy and G.H.Q. buildings. Egypt remained calm, and when the peril was at its greatest, British troops even received waves of encouragement from the people as they journeyed to the front.

It was at this moment that the Revolutionary Committee of the Free Society of Officers, having made contact with the Germans, decided to strike. Their somewhat hazy plan was forcibly to overthrow Nahas's Government, install Aly Maher as Prime Minister, and get the flags ready to welcome Rommel as he rode his legendary white horse into Cairo. The signal was to be given by two of Rommel's agents who had established themselves, complete with massive aerial, in the voluptuous houseboat of an Egyptian dancer. Unfortunately the lure of flesh proved stronger than the lure of glory and, to the shame of the Aryan race, the agents were caught in the houseboat with the aid of two seductive Jewesses. Widespread arrests were made on their information, but they did not embrace Captain Nasser. It was perhaps as well for his lieutenants that they had not had the time to draw their revolvers, for only prison sentences were imposed.

Meanwhile, guns, tanks, and thousands of reinforcements readily distinguishable by their pale knees and regulation, unsophisticated apparel, swarmed into Egypt to join the Eighth Army under its new commander, Lieutenant-General B. L. Montgomery. Eschewing the harum-scarum tactics that had become the vogue in desert warfare, they ponderously and methodically engaged the enemy in battle, crushed him and carefully chivvied his remnant out of Egypt, out of Libya, out of Tripoli. Egypt became one of the war's backwaters, but it was a very busy one. Alexandria remained a bustling, all-important base for ships and aeroplanes;' Cairo contained not only the headquarters of the Middle East Command, but the massive Middle East Supply Centre, which catered for the needs of every country affected by war shortages, from Turkey to Abyssinia, and also in Cairo was the hotpotch flotsam from the German-occupied countries of South-east Europe, including three unthroned kings; and the Delta as a whole was the depository for wounded men and broken vehicles, for reinforcements destined either east or west, and for divisions in need of a rest from the battle zone.

There was little trace of friendship now between the Egyptian people and the British soldier, whose outlook was in any case bound to be different from his peacetime predecessor's. Ever since the war began he had despised the Egyptians for leaving the defence of their country to the British—it never occurred to him that they had not asked the British to intervene, nor was it ever explained to him that it was to Britain's advantage that Egypt should not declare war—and scorn turned to rage at the extortions of the vendors, tricksters and thieves who preyed upon the troops like insatiable hyenas. As in the first war, the Australians had organized a systematic beat-up of part of Cairo. The Irish Brigade, on rest from Italy, did the same. More restrained Englishmen contented themselves with booting the occasional bottom, expressing the oft-repeated wish that they had let the Nazis into Cairo, just to teach the wogs a lesson, and loudly and boisterously singing their own doubtful version of the Egyptian national anthem.

As the war drifted far into the distance, Nahas turned his mind to fresh distinction and sought to implement the plan, for which Eden had promised his Government's full support, of bringing the Arab states into closer unity. Egyptians did not regard themselves as Arabs, however strong the Arab influence left by medieval conquest, and ever since the abrupt curtailment of Mohammed Aly's empire Egyptian ambition in that direction had been dormant. But the war had stirred it afresh. Not only had Eden spoken, but the

British had themselves used Cairo as their centre of control, political, military and logistic, for all the countries of the Middle East, even establishing a Minister of State to supervise the affairs of neighbouring countries. Nahas was not the man to let slip a chance to extend his influence. Cairo must remain the capital to which the Arab states turn, and Nuri-as-Said of Iraq, who had long been working on plans for a much narrower form of union, under the title "Fertile Crescent", could not decline the wider proposal. Under the auspices of these two protégés of Britain, a conference was convened to be held in Alexandria in October 1944.

The representatives of five Arab states assembled, outwardly optimistic but inwardly suspicious of British intentions. When they got down to talking they found there was only one thing on which they could agree: the need to keep Palestine an Arab state. And the more they disagreed on other matters, the stronger did they pledge themselves to save Palestine from the Jewish menace. There was little prospect that they would have to fulfil their pledge with anything stronger than their voices, since Britain was under obligation to remain in Palestine until stability was restored, and it seemed a safe and convenient means of presenting a semblance of unity. The Covenant of the Arab League was duly signed and its headquarters established in Cairo. No one could have imagined then that Britain's baby would cause such torment to its mother.

Ten minutes after signing this convention, which owed so much to his leadership, Nahas was dismissed. He and his party had been much reviled for their allegiance to the British and at last Farouk felt strong enough to be rid of him, choosing a moment when Lord Killearn (as Lampson had become) was out of the country. Podgy Ahmed Maher, an ex-Wafdist, succeeded him.

In February 1945 Egypt declared war against Germany and Japan. The object was to gain entry as a founder-member of the United Nations, a prize promised at the Yalta Conference to any nation that came into the war before March 1. It was a chance of getting something for nothing to delight the Egyptian heart, and in any case Egypt had already made a very considerable contribution to the Allied cause. Yet the victory was not gained without loss. Ahmed Maher was shot dead as he left the Chamber of Deputies after announcing the declaration. The frustration and impositions from an extraneous war had once again generated their great store of latent violence, and this was its first release on the toadies who heeded to the wishes of the West.

CHAPTER ELEVEN

Withdrawal

(1945–7)

VARIOUS AGENCIES PROVIDED fresh fuel to inflame the volatile passions of the Egyptian people. The Moslem Brotherhood had been originated, in the early thirties, as purely a religious body. It began as one of those recurring movements for the purification of the faith of Islam and, like its forerunner in the 1880s, it gradually broadened into a nationalistic movement, dedicated to the removal of all foreign influence. Its strength grew as the inevitable stain of involvement in government weakened support for the Wafd. The Supreme Guide, Sheikh Hassan El Banna, wisely refrained from putting forward his own political candidates. There were surer, more dramatic means of arousing the crusading zeal of people who, like children watching television, had had their appetite for violent heroics whetted by the spectacle of a world fighting a war in which they had played no combatant part.

Those with a taste for violence were enlisted into secret terrorist gangs, while the devout Brethren publicly propagated their faith in the coming triumph of Islam over the infidel. There was no close alliance between the religious and military revolutionary leaders, as in Arabi's day. Vague proposals for a union were made by the Supreme Guide but the Free Officers' Society rejected them, on Nasser's advice, through fear of being swallowed up. Officers could join the Brotherhood if they wished. Their enthusiasm waned when they found they were required to undergo recruit's training in the handling of fire-arms. In any case, Nasser was not keen on assassination, partly, it seems, because of a certain tenderness of heart, partly through fear of reprisal, and partly from experience of the amateurism of the would-be assassins in his ranks.

Association with violence was not the only unsettling influence of war. The needs of the belligerents had brought employment for thousands, unbelievably good wages, moves of home, and finally, with the rundown of the war effort, unemployment and the erection of shanty towns. Their ambitions had been widened not only by contact with the ubiquitous British soldier but by the strange sight of the familiar Greek suddenly turned hero as he fought in the desert for the liberation of his country, and their sense of national importance was nourished by the stream of Arab officials and hangers-on come to Cairo to pay court first at the Middle East Supply Centre and then at the Arab League headquarters. British propaganda had made much of the Beveridge report, extolling the principle of social security as much for the Egyptian as for the Englishman. It was a weapon that could backfire, for the mood of questioning it provoked soon turned to criticism of the ruling class and of the British régime which in the minds of most Egyptians it represented. What right, it was asked, had Britain to interfere in the affairs of the Middle East at all, involving it in war by pursuit of her own interest? Egypt was astir. The middle class was emergent, and primeval customs and attitudes were being discarded. Instead of the yashmak and black, women sallied forth in gaily coloured frocks, and their menfolk were just as eager to adopt the habits, tastes and ideas of the West.

Never was it more important that Britain should make some swift gesture of goodwill towards Egypt, showing sincere recognition of her aspirations as a truly independent state. But victory had brought its crop of baffling new problems, and minds already overtaxed by the task of winning the final battle had no inclination to give new study to a question which had been settled, with apparent amity, in 1936. Egyptian agitation had the status of a hardy annual, a thing to be tolerated with good-humoured resignation and a symbolic pat on the back. As Elizabeth Monroe put it, "No other country affords such clear proof that force of habit kills political sensitivity and imagination."

What mattered most from the British viewpoint was not that the Empire had survived two years' severance of the supply route through Suez and the Mediterranean but that it was in Egypt that Hitler had been halted and defeated, and indeed Churchill had given such priority to its defence that he had sent it troops and tanks which could ill be spared from the defence of Britain. It seemed unthinkable to the military mind that Britain should ever yield such a vital link in the imperial defence scheme, and even withdrawal from the cities, in implementation of the Treaty, seemed a remote speck on the horizon of time. After all, the Egyptians had accepted responsibility for building the barracks and roads by the Canal, and until they had done so the British were under no obligation to bestir themselves. G.H.Q. Middle East was in any case far too occupied with problems of redeployment to risk the disruption involved in a move from its own intricately entrenched establishment at the Grey Towers, and the same applied to Headquarters British Troops Egypt at the Samirimas Hotel. India was already being run down as a base, and from there to Greece and Tripoli units in process of disbandment or transit turned to Egypt as a sorting-house for their personnel and a dumping-ground for their stores and vehicles. Further bolstering the need to remain in Cairo, and typifying the Army's sense of its own permanence, were all the flats that had been hired as married quarters. These made an important contribution to contentment at a difficult period and the Army was in no mood lightly to surrender them.

Nationalist pressure was directed, not so much at the British themselves as after the Great War, but at the politicians and notables, the "traitors" who by apparently condoning the British presence stamped themselves as their lackeys. The murder of Ahmed Maher was the first expression of the new fervour, and the fact that El Banna, the Supreme Guide, was released after arrest for lack of evidence emphasized the power of intimidation wielded by the Brotherhood. The result was that the politicians vied with each other in demanding the complete evacuation of the British. Nahas, attempting a come-back, presented himself before Lord Killearn with great flourish and demanded unconditional evacuation both from Egypt and the Sudan. He received the refusal he obviously expected.

Hope rose in Egypt when the British Labour Party came to power in late July 1945. It soon turned to intensified frustration. Ernest Bevin, the new Foreign Secretary, proclaimed his Government's wish "to leave behind for ever the idea of one country dominating another", but he showed himself as adept at throwing cold water as any of his predecessors when fresh demands were made. Nokrashy Pasha, Prime Minister of Egypt, sent a note to the British Government on December 20, earnestly requesting revision of the 1936 Treaty on the grounds that "the presence of foreign troops on our soil, even if stationed in distant area, is wounding to the national dignity". Bevin kept him waiting five weeks and then sent a reply which dwelt on the mutual benefits derived from the Treaty and offered no more than "preliminary conversations" to examine possible means of revision in due course.

The Egyptians were well accustomed to this form of response. With yells of "Down with England! Down with Bevin!" the mobs broke loose in the cities, looting, burning and destroying all things British they could grasp. A number were killed in the task of pacification, and there was further bloodshed when a commemoration day was staged for the "martyrs" in Alexandria on March 4, 1946. Two British soldiers were stoned to death that day, defending a post at Ramleh. Nokrashy had meanwhile resigned, rather than incur further odium by accepting such an unenthusiastic offer of negotiation.

He was succeeded by the old hand Sidky Pasha, a Turk by origin, not easily intimidated by the mob. His task of easing tension was aided by a change at the British Embassy: Lord Killearn was appointed in February as Special Commissioner in South-east Asia and Sir Ronald Campbell came to Cairo in his place. Killearn's organizing ability had prevented much suffering throughout the Middle East during the years of wartime shortages, but the Egyptians saw him only as the symbol of Imperialism, and whenever his commanding figure was seen in Cairo it served as a reminder of the humiliation the King and Government had suffered at his hands. Campbell came with hands outstretched, determined to make friends with every Egyptian he met.

Although his former party, the Wafd, put a boycott on participation, Sidky reopened negotiations with London, and he received such response that by May a delegation under Lord Stansgate (Wedgwood Benn) was on its way to Cairo, and the Prime Minister, Clement Attlee, who did not share the soldiers' belief in the all-importance of Egypt as a base, was rousing the Opposition to fierce protest in the House of Commons by announcing that the Government accepted the principle of complete evacuation of British troops. "Things are built up with great labour and cast away with great shame and folly," rebuked Winston Churchill when interrupted by a Communist Member as he commented on the "very grave statement" the Prime Minister had made. The only comfort he could find was from Attlee's assurance that unless safeguards for the defence of the Suez Canal could be effectively negotiated the terms of the 1936 Treaty would still stand.

Terse orders, emanating from Bevin himself, had meanwhile been received by G.H.Q. that immediate arrangements to move must be made and that they would have to provide new quarters themselves. Troops, headquarters, depots, factories, workshops, cold-storage installations, hospitals, family hostels—all had to be uprooted and transplanted into the desert by the Canal and finally to Palestine, which, as then envisaged, was to be the new centre for the Middle East Command. The staff officers heaved a sigh both of nostalgia and of awe at the task in hand.

News that the British were really leaving the capital was brought by Field-Marshal Lord Montgomery when he visited Sidky in June. The withdrawal began on July 4. The Citadel, first of Cairo's fortresses to be entered by the British, and symbol of Egyptian pride, was handed over, and on August 9, anniversary of Mohammed Aly's death, King Farouk himself ceremoniously hoisted the Egyptian flag. By now, General Sir Miles Dempsey, the Commander-in-Chief, had announced that his headquarters would be out by the end of the year. Tradesmen and shopkeepers apart, most of them Greek, Maltese or Levantine, the Cairenes revelled in contemplation of the hardships the British soldiers would endure.

The negotiations jerked, fizzled, broke down and were reopened, to the accompaniment of much rough play by agitators which Sidky took firm measures to keep in bounds, even having the courage to make widespread arrests among the Moslem Brotherhood hierarchy. The climax came with Sidky's visit to London in October. He returned with a draft treaty which was said in Cairo to give Egypt full possession of the Sudan. This was immediately denied in London; "the development of self-government" was the policy prescribed in the draft and Attlee announced that no change was at present contemplated and "no impairment of the right of the Sudanese ultimately to decide their own future". British administrators in the Sudan were, with good reason, proud of their work and were as determined to preserve the integrity of their child as the Egyptians were to procure her, and of course in the view of the latter the British were motivated purely by imperialistic designs. Full possession of the Sudan was an essential complement to the evacuation of the British troops, and Sidky could never obtain ratification of a treaty which did not provide for both. He resigned to evade the rage which inevitably flared from the breakdown of negotiations.

Military planning was now in confusion. Despite the prevailing chaos in Palestine, so vividly expressed by the blowing-up of the requisitioned headquarters building, the King David Hotel, in July 1946, the War Office had persevered with its plan to move the Middle East headquarters there, combined with the opening of a supplementary base at the McKinnon Road, Kenya. Now the situation was altered, and in the meantime G.H.Q. had moved into makeshift accommodation at Fayid, on the banks of the Great Bitter Lake. Headquarters British Troops Egypt was rather better placed, having occupied existing barrack accommodation at Moascar, a suburb of Ismailia.

The construction of the camp at Fayid was a considerable feat of resource. Regarded as permanent at its inception, temporary after the policy statement on complete evacuation, and then again as permanent, the work had been entrusted largely to prisoners of war who were paid for their labour. Germans and Austrians did most of the building work with great will and efficiency, while Italians helped with the mechanical work, which included the installation of massive turbo-generators, originally destined for Russia, and a water and chlorination plant. Even so, it was a bleak and barren life after the joys of Cairo. On the arrival of G.H.Q. the Commander-in-Chief was the only man who could sleep with stone walls around him and enjoy the luxury of pulling a lavatory chain. Everyone else had a tent to sleep in, a hut to work in, and rock and sand all round him, alleviated only by the balm of the lake. Communal, Butlin-style centres were constructed for the families, serviced under protest by N.A.A.F.I. Those wives who could, found relief from boredom by taking typing jobs on G.H.Q.

One by one the old fortresses fell. Fort Ras-el-Tin, the first to be captured, was handed over to the Egyptian Navy on January 8, 1947, and the last of the barracks in Alexandria to the Egyptian Army on February 9. It fell to the Life Guards to perform the last rites in Cairo. A farewell cocktail-party was held, with many Egyptian guests, and among the English a lady who had, as a girl, welcomed Wolseley's troops into the city. No invitations were issued for the final departure a few days later. The last armoured cars slipped out of Kasr-el-Nil barracks at 5 a.m. on March 28, yet a large crowd had gathered to gaze calmly at them through the pre-dawn gloom. As daylight came, Egyptian soldiers were to be seen at every window of the barracks, tirelessly waving their flags to celebrate the re-occupation of this, the most conspicuous symbol of the British raj, once the scene of Arabi's first great triumph, always a magnet for bugs, and soon to be pulled down to make way for a skyscraper hotel.

British troops were, of course, free to return for a few days' leave, dressed in civilian clothes, but the first officers to try were subjected to aggravating scrutiny at check-points—the police, once browbeaten with ease, seemed to have become so officious since Russell Pasha, the imperturbable Englishman who rode the grey, had been relieved from command in Cairo. When they did reach the city the place did not seem the same, the old strongholds overrun.

Nearly eleven years had elapsed since the British had solemnly undertaken to withdraw from the two cities, and though there were compelling reasons for "the military capacity for delay", as Lord Attlee termed it, they had done themselves much harm in Egyptian eyes by their apparent disinclination to honour their word. If Allenby had had his way, the move would have been made at least twenty years earlier, and it may be that the Egyptians would have grown accustomed to the contained British presence and not regarded it as such a stain on their pride. Lloyd maintained, however, as he declared in a speech to the Lords after his resignation, that "the only place from which the Suez Canal can be economically and adequately defended is from Cairo". For him it was complete domination or nothing, and the logic of his contention was to become increasingly apparent.

In July, Egypt took advantage of the status she had acquired by her last-minute entry into the war to arraign Britain before the Security Council of the United Nations. It was a brash gesture, presumably made more to impress opinion at home and the world at large than with any hope of redress, and it certainly came as a shock to the die-hards in Britain to know that it was within the power of Egypt to take such an insolent step. Nokrashy, who had stepped in again as Prime Minister when Sidky stepped out, presented his case in person and spat forth the venom in a manner to win praise from the most ardent nationalist at home. He could at least claim that Britain had no right to station troops in any country against the will of its people or to interfere, as in the Sudan, in the administration of a country which had never legally been hers. But he lost sympathy by overstating his case, by making accusations which were palpably false, and by embroiling the two separate issues into one. Britain merely had to claim her rights under the two treaties, that of 1936 and of 1899, and as the sanctity of treaties was one of the things the United Nations sought to preserve, even Russia was obliged to take her side.

Meanwhile Britain had herself referred a Middle East problem to the United Nations, the anguished one of Palestine. She did so in desperation, and her desperation was to have calamitous consequences on her standing in the whole of the Middle East.

CHAPTER TWELVE

Defeat

(1947–50)

THE BRITISH GOVERNMENT had for long been groping in the murky impasse into which they had been led by their vague, incompatible promises made to Jew and Arab under the Balfour Declaration of 1917. As Jewish immigration into Palestine gained stimulus from Nazi persecutions, realization of its ultimate effect drove the proud, intransigent Arabs to rebellion. It cost them the expulsion of their leader, the Mufti of Jerusalem, and the arousing of a new spirit of belligerence among the Jews. The war brought further strength for the Jews, in the form of fresh immigrants, battle experience, illicitly acquired equipment, and further sympathizers. It was their turn now to rebel against the infuriating restraint on their ambitions imposed by the allegedly impartial hand of the mandate power, Great Britain. They demanded Palestine as their national state, not just a shared home, and backed their demand with gelignite, knife, rope and bullet. Great was the destruction, suffering and vexation they wrought.

Coming to the Foreign Office with all the confidence born of victories won in labour disputes, Ernest Bevin declared in the Commons that he would stake his political future on solving the Palestine question. He was soon made to look foolish. An Anglo-American committee went to Palestine and, having made the profound observation that it was essential to establish friendly relations between Jew and Arab, proposed measures which could only exacerbate the hostility between them. Representatives of the Jews and of all the Arab countries came to London but could not be persuaded to enter the same room. Their demands were irreconcilable: the Jews were prepared to accept partition, the Arabs nothing short of complete annexation. In despair, the British Government referred the matter to the United Nations, and in September 1947, before any decision had been reached, they startled the world by announcing their final act of abrogation. Come what may, they were surrendering their mandate and would leave Palestine the following May.

It is easy to sneer at Attlee's Government for taking the coward's way out, but they were impaled on a goring dilemma. The Jews had the support of the United States and of Russia, and both countries found strange unison in their maddening, unsympathetic censure of Britain's imperialistic oppression of an emergent race. It was no time for conflict with the United States, with Russia making menacing gestures in Europe. Yet any solution giving a stake in Palestine to the Jews would require enforcement by British arms and would arouse the fierce enmity of Egypt and her Arab allies at a time when their friendship was dearly needed. The only alternative was to stay on indefinitely in Palestine, incurring ever-increasing odium, tribulation and expense. The British people, revolted by macabre atrocities on soldiers, police and administrators by Jewish murder gangs—127 had been killed and 331 wounded since the war—were in no mood for heroics in support either of Jew or Arab and were glad to be rid of a thankless task. The Exchequer called for disengagement just as loudly. Britain's economy was at its lowest ebb.

Thus Attlee decided to abandon Palestine while the blood was still flowing in its torrents from his abandonment of India. But there was one big difference between the two decisions, making the one courageous, the other weak. In India he was able to impose agreement on the division of territory between the two claimants; in Palestine he recognized neither claims nor claimants. He wanted, above all else, to antagonize no one, and he succeeded in antagonizing everyone. "If the British hope was to ... encourage the Arabs to push the Jews into the sea so that the imperial position could be recovered, this was exactly the course of action best designed", was the Jewish view, as propounded by Dov Joseph, a member of Ben Gurion's Provisional Government. The aim, according to Nasser's lieutenant, Colonel Anwar El Sadat, was "to weaken the Arab world". "England had provoked war," he wrote. "She was, of course, only too willing to set the Arabs on the Jews, believing that this would be to her advantage." There could be no escaping the mantle of Machiavellian imperialism which the anti-imperialist Socialists had inherited with the cares of office.

Just as Eden's statement in 1941 served as complement to the Balfour Declaration, so Attlee's surrender of responsibility set alight the kindling wood unwittingly laid by Eden. After all the indignities of military occupation, leadership in the Arab League tasted like champagne to Egypt. Her voice had to be loudest in demanding freedom for her new-found brothers in Palestine, her crusader's zeal the brightest and most virtuous. Both King and politicians passionately proclaimed their ardour for the cause, seeing it perhaps as a convenient outlet for the militant patriotism of the people, which might otherwise explode against them. Now, with Britain's sudden announcement of the surrender of her mandate, words had to be turned into deeds. It was as though Britain, having encouraged Egypt to dress up in the armour of champion, had without warning shoved her into the tournament ring.

It remained to be seen how the United Nations would react. After much deliberation, lobbying and postponement, the General Assembly cast its vote on November 29. By a majority of 33 to 13, with 10 abstentions, a plan for partition was accepted which gave the Jews more than half the country, though they comprised only a third of the population. It was a slap in the face for the Arab countries that was nonetheless tantamount to an open invitation to aggression, since none of the member countries dared take steps to enforce their recommendation, other than through the agency of an unarmed commission. Britain, playing the role of Pilate, publicly washed her hands. She refrained from taking part either in the debate or in the voting.

There could be no direct intervention by the Arab countries until the date stipulated for the ending of the mandate, May 15, 1948. In the meantime, Abdul Rahman Azzam, the Egyptian Secretary-General of the Arab League, organized the raising of an irregular force, predictably named the Arab Liberation Army, and toured the capitals to instigate some form of concerted action when the great day arrived. Five thousand freedom fighters, including shock phalanges of the Moslem Brotherhood, filtered across the borders of Palestine, unimpeded by the British, whose policy now was merely to protect themselves and keep open their lines of communication with Haifa, their evacuation port. They would not even allow the United Nations commissioners to enter until the eleventh hour, for fear that their troops might have to go into action to rescue them from the fury of warring factions.

The Arab Liberation Army displayed dash and courage but made little headway. The vigour with which the Jews struck back bewildered the Arabs and surprised the world at large—but not Major-General H. C. Stockwell, commanding the 6th Airborne Division at Haifa, where he acquired as much respect for their fighting prowess as disgust at their brutality. Early in April the British withdrew to a compound around the port of Haifa and let the two sides fight it out. The Jews won a fierce battle and the Arab inhabitants of the nearby villages thereupon made mass, pathetic exodus, trusting their leaders' promises that they would soon be able to return. This was exactly what the Jews wanted, and further to precipitate the trend Jewish irregular gangs were allowed licence to strike terror into a village gained during the course of hard fighting to open the road to Jerusalem. The Arab League had a new and worthy cause to fight for, the restoration of the refugees.

The British High Commissioner and his troops left Jerusalem on May 14, leaving it to the combined consuls to maintain a fragile truce. Next day the mandate was declared at an end, though a British rearguard temporarily stayed on in the Haifa compound. The United States and Russia hastened to recognize the new state of Israel, and the regular troops of the Arab countries crossed the frontiers to the accompaniment of exuberant clarion calls from their radios and press.

Hidden beneath the boasts and prophecies that blared from Cairo were doubts sown by the brief revelation of Jewish strength. They had already found veiled expression in a mission to Amman, capital of the newly independent state of Trans-Jordan, made by Azzam and the Arab League secretariat only two days before the invasion began. General Glubb Pasha, British commander of the fine but diminutive Arab Legion, was to his great amazement asked if he would act as commander-in-chief of all the Arab League invading troops. He declined, and eventually his King, the staunch Abdulla, was assigned the post, though he was denied information about the troops under his nominal command. Azzam's motive dawned on Glubb when the war ended amid bitter recriminations between the allies. Egypt had foreseen that there might be need of a scapegoat.

The offer indicates how slapdash the arrangements for the campaign were. Trans-Jordan was the only country with clear purpose.

Her army of some 4,500 British-led men came at the request of the Palestinian Arabs in order to occupy that portion of Palestine assigned to the Arabs under the United Nations' agreement. The others attacked as much to prevent Trans-Jordan gaining all the glory as with any other object in view, and of course early estimates of the Jewish strength, backed by inherent Arab optimism, made it seem likely that glory would be easily obtainable. To make sure that Trans-Jordan did not get too large a share, the Egyptians confiscated a consignment of much-needed ammunition despatched by ship from G.H.Q., Fayid, on Glubb's request.

Egypt launched a force of two brigade groups, with tank and artillery support—perhaps ten thousand men—across the frontier near the coastline. With them was a token force provided by Saudi Arabia. The Arab Legion, advancing on a convergent axis, were some 80 miles to their right, and right of them, spread over a frontage of 90 miles, the Iraquis put in an armoured-car regiment and an infantry battalion, with considerable reserves as yet uncommitted, and the Syrians an augmented mechanized brigade, while the Lebanese Army formed a defensive screen across its frontier, acting as base for operations by the Liberation Army irregulars. The Jews had trained some sixty thousand men, excluding the Irgun and Stern group irregulars. There were rifles for about only fifteen thousand, two pieces of artillery and no tanks, though they had plenty of armoured cars and mortars. In terms of the total troops which the Arab countries claimed to have available, they had superiority of around eight to one, backed by tanks, aircraft and guns, which theoretically gave them crushing advantage. Anyone who did not predict crushing victory was denounced as a traitor.

Since Omdurman, its last major action, the Egyptian Army had first shrunk and then expanded. It was of course a conscript force, and such was the effect of bilharzia and other endemic diseases, not to mention graft, that it received only a fifth of each age group into its ranks; its total strength fell short of its publicized fifty thousand. It was British armed, equipped and organized, though it no longer had the advice of the British military mission, which had been discarded, for reasons of pride, in 1947.

There was no need to distort the initial communiqué. On the opening day, May 15, one of the Egyptian brigade groups advanced 17 miles along the coast and captured Gaza! (There was in fact no opposition except in some inland villages which, though by-passed,

Tewfik Pasha, who succeeded
his father, Ismail Pasha, as
Khedive of Egypt and dec-
lared Arabi Pasha a rebel

Evelyn Baring, first Earl of
Cromer and virtual ruler of
Egypt from 1883 - 1907

Abbas Hilmi, Egypt's last Khedive, who chose loyalty to Turkey in 1914

Saad Zaghloul Pasha, successful agitator and calamitous Prime Minister, seen here in hospital after an attempt on his life

eld-Marshal Earl Kitchener of hartoum, avenger of Gordon, iend of the Fellah, suppressor of the Khedive

Field-Marshal Viscount Allenby on his departure from Egypt in June 1925, 'richly endowed with tribute from Egyptians'

King Farouk I, exiled grandson
of Ismail

Miles Wedderburn Lampson,
first Baron of Killearn, ambassador with unusual powers

stubbornly and aggravatingly repelled assault.) The other brigade, directed on Jerusalem in hope of being present at the fall of the New City, made almost as rapid progress, reaching Beersheba on May 20 and Bethlehem, where they linked up with the Arab Legion, on May 22. They too encountered no opposition.

Northwards of Gaza resistance stiffened. There was some hard fighting. Three times the Egyptians made successful attacks on prepared positions, showing increasing skill in the use of tanks and artillery, and by May 29 they were at Isdud, only 20 miles from Tel Aviv, the Israeli capital. The Israelis, seriously alarmed, rushed up reinforcements and brought the advance to a halt. Now, on June 11, there was a truce.

It was ordered by the United Nations Security Council and accepted because both sides were in need of a breather, though the Arab League were able to conceal their relief behind strong protest. The fiercest fighting had been in and around Jerusalem, where the Jews had been courageously held by the Arab Legion, which had itself been stretched to the limit of its four-battalion capacity. Elsewhere, the fighting had been just as indecisive. The Iraqis, Syrians and even the Lebanese had gained some ground but had not accomplished very much. The Jews were confident that with aid of the arms on their way from Czecho-Slovakia (in violation of the terms of the truce) and with some training and re-organization they would soon put the invaders to flight.

The Egyptians had not been disgraced. Indeed, Major Edgar O'Ballance, in the one impartial account of the campaign available, praises the fortitude of the soldier in action, though he notes the officer's traditional disinclination to "rough it". However, serious deficiencies in the supply and medical services caused such peril and hardship that the truce was welcome, hard though it was to explain its acceptance to a public fed on stories of sweeping victories. The forward troops were in a precarious position. They had been taken aback by the tenacity of the resistance in the Jewish settlements adjacent to their axis and, rather than waste time in reducing them, had left the Jews in occupation. Tough, mobile patrols of Jews buzzed from strong point to strong point, presenting constant menace to the Egyptian lines of communication. If the Egyptians had been wiser, they would have concentrated all their strength on the coastal thrust.

A month was the limit agreed for the truce and both sides strove hard to build up their forces. King Abdulla visited the Arab capitals in his role as Commander-in-Chief, but the Egyptians refused to allow him either to know the strength they deployed or to visit their field headquarters. King Farouk meanwhile attended to such important details as the size of the flag displayed by each ally and the construction by his engineers of a palace at Gaza, where he intended to preside over the "Palestine Arab Government". On June 30 the bark of guns and roar of aircraft were heard in Haifa. They were sounded in salute to add ceremony to the departure of the British rearguard, under the G.O.C., Lieutenant-General G. H. A. MacMillan. "Thus with dignity, with precision, without incident and entirely according to plan, ended thirty years of British occupation," wrote the General, without apparent attempt at sarcasm.

Count Bernadotte had now arrived in Palestine as United Nations mediator and was throwing his powers of persuasion into obtaining an extension of the truce. He failed. The Israelis were willing, still needing time, but the Arab countries, Egypt in particular, were in the grip of the frenzied belligerence which flowed non-stop from press and radio, and their leaders were prisoners of their own agitation. The Egyptians leapt into the attack on July 8, a day ahead of the expiry of the truce. They found the Jews had not been wasting their time. The attacks foundered, even on a position near Gaza held by barely a hundred men. The Egyptians were thrown on the defensive and hard pressed to retain their original gains. After ten days' fighting, in the course of which the Israelis strengthened their positions in all sectors, another truce was agreed.

With the aid of three hundred officers drafted in by the United Nations, Bernadotte renewed his endeavours to reach a settlement, while the combatants licked their wounds, pulled every political wire they could manipulate, and prepared for the next round. Egyptian ambitions were by now somewhat shrivelled. Her dispositions consisted of three narrow belts. One stretched along the coast road to Isdud, another inland to Bethlehem, and the third precariously connected the two forward positions, running through Feluja at a minimum depth of two miles. In the middle were the defended Jewish settlements of the Negev, still as active and resolute as ever. With typical optimism the Egyptians aimed to force them into submission merely by containment. The Negev was a desirable prize. It constituted a larger area of Palestine than any of the other armies held, and with the "Palestine Arab Government" securely established at Gaza under her patronage, Egypt could yet emerge from the war with strengthened prestige—at any rate in comparison with her allies, of whom she was so jealous.

Bernadotte's proposals accommodated Egyptian ambition in the Negev while piquing it by their favours to Trans-Jordan. The Jews rejected them with contempt. On September 17, the day after their publication, Bernadotte was murdered by Stern Group gangsters. Ben Gurion's Government made wholesale arrests, the only outcome from which was a riotous party in the prison, given by the gangsters and attended by press and public. Such was Israel's mood of exuberant aggression that there was bound to be another eruption. It came on October 15, wearing the whimsical code-name "Ten Plagues". The object was to relieve the Negev settlements.

The Egyptian force had by now swollen to a strong division of thirteen infantry battalions, some of them Sudanese of the long-established Frontier District Force. The thin Feluja belt, some twelve miles long, was the most vulnerable part of their line. For five days the Israelis, also at divisional strength but with much greater mobility, strove to pierce it, aided by effective air support and by diversionary attacks from the Negev itself. The Egyptians resisted stubbornly, making good use of their artillery and launching a number of brisk counter-attacks. But they had neither the dash nor resource of the Israelis who on the night of the 19th at last cut a narrow corridor, not far from the coast road, through to their Negev settlements.

They now used their mobility with stunning effect. On the night following the breakthrough, they dashed southwards in their jeeps and by a surprise dawn assault seized Beersheba, midway between the Egyptian frontier and Jerusalem. The Egyptian right-hand prop was severed, and the troops holding it, as far north as Bethlehem, sank into demoralized apathy. Rather than mop them up, the Israelis struck westwards and on October 22 cut the coast road just to the north of Gaza. while out at sea the *Emir Farouk*, flagship of the Egyptian Navy, was sunk by one of the dilapidated craft hastily armed and refurbished by the Israelis. Only around Feluja was there any cause for Egyptian pride. Although quite surrounded and compressed into an area only five miles by one, the three battalions here bravely held on, under their magnificent Sudanese commander, Colonel Sayyid Taha, the "Black Wolf". Captain Nasser, who had received a superficial wound during the fighting in July, was with them, serving as a battalion adjutant and alternately experiencing disillusionment, rage at the sins of the High Command, most of all at the distortions broadcast from Cairo, and odd moments of uplift at the repulse of an attack.

The Israelis now agreed to a truce which did no more than reduce the tempo of fighting. The Egyptians were obliged to fall back on Gaza, and on November 8 the Israelis succeeded in further reducing the size of the Feluja pocket. Unable to bring relief to its dauntless garrison by peaceful means, the Egyptians turned to the offensive but could make little headway against the settlements round Gaza. The Israelis eagerly planned reprisal. After a feint attack towards Gaza on the night of December 22, they tore at the very guts of the Egyptian defences, aiming at the base of the U-shaped line. By using a Roman road to cross desert which the Egyptians thought impassable, their mobile columns swept in behind the enemy positions south of Beersheba and in three days' sharp fighting forced the defenders, numb with cold and bewilderment, into submission, while their rulers called in vain for aid from their allies of the Arab League.

By December 28 the Israelis had crossed the frontier and were plundering the Egyptian base at Abu Ageila. They then darted for the port of El Arish and, having seized the airfield, were about to enter the town when they yielded to formidable political pressure and turned back into Palestine. Britain had stepped in to return the cock to the pit. She did so on her own initiative. Egypt could have invoked her aid under the 1936 Treaty, but bruised and shamed though she might be, she would never humble herself to that extent. The Israelis turned on the remainder of the Egyptian forces lining the coast route to the north. On January 7, 1949, Egypt asked for an armistice and the fighting stopped. On this same day five British aircraft, making a reconnaissance near the frontier, were shot down by Israeli planes.

Unity among the member states of the Arab League was no longer even a fiction. Their delegates came to the island of Rhodes and separately made terms with those of Israel, with the exception of Iraq, who, having no common frontier, had no need of terms. The Egyptians came first. After much haggling over Beersheba and other places which the Egyptian public believed still to be in their hands, they were allowed to retain Gaza and the coastal strip. The Feluja pocket, still unconquered, was their one trump card. With the armistice signed, on February 24, the heroic garrison proudly marched out with bayonets fixed and colours flying.

Egypt's humiliation was made the more shaming by the success achieved by the adjacent, infinitely smaller army of Jordan, as the enlarged state of Trans-Jordan had become, with the consent of the Palestinian Arabs. Deprived though it was at an early stage of its officers in British service, by order of the British Government, the Arab Legion had fought magnificently and had acquired for its Government the treasured prize of the Old City and extensive areas to north and south. Jordan's jealous allies denounced her as a traitor, both for claiming this territory for herself and for con- ceding a strip of land to Israel at the armistice talks. Egypt, de- feated more decisively than Iraq or Syria, was loudest in denuncia- tion. Her pride had skilfully been rasped by the Israeli radio. Typical of its power at provocation was an assessment of the oppos- ing armies made by a military commentator when the autumn fighting was at its height. One Israeli soldier, he claimed, was the equal of one Arab Legionary, of three Iraqis and six Egyptians.

Firm measures had meanwhile been taken in Egypt to throttle subversion as news of defeat and scandals at the front began to seep through the heavy screen of censorship. The Moslem Brotherhood had been getting increasingly obstreperous and when the fighting seemingly died down in December, Nokrashy, the Prime Minister, felt himself strong enough to decree its suppression. He was mur- dered for his daring, shot dead on December 28 while standing in his own Ministry of Interior surrounded by his police. His succes- sor, Abdul Hady, struck hard. Brethren were flung into prison wholesale, and on February 13 El Banna, the Supreme Guide, was murdered, supposedly by Government agents.

The purge spread beyond the Moslem Brotherhood and would have overwhelmed the Free Society of Officers if it had not been for the painstaking attention to security that Nasser had paid, com- bined with the distinguished part he had himself played in the fighting, gaining him promotion to major. Nonetheless he was brought before the Chief of Staff and cautioned for his insubor- dinate outlook. Though the defeat of the army had harmed the cause of the Free Officers' movement, reducing its potential for popular support, its members had been given fresh impulse by the tribulations they had endured, the bad rations, the ammunition shortages, the hopeless inadequacies of the medical services, the misappropriation of stores and most of all by the confusion, be- wilderment and anguish of defeat. All were blamed on the King

158

and his Government, on the "greed, conspiracy and lust" which, as Nasser claimed in his book *Egypt's Liberation*, "created . . . a tighter and more crippling siege than anything we experienced while dug in at the Feluja pocket". Conveniently posted to the Staff College, he began to plot in greater detail and with renewed ardour for the overthrow of the guilty men.

It obviously did not occur to these angry young officers that their defeat had deeper cause than mere administrative failings. Some of them are reported to have shown great courage, as no doubt Nasser did himself, but it was in deficiencies in tactics and leadership at all level of command, that the basic failure lay. Against an enemy aggressive, mobile and imaginative, the Egyptians showed none of these qualities themselves. They made some gains by assaults in the ponderous style taught them by their British advisers, but were disinclined to venture away from the roads and made no apparent attempt to dominate the enemy-infested areas around them by patrol activity, infiltration and deep-penetrating raids. As a result the Jews could strike when and where they chose, and the Egyptians allowed themselves to be in turn hemmed in, surprised and demoralized by an enemy who admittedly was fired with all the fervour of a nation born and showed tenacity, dash and resource which can seldom have been excelled in the history of war.

Yet it seems that deeper emotion had been stirred in Nasser than shame at the shattering of the Army's prestige. He had always been ardent for the Arab cause and had volunteered for the irregular Liberation Army, but had been turned down because he could not be spared from his staff appointment. His war experiences turned ardour to passion. He witnessed the ruthless ambition of the Jews where it was revealed at its starkest, saw the streams of miserable refugees, and described the plight of homeless children, starving in the battle zone, in a manner which defies suspicion of cynicism. Here indeed was a cause calling for a champion, and the enticing path towards it led through revolution at home, re-invigoration of the Army, and leadership of the Arab League.

Though defeated and embittered against each other, the states of the Arab League at least remained firm in their continued hostility against Israel. They refused to negotiate a peace treaty. The armistice was acknowledged merely as a temporary cessation of hostilities, and in the meantime war was waged by adventures across the frontier and by blockade. Ships bearing cargo for Israel were denied passage through the Suez Canal by the port authorities at its entrance, and Britain could do no more than protest, even though she was still responsible for safeguarding free navigation in co-operation with Egypt, under the terms of the 1936 Treaty, and indeed kept troops in Egypt for that primary purpose. Egypt was betraying the trust she had accepted when she gained independence. She could retort that Britain herself had violated the Convention during two world wars, and as long as no one was prepared to take positive measures on Israel's behalf, Egypt could be as defiant as she wished. Britain was the principal sufferer. Israel could get oil from Rumania: the Haifa Refinery was a source of sterling for Britain, and Haifa was now cut off from the Persian Gulf oilfields, both by pipeline and ship.

The United States and France became as concerned as Britain about the peril of a sudden flare-up of the smouldering conflict, and having failed to bring the rival parties to the peace table, the three countries signed a joint policy statement, the Tripartite Declaration, in May 1950. It restricted the supply of arms to the contestants and naïvely requested assurance from the recipient that they were needed for self-defence, not aggression. It also declared the three Governments' "unalterable opposition to the use of force or threat of force" and pledged themselves to take immediate action against any state which violated its armistic line. It was intentionally an impartial document, showing favour to neither side, but it could never seem impartial to Arab or Egyptian eyes, offering as it did protection to the brigand state of Israel. The arms' limitation stifled Egypt's prospect of regaining prestige and caused much aggravation.

It was the final signpost to collision. The first was Balfour's finger directing Jews to Palestine; the second, that of Eden pointing to Arab unity; the third, the infuriating diversion of the British occupation which gave such reckless impulse to Egyptian ambition; the fourth, Attlee's hand of surrender hustling Egypt headlong to a hazard which it was far beyond her capacity to cross; and the fifth was the blaze lit in the heart of Nasser by the crash.

CHAPTER THIRTEEN

Explosion

(1949–52)

EGYPT RELAPSED INTO a state of sullen inertia. The zealots of
the Moslem Brotherhood were either safely locked up or dispiri-
tedly skulking the alleyways, while with the Army not exactly the
hero of the nation, there could be little popular support for the Free
Officers' movement, pent with ardour and indignation though its
members might be. Meanwhile the King and the politicians could
continue their perennial joustings in a more relaxed atmosphere,
and the longer they jousted, the brighter the prospects of the
revolutionaries became. The landowners were the real rulers of the
country. They held sway in both Houses of Parliament, controlling
both Wafd and King's men by their skilful manipulation of elections, and they knew how to look after their own interests and to
evade even the mild taxes which they apparently imposed on themselves. The ever soaring cost of living did not greatly trouble them.
It made life a struggle for the lower classes who, by indirect levies,
shouldered the main burden of taxation, but the landowners
merely made corresponding increases in the rents demanded from
their unfortunate tenants. Thus the gulf grew ever wider between
rich and poor.

Striving to regain office after five years in the doldrums, the
Wafd took the eccentric step of advocating social reform, rather
than concentrate on nationalistic aspirations, when a fresh election
was held in January 1950. Nationalism, it had been found, was a
theme rather too hot for the politicians to handle. With the Moslem
Brotherhood still ineffective, the Wafd were swept back into power,

and Farouk had no option but to appoint old Nahas, his wartime enemy, Prime Minister for the fifth time. Government followed a familiar pattern. Progress on the social front foundered in face of steeply rising prices and Nahas once again sought diversion by negotiating a treaty with Britain. Talks began, at Foreign Minister level, in the autumn.

Britain's Labour Government were no longer so keen to give up their foothold in the Canal Zone. The Russian menace had grown, and the emergence of the state of Israel had shattered all illusions that the Arab League might provide a shield. The Canal was still Britain's lifeline. With the independence of India, it had lost value as a link with the Empire, but as a channel for Britain's oil it had gained importance immeasurably. The development of the Persian Gulf oilfields, for Europe's benefit, formed an essential feature of the Marshall Aid plan of 1948. Before the war they had provided merely a twentieth of the world's supply. Now the proportion was more than an eighth and fast increasing every year. It was here that Britain was most vulnerable to Russian intrusion.

As the negotiations floundered in the familiar mire of incompatible requirements, Russia at last awoke to the possibilities of the impasse and began to coo in Egypt's ear, like Little Red Riding Hood's spurious granny, posing as a "noble ally in the struggle against Western imperialism". Ernest Bevin broke physically under the strain of office and Herbert Morrison took up the running, bringing fresh vigour to the task of finding a solution. He offered gradual evacuation, subject to the right of return in an emergency, together with participation in a scheme to advance the Sudan towards self-government. It was all in vain. The ban on the Moslem Brotherhood had been lifted, and the furore of nationalist emotion gained momentum every day, and Nahas could not resist the goad from behind: evacuation must be immediate and unconditional. In August 1951 the Persian Government spurred on the nationalist frenzy throughout the Middle East by their brash expulsion of the British employees of the nationalized Anglo-Iranian Oil Company, and all Britain dared do about it was to send a ship to take her bereft subjects away.

Still the negotiations continued, and Morrison now turned to his N.A.T.O. allies for a means of safeguarding his oil supply line without offending the super-sensitive occupants of the zone it crossed. Turkey joined the Alliance towards the end of September, and she agreed to a plan under which the Canal Zone would become

11

an inter-allied base, with France also participating. Egypt was to be invited in as an equal partner, sharing responsibility for, and control of, this multi-racial strategic force. Those who were aware of the mood of defiance which had the whole of the Middle East in its grasp had little doubt how Egypt would respond. Any tie with the West bore mark of ignominy that no leader dare incur.

Nahas's Government had by now fallen sadly into disrepute. Its inefficiency was notorious even by Egyptian standards, inflation ran riot, and revelations of corruption had forced two Cabinet Ministers out of office. But old men are hard to shift. Craving for public acclaim, Nahas did the thing best calculated to distract attention from the home front, rouse the crudest and most combustible instincts of the people, and erase for ever the stigma of lackey-imperialism which he had borne for his staunch stand for the Allied cause during the war. In an impassioned speech to the Chamber of Deputies on October 8 he tabled decrees abrogating the 1936 Treaty and the Sudan Convention of 1899.

Treating this as an immature outburst best forgotten, the N.A.T.O. Governments, the United States among them, blandly presented their invitation for Egypt to join their Middle East defence scheme, adding a provocative rider to the effect that the British must stay in the Canal Zone if the proposal were not accepted. It was rejected with contempt. The decrees of abrogation were made law, King Farouk was proclaimed King of Egypt and the Sudan, and a state of emergency was declared. Next day, October 16, there was rioting in the Canal towns, with the most violent in Ismailia. While the civil police stood by, buses and cars belonging to the British were overturned and set on fire, houses were pillaged and burnt, and Army wives and children, besieged by looters in the N.A.A.F.I. grocery store, were rescued by the timely arrival of a platoon of Lancashire Fusiliers who dressed them in their steel helmets and escorted them home. Troops opened fire on occasions but they aimed, with effective disregard for military principles, at the sky.

No sooner had this pip been flicked in Britain's face than (on October 25) the Conservatives beat Labour in the general election and the old team was back, Churchill as Prime Minister, Eden as Foreign Secretary. Thus Nahas, having torn up the treaty he had signed fifteen years previously, was confronted by the man who had partnered him in signing. Eden played it cool. He was willing to negotiate a fresh treaty, he told Nahas, but as no provision for unilateral renunciation had at any time been made, the old one in the meantime remained effective. The Egyptian Government would be held "responsible for any breach of the peace and any damage to life and property that may result from their purported abrogation".

Nahas also played it as cool as the fires he had lit allowed. There was nothing much he could do about the Sudan. His predecessors in office had refused to participate in a scheme for constitutional advancement, fearing that the Egyptian-backed party might be worsted, and it had been left to the British to lead the Sudanese happily towards self-government on their own. It would obviously be unwise to send Farouk upriver in the royal barge to claim his kingdom, glorious though the spectacle might be in its early stages. As for the Canal Zone, it was equally undesirable to force the issue to the point of war, or for that matter to any point which might lead to a clash between the two armies. The Egyptian Army was in delicate health and a delicate situation. Half of it was deployed east of the Canal, making rude noises at the Israelis, and the other half to the west, mainly around Cairo. The British stood between them and had only to close the El Firdan swing bridge, near Ismailia, to reduce the eastern half to starvation. In a clash for possession of this bridge the Egyptians lost two soldiers killed, after which they obediently kept their distance behind a line arbitrarily drawn by Lieutenant-General Sir George Erskine, commanding British Troops Egypt, round his zone of action, and known as the Erskine Line.

It was therefore left to that master manipulator of the underworld, Fuad Serag El Din, Minister of the Interior, to wage a war of blockade and terrorism against the British forces, officially described as "non-co-operation". There was a splendid outlet here for the energies both of the Moslem Brotherhood and its fellow trouble-maker, the Communist Peace Party, and they could be assured of enthusiastic aid from the professional brigands, of mixed fallah-bedouin blood, that inhabit the Delta fringes. In an attempt to prevent misdirection of the non-co-operators' zeal, a training and indoctrination centre was opened at Zagazig and as many as possible were enlisted into the auxiliary police, the Bulak Nizam, where El Din could feel surer of their allegiance.

The British troops were in a weird position, weirder indeed than most realized. Technically, the only reason for their presence, as stipulated by treaty, was "with a view to ensuring in co-operation with the Egyptian forces the defence of the Canal". Now the Egyptian Government were trying forcibly to rid themselves of their co-operation, and instead of the conventional role of aiding the civil power, the task of the soldiers was to defy it. But it carried the same obligation of restraint, whatever the provocation caused by acts either of blockade or banditry. Nonetheless Erskine made it clear enough in typically forthright style that every step necessary to ensure the safety and supply of his troops would be taken. He had one powerful weapon of retaliation available in the control of the oil pipeline from Suez on which Cairo depended for petrol and power. He was tempted to use it as a counter to such measures as the dislocation of his domestic railway service, the withdrawal of labour, and an embargo on supplies of fresh food, but he was persuaded by the Ambassador to hold it in reserve. The Egyptians also kept their most damaging weapon in reserve, control of Nile water through the Sweet Water Canal.

The first achievement of the besiegers showed itself towards the end of October in a stream of refugees heading away from the Canal Zone with livestock and possessions piled to haystack height on lorries and handcarts. Forty thousand Egyptians had been directly employed by the three services, not counting contracted labour, and these were the first target of intimidation exerted by press, police and thugs. A few brave ones stayed on—a very few— granted protection inside wired-in garrison encampments which also contained service families hastily moved out of isolated homes. The bustling trading centre that had once been the village of Fayid became a desolate clump of boarded houses, and in power stations, water filtration plants, sewage works, bakeries and hospitals, soldiers took over strangely unmilitary duties, working a 12-hour day.

The R.A.F. flew in reinforcements fast, evincing a higher state of readiness than when crisis came four years later. An infantry brigade, a mixed brigade and an artillery group were the only fighting troops immediately available—a stronger force nonetheless than the ten thousand agreed by treaty—and in a short time they were joined by two other infantry brigades, completing the 1st Division, and by the 16th Parachute Brigade, followed by a brigade of the 3rd Division. Their arrival accentuated the supply and maintenance problem, but it was alleviated to a certain extent by the despatch of civilian labour from Cyprus and pioneer units from Mauritius and solved by the determined exertions of the troops themselves.

So far El Din's storm-troopers had taken little offensive action except to commit the occasional murder and take pot-shots at encampments, a task facilitated by the ease with which a rifle can be concealed beneath a galabiya. But in mid-November there was a big flare-up in Ismailia, during the course of which the auxiliary police were seen deliberately to open fire on their British military colleagues; three British officers were among the killed in two days of tumult and endless firing. The battle then switched to the Suez area where the auxiliary police again openly came into action. While the Buffs and the Royal Sussex quenched their ardour, a party of an officer of the Royal Engineers, two sappers and eight Mauritian pioneers were ambushed nearby, and apart from one sapper, who made his escape, all were brutally murdered.

The main objective here was the water filtration plant which was overlooked from the village of Kafr Abdu, across the Sweet Water Canal. It was impossible to relieve the guard on it without a hot exchange of fire, which from the Egyptian side did not always miss target, and Erskine was obliged to order the demolition of the houses which gave the bandits such cover. After some lengthy parleying, operation Flatten, as it was aptly called, was carried out on December 8. So far the troops had shown exemplary restraint under provocation; now restraint was discarded. Covered by paratroops, engineers laid low the complete village, some solid two- and three-storeyed houses included.

At a press conference the previous evening correspondents had been told that it was necessary to "bulldoze several mudhouses". When the extent of the destruction became known, duly magnified in transit, rage flared in Cairo. At last the dangerous game of baiting the British had drawn retaliation, with its dividend of indignation, and Nahas made protest against the outrage by withdrawing his Ambassador from London and dismissing the two hundred odd British subjects, most of them school-teachers, still in Egyptian Government employment; eight years were to pass before they were able to obtain compensation. An offer to pay for the damage, made by the British Government, was contemptuously rejected by Nahas. When, however, the owner of the village sued the British Army and was awarded mighty damages, the Army claimed immunity from such proceedings under the 1936 Treaty and refused to pay. The result was that its banking account was blocked and N.A.A.F.I. tokens had to be introduced as currency for the soldier's pay.

The British community in Cairo, having stronger evidence of the consequences of the demolition than of its justification, were disinclined to be convinced of its military necessity, and from the Embassy comment leaked out about "a psychological blunder" and "a political disaster". On the other hand, there was a feeling at Erskine's headquarters, inspired perhaps by nostalgic memories of Lord Killearn, that a few firm words to King Farouk could long since have brought the crisis to an end. It did not promote harmony between the Army and Embassy that each had its own channel of communication with London. Over the military one came a personal telegram for Erskine bearing the Prime Minister's congratulations on the action he had taken.

In the new mood of defiance, the Egyptians enlisted schoolboys into "youth commandos" and despatched them to the front with heroic fanfares. Anxious parents sought some means of discouragement, and in the typically droll and paradoxical manner of the Anglo-Egyptian relationship, an approach was made to Erskine in response to which he publicly appealed to parents to stop "this criminal waste", and warned, "I shall be obliged to crush the youths with the powerful forces at my disposal which have not yet been brought into action." One result was that he was rebuked by the more liberally-minded section of the British press, another that a number of the young heroes were soon safely detained in prison cages, to which their school-books were despatched from Cairo.

With the bitterness intensified, British troops were constrained to strike harder yet. In January, the 1st Guards' Brigade refought the Battle of Tel-el-Kebir, though without claim to glory, and rounded up 131 armed policemen in a single village. The spotlight then fell back on Ismailia for the finale, the prelude to which consisted of a bomb explosion from a barrow of oranges that killed two British soldiers and wounded six others, whereupon gangsters submitted the town to frenzied firing, in the course of which a much-loved English nun was killed apparently while shepherding children to safety. The troops then moved in to search the Arab quarter, returning fire with interest, and with the Egyptian press accusing them of crucifying their prisoners and throwing their bodies to wild dogs, Serag El Din gave warning of fiercer reprisal if they did not desist. Erskine resolved to disarm the police whom he had such good cause to regard as the root of evil.

The deed was done on the morning of Friday, January 25, 1952. Both police barracks, the Caracol and the Bureau Sanitaire, were surrounded at first light and their occupants ordered to parade outside unarmed. There was no response. The Egyptians were cut off from escape but (as was to happen again on an even more momentous occasion) they were not cut off from communication with Cairo, and from Cairo came the orders of El Din: fight to the last. The Bulak Nizam were in the Bureau Sanitaire, a sprawling modern building normally part of a hospital, and just after seven they opened fire with rifles, shot-guns, sub-machine-guns, riot-guns. They were answered by a round of blank from a Centurion tank, such was the confidence of the British that a show of force would prevail. Loud-speaker warnings followed. There were more shots, more warnings. Pleas were made to the police commandant, outside the barracks, but Cairo had spoken and it was not for a junior to countermand orders from above.

Force had to be felt as well as seen. A Centurion crashed through the gate into the hospital grounds and slewed into a side wall beyond. A platoon of the Lancashire Fusiliers rushed past it into the courtyard and were sent spinning and sprawling by a hot fusillade. The tanks opened up with their 20-pounders bringing masonry down with crash and dust cloud, armoured cars belted the building with machine-gun fire, mortar bombs whistled and crumped, and infantrymen climbed into position on surrounding rooftops to shoot up the policemen's sandbagged positions on their rooftop. Still the Lancashire Fusiliers encountered opposition, until eventually the vicious crunch of their grenades gained them their first entry through holes blasted by the tanks. After a burst or two from a tommy-gun and the crunch of more grenades the survivors came out, stark-eyed and unsteady, their jerseys, black trousers and not-so-dark faces coated with dust and flecked with blood. They were marched away, forlorn but still proud, some displaying wounds that would have placed the ordinary soldier on a stretcher. Inside the barracks and on the rooftop a pathetic jumble remained to be cleared up, of corpses, wounded, squalid blankets, upturned kitboxes, knick-knacks, rubbish, weirdly assorted weapons, and a mass of ammunition spilled everywhere.

This battle was over soon after half past ten. The other barracks, the Caracol, held out until noon, when, after much patient parleying and some intensified small arms fire, the policemen began to come out with hands up, in defiance of a brave and resolute officer. They were regular police here, and most were found sheltering in the cells with civil prisoners. Of the total Egyptian casualties, nearly fifty killed and a hundred wounded, only one and three were incurred at the Caracol. The Lancashire Fusiliers' losses, five killed and nine wounded, were all suffered at the Bureau Sanitaire and bespeak the vigour of the ill-furnished resistance.

The battle left British officers stunned and disturbed. Not realizing the effect of Egyptian propaganda and having always despised the fighting quality of the opponents they had so unwillingly fought, they were amazed that these men should have sold their lives so dearly when so little was at stake and the outcome so inevitable. There was much heart-searching to decide whether the casualties could have been avoided, but if Cairo demanded sacrifice and could evoke such response there seemed to be no alternative. Not everyone was so surprised at the result. General Sir Brian Robertson, Commander-in-Chief of the Middle East, was well aware of the fortitude of the fellahin and when Churchill had some months earlier belittled the likely opposition, he had referred him to his book, *The River War*. The point was taken with grace.

The reaction in Cairo was as predictable as it was traditional: swollen by the workless thousands from the Canal Zone the mob broke loose next day, Saturday, January 26. It is not certain who provided the instigation, but the methodical beginning gave more than a hint of official connivance and certainly the police, listless and indifferent, made little attempt to intervene. Indeed the auxiliary police were in open mutiny, having marched from Abbassia to Abdin Palace to protest against the callous sacrifice of their colleagues in Ismailia.

Around noon, groups specially equipped for the task began industriously to set fire to the buildings of British firms and institutions. At the Turf Club, exclusive hide-out of long established British residents, arson was supplemented by murder. All British subjects had been warned by the Consulate to stay at home, but little heed was paid and eleven members of this club, including a Canadian diplomat, were either suffocated amid the flames or battered to death trying to escape. The arsonists now enlarged their target area to include all places where Western customs exerted their corrupting influence in violation of the pure doctrine of Islam, as expounded with such fervour by the Moslem Brotherhood. Shepheard's Hotel, haven of Englishmen for 120 years, was gutted while guests cowered together in its tiny garden. Bars, restaurants, cinemas, the shops of Jew, Maltese and Greek, were smashed, ransacked, ignited, and separate bonfires were made out of documents flung from European offices. Thugs swarmed out of the alleyways in exuberant cry for loot, while those without criminal tendencies merely danced in ecstasy round the flames, pausing to cut the hoses of the fire brigade. A great black cloud hung lethargically over the city, plunging it into premature darkness—it was "Black Saturday" quite literally—and Nero-like, the King and his Ministers gazed on the scene just as lethargically.

It was a worrying day for General Erskine at his headquarters at Moascar. It had long been agreed at highest level that if the Ambassador considered British lives in Cairo to be in danger he was empowered directly to call on Erskine's troops, and indeed most of the 1st Division, with the 16th Para Brigade, armoured cars and a tank battalion, were concentrated astride the Suez road, awaiting the signal to advance. But now came signs of cold feet. Eden refers in his memoirs to a message "from the British command in Egypt expressing concern at the resistance shown in the recent fighting at the police station". After summoning the only other member of the Cabinet in London that Saturday, he gave orders that if the call came from the Ambassador it must be answered, whatever the risk.

The Egyptian Army had two brigade groups, with tank support, dug into hill positions astride the Suez road. The troops resented the spectator's role they had so far played in the struggle and were keen to prove their mettle. Erskine admitted shortly before his death (in a letter written to the author), that he was anxious to avoid a showdown, but claimed that it was more the consequences of a deliberate act of war than fear of the opposition that daunted him. The British were as familiar with the Egyptians' dispositions as with the ground on which they stood, and it was planned to make a flanking attack under cover of smoke and air attack. Despite a shortage of armour, there was high confidence of swift success at all levels of command—indeed the story current at the time, which well illustrates the prevailing mood, was that when asked how long he needed to enter Cairo Erskine replied, "Twelve hours if unopposed, six hours if opposed."

There was more behind this distorted quotation than facetious insult. What Erskine meant was that his task would be that much easier if the Egyptian Army stood to fight him in the open rather than disperse into guerrilla bands and resist house by house in the manner to which the Egyptian temperament is so much better suited. The occupation was the problem that daunted. Street-fighting could quickly absorb the whole of the 1st Division, and in the probable absence of any form of governmental co-operation, the task of administering to the needs of a hostile population, of maintaining supplies, power and communications, not to mention order, was far beyond Erskine's resources, however fast reinforcements might be flown into Almaraz aerodrome, to which the paratroops were to race on wheels. (Another plan some time considered was to drop them on Gezira Island, to form a protective compound for British subjects, but it was not popular because of the risk of their being blown into the Nile.)

In the event the call did not come. Sir Ralph Stevenson, the Ambassador, was even more reluctant to send for the troops than Erskine to bring them in, and he pinned his faith instead on the Egyptian Army, hoping that knowledge of the British troops' readiness would act as a spur. It was fortunate that the Embassy itself was not greatly endangered. The staff were prepared for siege. Sandbagged positions had been prepared on the roof by the military attaché, rifles issued, fire appliances manned, and a hundred people (including families) allotted their posts. Around half past three in the afternoon the mob was heard to be approaching from Kasr-el-Nil. Three rifle shots, aimed to hit, dispersed them. They were fired by Egyptian policemen, one of whom had earlier received a pep talk from a former commander of Egyptian police, the elderly British resident, Major Alec Wise Bey, whose house was next to the Embassy. Showing all the independence that so characterized the veterans of Kitchener's Egypt and exasperated consular officials, Wise had been out that morning to buy some cartridges for duck shooting, had called in at the Turf Club and left shortly before the arrival of the fire-raisers.

Did Wise's exhortation change the course of history? It is a tempting thought for a romanticist with faith in the magnetic influence of the British raj, for it was a lone act of firmness in a day of anarchy, and there can be no telling the consequence if an assault on the Embassy had been made. On the other hand, it does not necessarily follow that these particular policemen needed an Englishman's prompting, nor does it seem very likely that the mob they scattered so precipitately were bent on serious destruction. The organized gangs concentrated on targets in the centre of the city. Private houses and individuals were unmolested, and Gezira Island, the main residential area for Europeans, was left in peace. Some British subjects, caught in the streets, were even escorted home by brave Egyptians. It was an unusual day of violence, part staged demonstration, part opportunist hooliganism, in which, despite the excesses of the riff-raff, hatred does not appear to have been the dominant motive.

With grotesque disregard for the realities of the situation, King Farouk spent the afternoon in giving a banquet at Abdin Palace to six hundred army and police officers to celebrate the birth of a son. He was aware of treacherous inclinations, even among some of his guests, and on the advice of his Chief of Staff he forbade the intervention of the Army through fear that they might snuff him out as well as the fires. At length, after sultry exchanges with Nahas, he had a call put through to the British Embassy to ask if it were true that British troops were moving in. The answer was designed to make him think that they probably were. Whatever the risk in the loyalty of his own troops, his regime was bound to topple if the British had to come in to clear up the mess. Egyptian troops were ordered in during the closing hour of daylight. The first were recruits and could do nothing. Regular units then arrived from Bilbeis, on the Ismailia road, and marching shoulder to shoulder they speedily cleared the streets, shooting anyone still too intoxicated by the occasion to heed their warnings. Most had had enough fun for one day and were content to go home.

Next day, Sunday 27th, Farouk consolidated his position. He sacked Nahas and the whole of the Wafd Government for their failure to maintain order and made his old collaborator, Aly Maher, Prime Minister. Farouk could chuckle. An armoured car at the gate of Abdin Palace had compelled him to drop Aly Maher for Nahas in 1942, and now by ridding himself of Nahas in favour of Maher he had prevented the British from bringing their armour back. Though he did not realize it at the time, he had also earned himself a few months' reprieve as King. Encouraged by Nahas's bellicosity, the Free Officers had made tentative league with the Wafd and planned to strike in March. Now they had to revise their plans, but their position had been strengthened. The reluctance of the British to intervene, when life and property were under assault, was a matter of great encouragement to aspiring revolutionaries, and instead of suffering further humiliation, as at one time seemed so likely, the Egyptian Army was the one power that gleaned prestige from this shameful day of destruction.

With the Wafd gone, an uneasy peace returned to the Canal Zone. The boycott on civilian labour was maintained and there was still spasmodic thug activity, but living was no longer a problem in itself for the troops, even though comfort and variety were in short supply. Guard duties formed the most tormenting task, especially on the great depot east of Tel-el-Kebir, with its workshops and rich store of mobilization equipment. Patrolling the seventeen-mile perimeter was a nightmare, calling for the employment of half a brigade. The thieves were as daring as they were resourceful, and were so light of touch that they could detect the mines laid within the network of protective wire by massage with finger or bare toe. It occurred to one officer at least, his taste for history whetted by his surrounding, that Wolseley's task could have been made very much harder if Arabi had made better use of the superb material for clandestine warfare always available in Egypt.

CHAPTER FOURTEEN

Revolution

(1952-3)

WITH NAHAS CONVENIENTLY discredited, Farouk could spend more time from the pleasures of the flesh to indulge his taste for power politics. Maher, with his talent for accommodation, showed himself too eager to treat with the Wafd, and early in March the King replaced him with Neguib Hilaly, a former Wafd Minister who could strike at his old party with all the animosity sown of recent disagreement. Parliament was dissolved and Serag El Din placed under house arrest. In the sunnier atmosphere thus created, Hilaly reopened negotiations with the British, but as he would not renounce Nahas's act of abrogation there was little scope for manœuvre. He then turned his attention to the more fruitful field of investigating the Palestine War munitions scandal. This was contrary to the royal will and pleasure, and such pressure was brought to bear on Hilaly that towards the end of June his government resigned.

The King now stirred himself into a gallop towards the unseen abyss. A purge of the dissident elements in the Army, whose ominous rumblings could plainly be heard but not accurately located, was his great desire. Such a course had no appeal to the politicians with their sure instinct for the feel of dynamite. They preferred appeasement, and because no one was prepared to carry out his purge, through the agency of his own nominee as War Minister, Farouk had great difficulty in finding a successor to Hilaly. The veteran Sirry Pasha—there were no up-and-coming young men in the political ranks—eventually agreed to take office but was soon in conflict with the King who, despite promises, could not resist interfering.

Farouk showed reckless confidence. Though he expected every tree around his palace to conceal an assassin, he had high opinion of his own standing in the country, falsely buttressed as it was by his own intricate security shield which kept him at such distance from his people. There was no one at hand to tell him of the harm done by his wartime humiliation, his part in the Palestine war, his divorce of Farida, his honeymoon with Narriman during the fast of Ramadan, and above all his palpable cynicism which was harder to conceal even than his preoccupation with lust. In the course of twelve years the boy who had enjoyed greater popularity than any of his predecessors of the Mohammed Aly dynasty had wantonly tossed it all away.

Ironically, his interference in army matters gave the Free Officers the very thing they so much coveted, a respected senior to act as figurehead. Mohammed Neguib was their choice, a middle-aged brigadier, brave and ambitious, and a likeable, cheerful man with all the best qualities of the emergent middle-class Egyptian. Thanks to the backing of the Free Officers, Neguib had defeated the King's nominee in the poll for President of the Military Club, a semi-official Army organization, held the previous December. The King was furious. He was thwarted in an attempt to get Neguib posted to the Sudan frontier but succeeded in blocking him for promotion—at any rate, in the eyes of Neguib. The Free Officers had been presented with the instrument they needed, but they were far too astute to bring him into their counsels. Neguib was to be kept on ice, for serving when the master of ceremonies ordered.

Further interference forced the Free Officers to act rather sooner than they planned. On July 15 the committee of the Military Club was ordered to be disbanded, and as it consisted almost entirely of Free Officers they naturally assumed that direct action against their clandestine activities would follow. There was a tense meeting of seven officers, under Nasser's presidency, held in Cairo. They resolved to act—though exactly how, at that moment is not clear. For these ardent men, who had so assiduously infused the lower ranks of the Army with fervour for their cause, the hour had come, the hour of fulfilment of the design to which they had dedicated themselves fourteen years previously. They took up action stations, earnestly chanting their slogan, "Resolution and Boldness", as they awaited final orders from their chief.

After only eighteen days in office Sirry resigned the Premiership in protest against the King's obstinate interference in the appointment of War Minister, and like a batsman facing rout on a sticky wicket Hilaly returned for his second innings. He had extracted from the King an undertaking that his own nominee, the staunch Mortada El Maraghy, should be War Minister, but when on July 22 he and his Ministers went to the Palace to take their oaths, the King's brother-in-law, Colonel Ismail Sherine, was presented to them as holding this post. Farouk had played his last shot, and it was a wild, panicky swipe.

Revolt was unmistakably in the air, adding oppressive weight to the sultry summer's heat in Cairo, to evade which the King and his Ministers had as usual moved to their quarters at Alexandria. The Free Officers had planned to strike the previous night but had been obliged to postpone action by twenty-four hours, and now the Army High Command had assembled to decide how to deal with the trouble which all knew to be brewing. They decided to send a company of infantry round to arrest Nasser and his accomplices. The company went, and its commander placed his men at Nasser's disposal. Nasser sent it back under command of the trusted Major Hakim Amer, and the High Command found themselves detained in their operations' room at pistol point. It was the easiest victory ever won. Troops in Cairo, already committed to the cause, marched in to occupy government offices and communication centres, and at 5 a.m. (July 23) Neguib was awakened and offered the post of Commander-in-Chief. He blinked, rubbed his eyes, and accepted. Two hours later a lofty, broadcast proclamation told the people that the Army had taken over government and delivered the country from "one of its darkest periods of history". Wisely, foreign nationals were assured "that the Army considers itself entirely responsible for the protection of their persons and property. May God sustain us all!"

There was no great excitement in the city; it was just another change of government. But there was jubilance in all military centres, most of all in Abbassia Barracks, where Neguib had set up his headquarters and was embarking on such important business as the presentation of his demands to the King and the appointment of an amenable Prime Minister, keeping a wary eye meanwhile on troop movements beyond the Erskine Line, where Lieutenant-General Sir Francis Festing now held command. Neguib had sent official notice of the *coup d'état* to the British Embassy at 10 a.m., and at 10 p.m. he received official reply. Her Majesty's Government, it told him, had no intention of interfering with the internal affairs of Egypt, but were concerned about the safety of foreigners and had troops at high readiness in case of disorders, but with no "hostile intention against the Egyptian Army". John Hamilton, who as senior Embassy official in Cairo delivered the note, was much impressed by Neguib's calm and humour after all the stresses of the day. "Y'know, Hamilton," he remarked as he wrote down the contents of this rather schoolmasterish message, "this reminds me of taking down dictation at Gordon College." (For he was half Sudanese and was a product of the college founded by the British in Khartoum.) He expressed thanks for the note, which indeed simplified his problems, and gave calm assurance of his resolve to maintain order.

Farouk proved embarrassingly co-operative. An envoy came to Ras-el-Tin Palace with the Junta's demands and he accepted them all without demur: the appointment of Neguib as Commander-in-Chief and of Aly Maher as Prime Minister—he had been earmarked for the post in 1942 and on neither occasion had been in the plot—and even the dismissal of his complete entourage. The revolutionaries were in danger of being entrapped by their own moderation. A heated meeting was held by the Executive Committee to discuss the King's fate. The more fiery ones favoured public trial and execution, but Nasser's aversion to bloodshed prevailed and a majority were persuaded to vote for removal.

In the early hours of July 26 troops surrounded Ras-el-Tin, and after firing a few token rounds the palace guard surrendered. Farouk was presented with a humiliating document by his old friend Aly Maher, now the faithful servant of the Revolutionary Committee. It listed his sins, demanded his abdication in favour of his infant son, Ahmed Fuad, and ordered his departure that very evening. He was in no position even to protest and later an instrument of abdication was laid before him, under which he declared that, having "always sought the happiness and welfare of our People," he submitted to their will. Like his grandfather before him, he sailed for Naples in the royal yacht *Mahroussa*, which was laden with hastily packed treasure, taking with him his son, the King, and his wife Narriman. He departed unbewailed, but not without dignity. Eager to present an appearance of constitutional decorum, Neguib came aboard to bid his ex-King farewell and received a friendly, though loaded, expression of good wishes. As the yacht sailed out of harbour, with Farouk on the bridge resplendent in the white uniform of an admiral, a twenty-one-gun salute was fired. Press and radio followed it up with a barrage of vituperation next morning.

There can be little doubt that Farouk expected, and angled for, aid from the British. "I must press you to leave—but please don't go too far," he is said to have told the British Ambassador while the British troops were still in Cairo. It would have been too dangerously blatant to have made direct appeal to the British when the Junta seized power, and instead, from 8 a.m. on the day of the coup, he called constantly for help to the American Ambassador, Jefferson Caffery, even telling him that without foreign intervention (which only Britain could provide) he and his dynasty must go down. The British had, after all, originally come to Egypt for the express purpose of keeping Farouk's uncle on his throne in face of a military revolt. But they had long since lost enchantment with such a role.

The Junta would never believe this. It formed an essential part of their creed that the function of the British army of occupation was to act as prop for the hated, reactionary regime, and its failure to provide the prop could only be attributed to weakness, not to disinterest. El Sadat's book throbs with exultancy at the discomfiture of British Embassy officials when warned by the Junta, in the early hours of the coup, "that the least sign of intervention would be regarded as an act of hostility". (Sir Walter Stuart, who is said to have received the warning, is presumably a mis-translation of Sir Walter Smart, who was no longer on the Embassy staff, and the military attaché, Brigadier Goulburn, who "was furious", was in fact on leave in England.) And when, after Farouk's abdication, the British *chargé d'affaires* called—since Stevenson was also on leave—to suggest that the Monarchy be maintained for its stabilizing influence, El Sadat proudly claims that he personally rebuked him for lack of tact. Beacons of defiance had been lit, illuminating the road ahead.

It was not surprising that the Junta should be cock-a-hoop. They had achieved their great design without bloodshed, molestation or even protest; not since the days of Mohammed Aly had such daring been show, such precision achieved. They had struck swiftly, painlessly, and above all tactfully, whatever El Sadat might maintain, and it is here that the statecraft of Gamal Nasser so reveals itself. The Egyptian people got the change they wanted,

12

but without any drastic jolt to upset the easy-going, conservative-minded majority. A despised King had gone but his dynasty lived on; a doyen of the old political school had become Prime Minister, renowned as a skilful team manager, and Nahas himself had flown from holiday in Europe to hail the new regime; and there could be no fears about the intentions of the Army with such a benign and distinguished man as Neguib, hero of the Palestine War, at its head. What was not so apparent was that the young bloods around him, bouncing with melodramatic exuberance, had merely scaled their first objective.

Their aims were made manifest step by step and their attainment caused little initial alarm, thanks again to Neguib's amiable personality and Nasser's flair for timing. Farouk's most active and disreputable agents were rounded up, but no vindictive punishment was as yet prescribed, and the only immediate reform, acting as aperitif to the revolutionary menu, was the abolition of the old Turkish titles of pasha and bey. This was accepted with a shrug. The Prime Minister and all his political colleagues were affected, but they were not going to lower their standing with the people by protest against an egalitarian measure, and in any case official abolition could not banish the pasha mystique.

Sharp retribution fell on the textile workers of Kafr-el-Dauwar when they sought to hasten the revolution along by seizing their factory and driving the owners' representatives out. Two ringleaders were hanged for their rapacity, the first to die either for or against the revolutionary cause. Neguib meanwhile toured the country, using his pipe and friendly grin to win acclaim from the people that put even Nahas to shame. Foreigners received almost as hearty an embrace. "Egypt will always treasure the friendship of the British people," he publicly declared in mid-August. These brave words, such as no politician had dared use since the war, gained prompt reward. £10,000,000 sterling was released by Britain to save Egypt's tottering finances from complete collapse.

By mid-September the Junta felt strong enough to enforce a modified land reform in pursuance of one of their most cherished aims, the ending of feudalism. Land ownings were reduced to 200 acres, a holding large enough to bring in a comfortable income but a mere particle of some of the larger estates. It was the death blow to the ex-pasha politicians. Aly Maher resigned and Neguib became Prime Minister. The revolutionaries could now lengthen their stride.

Neguib spent the autumn months in exposing the corrupt practices of the parties, with the Wafd his main target, and in December he abolished the constituion, dissolved the political parties and confiscated their funds. Swift arrests of influential party members and the cashiering of 450 senior army officers bared the neck for this mighty sweep of the axe, made in violation of the inaugural proclamation of July 23, and the victims' squeals had no power of penetration, partly because of their own manifest failings, partly because of Neguib's propaganda campaign, in which he had beaten Nahas pointless, and partly because the Free Officers were still in fragile alliance with the Moslem Brotherhood. In January 1953 Neguib told the people of the new constitution which had been formulated on their behalf. For the next three years at any rate power would be exercised by a Congress. This sounded cosy enough, but it was soon revealed that power within the Congress was vested in the Revolutionary Command Council, consisting of Neguib and twelve young officers who were officially presented to the public for the first time. Neguib had been usurping rather more of the limelight than intended.

For another six months these men still incongruously owed allegiance to King Fuad in his Italian nursery. Then, in mid-June, the final act of severance was done: the monarchy was declared at an end and Neguib became both President and Prime Minister. Major Hakim Amer, Nasser's vacant-faced but staunchly loyal henchman, jumped to Commander-in-Chief, with the rank of major-general, while Major Salah Salem, who like his brother, Wing Commander Gamal Salem, combined a taste for buffoonery with contempt for discretion, bounced nearer the centre of the stage as Minister of National Guidance. Less prominent publicly, but of greater power within, were Nasser's shrewd adviser, Captain Aly Sabry, and the sinister figure of Colonel Zakaria Mohieddin. Nasser himself was raised to Deputy Prime Minister, but he already held the post of Minister of the Interior, always the seat of power in Egypt, and this he did not let go.

Members of the British Embassy did their very best to get on friendly terms with Egypt's new leaders. The old pasha politicians may have hurled invective at Britain in public but they always had a happy personal relationship with the Embassy officials, spiced with inconsequential touches of humour, and for those few British advisers who still served them they showed both trust and affection. Indeed, this blend of personal friendship and political antagonism had deep roots in Egypt, and the former acted, and was still to act, as a safety valve when the political temper ran high. At governmental level, as between the Junta and the Embassy, the relationship now was formal and rigid. There was little social contact, little sharing of jokes. The Egyptians were on the defensive, most of all to any Englishman who could speak Arabic.

This was not so remarkable. The young officers, so long conditioned to the separateness of conspiracy, were very conscious of the mighty responsibilities they had grabbed and inevitably showed the touchiness that accompanies accelerated promotion, which in their case took the form of a bound of absurd proportions, from command of a few hundred men or some aircraft to the control of a ministry of state. They did not want to be patronized, and above all they were determined to remain free of the taint of corruption, the removal of which had provided their crusade with its main driving force. In their view nothing had such power to corrupt as the British handshake, the evil influence behind the old regime.

CHAPTER FIFTEEN

Evacuation

(1953–6)

No sooner had Neguib become Prime Minister of Egypt than he applied himself to the eternal problem which had caused such heartbreak to all his predecessors, the removal of the British from Egypt and the Sudan. The Sudan was dear to him, and he had the great wisdom to treat it as a separate issue, taking advantage as he could of freedom from pressure either by the King or the masses. Eden had made clear his determination to advance the Sudan to self-government under the scheme in which Egypt had refused to participate. Neguib realized that only by participation could Egypt acquire any influence in the land of his birth. He renounced claim to the kingdom of the Sudan, had talks with the leader of the British-groomed Umma Party, who amazingly was a son of the Mahdi, Sir Sayed Abdul Rahman, and on February 6 reached agreement with the British Government, under which the two countries shared responsibility for supervising the coming elections and the subsequent transfer of power.

Egypt stretched her concept of supervision to blatant electioneering for her own candidates and their cause of union with their sisterland of the Nile. Britain was reviled and every clumsy ploy was used to woo the simple Sudanese, such as the comic capers of Salem which earned him the name of the Dancing Major. Protests were soon flying fast; but the principle of partnership, formally declared under the 1899 Treaty, had for the first time become accepted fact, and one of the twin boulders blocking the course of Anglo-Egyptian relations had at last been reduced.

The other boulder remained jagged and firm. Like Morrison before him, Eden offered withdrawal subject to the maintenance of an emergency base and Egyptian participation in a Middle East defence organization. The United States were to co-operate, their pockets bulging with attractive offerings, and were to join the negotiations. But Neguib said no. He would negotiate only with the British and insisted on getting agreement on evacuation before the problem of joint defence of the canal was discussed. The Americans, whose aid Eden had been so keen to enlist, were no help at all. They exasperated the British by supporting the Egyptian demand for unconditional evacuation, and by their patronage of the Egyptians they aroused more suspicion than affection. It was no help that their Ambassador, Jefferson Caffery, was of Irish extraction and a proud kinsman of the drafter of the American Declaration of Independence. Negotiations ground to a halt early in May before they had really got in motion. Nasser declared that he would "pull down the pillars of the temple". But the terrorist campaign was not re-opened.

Eden now fell ill with internal trouble, and Churchill assumed direction of the Foreign Office. Referring to the breakdown of negotiations, he made slighting remarks in the Commons about General "Nee-gwib" and in repeating them in the course of a broadcast to the nation he drew many a chuckle from the ex-army legions for whom Egypt's leaders would always be figures of fun. Churchill regarded Egypt virtually as a colony. The thought of evacuation pained him, but he boldly faced the facts, and the facts were that the occupation of the Canal Zone was bedevilling relations with Egypt, tying down troops that should be forming a mobile strategic reserve, jeopardizing army recruitment by the unpopularity of service there, and causing the Government exorbitant expense. It was in the interests of the soldiers themselves, more than anyone else, to make a dignified departure, and it seemed likely that Egypt's military rulers would as soon treat with men of their own profession as with diplomats. Churchill had already recognized this by bringing Field Marshal Sir William Slim into the negotiations that had broken down.

He tried again within a month. The Commander-in-Chief of the Middle East, General Sir Brian Robertson—a man with radical views on Britain's strategic requirements—was in London for the Coronation, and Churchill called him into conference and appointed him special delegate in Cairo to assist the Ambassador, Sir

Ralph Stevenson, in new negotiations. The military plan for re-deployment envisaged the transfer to Cyprus of the Middle East Command, with the continued use of the Canal Zone installations for maintenance and emergency purposes. Churchill asked only that the base should remain under military control.

After formal preliminaries, attended by Neguib, negotiations were conducted privately in a villa lent to Robertson in Cairo, with Egypt represented by Nasser and members of the Junta, and Robin Hankey, the *chargé d'affaires*, taking the place of Stevenson, who retired home on sick leave. Robertson was impressed by Nasser; he found him friendly, reasonable, calm and of calibre which dwarfed his colleagues. Great strides were made, but after more than three months of progress it all ended in frustration once again. A mere pebble caused the collapse, the question of identity and all it means to national pride. The Egyptians agreed that a skeleton organiza-tion might be retained, with the right of re-entry under certain circumstances, but insisted that the base formed part of Egypt and must bear no mark of a foreign power. The British Government insisted for their part that their soldier-technicians must have some form of emblem, even if only a badge on their overalls and a flag at their headquarters, as token of their loyalties and reminder that they were still subject to military discipline.

Control of Egyptian affairs was meanwhile slipping from Neguib's grasp. Following the abolition of the Monarchy in mid-June, the property of the entire royal family was confiscated, bring-ing many millions to the Exchequer, and in September revolu-tionary courts were set up. Having drawn up their own charges and rules of evidence, they indulged in the ritual of public trials designed to bring home the wickedness of the former regime to a people always as eager to boo the loser as to cheer the winner, and in particular to transfer any blame which the Army might have incurred for the defeat in Palestine firmly on to the shoulders of the ex-King and his corrupt Ministers. Among those who received harsh sentences were ex-Prime Minister Hady (for his fearless sup-pression of the Moslem Brotherhood after the Palestine War), Nahas's wife Zeinab Wakil, Serag El Din, and many members of the royal entourage, one of whom was thrown in chains. There were no executions. Nasser's aversion to bloodshed still held good.

Neguib was unhappy. He had not wanted these trials, the crudity of which offended his sense of justice. But though he was President of the Republic, Prime Minister of Egypt, and acknowledged Leader of the Revolution, the only technical means of power at his disposal was his single vote on the Revolutionary Command Council, and this of course was of no value whatever when all twelve of the "boys", his fellow revolutionary councillors, voted the other way. His potential power was very much greater. So popular had he made himself in the country that he had become imbued with a sense of mission, seeing himself as the saviour father for whom the whole of Egypt yearned, and it was to combat this personality cult that the Free Officers had shed their anonymity and thrust themselves into the public gaze as ministers of guidance and welfare, and so on. These ardent military zealots, whose earnest dedication seemed so alien to the shambling, easy-going Egyptian scene, could never rival the cosy, paternal appeal of their chief. There was danger that the instrument they had so cynically taken up—"We had constructed a legend around him. . . . We did not wish to explain that he was simply a puppet," Sadat points out in his book—might be used against them. Wafd, Moslem Brotherhood and Communists were growing increasingly restless, and all saw in the patronage of Neguib their only hope of gaining power. There was friction, too, within the Revolutionary Council itself.

Crisis came on February 23, 1954. Thwarted in his desire to reshape the constitution on a wider, more representative basis, Neguib tendered his resignation to the Council with expressions of goodwill and thanks for past services. It was accepted and he was placed under guard in his house. Next day the cavalry officers at Abbassia barracks prepared their men for revolt, under the somewhat incongruous instigation of the Communist member of the Council, Major Khaled Mohieddin, cousin of Zakaria. Nasser harangued them but nonetheless accepted their demands and promised to make Mohieddin Prime Minister and reinstate Neguib as President. Instead he had himself made Prime Minister and Mohieddin exiled, the cavalry officers having been temporarily subdued by Amer, the Commander-in-Chief, and Neguib was in due course released from custody and reinstated as President in the manner of a puppet. A vast gathering of the Moslem Brotherhood, Wafdists and Communists made their disapproval of this arrangement apparent in characteristic style. Neguib promised them that parliamentary government would soon be restored.

On March 1, Neguib and his outspoken critic Salem went to Khartoum, where their presence caused such violent commotion that they had speedily to return. Nasser had meanwhile been busy. He made sweeping arrests of cavalry officers and party leaders, while alerting his own revolutionary party, the Liberation Rally, which as the name implies was organized on Nazi lines. With true Machiavellian instinct, he gave Neguib the rope to hang himself on his return. At a banquet held in his honour, Neguib expanded on his promise of a return to parliamentary rule. The Council, with touching meekness, accepted his lead and announced in effect that the revolutionary regime would come to an end on July 24. Now, as politicians grown rusty in the art practised their histrionics and editors set loose opinions long bottled up, the Liberation Rally came into action with trade-union support. A national strike was organized, and soldiers and policemen marched in mass protest against the abandonment of the great cause. The people had spoken and Nasser of course had to obey. On April 17 he had himself reinstated as Prime Minister, having handed the job back to Neguib, and the Council happily declared the continuation of the Revolution and with cruel severity silenced re-emergent parties and press. Neguib carried on as President but there could be no disguise now of his puppet's role.

Nasser's long climb to dictator was complete at last, bringing him the power to which Arabi was said (probably unfairly) to have aspired. There is close affinity between the two men in their character, background, driving impulse and means at their disposal, but Nasser had immeasurable advantage in his patient cunning, in the circumstances of a discredited monarchy and the disinclination of foreign powers to intervene. He also had wider and more precise ambition. A devoted student of national history, he was deeply conscious of the humiliation Egypt had endured not only during the British occupation but in the 1,900 years of slavery that had gone before. Ardently pan-Islamic, he was just as conscious of the humiliation endured by the whole of the Arab world. He would burst "the shackles of history" with a bang, those binding Egypt as represented by the continued British occupation, those binding Islam as represented by the unrecognized state of Israel. All this is evident from his writing. And the discontent at home, the seething resentment of the Brotherhood and political parties, the continuation of primeval poverty, and shortage of food for an ever expanding population, gave classic urge to his military ambition.

To achieve his first objective, the removal of the British forces, Nasser employed an effective, if brazen, mixture of concession and duress. In the face of considerable opposition within the Junta, he agreed to allow the British re-entry in the event of an attack not only on an Arab country but also on Turkey, and to hasten their departure he set loose the thugs again early in the new year, 1954. Murder lurked round every corner, and although less disruption was caused than in 1951–2 wearisome restrictions had to be observed as the price of survival, and irksome watch maintained on property. It was a testing time for tempers, and there were many who yearned for tough retaliatory action when an old Egyptian retainer of the British forces, who had been earning pocket-money from R.A.F. Intelligence, was tried for treason after a year in the cells of a Cairo jail and hanged on the day following conviction. Nasser had tired of his self-imposed ban on bloodshed.

Political opinion in Britain hardened to a mood of determined obduracy against Nasser and his gangster methods, combined as they were with a vicious propaganda campaign in Arab and East African countries. But Britain's top soldiers could see no future in maintaining a peacetime station continually under a state of siege, and whatever the feelings among the Government's supporters, the Cabinet—Eden in particular—fully appreciated the soldiers' views. There was a political factor even more compelling than the military ones. The 1936 Treaty was due for revision in 1956, and the British would then be illegal occupants, liable to unconditional eviction.

Stevenson returned from sick leave in January 1954 and with the aid of another soldier picked for his knowledge of Egypt, Major-General E. R. ("Lofty") Benson, he kept a channel of negotiation quietly open. At the end of May Nasser called a halt to his campaign of violence, thus opening the door for Britain's final concession. It had been decided now that instead of soldiers, civilians should man the base installations, bearing no mark of their nationality: a point that might have saved lives, rage and anguish if it had been conceded earlier on. Junction point at last! Negotiations went ahead at a gallop and on July 27 Antony Head, Secretary of State for War, initialled the Heads of Agreement in Cairo, thus emphasizing the Army's part. (The Egyptians would not have it called a treaty because of the distasteful association the word had for them.)

Nasser had on the surface given almost as much as he received. He had accepted a thing despised by every nationalist in the Middle East: obligation not only to Britain but to the N.A.T.O. alliance.

Egypt was to remain an arsenal for British arms (which would of course afford employment for Egyptians) and Britain had the right to place it on a war footing "in the event of an armed attack" on Turkey, as well as any country of the Arab League—and this, in view of Communist pressure, was a very considerable concession. It would have been hard for the old politicians to have accepted such a commitment in face of agitation by a hostile press and the mob hysteria it could provoke. Nasser, having the freedom which dictators enjoy, had these agencies well under control. The doubt from the British viewpoint was the value of his word. So far his personal charm had allayed such doubt. General Glubb Pasha had yet to write, "He is delightfully frank and sincere in appearance, but is nearly always telling lies", and in those midsummer days of 1954 such words would have been regarded as outrageous. Yet there were those who could point to the evidence of the days when Egyptians last had control of their own destiny and quote from the Second Book of Kings (XVIII, 21), where Egypt is described as a staff, "on which if a man lean, it will go into his hand, and pierce it".

Indication of Nasser's cynicism was to be found in another heading, under which Egypt expressed determination to uphold the 1888 Convention guaranteeing the freedom of the Canal. She still refused it to Israel and since September 1951 had stood condemned, on Britain's initiative, by the Security Council and had remained indifferent to such august stricture. Israel was deprived of her cargoes, and so eager was Britain to reach agreement over her base that she was prepared to condone Egyptian defiance, even though it affected her economy quite as much as Israel's.

There could be no concealing this weakness, and from Eden's point of view it made the task of obtaining parliamentary ratification all the harder. The die-hard Tories needed stronger persuasion of the case for withdrawal than was provided by the Egyptians' manifest ability to make life unbearable for the occupying troops. They had been nettled by a typical and highly pertinent indiscretion by the dancing Major Salem when he publicly stated, "We cannot fight in Palestine with the British lurking behind our backs." The thwarting of such obvious ambition appeared to justify the retention of troops in the Canal Zone, whatever the hardship and cost.

Again the military came to the Government's aid. A report by the Chiefs of Staff Committee, which has never been made public, called for strategic reappraisal. The hydrogen bomb was invoked, the horror of which was still in process of revelation. Such was its power that the entire Canal could be devastated at a single drop, and it was for this reason that the Middle East Command had to be moved to an older base, the peaceful and apparently sleepy (though equally vulnerable) island of Cyprus, which was handily placed for the despatch of aid to the treaty countries of Jordan and Iraq. Thus, as a time-honoured cornerstone of Imperial strategy, the Suez Canal was made obsolete at a stroke of the pen. It was an argument that could just as well have been used nine years previously, since the less pretentious atom bomb could cause sufficient havoc to block the Canal for months, and it made nonsense of the case for re-activating the base at a moment of crisis, thus increasing the attraction of the Canal as a target for a hydrogen bomb.

However, the Chiefs of Staff had spoken, and the Prime Minister used their report as his principal weapon to dragoon his wavering ranks when the agreement was debated in the House of Commons on July 29. It was a painful day for the Conservative Party. Twenty-eight Members had issued a statement a fortnight earlier, declaring their resolve to "vote against any treaty with Egypt which involved the withdrawal of all fighting troops from the Suez Canal area" and they sat grim and obdurate as the War Minister, having come post-haste from Cairo, suavely presented the Government's case. He did not speak only of the H-bomb. He stressed the importance of Turkey's entry into N.A.T.O., which in fact restored the shield on which Britain had relied to protect her route to India against Russian encroachment in the days before her occupation of Egypt, and of course with its reinforcement by American obligation the shield was stronger than it had ever been before—at least, against direct attack. Head also touched briefly on the crux of the matter, the drain on manpower and the tying-down of reserves caused by the occupation of Egypt.

Attlee followed. The Opposition could not very well oppose an agreement which they had themselves repeatedly tried to bring about, and Attlee therefore concentrated on stinging Churchill with his own words—"Things are built up with great labour and cast away with great shame and folly"—and with grim relish, and to the delight of his followers, pointing to the "immense difference between the Prime Minister in office and the Prime Minister in Opposition". The tormented one retaliated with looks of thunder.

Attlee did not neglect the Government's failure to eradicate Egypt's default of the Suez Canal Convention (which he had himself referred to the United Nations) and with words that belie his party alignment he unwittingly emphasized the difference between his own line as Prime Minister and Opposition leader: "When on this side of the House we asked, we were told that this is a matter for the United Nations and not for us. But this is our great imperial lifeline."

The jabs were replaced by bludgeon blows when Captain Charles Waterhouse, leader of the Suez rebels, rose to speak. These great traditionalists felt a sense of bereavement; it was as though the Empire had been murdered by the severance of her jugular vein. (Empire—or Commonwealth—still featured more prominently in discussion than the more vital issue of oil supply.) But though emotion may have clouded their eyes to strategic realities, they could see danger clearly enough. They were aghast at the haste with which the agreement had been signed and the frailty of the safeguards, and they were deeply concerned about the immediate consequences of withdrawal. "This is not a sell-out. It is a give-away," said Waterhouse, and later, "We have handed over £500,000,000 worth of stores and buildings to the Egyptians [a great exaggeration, based on out-of-date figures] and if they like to use them against Israel or against anyone, who is going to say 'No, you will not'?"

Churchill, sombre in demeanour, took no part in the debate except to intervene when a Labour Member most unjustly accused him of encouraging "the back-bench cabal . . . under the table". As his anger turned to reasoned gravity he silenced the House by falling back on the H-bomb and pointing out "how utterly out of proportion the Suez Canal and the position we hold in Egypt are to the appalling developments and the appalling spectacles which imagination raises before us". Eden, on the other hand, spoke with buoyant optimism of his "act of faith" when he wound up for the Government. "It is politically sound because it enables us to re-establish conditions of friendship with all the Arab lands, without losing our friendship with Israel. No one can say how it will work out, but I want the House to say plainly to Egypt that we are going to enter the new era with a real determination to try to make it successful."

The House duly gave its verdict, but with no great display of determination. The rebels voted as they had vowed, and only six

Labour Members voted with the Government. The remainder abstained.

There were still many points of detail to be decided and for more than two months the negotiating teams were hard at work in Cairo, where Stevenson and Benson were joined by a tall young politician newly promoted within the Foreign Office to Minister of State, Anthony Nutting. Some installations, such as all nine of the airfields, Navy House, Port Said, and the headquarters barracks at Moascar, were to be handed over to the Egyptians without obligation; others were to be maintained by them on the understanding that they would be made available for the British in an emergency; and the others were to be kept active by British civilian firms, and consisted primarily of the workshops at Tel-el-Kebir, which was to remain the repair centre for the Middle East Command, an ordnance depot there containing maintenance stores, and various depots around Fayid and Ismailia containing petrol, ammunition and the means of providing camps with light and water. Most of the work went into the preparation of a programme for the withdrawal and hand-over, to be completed within twenty months of the final signing; most of the dispute into the question of cost and the allotment of quarters to the civilian staff. There was some tough bargaining, but the atmosphere was friendly and, with the one side as eager to find solutions as the other, differences were soon moulded into agreement. The British shared with their Egyptian colleagues the invigorating sense of standing on the threshold of a new era—as indeed they were!—and were in no mood to pay heed to grating noises from Israel, whose Prime Minister, Moshe Sharett, described the pending agreement as "an abandonment of Israel to her fate, as if she had no place among the countries of the Middle East".

Israel indeed had no place in the new arrangement. Not only was she excluded from those countries on which an armed attack gave Britain the right to re-activate her base, but by a special annexure Britain was also denied this right if Israel herself attacked one of the protected countries. Egypt, in other words, was free to deal with such a situation as she chose—which did not exactly tally with Eden's claim that he was re-establishing friendship with the Arab countries "without losing our friendship with Israel". He hoped, however, that the United States might show approval of the British withdrawal by exerting increasing influence to bring Jew and Arab nearer peace. Anyway, Israel was protected under the

Tripartite Declaration, and it seemed absurd at that stage to suppose that she should have any fear of the armies she had in her
infancy so triumphantly defied.

Rather as if to deflate the importance of the occasion and the
Egyptian's overweening pride, the British Government sent no
senior Minister out for the signing ceremony which took place,
after some anxious last-minute delays, in the Egyptian Parliament
House on the evening of October 19. Nasser signed and Nutting
signed, the one dressed in British-style khaki drill bush-shirt and
attended by his dashing young colleagues similarly attired, the
other (like his colleagues) in sober lounge-suit. There was a
dazzlement of camera flashlights and hearty handshakes all round,
then fireworks in the open and the roar of the crowd. It was such
contrast to 1936, and it is not so surprising that Eden should shrink
from attending a ceremony which was bound to lack the stately
dignity that marked the culmination of his former great *détente*. "I
am delighted," he nonetheless told Nasser in a personal message,
and Nasser for his part told his followers, "The ugly page in Anglo-
Egyptian relations has been turned and another page is being
written. British prestige and position in the Middle East has been
strengthened. There is now no reason why Britain and Egypt
should not work constructively together."

To the British negotiators in the hour of triumph, Nasser spoke
with disarming candour about the handicap imposed on himself
and his colleagues by their inexperience in the affairs of state. They
were simple officers, of the Army or Air Force, and their first duty
was to the men who had borne them into power. These men
needed arms, and could not the British increase their allotment?
The answer was a polite no. The British people, it was explained,
were not keen to send arms from the country when there was a
danger that they might be used against their own soldiers, sent to
the aid of Israel.

Exactly a week later six shots rang out at a Liberation Rally
meeting at Alexandria. They were aimed at Nasser as he stood
speaking on the platform under the spotlights, and they all missed.
With the shooter removed, he calmly continued, winning fresh
adoration from the faithful, and even as he spoke his police were at
work. The Moslem Brotherhood, with all its Communist associates, was incarcerated root and branch, and four of its members
were hanged (which was the same number as for the never-
forgotten Denshawi affair of 1906, in which at least murder was

done and injury inflicted). There could be no one to protest now if Neguib were removed, and on November 14 he was placed in detention in a villa just outside Cairo. Nasser obediently awaited the command of the people before accepting the Presidency some eighteen months later. All were made to vote and there was only one candidate.

Eden was now nearing the end of his third term as Foreign Secretary. Never had his serene and polished professionalism won such rich reward. All the entangled residue of war seemed to fall apart at his magical touch. In Europe, Trieste was freed from the clutch of Tito after a decade of dispute, and Austria was placed well on the road to a treaty that would entail the withdrawal of Russian troops. Egypt had been turned from an irate rebel into an accomplice, if not an ally, in the N.A.T.O. alliance, and Iran had miraculously been recovered to the fold of friendship. In the Far East the rebels had been vanquished in Malaysia, peace with honour had come to Korea, and South Vietnam had been rescued from the debris of French Indo-China at the Geneva conference table, where the deft diplomacy of Eden, co-chairman with Molotov, so exposed the bludgeon tactics of Secretary of State Foster G. Dulles that this man of low tact and high principle left the conference in a huff.

Eden was made Knight of the Garter, the highest honour the Queen could bestow and a rare distinction indeed for a man whose career was still in full flow. The office of Prime Minister was nearly ready for his undisputed inheritance from his friend and admirer, Sir Winston Churchill, and in the meantime Eden, the Foreign Secretary, achieved one further triumph, as it was hailed at the time. Containment of Russian expansion by an extension of the N.A.T.O. alliance had long formed one of his aims, and he was delighted when Nuri, Prime Minister of Iraq, made a defensive pact with the new member of N.A.T.O., Turkey. Eden took the chance to visit Nuri on his return from a flight to Bangkok, and on March 30, 1955, he announced to the House of Commons that Britain was joining the Baghdad Pact with Turkey and Iraq. Pakistan and Iran were soon to follow her example, forming a continuous defensive belt from the Mediterranean to the Himalayas. The Bear enchained!

On the way out to Bangkok Eden gave dinner to Nasser at the British Embassy in Cairo. He was much impressed by his fine physique, his friendliness and his readiness to support the West, but was unable to convince him of the wisdom of the Turco-Iraqi pact, which Nasser described both as ill-timed and ill-designed to further the cause of collaboration between the West and the Arab countries. Eden ascribed his opposition to jealousy and "a frustrated desire to lead the Arab world". He did not regard his founder plan for the Arab League and his more recent one, embodied in the Baghdad Pact, as incompatible, nor does he seem to have appreciated that the outlook of the young nationalist Nasser was bound to be very different from that of Nuri, who belonged to a country that had not smarted under British domination and to a generation prepared to accept British leadership.

According to testimony given his biographer, which may have been coloured by after-events, Nasser was incensed by the pomposity of this dinner party and by his host's air of superiority. He was enraged by the Baghdad Pact, cutting as it did across his dearest ambitions, and Cairo Radio blared forth its opposition in very different terms from those expressed personally to Eden, swiftly rousing hatred. Though shaky and discredited as an alliance, the Arab League still had emotional appeal which admirably suited Nasser's purpose. He would lead it into ever closer unity, and the essence of his plan, and indeed the great attraction of the League to its members, was its independence from commitment to the power groups either of West or East.

No sooner had Eden left Cairo than fresh fuel was added to the reviving embers of conflict. Raids across Israel's frontiers had been a regular occurrence ever since the signing of the armistice agreements, but they were launched for the most part from Jordan and Syria. Egypt's principal contribution lay in her power of blockade which she exerted not only at the mouth of the Suez Canal but at that of the Gulf of Akaba, where she constructed gun emplacements and effectively blocked the passage of ships to the Israeli port of Elath. On the frontier around Gaza she indulged in spasmodic hostilities without maintaining large concentrations of troops. It was here, however, on February 28, that the Israelis launched a savage reprisal raid, in which they seized an Egyptian fort and killed thirty-eight Egyptian soldiers. It announced the return of Ben Gurion, brought back from retirement to meet the new threat created by Britain's withdrawal, and for Nasser it sounded fresh clarions of challenge.

One result was the formation of the fedayin—the self-sacrificers

13

—made of the mixture of criminals and patriots who had won their spurs with the Arab Liberation Army and sharpened them against the British in the Canal Zone. A second was of even greater importance: the Regular Army called more shrilly for weapons. More tanks, guns and aircraft had to be provided than would ever be eked out of the Western powers, with their inhibitions under their Tripartite Declaration, favourable to Egypt though the proportion normally was. Their meanness was duly reported to Dimitri Shepilov, editor of *Pravda*, when he came to Alexandria for the July revolutionary celebrations. He listened attentively. He knew that Nasser had recently been to the Bandung conference, where he was eagerly patronized by Nehru and Chou-en-Lai, and he may have guessed that the latter, too, had made offers of arms. Here was his chance, and the wonder was that it had not been seized before, with all its potential for endangering peace.

A deal was rapidly arranged with Czecho-Slovakia (who had so generously supplied Israel at her hour of greatest need). Though it was announced in September, its size and delivery dates remained secrets. There were enough tanks on order to equip an outsize armoured division, enough ammunition for a European campaign, and enough aircraft—120 M.I.G. fighters and 50 Ilyushin bombers —to turn the cities of Israel into dust, and destroyers, minesweepers, submarines and radar equipment besides. And to instruct the eager but inexpert Egyptians in the use not only of the military machines but of factory and agricultural ones too, Russian technicians, mostly Arab-speaking, began to stream into the mysterious Land of Paradox. The Bear had calmly stepped beyond the Baghdad line without resort to fighting, and the naïve Western powers were baffled and distressed.

Jordan, the twin kingdom of Iraq—each was allotted to a son of the Sherif Hussein of Mecca and was still under treaty alliance with Britain—now became the target of rival advances, brash and subversive by Nasser, correct and tactless by Britain, under the auspices of her new Foreign Secretary, Harold Macmillan. Jordan expressed willingness to join the Baghdad Pact, coupled with the hope of an increase in British aid which already amounted to an annual £10,000,000. Since military matters predominated the C.I.G.S., General Sir Gerald Templer, suppressor of the Malayan rebellion, was sent out in December to arrange terms. It was bad psychology. Templer was at pains to point out that he came merely as a plenipotentiary, but plain clothes could not disguise the soldier, and Nasser portrayed the move as an arrant, atavistic attempt at military domination. Radio Cairo yelled its fevered protest—it was all a trick to aid Israel—the nationalist bull bellowed, and with the Government wavering, the young King Hussein, grandson of Abdulla (who had been murdered), turned to a new Prime Minister for the decision he so much desired. Wild rioting broke out in Amman, conducted in person by the Egyptian military attaché. The King was forced to give way; Jordan, it was announced, would not join the Baghdad Pact.

Soon afterwards, in January 1956, Russian tanks, said to be the massive Joseph Stalins, lumbered into position on the Egyptian side of the Sinai frontier. There had been great increase in activity during the previous months. Fedayin gangster bands roamed across Israel from Gaza to Jerusalem, murdering innocents as opportunity offered, and the Israelis struck back, less frequently but more lethally, with occasional, well-planned raids. The United Nations observers, there to enforce the armistice agreements, industriously made report and protest. But this latest apparition cast a new and sinister shadow across the jumpy wastes of the frontier, calling for stronger deterrent than report.

Dag Hammarskjold, Secretary General of the United Nations, therefore visited both Egypt and Israel. Nasser was all charm, blandly denying that he had any aggressive intent against Israel and promising to withdraw his troops back from the frontier if Israel did the same. Ben Gurion, on the other hand, was as blunt and rugged in manner as in shape. He refused to retreat from a key frontier position because he did not believe that the Egyptians would do the same, whatever they might say. Such lack of faith, expressed so uncouthly, was painful to poor Mr. Hammarskjold.

One of Nasser's next visitors to Cairo, of which there was never any shortage, was Britain's new Foreign Secretary, Selwyn Lloyd. He was entertained to dinner at Abdin Palace and it was during this meal, on March 1, that Nasser contradicted a remark Lloyd made about Glubb Pasha's influence in Jordan to tell him, with obvious relish, that Glubb had been dismissed. It was a victory, as King Hussein has admitted, for propaganda from Cairo which had skilfully portrayed the once revered father figure as the evil influence behind the throne, making it a "hated tool of British imperialism". Hussein had to act to save himself, and it was not to Nasser's advantage that Glubb should go, providing as he did such fertile soil for subversion against a royal regime. Nonetheless it was chastening evidence, to British eyes, of Nasser's power to undermine, and Lloyd had further experience of it when he went on to Bahrein to be greeted by rioters yelling rage against Britain. It was from this point, it seems, that Nasser was placed on a par with Mussolini in high places, and for the Prime Minister, Sir Anthony Eden, the most aggravating aspect of reappraisal was surely the taunting, told-you-so look in the eyes of Waterhouse and his rebels.

The one streak of light through a gloomy horizon was lit by the friendly co-operation which the Egyptians accorded not only to the retreating British soldiers but also to the civilians who replaced them. The troops withdrew quite unmolested. The Grenadiers were the last fighting unit to leave, having spent the night on the Port Said golf-course, and as related at the start of this book the administrative rearguard sailed bashfully away at dawn on June 13, six days before the agreed twenty months expired.

About seven hundred employees (out of a permitted total of eight hundred) of ten different firms had come out to run the depots, with aid from a further 1,200 workers enrolled locally. Many of these "contractors", as they were rather inaccurately termed, were ex-servicemen, and all had handbooks telling them to respect Egyptian customs, be liberal with their tips, and avoid wearing khaki drill clothing, "so as to emphasize your civilian status". The top executives (thanks to pressure by the British negotiating team) lived with their families in smart villas in Moascar, the remainder in Kensington Village, Fayid or at Tel-el-Kebir. The Egyptian authorities did their very best to please, and there was good co-operation between the Egyptian Police and the contractors' private force, which included some Egyptian officers. Thefts from the workshops at Tel-el-Kebir, which had caused the British Army such anguish, subsided to the merest trickle. Yet apart from the workshops, which were kept busy enough with work from Cyprus and other stations, the installations and encampments had a ghost-like air about them, almost as of a museum. And indeed they had virtually become museum pieces, for it was hard to imagine circumstances under which the soldiers might be invited back.

CHAPTER SIXTEEN

Outrage

(1956)

ALL AUTHORITARIAN REGIMES are irresistibly drawn to military display as a means of stimulating the zeal of their people, impressing the world and inadvertently exhibiting the inferiority complex which provides the motive force for acts of conquest. Sometimes armies are maintained for this primary purpose of making the streets of the capital ring with applause—as was admitted by the President of Syria when his British military adviser mentioned the irrelevant problem of battlefield maintenance during the brief care-free days before the Palestine War. On other occasions the very might of the parading army evokes suspicion that it has other functions to fulfil.

Such a suspicion took forceful hold of the attachés, journalists and observers who watched the inevitable parade in celebration of the final departure of the British, held in Cairo on June 20. For four hours the troops marched past the multi-beflagged dais, the tanks rumbled by with impressive precision, the Valentines, Centurions and French light tanks providing the overture to, and emphasizing the strength of, the top-billed and deliriously welcomed stars, the Joseph Stalins, and overhead flew waves of Russian aircraft. It was an impressive display of strength, whether the drivers were Egyptian or not, and equally impressive was the evidence of Nasser's influence over his jealous Arab friends, for with the significant exception of Iraq, every member country of the Arab League was proudly represented on parade.

Quite as sinister (from the Western viewpoint) as this boastful manifestation of might was the bustling presence of Shepilov, who, now promoted Foreign Minister of Russia, held the stage as the most cosseted guest at the celebratory banqueting, self-congratulation and ebullience which lasted almost a week. He came, he announced on arrival, from "the land of Socialism, the country which totally repudiates the policy of colonial expansion, the country whose economic structure has no place for oil monopolies that suck the vitality of the less-developed nations", and wherever Nasser went this bumptious champion of the Arab cause was bound to be at his side. Russia had openly cast herself in the role of mother plentiful, and to the *Times* correspondent Shepilov gave some details of the offers he had made "with hands free and bountiful". Egypt, if she wished, could have a loan of $1,200,000,000, at a most generous interest rate, and was in addition free to sell the surplus of her cotton crop for transferable sterling. What he did not add, though news of it was leaking through, was that to obtain arms from the Communist countries Egypt had already mortgaged her cotton crop for many years ahead.

Britain might also have been represented by her Foreign Secretary, but the Government were more in the mood to snub than to patronize and the invitation was passed on to General Robertson, who accepted with reluctance. (It did not originate as a personal invitation from Nasser.) He was little in evidence and though he played his part with dignity the right-wing press in Britain expressed the view that it would have been more dignified if he had stayed at home. As little attention was paid to Britain in the endless speeches that were made. Nasser, in his one reference, condescendingly conceded that she had fulfilled her obligations, and added both with patronage and menace: "We have no aggressive intentions towards her. But we shall be hostile to those who are hostile to us, and peaceful to those who are peaceful to us." This was tantamount to saying woe to those who interfere on behalf of Israel, and a *Times* leader showed realistic foreboding by quoting "a senior administrator": "The Army rules Egypt . . . Many a fire-eater wants war."

It was known by now that the delivery of arms from the Communist countries was three times as large as had at first been imagined and that Syria was receiving a consignment too. British military intelligence was sceptical of the Egyptians' ability to put their new equipment to effective use, yet it was nonetheless an alarming situation. The weapons could be needed for one purpose only, and sooner or later Egypt was going to be forced by her own chauvinism to lead her allies against the common foe, with infinitely greater offensive power than they had previously possessed, and quite probably with Russian backing too. If Israel called for aid under the Tripartite Declaration, Britain stood to lose very much more than her two allies. Not only would cherished alliances be in jeopardy but her oil supply as well.

Perusal of Nasser's book *Egypt's Liberation* added gloom to such brooding. It had caused little stir when published over a year earlier, but it was now being likened to Hitler's *Mein Kampf*. Those who have studied the two books regard the comparison as absurdly facile. Yet it is true that Nasser in his book envisages a role of leadership for Egypt in the three connected circles of the Arab, Moslem and African communities, and he was daily providing evidence that the type of leadership he had in mind was of the bombastic, imperialist type.

He was also displaying the same taste for ostentation (though not for corruption) which had brought the old spendthrift Khedive Ismail tumbling down. America, not France, was now the model. Skyscrapers rose up in Cairo, incongruously advertising the glory of the pan-Islamic officials they housed, and great roads were being built, on which the limousines provided for visiting kings, presidents and plenipotentiaries could develop their full speed. All this, and the mighty armaments too, could be provided partly from the vast bounty acquired by confiscation, most of all from the Khedival family, and partly because favour, not financial gain, provided the motive for advance of credit, and with suitors vying for favour from East and West the credit came in spate. Such glorious competition would have delighted the heart of old Ismail.

Yet people cannot be fed entirely on a diet of promises and exhibitionism, and the time was at hand for Nasser to make a dramatic stroke, with true Ismailian flourish, that would silence the undercurrent of muttering and bring prosperity both to industry and the land, produce from which lagged sadly behind the rise in population, which now stood at 22,000,000, having doubled itself in the last fifty years. He would build a mighty dam at Aswan which would make the existing ones, built under British inspiration, appear mere breakwaters in comparison. The project had for long been under consideration and it had been tentatively agreed in January that an initial loan of $270,000,000 should be advanced,

$56,000,000 by the United States, $14,000,000 by Britain, and the remainder by the World Bank. Egypt, however, objected to the terms of the offer, one of which was that the Communist countries should not contribute, and negotiations degenerated into prickly and extended dispute.

The offer was finally withdrawn on July 19, abruptly, bluntly and entirely on the initiative of Secretary of State Dulles. He had become thoroughly disenchanted with Egypt. He had brought her aid with all the confidence of anti-colonial patronage, but instead of keeping the Communists away it had brought them custom. Egypt, it had been revealed, was in debt to them to the sensational tune of $450,000,000 for the arms she had ordered, and had many other commodities on order too, most of which could be put to warlike uses. It was hard to take the Aswan request seriously when the country's revenue for many years to come had already been squandered on arms, and it was certain that the grant would cause adverse comment at home in America, which with a Presidential election due in the autumn was not a thing to be heedlessly provoked. Even so, it seems quite probable that Dulles had not yet made up his mind, as one account asserts, until he saw Ahmed Hussein, the Egyptian Ambassador, on the morning of July 19. Hussein had just returned from consultation in Cairo and had publicly announced that Egypt had agreed to the terms of the loan. Dulles confronted him with the full list of his country's commitments with the Communists, whereupon Hussein brashly retorted that he had a firm offer from the Russians to finance the dam as well. This rasped Dulles where he was most sensitive. "Well, as you have the money already," he replied, "you don't need any from us. My offer is withdrawn!" Nasser had carried his game of courting competition one stage too far. The Russian offer had not as yet been made.

The communiqué issued by the State Department added sting to rebuff. "Developments have not been favourable to the success of the project," it stated, "and the adequacy of Egypt's resources to assure that success are more uncertain than at any time since the offer was made." It was a scathing indictment of profligacy that the conventional expressions for the welfare of the people of Egypt could not tone down.

Britain followed suit next day, as curtly announced by a Foreign Office spokesman: "We have concluded that in present circumstances it would not be feasible to participate in the project." Eden states in his memoirs that he had no option, since the three offers were interdependent. He thought it a pity that the American rejection should have been so abrupt, but fully agreed with it in principle, mainly because of the envy the loan would arouse among the Arab countries he counted as friends. "Already the Iraqui Government were complaining that the Egyptians had done better out of the West by bullying than by co-operating." After all the years of co-operation with Egypt over developments of this nature, it marked the end of an epoch even more starkly than the evacuation of the troops, and the manner of the ending seemed specially calculated to give offence. It is significant that no critical question about the withdrawal of the offer was asked in the Commons, not a word of protest raised. Nasser had cut himself off from his British friends.

Nasser learned of Dulles's rebuff just as he returned to Cairo, in company with President Nehru, after a state visit to Marshal Tito. There is little doubt that he had foreseen that the loan might not be forthcoming; he had made his plans but had not yet decided how to put them into effect. The manner of refusal fashioned that of reprisal. Nasser would deliver slap for slap. Full ownership of the Suez Canal had always been an ambition of the revolutionaries, had in fact been the most natural aspiration of all Egyptians. Some amends had already been made for Ismail's squandering, which for years had denied Egypt a piastre of the Canal Company's swelling profits. By various stages of negotiation Egypt had gained some seats on the board of management and a share of the profits, and since Nasser came to power he had with some success been pressing hard for an increase of the Egyptian share, both in influence, benefit and operation, particularly in the matter of pilots. The Canal would fall into Egypt's lap, to be run as she chose, when the company's concession ended in 1968, and there was no reason why she should not acquire full control, as part of the policy of nationalization to which she was as entitled as inclined, well before that date. So long as the transfer was tactfully and gradually handled, there could be no complaint by the users of the Canal. Nasser had in fact taken full possession of the Domain Commune, the canalside territory owned jointly by Egypt and the Canal Company, even before the British evacuation was complete, and because there had been no accompanying trumpet call this act of nationalization had passed unnoticed.

Now it was to be different. For a week Nasser hurled abuse at

America and vainly tried to jostle the Russians into making a clear-cut promise that they would provide the money to finance the dam. Now came July 26, anniversary of the revolution and top day in the calendar for the outpour of emotion. Alexandria was the chosen scene, traditional saucepan of racialist passion, and all the ingredients were prepared as if by the hand of a master chef trained in the Nazi school of *haute cuisine*. The searchlights blazed (for night was chosen), the flags flew, the ranks were marshalled and the cheer leaders bellowed their applause.

Nasser had little natural flair for demagogy. His early speeches had been too earnest, in the manner of Arabi, and lacking the flourish to arouse much fervour. But he was an ardent self-improver, and gradually he developed the pauses, the gestures, and the falsetto crescendo that transports a simple audience into a state of delirium. Tonight he gave a virtuoso performance, reminding one observer of "a daemonic sorcerer conjuring up from the bowels of the earth the legions of hate and fury". For over two hours the inferiority complex of a people perpetually under the commercial domination of foreigners was whetted and nourished by a hackneyed recital of the cunning of imperialism, of its attempts to shatter Arab nationalism by the creation of the state of Israel, "stooge of imperialism . . . vanguard of imperialism", of the width of the battle that Egypt was fighting for the Arab world—this was the recurring theme—and of the brave deeds that had been done "to render the British force—88,000 strong in the Canal Zone—not only unable to defend the Middle East or the Canal, but even to defend itself". Having treated the United States, Britain and the World Bank to individual chastisement for their parts in the rejection of the loan, he turned to the Canal and the 120,000 Egyptians who he claimed died in the process of building it "for an usurping company . . . who sucked our blood and stole our rights". On and on his phrases rolled, like waves smiting the sea front. "Americans, may you choke in your fury! . . . We shall build the High Dam as we desire. The Canal company annually takes £35 million. Why shouldn't we take it ourselves? . . . The Suez Canal was one of the façades of oppression, extortion and humiliation. Today, O citizens, the Suez Canal has been nationalized . . . and it will be run by Egyptians, Egyptians, Egyptians!"

The people swayed and yelled in hysteria of delight. Defiance was their favourite wine and Nasser had filled their cup to overflowing. Never had there been such cause for inebriation. Only five weeks ago they had been celebrating the departure of the cur-dogs with tails between their legs, and now here were the full fruits of deliverance. Egypt at last was true mistress of her destiny.

Even as Nasser spoke, the act of seizure was effected, and with most un-Egyptian speed, co-ordination and decision. It was the work of Major Mahmoud Yunes, a former army engineer who had once been Nasser's commanding officer. He sat in Moascar listening to the broadcast and at mention of the grasping de Les-seps parties of soldiers simultaneously rushed into the company's offices at Cairo, Port Said, Ismailia and Suez, brandishing tommy-guns in the face of startled officials. With them came engineers briefed by Yunes for the task of organization which he had spent many months studying. It was the gangster grab, so reminiscent in its stage management of those deceased master gangsters of Europe.

Eden was at the time dining in Downing Street with King Feisal of Iraq and his Prime Minister Nuri, hardened absorber of Nasser's vitriol. For both host and guests there was as much to hearten in the news, when fully digested, as to shock. Surely Nasser had over-played his hand at last. He had spoken so much about Arab unity, riding high on the prestige that accrued from his severance of the bonds of British occupation, and yet now he had committed a brazen act, which might affect all his Arab allies, without consult-ing one of them. The advice tendered by Nuri was that so long as Israel was kept out of the controversy there would be no complaint from Iraq against any measures deemed necessary to humble the delinquent.

Eden learned next day that the French, who were much incensed with Nasser's championing of the rebel cause in Algeria, were just as appreciative of the opportunity to strike down the common enemy, and he derived further encouragement from the Oppo-sition benches in the House of Commons. Hugh Gaitskell, their leader, deeply deplored "this high-handed and totally unjustifiable step by the Egyptian Government", and another Labour Member, R. T. Paget, pointed to the similarity of "the technique which we got used to in Hitler's day" and spoke of "the consequences of not answering force with force until it is too late".

Gaitskell himself took up this theme when the matter was debated the following Thursday, August 2, before the adjournment for the summer recess. "The pattern", he said, "is very familiar. It is exactly the same that we have encountered from Mussolini and tler in those years before the war". (Admittedly he concluded with words of homage to Britain's obligations under the United Nations' Charter, having agreed that the use of force should not be ruled out, but the tone of his speech was set by his former words.) Eden had for several months been struck by the comparison, and Herbert Morrison won him a further debating point by vehemently denying, in response to a left-wing claim, that "what the pocket dictator in Cairo had done had any resemblance with the orthodox beliefs of the Labour Party on the process of nationalization".

Earlier Eden had vaguely pointed the way ahead in a manner, for which he had a gift, evocative of the inexorable majesty of the Thames flowing past Windsor Castle. He spoke of the need for "firmness and care" and told the House how "in view of the uncertain situation created by the action of the Egyptian Government, Her Majesty's Government have thought it necessary—and I wanted to take the first opportunity to tell the House—to take certain precautionary measures of a military nature". A proclamation for the recall of selected reservists was signed by the Queen at Arundel, where she was staying for Goodwood races, and—shades of 1882—the Life Guards were among the units reported to be on their way to battle stations while Members of Parliament set out for their holidays. As if in the days of Palmerston, the might of Britain seemed to be sailing for its rendezvous with destiny, causing scarce a ripple on the water, while the nation applauded wholeheartedly and the world watched expectantly, approvingly, with even Russia issuing no more than a belated, mildly worded broadcast warning. Nasser had dug himself a pit, and it only remained to tip him into it.

CHAPTER SEVENTEEN

Plans Frustrated

(1956)

ONE OF THE busiest men at the War Office was the Director of Plans. It was his job to prepare for every emergency which the Chiefs of Staff thought fit to guard against, from a rising in Northern Ireland to the invasion of Hongkong. But there was no plan for the reoccupation of the Canal Zone. Although Nasser's act of seizure should have been easy to foresee, the Army was not ready. It did not occur to the service chiefs that, having at last achieved their long-cherished withdrawal, they might be required to force a re-entry.

Plans, however, now had to be made, and on the very morning following the theft Eden personally ordered his Chiefs of Staff to prepare for military intervention, should it be proved necessary as a last resort. Eager collaborators were at hand in the French. Emotional patriotism ran high in France, just as it had done at the time of Arabi's revolt, and it is a strange coincidence that both Arabi and Nasser should have brought Egypt to the forefront of world politics when the national pride of France was at the same stage of recuperation after defeat in war. Like Gambetta, Guy Mollet, the Prime Minister, had won distinction as a resistance leader, and so had his two tough and determined colleagues, Christian Pineau, the Foreign Minister, and Maurice Bourgés-Maunoury, Minister of Defence. Like Gambetta, too, these men were eager to bustle the British into joint military intervention in Egypt, and they had the great advantage which he did not enjoy of having behind them a nation united in its resolve to strike. Cairo

Radio had been smiting France as hard as Britain, and Cairo itself openly and proudly harboured the seat of government of the Algerian rebels. Nasser had, in deed if not in word, declared himself at war with France.

The British were as usual disinclined to be bustled. Eden was concerned about world opinion, and in particular the opinion of the Arab states, which was of such greater importance to him than to the French. He proposed that all the nations that used the Canal should be summoned to a conference and there make combined condemnation of Egypt's crime, backed by which Britain and France should have resort to military measures if the mere threat of them were insufficient to make Nasser retract. The French distrusted world opinion, but they were bound to agree. They too were in no position to mount a quick operation and could not in any case do so without use of the Cyprus base. Possession of this base, combined with the dominant part she had played in Egypt and her greater reliance on the Canal, automatically put Britain in the position of senior partner, and France was obliged to concede to Britain command of the combined invasion force that they agreed to prepare. It was a decision that the French were to rue, but with unity of command an established and unquestionable principle it was a case of Hobson's choice.

American representatives were also early brought into consultation, and on July 30 Dulles himself arrived in London, having cut short a visit to Peru. After three days in conference the three Foreign Secretaries issued a joint statement which gave a forceful impression of united resolve. "The arbitrary and unilateral seizure by one nation of an international waterway" was condemned as being far beyond the sovereign rights of any nation, and a users' conference was announced, to be held in London on August 16 with the object of restoring the Canal to international control. What of course was not revealed was the wide divergence of view as to how the final aim should be attained. The French were all for rushing in to recover the stolen property, which they regarded as their own, with minimum formality; the British were willing enough to carry out punishment but not until the full course of justice had been run, and seen to be run, and the criminal offered every chance to repent; the Americans shuddered at the prospect of enforcement and made it clear that they would not be involved if they could help it, but they could not deny that it might eventually be necessary. By his lavish expressions of indignation, and of the need to make Nasser "disgorge the Canal", Dulles made some amends for the immediate American reaction, the coolness of which had worried and perplexed Eden. Having promoted the crisis by his rude rejection of the loan, it was incumbent on Dulles to protest at its consequence, but he privately admitted his amazement at the passion it had aroused. "I just can't understand why you people are willing to risk so much for the sake of this damn canal," he told Pineau.

Within a week of the seizure the first staff officers arrived in London, hastily summoned from various regiments and headquarters, to make the first "appreciation of the situation" in the approved military style. They met in the oppressive atmosphere of the tunnelled catacomb under the Thames, entered through the Ministry of Defence, which had formerly been used by the War Cabinet. They wore civilian clothes of course and hid their activities beneath the weird and not inappropriate code-name of Terrapin, the American-Indian name for a turtle. Initially they were lost within the massive network of cabins and passages, but Parkinson's Law rapidly asserted itself and the headquarters grew and grew until there were over a hundred British Army officers on its staff, not to mention their French, naval and air force colleagues. The plans they produced showed the same capacity for increase, both in number and detail.

Hard on the heels of the pioneer planners Lieutenant-General Sir Hugh Stockwell arrived from Germany to take command. Elegant of build, and with a volatile, bluff-gruff personality, he had been brought up in the Royal Welch Fusiliers and had an infantryman's understanding of the common soldier. He was not regarded as one of the great brains of the Army but he had an endearing way about him which was to prove a valuable harmonizing agency between allies who took a different view of the situation. The French land-force commander, General de Beaufre, was appointed deputy to Stockwell. Calm and urbane, he was well endowed with tact, and he needed it all, since his Government, convinced that the British overestimated the ability of the Egyptians, were always urging speed and daring.

Powerful forces were put at the disposal of the planners, indicating a very natural reluctance to take risk. The British made available the 3rd Infantry Division and two tank regiments in England, the weak 10th Armoured Division in Libya, and the 16th Independent Parachute Brigade and the 3rd Commando

Brigade, both of which had two thirds of their strength deployed in Cyprus, while the French could provide a powerful airborne division, the 10th Aéroportée, and a mechanized division, the 7th Mécanique Rapide, from Europe and Algeria. The Egyptians had ten active infantry brigades and two armoured ones (with a third forming) available, half of which were deployed on the Israeli border, and they also had a numerically strong territorial force, the National Guard, and various irregular units. They had many more tanks and anti-tank guns than the allies could hope to concentrate with any speed and they had great potential strength in the air, to combat which the French quietly removed aircraft from their N.A.T.O. commitment to reinforce the powerful striking force that the British were assembling. At sea the allies could muster monumental strength, topped by the superstructure of an old French battleship, the *Jean Bart*, and with swarms of carrier-borne aircraft overhead.

When they turned to launching equipment, the planners were confronted with a daunting poverty of material. Like the armoured battle after the 1914 war, the combined operation was an art which the British had mastered but had since neglected under pressure of the compelling problems of a world half at peace, half at war, darkened by the sombre menace of the nuclear bomb. All but a handful of the old landing craft had been cast away and no new ones built, transport aircraft for the paratroops were in pitifully small supply and out-of-date, being side- not back-loaded, and worst of all, the old know-how had decayed. No one had had recent experience in the preparation of loading, marshalling and movement tables on the scale required, and the task on hand was one to exasperate even the most experienced planner. The commandeering of ships had to await their availability and there were scant records of their hold capacities for military purposes. Peacetime loading regulations, laid down both by the Board of Trade and individual insurance companies, gave further cause for exasperation unknown to the wartime experts.

Another drawback was the inadequacy of Cyprus as a base. Only from here could a quick blow be struck, either by seaborne or airborne troops, but Cyprus had been allowed to lie fallow since the days it had been acquired for this very purpose. The only real port, the ancient one of Famagusta, had very limited berthing space, and the other harbours were mere open roadsteads, vulnerable to onslaught by gale and lacking facilities for vehicle loading. The political climate gave further discouragement to the concentration of large forces. No sooner had the Middle East Command been established there than it was inflicted with the same type of trouble as had obliged it to move from Egypt. EOKA opened their terrorist campaign in 1954 and soon the strategic reserve was fully committed to the protection of its own homestead. To assemble an assault force there, with all the requisitioning it would entail, would further inflame the passions of a proud people.

This factor made Malta, with its well-developed facilities, all the more tempting as a base and the 16th Commando Brigade were moved there from Cyprus, where they eventually formed the sea-borne spearhead in company with the 6th Royal Tanks. But there could be no substitute for Cyprus as an air-base, lying as it does 900 miles east of Malta and 250 miles north of the Egyptian coast. Nicosia was the only operational aerodrome initially, but by urgent endeavour full runways were built at Akrotiri and Tymbou, the latter of which was offered to the French and accepted with exuberant alacrity.

Cyprus also seemed the obvious place from which to direct the assault, and on August 11 General Sir Charles Keightley, C-in-C. of the Middle East—a former cavalryman, big, bland and imperturbable, who had begun his tenure of command in Egypt and acquired respect for the Egyptian Army and the dedicated young officers in control—was appointed Supreme Commander of the forces that were being prepared. This arrangement made for cohesion, in that land, sea and air task force commanders now had an overlord, but it created further problems of control, since London, Paris, Cyprus, Malta and Algeria all contained important centres of command. Keightley set up his own headquarters in London and remained there until plans were firm. He too had a French deputy, the small and jovial Admiral Barjot, who tirelessly flitted from centre to centre, pollinating brains with fresh and imaginative ideas.

The first plan considered was a direct assault through Port Said to achieve the task laid down in the politicians' directive, "occupation of the Suez Canal Zone for an indefinite period". This was quickly rejected, for reasons which were to be proved sound, and adopted instead as a cover plan. One reason was the difficulty of breaking out from Port Said along the 25-mile causeway through Lake Manzala; another, the lack of berthing space; another, the likelihood that the Egyptians would block the Canal; and another,

14

the danger of their cutting off the water supply through the Sweet
Water Canal. It was therefore decided that Egypt itself must be the
objective and plans were made for an invasion from Libya. This
plan—Hamilcar to the British, Amilcar to the French—was discarded through doubt of the co-operation of Libya, who, however
scornful of Nasser, would not relish the role of traitor to the Arab
world, and there were also doubts about the ability of the tanks of
the 10th Armoured Division to stand up to the 800-mile journey
into Egypt without support from tank transporters.

A much more spectacular plan, bearing mark of its begetters'
sense of daring in its code-name "Musketeer", was therefore
adopted. The commandos were to smash straight into Alexandria
harbour, on the western side of the city, in conjunction with parachute landings designed to seize the short causeway south-west of
the city and open up the desert road to Cairo from which it leads.
Led by its two tank battalions, the 3rd Infantry Division would
then break out with all possible speed. The strongest concentration of Egyptian armour was around Giza and it was hoped that it
would come out to refight the Battle of the Pyramids in the clean,
open desert. The Nile would then be crossed with the aid of a
further parachute landing, and the troops would dash through
Cairo and make a two-pronged drive for Suez and Ismailia, and
thence on to Port Said. Such was the outline of a plan which
developed many permutations in detail, and inevitably became
more elaborate with each one, and ever heavier in its administrative accompaniments.

Politically, it was a plan of staggering audacity. Yet if force were
to be used this was the surest way to achieve swift and clean success;
indeed, the lesson emphasized by Britain's previous entries into
Egypt, in 1801, 1807 and 1882, is that Cairo is the key. Militarily, it
afforded far the best opportunity for rapid build-up and exploitation, though the prominent part assigned troops direct from
Britain precluded rapid implementation once the decision had been
made. There were two difficulties that may have been underesti-
mated. One was the clearance of Alexandria, both of foreign shipping from the harbour—there were American warships among
them which were unlikely to skelter seawards with the alacrity
shown when Admiral Seymour issued his warning in 1882—and
of guerrillas from the bridgehead, since there is endless scope for
infiltration in this city famed for the ferocity of its mob. The other
was the crossing of the Nile. Since the Palestine War the Egyptian

Army had employed German advisers, headed by the able General Farnbacher, who remained to advise on tactical matters while the Russians concentrated on the technical side. Farnbacher had no illusions about the prowess of the Egyptians, and if he could have persuaded them to withdraw their tanks across the Nile, rather than be caught with their backs against it like the Mamelukes, it can be guaranteed that the Russian technicians would have rendered eager assistance in the task of bridge demolition. It would have been a poser for Stockwell, stranded on the western bank.

But the greatest problem facing the soldiers, greater than fighting any battle, was the control and care of a hostile population twenty-two million strong. A great deal depended on the measure of the political success gained. Nasser had ground political opposition to dust, and with the Army firmly under his control apparently had no rival. Yet the Egyptians are a notoriously fickle people, and if retribution fell on Nasser for overleaping ambition he could descend overnight from hero to villain. A responsible leader might have come forward—Neguib, for instance, had all the qualifications required—and the promise of the swift withdrawal of the Anglo-French forces could have won him the wild acclaim of the people. Some such solution was the ardent hope not only of the Military Government team that was being assembled but of every officer in the force with experience of the Egyptian people.

On August 8 Eden made a broadcast to the nation. He spoke of Britain's reliance on the oil transported through the canal: "This is a matter of life and death to us all." He told how Nasser had responded to friendly advances with vicious propaganda assaults and broken faith, and echoing Gaitskell's words, "The pattern is familiar to many of us, my friends. We all know it is how Fascist Governments behave." He spoke confidently of the user nations and their combined influence. "We do not seek a solution by force, but by the broadest possible international agreement." But he added the stern warning: "We cannot agree that an act of plunder which threatens the livelihood of many nations will be allowed to succeed."

Eden was committed: Nasser must retract or fall. He spoke as the man who had stood out against Munich, and he spoke too as a man who needed to re-establish his reputation for firmness, for not only had the Suez rebels been sniping at him but he had been under criticism from many quarters for lack of leadership on the home front—the very goad which had driven so many of Egypt's leaders to rash deeds of daring in the international sphere. "There seemed one strong young figure standing up against long, dismal, drawling tides of drift and surrender," Churchill had written about Eden in the pre-war era. These words must inevitably have rung out their clarion call, made all the shriller perhaps by the suspicion that such famous praise might have been harder earned. Eden had after all been Foreign Secretary when Hitler committed his most punishable offence in reoccupying the Rhineland, and he had also been obliged to accept Mussolini's seizure of Abyssinia, despite the stranglehold that occupation of the Suez Canal gave Britain the power to exert. It must be proved now to Mussolini's imitator that the days of appeasement were ended.

Historical analogies set their own pitfall in that they can never be exact. Nasser resembled the Fascist dictators in many ways: in his hysterical rhetoric, his hateful propaganda and his sanctimonious pledges of good faith; but in appropriating the Canal Company he had merely ended a trade concession, which was embodied in no international treaty, and means of redress for the dispossessed shareholders, the British Government and thousands of individual Frenchmen, had already been taken by the freezing of Egyptian credit. Only if he held up shipping would he be in breach of international treaty, and this, by successful pressure on the company employees, he had successfully avoided doing. He had, of course, been selectively blocking shipping for years, proving that control depends on possession, not of the Canal Company, but of the ports at either end. The Tory Government had condoned the offence in their haste to get their troops away, and yet were now planning to send them back merely because Nasser had taken possession of the operating machinery. It became harder, as indignation subsided, for Eden publicly to justify this strange anomaly, except by pointing to the threat, as yet unfulfilled, that Egyptian capacity for mismanagement, financial extortion and mischief presented to those nations whose dependence on the Canal far exceeded her own.

In private, both to his Cabinet and by letter to President Eisenhower, Eden could give stronger reasons for his determination to humiliate Nasser. It was not so much the direct consequences of the act of seizure that he feared, as the next move ahead. By taking independent action, Nasser had jeopardized his standing in the Arab world; Nuri had already given Britain the go-ahead, subject to the proviso about Israel, and even King Saud, once Egypt's staunchest ally and financial promoter, was showing concern about the peril that faced his own country's economy as a result of Nasser's precipitate act. Yet if the crime went unpunished, after all the furore it had caused, Nasser's prestige would rocket. Young officer revolutions, which he was known to be preparing, would follow. They would then all turn on Israel, Britain would be forced to intervene, and for her pains be deprived of her oil supply, in all probability permanently, much to the joy of Russia. Whatever the risk now, the long-term one was infinitely greater; but this was a motive that could never be publicly explained, because it would defeat its own object in its inflammatory effect on those very Arab countries that had the power to cripple.

Unfortunately the Leader of the Opposition had become disenchanted with his own noted analogy between Nasser and the Fascists, and Eden was unable (if he really tried) to make him appreciate his secret motive. There was in any case singularly little ease of communication between the two men. They were similar in respects more likely to cause friction than harmony, having stiff, inhibited personalities, stubborn and proud, further tensed by their struggles to establish ascendancy as party leaders. Eden admits in his memoirs that he could make no headway with Gaitskell. "This was one of my failures . . . We never seemed able to get on."

Support for Nasser was quick to accumulate as soon as it was seen that the traffic was still flowing through the Canal. His great patron, President Nehru, made strong condemnation of the military measures taken by France and Britain and spoke of the great resentment they had aroused in those with "colonial memories", while Nasser himself, showing consummate skill as a tactician, no longer shrieked defiance, but calmly and with sweet reason spoke of Egypt's "sovereignty and dignity". He declined the invitation to participate in the users' conference, calling it a scheme for "collective colonialism", and yet at the same time he pledged his determination to maintain free navigation and his willingness to discuss means of co-operation with all interested parties.

Such expressions of reasonableness enabled left-wingers in Britain to heave the bulk of the Labour Party over to their side, aided by a press campaign in which such papers as the *Guardian* and *Mirror* exhorted the sanctity of the United Nations and raised the cry, "Britain must not go it alone". Gaitskell was constrained to point out that his speech in the Commons appeared to have been misleading, and on August 13 he issued a statement on behalf of his party that "apart from the continued stopping of Israeli ships, Colonel Nasser had not done anything which justified the use of armed force against Egypt". It was the start of a countermarch that daily gained momentum.

Representatives of twenty-two user nations came to London for the conference on August 16, Egypt being represented merely by an observer and Israel not at all, since her presence, to quote a French Embassy official, "would have only caused trouble". There was no great excitement. Eighteen supported Dulles's motion for the restoration of the Canal to international control, under financial terms favourable to Egypt, Russia and India being the main opponents. It was agreed that Robert Menzies, Prime Minister of Australia, should negotiate a settlement on these lines with Nasser, taking four other representatives with him. Nothing was said about enforcement, and indeed the subject scarcely seemed pertinent, so conciliatory was the tone, so frequent the references of respect for Egypt's "sovereignty and national dignity". The tension subsided. Wars did not begin with conferences, and most Englishmen turned their minds to more important matters, such as the Fifth Test at the Oval against the Australians.

Yet the soldiers seemed to be in earnest. They fired their weapons, marched, trained, packed, unpacked, drew equipment and handed it in again, and were to be seen all over England and Wales driving sand-coloured vehicles. A look of exasperation often showed itself on the faces of officers. They suffered many trials, caused sometimes by the closing of mobilization depots for the week-end, sometimes by lack of liaison between embarkation staffs and units, and sometimes by the overlapping of the operational chain of command with the static system through War Office, commands and districts, which was apt to result in the issue of conflicting orders. Vehicles often arrived at a port, with groaning springs, only to find the boats all full, as in the case of the tail-enders of a certain unit's convoy which were routed first to Plymouth, then to Liverpool and finally to Selsey, in Sussex, before they could find a berth. It was the start of a long period of separation between the men and their vehicles and equipment of war, some of which went on to Malta, awaiting shipment straight into battle, although not loaded with such a thought in mind, while others remained off the shore of Britain, tight packed aboard some tramp-ship at anchor in estuary or bay.

The mobilization of the armour, the key arm in the break-out from the bridgehead, caused the greatest tribulation. Although there were units ready for war in Germany, conscience demanded that full reliance be placed on those in England and these were quite unready for battle, being dispersed on various menial duties. (Initially the formation of a brigade headquarters was ordered but no sooner had its personnel assembled than it was decided that its regiments should come directly under divisional command, for allotment to infantry brigades.) Reservists had to be absorbed into tank crews, guns zeroed and special ammunition allotted for use against the mighty Joseph Stalins, before the Centurions of the 1st and 6th Royal Tanks were trundled to their ports in transporters supplied by Pickfords, working trade-union hours. Late instructions about waterproofing caused further confusion, and not until September 4 were the 6th Royal Tanks ready to sail for Malta, though intended operationally to follow up the 1st, which were still loading at Southampton.

Meanwhile the staff officers under the river grappled with their instructions, task tables and plans, burdened by a sure sense of foreboding that fresh alterations would be decreed from the summit to keep them busy every week-end—for reluctance to delegate was a failing of the Prime Minister, and the planners suffered from the close and fussy hold he maintained on the reins. As they emerged from their strip-lighted warren a strange Alice-in-Wonderland feeling of unreality (as one of them described it) assailed them. Here were Londoners unconcernedly going about their business, talking business gossip and searching the evening papers for racing results and cricket scores. Egypt seemed as far distant as the moon, war even further. Yet it was war they were preparing down below.

Fresh wonders were in store for the planners. No sooner had the final version of the Alexandria plan received Downing Street approval than they were told to switch to the one that had been discarded at such an early stage—the direct assault through Port Said to seize merely the line of the Canal. The political nerve (in London but not in Paris) had, it seems, weakened under pressure, and further there was evidence of a security leak, for the Egyptians had moved an armoured regiment to El Amiriya, the key objective of the paratroops commanding the south-west exit from Alexandria. Thus cover plan and real plan changed places, retaining the name of Musketeer, and with memories of Wolseley's crafty deception of Arabi, the planners hoped that the interest they had shown in Alexandria (and could sustain, if fulfilment came, by air activity) might similarly fox Nasser.

Doubt as to the exact political objective made the task of military planning no easier under the latest scheme, and it appears to have been from this stage that increasing faith was pinned by some in the air arm to achieve the submission that the direct thrust on Cairo would so swiftly bring about. The air offensive was an essential preliminary to any landing, first to knock out the opposing air force and then to incapacitate and demoralize the ground opposition, and certainly there were those who believed that it would be sufficient on its own. Though it is hard to establish how prevalent this belief was, it seems to have been held more strongly by those only indirectly concerned with the planning—a general of great importance at the War Office wrote across an appreciation submitted to him, "The wogs will pack in as soon as the first bomb falls; I am convinced of that", thus echoing an opinion long held of the Egyptian, despite such contrary evidence as the affair at the police-station, Ismailia. Keightley's commanders, both army and air force, were occupied more with realities than conjecture, but in order to carry the assault to the morale of the people, a Psychological Warfare team was formed and leaflets were printed, designed to make the Egyptian blood curdle. Their effect, of course, was bound to be influenced by the moral backing the world gave their intended recipients, and this was growing stronger every day.

Nasser agreed to receive Menzies' mission in Cairo on September 3. Egypt was making the most of the crisis. Citizens were being enrolled in the Liberation Army, and members of the National Guard and Auxiliary Police had been called up and were practising their skill at arms or evasion of duty, according to taste. Tanks rumbled to and fro, predominantly in a westwards direction to meet the British threat, and to maintain the enthusiasm of the people four British subjects were arrested and charged with espionage, to all the brash accompaniment of assumption of guilt. French nationals were recalled by their Government, and the British Embassy and the Suez Canal Contractors' Company evacuated their families and private firms were advised to do the same. Some did so. For the majority of British residents life carried on as usual, subject to such aggravations as the closing of Gezira golf-course for anti-parachute defence. Some sensed a certain air of unrest, and Nasser was freely criticized in private for leading the country into such peril.

Menzies' first meeting with Nasser gave him hope that the mere threat of force might win its dividend. When it was over he had a private chat with him and warned him that the British and French were in deadly earnest and that it would be wrong to suppose that they would not have the backing of the other user nations. Menzies believed that his words had considerable impact; Nasser was a worried man. Next day he had regained his buoyancy. A report had arrived of a press conference held by President Eisenhower in which he gave views already expressed to Eden, thus letting the world know of the chasm that divided the viewpoints of the two men. He told of his determination "to exhaust every possible, every feasible method of peaceful settlement . . . not to give up, even if we do run into obstacles". This proved Menzies wrong, and Nasser turned down the users' proposal, politely but quite without compromise, leaving Menzies to return grim-faced to London while Cairo Radio mocked him as "an Australian mule". Nasser at once sent a note to the United Nations, full of sober reasonableness, proposing that negotiations should at once be opened to solve the problems, including that of tolls, that so worried the Canal users. The cunning of the Egyptian was rivalled only by his nerve.

The next move should by rights have been to reconvene the users' conference and gain approval for the employment of the means that Britain and France had at their disposal to enforce acceptance of its original demands. But Eisenhower had virtually vetoed such a measure and now Dulles intervened further to divert Eden from his intended course. Glibly dismissing his own resolution, which the users had adopted for presentation by Menzies, as legally unsound, he proposed a counter plan whereby the Canal users should form their own club providing for an organization, complete with its own pilots, which would pass their ships through the Canal without aid or interference by the Egyptians. Eden saw it as a bait to land Nasser on the hook of obstructing free navigation and he presented the plan to the Commons, reassembled for an emergency debate on September 12, without realizing that he was himself swallowing the bait, attached to the American hook of inaction.

The interruptions that Eden encountered almost from the start of his speech emphasized the upsurge of emotion that had germinated since Parliament was last in session. Having explained the new users' club, he went on to say that "if the Egyptian Government should seek to interfere"—and amid cheers, groans and shouts of "Resign!"—"the British Government and others concerned will be free to take such further steps as may be required, either through the United Nations or by other means, for the assertion of their rights." At last, however, he reduced the House to silence by recalling the frustration met by the Labour Government when they referred the Abadan dispute to the Security Council.

The tone of Gaitskell's reply was so pacific, dwelling on the sanctity of the United Nations Charter, that a Conservative when his turn came, remarked that Parliament appeared to have been recalled "to enable the Leader of the Opposition to apologize to the House for making such a good speech on August 2". The pattern was hardening, with the ex-military men in the van on the Tory side and on the Labour side, far more militant, the pacifists, one of whom quoted a prediction made at the Trades Union Congress: "The nation will be roused to a deep, implacable, bitter anger such as has never been seen before if you take this country into an unnecessary war."

A more pertinent contribution from the Labour benches, neither sanctimonious nor emotional, came from Richard Crossman. He asked the Prime Minister to state clearly whether he still believed in negotiation with Nasser or aimed only to "topple him over", and pointed out that, if the latter, his method was having the opposite effect to the one intended. "Nasser is infinitely stronger in the Arab world," he said, pointing to a chastening truth, "because of the military posturing of Britain and France against him." But of course Crossman was quite confident that the posturing, which was making Nasser such a hero, would never materialize into a blow "because the Americans will not permit it".

The full weight of this second contention fell painfully on Eden's Government when the overnight news from America arrived next morning. Dulles had given jerk to his hook. Having given at a press conference the agreed statement about "such further steps as may be required", he deprived it of any meaning by saying that he knew nothing about a plan to shoot a way through. "We certainly have no intention of doing so . . . If we are met by force, we shall avoid it, that's all . . . The alternative for the United States is to send our vessels round the Cape."

Eden was stunned. The debate for him ended in personal humiliation which wounded so deeply that he wrote in his memoirs, "Such cynicism towards allies destroys true partnership." Yet

Dulles, in his clumsy and tactless manner, was saying no more than
Eisenhower had already said almost as tactlessly. Eden was well
aware of their allergy to force and should have known that with the
Presidential election drawing near they had no inhibitions about
giving it public expression at awkward moments. He was duped
more by his own optimism than by Dulles.

The soldiers were ready at last but opportunity was fast crumbling. However, there was one hope yet. Nasser had agreed to free
those pilots of the old Suez Canal Company who wished to resign
and there was to be a mass exodus on September 15, with many of
the old pilots hoping for enrolment with the users' club. Ten years'
training on the open sea and five in the Canal was said to be the
apprenticeship required, and such was the prospect of chaos that
Lloyds had (conveniently from Nasser's viewpoint) raised the
insurance premium by 15 per cent, with the result that many ships
were diverted round the Cape. Surely the user nations would
demand firm action now. But Nasser had a surprising card in his
hand—especially so for those who were ignorant of the fact that
only 40 per cent of the pilots on the company's books were French
or British. With Egyptian, Russian, Slav, Greek, German, Scan-
dinavian and American pilots at their helms, forty ships sailed
through on the day of test, four more than the daily average.
Sailors who had close knowledge of the problem were not at all
surprised, but many sages had been confidently predicting that
the Wogs could never do it, and for them and all who believed them
the explosion of this particular myth was perhaps the most humiliating feature of the entire crisis.

The representatives of the user nations came back to London
for another conference, but their enthusiasm had palpably waned
and the only course of action that had strong advocacy was reference of the problem to the United Nations. Eden's plan to
marshal the force of world opinion behind him had rebounded
against him, and the French were left to wring their hands in
frustration and remorse.

Surlily, and as if peevishly intent on proving the futility of such
a course, the British and French Governments referred the dispute
to the Security Council, deriving perhaps some grim consolation
from the disapproval of Dulles, who, seeing opportunity for Russia,
did not approve of such a move. On his arrival on October 5,
Selwyn Lloyd said that Britain had not discarded the possibility of
force as a last resort and then embarked on long private talks with

Hammarskjöld, Pineau and Egypt's Foreign Minister, Dr. Mahmoud Fawzi—a skilled waffler of the old Oriental school and an incongruous representative of the Revolutionary Government—which made that possibility seem ludicrously remote. Two resolutions were put to the vote on October 16. The first, laying down the principles for a settlement, was agreed unanimously; the second advocated the user nations' scheme for internationalization and was of course vetoed by Russia. It was agreed, however, that the British, French and Egyptian Foreign Ministers, having been brought together, should meet again to thrash out their differences. Ships continued to sail peacefully through the Canal, with no provocative insistence on cash toll payments by the Egyptians, and it seemed clear that the crisis had been suffocated beneath the weight of verbiage which had muffled the tom-toms long before the latter were fully ready for parade.

Yet the staff officers still fretted in their hide-away beneath the Thames, and the reservists—23,000 all told—waited vainly for release, occasionally making mutinous noises but displaying stoical philosophy in the main, and the tramps and transport ships creaked and strained against their moorings, placing even greater strain on the morale of the captive seamen and soldiers aboard. And as the tanks of the 1st Royal Tanks, the armoured cars of the Life Guards and the guns and vehicles of the 3rd Division rocked gently at their their offshore stations far spread around Britain's coast, their commanders turned anxious minds to such teasing problems as charging dormant batteries and preventing the pilfering of rations and stores.

And as October sluggishly sauntered towards November an enquiry from the Foreign Office reached Military Intelligence, asking how long it might take the Israelis to reach the Suez Canal if they made a sudden raid. Forty-eight hours was the verdict.

CHAPTER EIGHTEEN

Ultimatum

(1956)

GALLING THOUGH IT was for Eden to see opportunity slowly crumble beneath the weight of consultation, negotiation and tactless outburst, Israel found it even more painful to watch the process. The armies of the Arab League now had crushing power at their disposal, and along every mile of Israel's shallow land frontier they grimaced and made offensive gestures in eager anticipation of the promised day when the full assault would be renewed and vengeance gained for the humiliation of eight years back.

Egypt could bomb Israel to dust without fear of reprisal (for Israel had no bombers) and her tanks were strong enough to pound Israel's old Shermans to fragments; Jordan's army was four times as large as in 1948 and clothed in armour by British bounty; Iraq, Syria and Saudi Arabia had also been fast stocking their military cupboards, thanks to the combined munificence of Britain, Russia and America. Their ability to use their resources, especially in the case of Egypt, depended on the effect of outside training and the extent to which the assistants were prepared to turn aid to active, though occult, participation. This was a worrying imponderable. It was clear enough, however, that Egypt was preparing to renew the assault, whether or not with active assistance, and that each day's reprieve from retribution strengthened Nasser's influence over his allies and brought corresponding increase in fedayin activities, which placed stronger strain on the nerves of settlers than could be endured indefinitely. Israel was not the nation to wait passively for the blow to fall. She relied for survival on her fighting instinct, and her instinct told her to strike.

France was Israel's only ally. Both found common cause in their desire to overthrow Nasser, and the two countries were in close concert, unfettered by the inhibitions against giving offence to the Arab countries that so complicated British policy. Early in 1956 they made secret agreement, under which France shipped twice the amount of armaments to Israel that she declared to her N.A.T.O. allies.

As the Suez Canal crisis foundered in the bog of frustration, France's leaders came under strong criticism from a public more widely haunted by the spectre of Munich than in Britain. They therefore listened attentively when Shimon Peres, Director-General of Israel's Defence Ministry, made a proposition towards the end of September, having flown secretly to France with his Commander-in-Chief, Major-General Moshe Dayan, a youngish man of calm determination, gay serenity and good looks, the black patch over the eye he had lost on wartime service for Britain adding an appropriate air of romance. The Israeli Army was to attack Egypt on October 29: the French undertook to provide it protection in the air and at sea, and a joint planning staff was established in Paris. This, and details of the collaboration that followed, has been unashamedly revealed by the principal participants on the French and Israeli side, among them Ben Gurion, Mollet and Pineau, and the latter is claimed to have checked the account of their machinations compiled with their co-operation by Terence Robertson.

Eden was apprised of the plan, according to this account, when Pineau paid him a visit on October 3, just before going on to the United Nations to present the case for the internationalization of the Canal. The decision was made. France and Britain would jointly intervene. And a day or two later Eden was struck by a sudden and mysterious bout of fever: the first open protest, it transpired, by a stomach incapable of enduring nervous strain.

Fighting meanwhile flared up along Israel's sombre frontiers, strengthening her case for large-scale intervention but emphasizing the weird anomaly of Britain's position. It suited the Israeli purpose to draw attention to the menace from Jordan, and although fedayin murder gangs were just as active from Egyptian territory, it was against Jordan that the largest reprisal raid was directed, resulting in the destruction of a fedayin base during the course of fierce fighting on the night of October 10. Britain issued a sharp rebuke, giving warning that she would come to Jordan's aid, under her treaty obligations, if there were any further infringement of her territory. But Israel could claim provocation, of which she vigorously complained, and in which Britain, clumsily trying to play Nasser at his own game, was certainly an accomplice, if not the instigator. For the plan was to bring Iraqi troops into Jordan, although disallowed under the 1949 armistice agreement, in the hope that their presence might counter the influence of the pro-Nasser party at the coming parliamentary election, and Eden was quite as keen as Nuri that King Hussein should be persuaded to accept them. And as Britain strove for the cause of Jordan, France was flying fighter squadrons into the territory of her deadly enemy, Israel, staging them in Cyprus with the full connivance of the British.

Unappreciative of the Gilbertian niceties of the situation, the French hustled the British on to firmer decision. Thanks to the urging of his delegate, General Challe, who is reported to have found Eden still much preoccupied over the danger of an Israeli offensive against Jordan, Mollet persuaded him to meet him in Paris on October 16, two days earlier than previously planned. Here, in the ornate splendour of the Hotel Matignon, Mollet's official lodging, the two Prime Ministers determined the details of their combined intervention, in consultation only with their Foreign Secretaries. Eden insisted that it must take the form of an impartial parting of the two combatants with the object of freeing the Canal from the danger of their cross-fire. It was anticipated that the Israelis would be closing on the Canal by November 5, and operation Musketeer (revised version) was to be put into effect, with combined sea and air landings timed to go in on November 6, the day of the Presidential election in the United States. The ultimatum was not to be delivered until the Israelis had advanced far enough to imperil the Canal. Such is the gist of the account agreed by Pineau.

Military and Foreign Office staffs in Britain were soon made to realize that something was afoot, though for strangely different reasons. The soldiers, sailors and airmen of Keightley's combined headquarters at last left their hide-out beneath the Thames and flew to Cyprus, supposedly to carry out an exercise designed to test communications among the various components of the task forces. The Foreign Office, on the other hand, sensed crisis by the very lack of communication. Messages from France now went direct to Downing Street.

The drama mounted fast, both publicly and secretly. The results of the Jordan election, announced on October 22, gave Nasser another triumph over Eden. His adherents won strength enough in Parliament to put through their programme of the abrogation of the British treaty, union with Egypt and Syria, and war with Israel, and on October 25 Nasser's headstrong Commander-in-Chief, Hakim Amer, arrived in Amman and with hysterical clamour was declared Commander-in-Chief of the new unified command of Egypt, Syria and Jordan. "The time has come for the Arabs to choose the appropriate time to launch the assault for Israel's destruction," declared Jordan's Chief of Staff, Aly Abu Nuwar, ouster of Glubb and for long a protégé of Nasser, while from Cairo Nasser himself showed boastful jubilance, which was in marked contrast to the canny utterances he had been making before the threat of Anglo-French intervention apparently evaporated within the glass walls of the United Nations headquarters. "I have enormous forces at my disposal," he told a Lebanese journalist, "which make it impossible for any Power to stand against me."

As Nasser gloated, his arch-enemy Ben Gurion was being bundled, in the manner of Cleopatra in her carpet, into a villa at Sèvres, a suburb of Paris. He had come to obtain firm assurance of intervention and to tie up the final details of the plan. The appeal of this squat and shaggy old patriarch, so Churchillian in his rugged resolution, touched the hearts of the French. Nasser indeed had enormous forces at his disposal and if he acquired any aptitude at using them it meant death to the little democratic state of Israel, as Ben Gurion so eloquently pointed out; nothing else would satisfy the proud and impassioned Arabs and the ambition of their Egyptian leader. French chivalry was aroused as strongly as their own practical hostility to Nasser, which had received open declaration in the withdrawl of their Ambassador from Cairo as protest against a shipment of arms to Algeria, recently intercepted at sea. Mollet gave formal pledge.

Another visitor who flew secretly to this conference, according to Pineau's testimony, was Selwyn Lloyd. Pineau pressed that they should plainly state the cause of their intervention as the recovery of the stolen Canal. But Lloyd was not to be diverted. Britain could co-operate only under the pretext of separating the contestants and could afford to make no move that might indicate support for, or collaboration with, Israel. Since Britain's contribution included the all-important bombing of the Egyptian airfields, once the ultimatum had expired, Ben Gurion and Mollet were bound to agree to Lloyd's terms. A formal agreement was drawn up and signed the following day, October 24, by a Foreign Office under-secretary, Sir Patrick Dean, on behalf of Britain, since Lloyd had returned to London, where sensational news was streaming in from Hungary. The people of Budapest had arisen and were fighting Soviet tanks in the streets.

On Friday October 26 Eden gave his full Cabinet the information that Israel was about to mobilize. He outlined the measures he proposed to take in conjunction with the French if Israel should launch an attack on Egypt and endanger the Canal. Apparently they received general approval. Eden had a great reputation within his Cabinet as an expert on the Middle East and it had remained intact, since his failure as yet to discipline Nasser, as all had agreed he should, was blamed with considerable feeling on his American allies. Faith in his judgement was as strong an adhesive as traditional loyalty. Yet there was one hint that there might have been dissension within the inner circle responsible for detailed planning. Sir Walter Monckton, man of wide and liberal outlook, had recently been replaced as Minister of Defence by the War Minister, Antony Head. This, however, could be satisfactorily explained on the grounds of strain on an ageing physique, and of course Monckton remained in the Cabinet, taking the less exacting duties of Paymaster-General. The Ministers were going to march shoulder to shoulder, sublimely unaware (except perhaps for two or three) that there had been any plotting with Israel.

Ben Gurion returned to Israel on October 25, carrying inside him influenza germs caught in France, and as he did so men and women of Israel's territorial army—which forms the bulk of the national force—were summoned to arms by personal message, and a strange assortment of vehicles rumbled in to the report centres, their owners claiming their right to remain at the wheel, whether of military age or not. As civilians flowered ardently into soldiers and units headed for the Jordan frontier, news of the mobilization could no longer be concealed. Three times President Eisenhower cabled his concern, giving due warning of the consequences of aggression. Ben Gurion anxiously telephoned Mollet and, calmed by his reassurances, surrendered to the 'flu.

Contrary to the advice of their German adviser, General Farnbacher, the Egyptian forces in Sinai were concentrated in the forward zone. The Gaza strip contained the Egyptian 8th Division, of two ungainly brigades, National Guard and Palestinian, with various fedayin units under command, while the regular 3rd Division, of three infantry brigades and one armoured regiment, formed a supporting right-angular prop, from Rafah on the coast to the important pivot of Abu Ageila, 26 miles inland, covering the port and air-base of El Arish. Further south, the Desert Frontier Force garrisoned the odd village strong-point and provided mobile patrols, covering the approaches to Suez. The total troops in Sinai had apparently declined in number from around 45,000 to 30,000 as a result of Eden's military posturing, with the strongest drain on armour.

The armour had, however, begun to shift eastwards again. The "Russian brigade", the 1st Armoured—equipped with the medium T.34 tanks but not with the dreaded Joseph Stalins, which had not yet been made operational—had moved from the Pyramids to around Ismailia with the mechanized infantry brigade, with which it formed a vaunted, though scratch, armoured division. There was another armoured brigade at Kantara and an infantry one near Suez, both on the west bank of the Canal. There were three other infantry brigades and some untrained armoured units elsewhere in Egypt.

The Israelis' opening move was bold to the point of impudence. It was designed to rip open the Egyptian position, test reaction and establish a forward base for exploitation either to north, west or south. As the sun alighted on the horizon on Monday, October 29, Dakota aircraft flew low across the desert with a fighter escort zigzagging above them. (Though French planes joined the attack later, this opening blow was an all-Israeli effort, it seems.) A battalion floated down a few miles east of the Mitla Pass, which commands the approach to Suez. The aircraft returned to ferry in supplies. Without a shot being fired they had dropped their load almost into the mouth of the monster. Suez was 40 miles distant and so was the Egyptian aerodrome at Shallufa, and the other two para battalions, forming a relief column on wheels, had to come 130 miles along an uncouth desert track, interspersed by three strongly fortified positions, having already made a hectic journey from the Jordan frontier (as part of the cover plan) over ruinous going that took fearful toll of their vehicles.

This column managed nonetheless to cross the Egyptian frontier an hour or so ahead of their airborne colleagues, and with the setting sun behind them they swooped down on the first of their three strong-point objectives, riding jeeps and half-tracks, and captured it without loss. They reached the next at dawn next morning, after a hectic 40-mile journey. The position here covered a defile and was of great natural and artificial strength. The Israelis drove straight at it, killed sixty of its defenders, and put the rest to flight, at a loss to themselves of nine dead or wounded. They drove on more cautiously now, with anxious eyes towards the sky.

Another brigade of this amazing army, which has such an eccentric code of discipline, also went into the attack on the opening night. It consisted of territorials, and they had to make a ten-mile march through soft sand and attack the Kuseima position, 20 miles south-east of Abu Ageila, whence they would be as well placed to turn the flank of the main Egyptian position as to bring support to the paratroops. They encountered stiffer opposition, but captured their objectives just before dawn and an armoured column passed through. To the amazement of its commander, the Egyptians were found to have abandoned the formidable Daika Pass which led northwards towards the rear of the Abu Ageila position. It was a chance not to be missed.

Egyptian reaction was typically complacent. True, two battalions were ferried across the Canal, in accordance with plan, to reinforce the meagre detachment on the Mitla Pass, but no serious effort was made to destroy the paratroopers, who had not landed as near the mouth of the pass as intended and were in a most vulnerable position at daybreak. The mortar bombs fired at them and the odd, desultory air attack caused quite enough damage to emphasize their peril, and it was fortunate for the paratroops that their own aircraft, enlarging their target area, were able to smite the mechanized columns still toiling toward Mitla on the Tuesday afternoon—though perhaps not as destructively as they imagined.

Orders to send the three armoured and mechanized brigades across the Canal by the Firdan railway bridge or pontoon at Ismailia were not issued until Tuesday morning was well advanced, and although the move was carried out efficiently it had not been completed by midnight, with the leading elements still at least fifty miles short of the nearest battlefield. Cairo Radio was meanwhile telling the people, "We have annihilated the invasion forces." This of course exonerated General Amer's subordinate armies of Syria and Jordan from diversionary exertion, and not a bang was heard along their frontier lines.

Just before darkness on this Tuesday the relieving column of

Israeli paratroops, far bestraggled though they were by breakdown, attacked the last of the strong-points blocking their route, the old fortress village of Nakel on the Pilgrim's Way. Again they drove at it headlong, and again opposition collapsed, even though almost a battalion strong. Some four hours later, around ten o'clock, they reached their comrades in the fiery mouth of the Mitla Pass.

Just after the fall of Nakel, at around half-past six (local time), the terms of an ultimatum, issued jointly by the British and French Governments, reached Cairo and Tel Aviv from their Ambassadors in London. It required both sides to stop fighting and withdraw their forces ten miles from the Canal on either side. Egypt was temporarily to admit an Anglo-French force into the Canal Zone to ensure freedom of transit for the ships of all nations. An answer was required within twelve hours, and if either side refused to comply "British and French forces would intervene in such strength as would be necessary to ensure compliance".

Nasser had not expected this and he has claimed that he rapidly decided that it must be bluff—surely the British did not really mean to come back after all the trouble they had had when they had last been there. Around nine o'clock he handed a clear, categorical and defiant refusal to the British Ambassador, Sir Humphrey Trevelyan, who himself had had no prior indication that the ultimatum was coming. Nasser's manner was courteous, and Trevelyan was much struck by his air of calm confidence. The Russian and American Ambassadors were also summoned, but for a very different purpose.

The Government of Israel replied, without quite such alacrity, that they had the honour to accept the conditions and would take the necessary steps. They retained freedom of action, however, by adding, "In giving this undertaking it is assumed . . . that a positive response will have been also forthcoming from the Government of Egypt." If the assumption sounded cynical, Ben Gurion no doubt did not care.

Nasser could feel next morning that his confidence was well justified. Nothing happened. No declaration of war arrived, no bombers, no reports of invasion craft at sea. Defiance had won its dividend once again.

It had been a quiet night at the front, and now as dawn broke on Wednesday, October 31, it was Egypt's turn to strike a deadly blow. Whether or not the Russian technicians refused to take Egypt's Ilyushin bombers over Israel, the honour of piercing the homeland fell to the Navy, as represented by the destroyer *Ibrahim El Awal* (*née* H.M.S. *Cottesmore*). "Bombardment begun," she duly reported, "half of Haifa in flames; the oil refineries ablaze." But then, alas: "Under attack from a considerable force. We shall scuttle rather than surrender." Nasser made valedictory reply: "The name *Ibrahim El Awal* shall be written in letters of gold in the military history of Egypt."

The brothers Bromberger, those bustling French journalists who covered the allied operations and assiduously cross-examined every officer and man who would talk, claim that the attack was made by a modern French ship, the *Kersaint,* which chanced to be on the scene. Scuttling was attempted without success, and the *Ibrahim* was handed over to an Israeli torpedo-boat and towed into Haifa, with her unfortunate crew in their underpants ready to abandon ship. The inhabitants of Haifa deliriously acclaimed their prize, unaware that they had been the target of its guns. The shells had landed in the sea.

Egyptian counter-measures on land were no more successful. The diminished parachute brigade at the foot of the Mitla Pass should have been easy victims for the armour which for the last twenty-four hours had been crossing the Canal, at a point 80 miles distant. But no armour arrived, though reported moving, and as usual it was the Israelis who did the attacking, sending their half-tracks right through the first great defile with all guns blazing, while dismounted men made desperate efforts to prise Egyptians out of caves which they held with great determination. An Egyptian air strike, by Meteors and M.I.G.s, hurt the Israelis, and by nightfall they had suffered 160 casualties and were still not complete masters of the pass. Dog-tired, they dossed down where they fought and awoke next morning to find the Egyptians gone, having left 260 of their comrades dead in the caves. It was the first withdrawal of any significance to be made—but the paratroops, rather than the ultimatum, would appear to deserve the credit.

On the central sector the Israelis spent the Tuesday night in crossing the Daika Pass and at dawn an armoured group swept into the village of Abu Ageila, in rear of the Um Katef bastion. From here they could make little headway in some confused fighting, from which their effort was partially diverted by the need to guard their flank from a threat which also did not materialize. Having given up the quest for Mitla, the Egyptian "armoured division" had belatedly set off eastwards along the central road from Ismailia.

They were struck by a motley assortment of Mystères, Vampires, Mustangs and ageing M.I.G.s, and did not reach the Israeli Shermans waiting for them far inside the desert.

With darkness the bombs came down on two of Cairo's aerodromes, proving Nasser wrong. Warning had considerably been given by broadcast from Cyprus, but little heed had been paid and lights twinkled their defiance of black-out regulations to guide the Valiants and Canberras on to targets shrouded by thin layers of cloud. Egyptian aircraft were not the only casualties on the runways—and there were casualties too in a hospital next to Almaraz aerodrome, the one lapse from accuracy reliably reported. The bomber crews saw anti-aircraft shells bursting in the distance and also a lone fighter trying vainly to attain their height. Ilyushin bombers also took the air. They flew off to Luxor (where the bombs eventually reached them) from Cairo West aerodrome, which was spared from immediate attack, with the bombers diverted when already in the air, through fear of hitting a column of vehicles that was reported to be evacuating American refugees along the Alexandria road.

It was a bad night for Nasser's men. As the bombs fell around Cairo a new Israeli assault developed against the nodal point of Rafah, the coastal key to the Egyptian defences. All night through the men of four battalions and an armoured regiment grappled with mines and barbed wire, while the Egyptians, approximately in equal strength, pounded them with artillery, mortar and machine-gun fire. Midnight found the Israelis in sore need of respite—and it was brought with screams of fury by mighty shells from the opposite direction. The old French cruiser *Georges Leygues* was hurling in her block busters. Then, with the first streak of dawn, came the fighter-bombers. It was too much for the Egyptians. First on the right and then on the left the battalions yielded their great fortifications. By nine o'clock they were in full retreat. The Israelis had cut the base of the Gaza strip.

Around Abu Ageila, however, they had been repulsed. A fresh brigade had been brought up to assault the Um Ketaf position (also held by an Egyptian brigade) from the north-east and had rushed headlong in their half-tracks with headlights and machine-guns blazing. But the Egyptian field troops were not to be bemused by such tactics and every Israeli assault choked painfully out in the sand.

The air assault by Egypt's new enemies now developed full

momentum. From dawn onwards on this Thursday morning all eight of Egypt's operational airfields, around Cairo, Alexandria and the Canal Zone, came under non-stop assault from fighters and bombers, French and British, land-based and carrier-borne. Only now did Nasser order all units uncommitted in Sinai to come back across the Canal. Wisely recognizing that his capital was the key, he had resolved on a last brave stand around Cairo, and in the afternoon he interrupted the stream of fatuous claims churned out by his radio station—they were far wider of the truth than the ones that had so enraged him during the Palestine War—to make a personal exhortation which may have owed its inspiration to a British source. "We shall fight from village to village, from house to house. . . . We shall fight, fight, fight, and never surrender. I promise you, my brethren, I shall fight with you until the last drop of my blood." And to stir fire in the devout, in accordance with best tradition, a holy war against France and Britain was proclaimed from the Mosque Al Azhar.

It was also on this Thursday that the Russian tanks of the 1st Armoured Brigade at last came into action 100 miles down the Ismailia road, having not yet received orders to withdraw. The Israeli Super Shermans got in the first shot and knocked out eight T.34s without loss to themselves in a short, sharp fight which inevitably ended with the withdrawal of the Egyptians. Along the coast road meanwhile the Israeli progress was scarcely contested, until they reached the walls of El Arish, where they were halted for the night.

Surrounded for two days and fast running out of water, the gallant defenders of Um Katef slipped away when darkness fell. The order "sauve qui peut" was given, and with the Israelis not eager to take prisoners, escape was no problem for a man who had removed his boots (as fugitive Egyptians always prefer to do) and discarded his weapon. Most headed due west for Egypt and these unfortunates, who had fought the most bravely, died the most cruelly. They had no hope of reaching their beloved Delta and in the waterless desert they died the awful desert death, the lucky ones at the hands of cut-throat Bedouin, the remainder from thirst, crying with swollen tongues to the Israeli planes which occasionally circled over them, unable to ease their plight. It was a grim by-product of the dictator's ambition and of all his heartless propaganda designed to inspire fear and hatred of the Israeli, and the irony was that throughout their offensive the Israelis sought to prove their humanity by their restraint and punctillious observance of the rules of war. Out of a garrison estimated at three thousand, only seven hundred were fortunate enough to submit to the demonstration.

There was nothing to stop the Israelis now wherever they went. At dawn on the Friday, November 2, they drove at the mighty Gaza defences and in a few hours had forced the 8th Division into submission, fresh and unscarred though it was, and subdued all the Gaza strip except for one village held by Palestinians which did not capitulate until the following morning. Meanwhile El Arish had fallen, with all its workshops and ordnance depots, and, watched numbly by countless stragglers who had discarded uniform, arms and boots, the Israelis raced to within ten miles of Kantara, collecting 385 tanks and vehicles left by the roadside, often with engines running, by the sons of Nasser's pseudo-militaristic state. Only the 1st Armoured Brigade showed any fight. Though worsted in battle against the Israelis' Super Shermans, chivvied and battered from the air, and flummoxed by the desert sand, they at least clung to a rearguard position astride the Ismailia road until darkness allowed them to withdraw for the complicated task of recrossing the Canal, which Israel's observance of the ultimatum allowed them to do in comparative peace.

A vivid peep at the demoralization of the Egyptian Army was afforded an English doctor, on the staff of the Contractors' Company, who was impressed into service at a military hospital at Ismailia. Soldiers came in with open wounds, untended by elementary first dressing, and a very large number of them had tales to tell of abandonment by their officers, from whom the fellahin made a glorious profit by the sale of their galabiyas. It is an ironic reflection on the Young Officers' Revolutionary Government that the officer corps should once again have let the side down—but that perhaps was because the bravest and most ambitious of them now had political jobs. Between one and two thousand of their soldiers had been killed in battle, and a further five thousand made prisoner of the hated foe.

The Israelis' task was done, at a cost to them of 180 men killed and four captured—except for one final detail, the destruction of the blockading guns at the southernmost tip of the Sinai Peninsula, blocking the entrance to the Gulf of Akaba. Along a route strewn with encumberances eager children of Israel were bustling to this assignment, under the shadow of Mount Sinai, source of God's command.

Mustafa El Nahas Pasha, wartime friend of Britain, and post-war tormentor

Lieutenant-General Sir George Erskine, resolute defender of the Canal Zone during the siege by Nahas

Gamal Abdel Nasser, acclaimed on his return to Cairo after announcing
the seizure of the Suez Canal Company

Sir Anthony Eden leaving No. 10 Downing Street the day after issuing
his ultimatum in October 1956

Left, General Hakim Amer, Nasser's staunch henchman and Commander-in-Chief of Egypt, Syria and Jordan

Below, the Allied British and French commanders at Gamil airfield, Port Said, in November 1956. Left to right, General André Beaufre, Deputy Commander Allied Land Forces; General Sir Charles Keightley, Supreme Commander and Britain's Commander-in-Chief Middle East; Vice-Admiral Pierre Barjot, Deputy Supreme Commander; Lieutenant-General Sir Hugh Stockwell, Commander Allied Land Forces

CHAPTER NINETEEN

The Agonized Approach

(1956)

As THE ISRAELI troops sped to their battle stations for the opening assault, there were stirrings too around the central Mediterranean. The French were the first to move. Warships sailed from Toulon, and on the Saturday and Sunday, October 27 and 28, marine commandos of General Massu's 10th Airborne Division, part of which was already in Cyprus, embarked at Algiers under many curious eyes, followed by the 7th Mécanique Rapide. The ripples spread to Malta. Staff cars and jeeps roamed the island over the week-end, bearing summonses to the conference table which chilled the cheer at cocktail-parties and in restaurants. Some thought it an absurdly uncivilized way to start a loading exercise, which went by the home namely of Boathook; others thought a bit deeper.

By the Tuesday evening the 40th and 42nd Commandos were all aboard with their tracked amphibians—the Buffalos —and the 6th Royal Tanks with their Centurions, which together with various follow-up and command vehicles filled seventeen heavily laden landing-ships of various sizes. They set sail before dawn next morning under strong naval escort, with crews and passengers apprised of their destination after some briefing which added further complication to the embarkation programme. Ahead of them sailed four aircraft-carriers bound for the Egyptian coast, while behind at Malta two other carriers took on board men of the reserve battalion of the 16th Commando Brigade, the 45th Commando, who were to pioneer the fly-in by helicopter, the drill for which was still under hectic study.

Arrivals rather than departures activated the scene at Cyprus. The "new town" of Episcopi, the compound of tents, huts and austere white villas that housed the Middle East Command, almost burst with the immigrant staff officers, sailors, soldiers, airmen, French and British, who streamed in over the week-end. At last they were away from London, beyond the clutch of Downing Street, and though very few may have realized it, the moment of delivery was at hand, delivery of the plan that had been in such painful labour for so long. The order duly came: prepare to implement operation Musketeer; and though warning was desperately short, the preliminaries so conveniently arranged made the required date of landing, November 6, just attainable. The issue of the ultimatum, however, revealed weaknesses in the great master plan. In the first place the politicians had told the enemy the exact objective the soldiers were to seize, thus depriving the latter of any chance of deception, and in the second place the ultimatum had been delivered (apparently without military consultation) very much more impetuously than was desirable, necessitating an embarrassingly long period between warning and fulfilment.

It rapidly became apparent that the politicians were aware of this second drawback. A signal came from London, requiring the date of the landing to be advanced one day. It was for the sailors to decide, under the august and independent aegis of the Commander-in-Chief, Mediterranean, and the sailors firmly said that it could not be done. The timetable was too complicated to accelerate. It in fact allowed for the worst possible weather conditions— ships from Malta were routed at an average speed of under 6 knots —but with convoys sailing from Cyprus and Algeria as well, not to mention the supporting ones from Britain and France and the provision of the various escorts, co-ordination presented a problem of balance too easily upset by hasty, inconsidered alterations. Thus the tempo remained unruffled and all those complicated loading and movement tables intact.

The cause of this first setback, forerunner of many, to the calculations of the British and French leaders was a surprise over the Israelis' opening communiqué, issued on the Monday evening. It announced that the paratroops were within 25 miles of the Canal, 15 nearer than the truth. It had not been intended, according to Robertson's book, to make the threat appear so stark so early, and the announcement may well have been a ruse to precipitate the promised intervention. It achieved this effect. Mollet and Pineau came hotfoot to London and filled Eden with such sense of urgency that he announced the ultimatum to the Commons that afternoon, just after its presentation to the Ambassadors at 4.15. He would have been wiser to have waited twenty-four hours at least, and there was also a clause in the ultimatum, apparently added as an afterthought, which inevitably bred suspicion of its authors' good faith. Egypt was required to admit a force into the Canal Zone whether or not both sides accepted the demand to withdraw beyond the ten-mile range to east and west.

It was predictable that the announcement should be received with gasps, groans and boos by members of the Opposition. What had not been foreseen, for some strange reason, was that American reaction would be so hostile or so prompt. Eisenhower and Dulles had made it clear enough that they were opposed to armed intervention, and it was for this reason that they had not been made party to the Anglo-French plans, although the French believed that they knew well enough what was afoot. Yet Eden confidently expected American backing, despite the fact that Lloyd had discussed the situation with the American Ambassador that very morning and given him no hint of what was being planned with the French. In a telegram to Eisenhower, giving warning of the ultimatum, Eden stressed his acknowledged right "to defend our vital interests against Nasser's designs", the provocation Egypt had given Israel, and the manifest inability of the United Nations to take rapid and effective action. This was followed by a second telegram in which he said, with extraordinary optimism, "I think there is a chance that both sides will accept. In any case it would help this result very much if you found it possible to support what we have done at least in general terms." Neither had the slightest effect. Eisenhower, and Dulles too, seethed with all the rage of men personally insulted; they felt like guardians whose wards have played a dirty trick behind their back.

The Security Council, which had been trying to bring pressure on Russia to leave the people of Hungary alone, was at once convened and Cabot Lodge instructed to move a resolution calling on Israel to withdraw and member states to refrain from giving her any assistance. Ardently anti-colonial, Lodge eagerly grabbed the chance to prove to the Afro-Asian world that the United States no longer befriended the imperialists' tool, the pirate state of Israel.

Thus within a few hours of the delivery of the ultimatum Eden's Government was under attack both in the House of Commons and the United Nations. In the Commons the initial assault by the Labour Party was comfortably held, there being as yet no sign of dissension on the Government side. In the United Nations Britain had for the first time to make use of her veto to negative the American resolution, and of course France did the same. A Russian resolution which followed, calling for an immediate cease-fire and the withdrawal of the Israeli troops, was defeated by the same process. Even Australia voted for this resolution, although the United States preferred to abstain rather than register accord with Russia. The British and French representatives were treated as lepers. Sir Pierson Dixon was peremptorily brushed aside when he attempted to speak privately to Lodge, and Cornut-Gentille, who was President of the Council, was ignored even by old friends. Having presented France's case forcefully, he collapsed at the end of the session, soon after Sobolev, the Russian, had referred with dramatic menace to the "extremely grave consequences for all mankind".

The replies to the ultimatum were announced next day, Egypt's arrogant in its defiance, Israel's embarrassing in its co-operative tone. "The very real danger of fighting across the Canal", affirmed by the Prime Minister in justification of his action before the House, had subsided overnight, and it was impossible now to disguise the ultimatum's bias against Egypt. It cost Eden a serious breach in his defences. Anthony Nutting, Minister of State for Foreign Affairs, he who had signed the 1954 Agreement, had already issued his own private ultimatum, and he now went to Downing Street and handed in his resignation. The one concession he made to loyalty was to withhold announcement while the crisis lasted.

Parliament meanwhile, and for that matter the whole world, wanted to know what was happening. Had British troops landed, was the country at war? The Prime Minister was not prepared to say. "Answer!" yelled Opposition members. "Order," implored the Speaker. "This really is a fantastic situation," said Gaitskell, and after further exchanges Eden reluctantly admitted that a state of "armed conflict" did exist. Gaitskell, describing the decision as "an act of disastrous folly", pledged opposition "by every constitutional means at our disposal". But whatever Eden was planning and Gaitskell opposing it was clear enough that no armed conflict had as yet taken place, by land, sea or air.

The truth was that the air command, and the army too, had serious cause for anxiety. At dawn on the Tuesday, Canberra bombers had made a reconnaissance along the Egyptian coastline, flying at extreme height. They were intercepted by M.I.G. fighters with skill that belied their Egyptian insignia, and one had been hit, though not forced down. Eden felt confident, as a result of his talks with Khrushchev and Bulganin in London that spring, that Russia would not openly come to Egypt's aid, but Khrushchev had in September given warning that "if there is an attack on Egypt there will be volunteers". The "volunteers" were already available in impressive numbers on Egyptian soil, and here indeed was indication that they had more than an advisory role to play. It was a disturbing thought that placed the care-worn brake of caution on all military deliberations.

There could be no question of opening the air offensive in daylight. The Egyptian airfields were at extreme range for fighters from Cyprus and the planes on the carriers fast approaching from Malta could be no match for the land-based M.I.G.s. Air Marshal D. H. F. Barnett, the air task force commander, had in any case long since decided that the opening blow must be at night, when greater confusion and disruption were likely to be caused on the airfield targets by the difficulty of assessing the damage. The Canberras at Nicosia and the Valiants at Malta therefore had to wait until the approach of darkness before they took off with their loads, and the staff officers at Episcopi listened in dazed wonder as they heard them overhead. It was hard to believe that the long weeks of pretence were over and that the plan they had moulded, remoulded and again remoulded was at last taking active form. Hard as it was to work up much sympathy for the familiar and so long-despised Egyptians, it seemed ludicrous that it should be necessary to drop bombs on their heads. Surely they would pack in.

In the event no volunteer stepped in to offer resistance, and ever slow to react, the Egyptians were stunned into apathy when the assault on the airfields developed weight enough next morning to cripple any air force in Europe by the momentum sustained. Some four hundred aircraft zoomed off from the aerodromes and carriers, with the fighter-bombers from Akrotiri, the Venoms and the French long-range R.F. 84s, well to the fore. For two days they rained lead and high explosive on the runways, returning again and again, thanks to the exertions of maintenance teams. This part of the battle went entirely according to plan.

After their initial surprise the Egyptian ground staffs paid heed to the broadcast warnings and few human casualties were incurred, but nothing can equal the power of bombers at arousing indignation, and the verbal counter-offensive showed the same increase in momentum that the airmen had achieved. The announcement that the bombing had begun, made on the Thursday afternoon, brought pandemonium to the House of Commons. "Fascists!" yelled the Labour men, and their attempts to force the Government to commit themselves on the issue of a declaration of war degenerated into such uproar that the Speaker was obliged to suspend the debate for thirty minutes, something that had not happened for thirty years. Reason had collapsed before emotion, the Labour men letting loose all their atavistic rage against Tory imperialistic adventures, the Conservatives expressing disgust at their opponents' attempts to prejudice the success of military operations, which had already begun, for their own political gain. There was no room for moderates now in this battle between the patriots and moralists.

There was less noise but just as much bitterness when the debate was resumed on a censure motion against the Government. Eden made a significant contribution. "The first and urgent task," he said, "is to separate the combatants. . . . If the United Nations were then willing to take over the physical task of maintaining peace in that area, no one would be better pleased than we. But police action there must be to separate the belligerents." His words were greeted with derision but an idea had been sown—and, incidentally, used in rather different form by cartoonists who were quick to clothe Eden in policeman's uniform. The Tories were home by a comfortable majority, with no split as yet apparent in their ranks.

The United Nations General Assembly was at that moment being convened in record time by a vote of the Security Council against which there was no right of veto. Discussion lasted deep into this Thursday night on a motion, moved by Cabot Lodge in icily censorious tone, urging all parties to "agree to an immediate cease-fire, and as part thereof halt the movement of military forces". The debating included a splendidly lurid account of Anglo-French atrocities from the Egyptian delegate, and the motion was carried by the weightiest majority ever recorded, 64 votes to 5, with Australia and New Zealand among the dissenters and Canada among the six that abstained. Eden had little faith in the General Assembly, which in any case had not the authority of the Security Council. Nonetheless, it was a sad end to his dreams of rallying world opinion behind him, and with his stomach debility adding immeasurably to the strain, he showed signs of wavering.

Indication of it reached Cyprus in the form of instructions forbidding damage to life or property in the second phase of the air offensive, the disruption of troop movement and concentrations. Every target was liable to veto from London.

It was clear already that the bombers were failing hopelessly in the political tasks expected of them, however successful they had been militarily. The psycho-aerial offensive had been a flop from the start. The leaflets prepared by the psychological warfare team had been duly dropped, at some risk, by transport aircraft, bringing their blood-curdling message. "We are obliged to bomb you wherever you are," they ran. "Imagine your village being bombed. Imagine your wives, children, mothers, fathers and grandfathers escaping from their homes and leaving their property behind. . . . You have committed a sin . . . that is, you have placed your confidence in Abdul Nasser."

It was intended to resume the offensive over Limassol Radio—the Voice of Free Egypt—which so far had been trading milk for Cairo's venom. The Arab announcers decided otherwise and were not to be coerced. They therefore confined their messages to target warnings, couched in terms of such concern for the people, thus helping to keep that Alice-in-Wonderland feeling alive, while Cairo Radio blared forth its tales of the heroism of Egyptians and the cowardice of their enemies. The radio station was attacked once and partly disabled, but as it stands in Cairo's suburbs a second attempt received the veto. In the field of propaganda Egypt's victory was complete. The bombs were damaging enough to rouse the anger of the world against their droppers, but not the anger of the Egyptian people against their leader, because of the very lack of damage they inflicted. So far from jeopardizing Nasser's position, they consolidated it, enabling him to disguise Nemesis beneath a martyr's halo. Secure in his capital, he could turn his attention to the surest means of making fools of his enemies, blocking the Suez Canal.

Here indeed was a second failure of the air offensive—but then no one can have imagined that the Egyptians would do the job quite so thoroughly. The first blockship was spotted on the Friday morning wedged in the Canal from Lake Timsah, having survived an attack the previous evening. It was the start of a nightly mushroom growth, until finally seventeen obstructions were recorded in the Canal and twenty-one in Port Said harbour. Very probably it was on Russian instigation that Nasser consented to such lavish blocking of the Canal, and certainly a leading part in the scuttling at Port Said was played by a Russian pilot who was seen personally organizing the sinking of a very expensive ship with great relish. Yet it may just as well express the Egyptian's atavistic exasperation at the exploitation of his country as a mere passageway for the people of the world. Nasser had succeeded again where Arabi had failed, and no doubt the fact did not escape him.

Just as successful were his efforts, made largely through the medium of Cairo Radio, to cut the other lines of oil supply. In Bahrein the British Oil Company's buildings were set on fire, in Saudi Arabia all pumping was forbidden into British-held terminals, and in Syria the pipeline to the Mediterranean was cut and pumping stations blown up. Reserves in Britain were sufficient for barely six weeks. The country's "vital interests", so often invoked by Eden, were indeed in desperate peril.

Cyprus meanwhile was the scene of a tug-of-war between the British and French commanders, with Paris providing the propelling force from one end and London acting as sheet-anchor at the other. The paratroops formed the rope, the British brigade based on Nicosia aerodrome and the French at Tymbou. There was marked contrast between the two. So out of practice were the British, both aircrews and soldiers, that the battalions had returned to England, one at a time, for training during the months of crisis—and now, typifying the calls they were for ever answering, they were on operations in the Troodos mountains, winkling out bandits, while their outdated aircraft, eighteen Valettas and fourteen Hastings, were flying Red Cross supplies to Vienna for the benefit of Hungary's freedom fighters. Proud, eager and masters of the infantryman's skills though they were, the Red Devils had not floated into battle since the Rhine crossing in 1945 and had since had little chance to develop either their technique or equipment.

The French, on the other hand, had been constantly in action, either in Indo-China or Algeria, and whereas thirty drops was regarded as a veteran's tally by English standards, a Frenchman was hardly out of the beginner's class until he had accomplished a hundred. Their three regiments in Cyprus, the Colonial, Metropolitan and Foreign Legion, each sporting a different coloured beret, were twice as large as British battalions and could be organized into battalion groups. *Les Paras* had very much made their presence felt since their arrival in late August and Tymbou hummed with activity as they demonstrated their dropping skills with true Gallic panache, drawing gasps both at their expertise and at the risks they took. Though many were conscripts, they had the sure air of veterans, tough, battle-proud, brigandy and strangely colourful in their dull camouflaged smocks and baggy trousers. They fretted, almost too palpably, in their impatience to leap into battle against the despised Egyptian.

The entire length of the causeway from Port Said, 25 miles long, was originally to have been the first objective of the combined parachute forces. Then came news of the reinforcement of Port Said and the concentration of armour around Kantara and Ismailia, which, when the Israelis attacked, crossed the Canal but soon came back. It was decided, after the study of various permutations, to bring the paras' objectives nearer Port Said, to include the bridges at the head of the causeway and Gamil airport to the west, both to be seized simultaneously with the seaborne assault. But now with the disintegration of the Egyptian Army fast becoming evident, with the line from Paris a-sizzle with the word *"Vitesse!"* and with snorts from the old war-horse Massu, in command of all the airborne, frisking his eardrums, little Admiral Barjot made appeal to Keightley. *"Mon Général,* I present to you operation Omelette." Let the paratroops seize Port Said at once, blasted in by naval gunfire, and then release the remaining battalions all along the Canal. Keightley listened amiably—"God the Father sitting in the clouds", the French journalists unkindly christened him in their impatience for action—and in due course explained that it was not possible. The risk was too great, both of devastation in Port Said and of peril to the paras through overstraining the air arm. (The Joseph Stalins had not yet moved, but were being anxiously watched and attacked, where exposed, by fighter-bombers.) Keightley, it seems certain, had as strong backing as Barjot, both from his subordinates, especially Stockwell and the naval taskforce commander, Vice-Admiral D. F. Durnford-Slater, and from London.

However, the French were as resourceful as they were determined, and now Barjot offered operation Telescope, advocating that the para landings around Port Said should go in a day ahead of the seaborne, with the object of gaining the submission of the town without resort to naval bombardment. Politically, this was a most attractive idea to the British, and with the seaborne force close at hand to rectify failure it was militarily acceptable. Reports indicated, furthermore, that the Egyptian troops which had crossed

16

the Canal were being brought back to Cairo. At 4 a.m. on the Sunday morning, November 4, Britain's Defence Minister, Antony Head, and the C.I.G.S., General Templer, stepped out of a plane that screeched down at Akrotiri aerodrome. The plan was approved: the paras, one British and one French battalion, would fly in at dawn next morning. French pleading had borne fruit at last.

Two battalions of the 16th Parachute Brigade, together with brigade headquarters, had by now embarked on a troopship. Their loading, combined with that of the massive force headquarters, gunners and their guns, sappers and bridging equipment, medical units, supply units, and pioneers for stevedore duties, strained the resources of Britain's chosen base of Cyprus to the utmost, and there had been much scrimmaging and confusion around the open harbour of Limassol and the little port of Famagusta, as lighters chugged, soldiers shoved, officers fussed and Cypriots shrugged their shoulders, half in resignation, half in despair at the designs of the imperialists. Now, since the fly-in had been put forward, Brigadier M. A. H. Butler, commanding 16th Parachute Brigade, had to unload his headquarter equipment so that he too could fly in to take command. Against the stream of loading still in progress, this was not so easy and confusion veered dangerously near chaos.

Not until dusk on the Sunday evening were the ships ready to sail in convoy from Limassol, with Stockwell, Durnford-Slater and Barnett—the land, sea and air task force commanders—all aboard the command ship, H.M.S. *Tyne*, and Beaufre, Stockwell's deputy, on the *Gustave Zede*. By morning they had joined up with the plodders from Malta and the convoy from Algiers to form a great and weirdly assorted array of tramps and steamers, ringed by the serene might of the combined naval escorts. Behind them, in faster-moving troopships, sailed the spearhead of the British 3rd Division which had left Southampton on the night of November 2, preceded by its slower-moving tank landing ships. In Libya men of the 10th Armoured Division were preparing to follow, but on the very day of Stockwell's embarkation news arrived that the 10th Armoured could not after all be made available. Keightley asked him if he would like an infantry brigade from Malta instead. Stockwell said he thought he had enough infantry but might need more armour, and the War Office were therefore asked to earmark two more tank regiments. Such was the tempo of expectation within the military mind.

The political tempo was very much brisker. In the House of Commons, assembled for a Saturday session in response to the insistent demands of the Opposition, Eden gave his Government's reply to the General Assembly resolution, while the Opposition kept up a continual barrage of booing, febrile in their expectations that, with the United Nations on their side and cracks appearing across the Tory plaster, they were on the threshold of a sensational victory. Eden laid down three conditions for a cease-fire and British disengagement: that both Israel and Egypt should agree to accept a peace-keeping United Nations force; that the United Nations agree to maintain such a force until a peace treaty were signed and the Suez Canal dispute settled; and that until the U.N. force were effectively established the Anglo-French troops should divide the contestants.

Eden had a friend in the United Nations. Lester Pearson, Foreign Minister of Canada, was trying to secure a solution that would meet Eden's requirements, while the verbal bombardment grew in fury, with the Russians making the most of the chance of diversion from Hungary, where their tanks, having withdrawn the previous week, were returning to the capital to grind the bud of democracy into the dust. By urgent endeavour Pearson rushed a resolution through the General Assembly, at 2 a.m. on the Sunday morning, envisaging the formation of an emergency force "to secure and supervise the cessation or hostilities." Not one nation voted against it—but no more than exploration, rather than action, had as yet been resolved and there could be no guarantee that Egypt, who had not officially accepted the cease-fire previously demanded, would accept any such force once the danger of invasion was averted.

Eden spoke to the nation on this Saturday night. His words had their familiar patrician ring, to which his calm determination, weary yet unbowed, gave added effect—"All my life I have been a man of peace, striving for peace and negotiating for peace. I have been a League of Nations man and a United Nations man." It was effective, touching stuff, vividly conveying the agony that lurked behind his resort to such drastic action "to put out a fire . . . likely to inflame the whole of the Middle East". Action was called for, not consultation, yet "If the United Nations would take over this police action we should welcome it. Until the United Nations were there, we and France must be ready to go on with the job until the job was done."

Sunday was a day of angry meditation for Englishmen. There could be no waverers; everyone fumed with indignation, either against the madness of the Government or the treachery of an Opposition indifferent to the fate of their compatriots about to enter battle. The *Observer* provoked most indignation of all. "We had not realized that our Government was capable of such folly and crookedness", ran a leader which asserted that only by rebellion (as against Chamberlain) could the Conservative Party "save itself from obliteration for a generation".

Labour M.P.s, returning to their constituencies in expectation of praise for the stand they had made, met disappointment. Unlike many of the M.P.s themselves, large numbers of their constituents had seen military service in Egypt, and their attitude, as all acounts and opinion polls agree, was that the Gyppos had asked for it from the start and deserved what was coming to them. Rather than the Conservative Party, it was those who voiced the *Observer*'s views that were in danger of obliteration.

In Trafalgar Square a great rally was held, the first of the great meetings organized by Labour as part of the protest "by every constitutional means"—wisely no attempt was made to organize strike action as had been done when the Government contemplated aid for Poland against Russian attack in 1920. A vast crowd assembled, estimated by one source at thirty thousand, but the cheerleaders did not get quite the response required. "Law not war" was meant to be the slogan, but as one of them admitted to a spectator, "They won't wear it—it's very hard, very hard indeed." However, they had greater success with the simpler, purely political slogan of "Eden must go", and with this on their lips the demonstrators surged down Whitehall into Downing Street, where they showed their faith in "law not war" by fighting a battle with the police, having first rolled marbles to bring down their horses. Some seventy-five were either wounded or taken prisoner in this tussle which cannot have eased the tension within No. 10, where Pineau and Bourgés-Maunoury had come to sustain Eden's determination in the face of urgent pleas for a halt from his helpers at the United Nations. As the crowd drifted away, the Frenchmen went too, and the full Cabinet assembled.

The most telling miscalculation of opinion was made by Gaitskell himself. His right to reply to the Prime Minister's broadcast was stubbornly disputed by the Government, but the B.B.C.'s reputation for impartiality proved unassailable and after the nine o'clock news on this Sunday the Leader of the Opposition was announced. Like the *Observer*, he called on Tory M.P.s to throw over their leader in obedience to the United Nations' command. The Prime Minister, he told the nation very earnestly, "is utterly, utterly discredited in the eyes of the world. Only one thing now can save the reputation and honour of our country. Parliament must repudiate the Government's policy. The Prime Minister must resign." There could be no surer way of rallying wavering Conservatives—and there were waverers—back into line.

The ships doggedly heading towards Egypt had just been plunged into darkness, with urgent clanging of the action-stations bells. Intruders were near at hand. But they proved to be Americans, not the phantom Russian submarines—it was the Sixth Fleet which in evacuating their subjects from Alexandria to the Lebanon caused much irritation to the allied navies, whether intentionally or not. They were despatched off course with a ribald message from the convoy commander which caused much merriment when transmitted to the men, and crews and passengers stood down. Then came Gaitskell's unwise words, broadcast over the tannoy system. They proved an unorthodox but effective way of arousing anger on the eve of battle, and none expressed disgust more forcefully than the reservists of the Port Regiment who had stevedore duties to perform.

Just as aggravating for the Supreme Commander on this weird Sunday night was a message that reached him at 10.15 (local time) asking how much notice he would require to postpone the assault. The truth was that in the United Nations plans for the formation of the emergency force, which might or might not meet Eden's requirements, were going fast ahead, and a fearful dilemma faced the Cabinet as to whether to stop or go. For six days Keightley had been wrestling with the feasibility of many alternatives and now when all seemed set at last, with the paratroops having a final rest before climbing into their planes, here he was faced with yet one more change. He promptly replied that he must know by one (eleven in London). The paratroops were not due to land until after dawn and it would have been possible to call them back even in mid air, as had been done in the case of the bombers directed on Cairo West. But the time had come to put an end to indecision. One o'clock came and no cancellation arrived.

The calmest place at this moment of world crisis—at any rate by its own standards—appears to have been the storm centre itself,

Egypt. Soon after the start of the bombing, Nasser had ordered the seizure of all British and French property, and Trevelyan and his staff were made prisoners in their Embassy. But there was no savage expression of rage such as the people had so often indulged in, thanks partly perhaps to the accuracy of the bombing and the friendly issue of warning. Some 4,000 British subjects had heeded the warning to leave, issued when the crisis first began, and a further 2,000 citizens of the United Kingdom, and 9–10,000 colonial subjects, remained. In curious contrast to American subjects, they had received no further warning when the Israelis mobilized, and all were now at the mercy of the Egyptian police. Some were summarily arrested, while others, such as journalists, were placed under confinement. Most, however, went unmolested on their daily round.

Major Wise Bey, for instance, was still free to go where he pleased, subject to a curfew order which there were means of evading and an annoying ban on entry into the Gezira Club. He encountered no hostility as he walked the streets of Cairo, making his daily trips to shops and the Turf Club as usual. There was a certain coldness, a listless coldness, but no more. The citizens had literally taken up arms, but except for the predictable hotheads, with an air of resignation rather than defiance—and resignation turned to gloom when on the Saturday night the tanks rumbled through the streets back home to the Pyramids from the wreckage of Sinai. Normally so perky, the wooden look of dejection worn by the defeated soldiers told a story to belie which was beyond the prowess even of Cairo Radio. Near Wise's house four tanks and six armoured cars stood deserted for many days.

There was a shortage of comfort at Kasr-el-Doubara, the British Embassy, where armed policemen stood on guard. There was a shortage of food and bedding, and to ensure that there could be no communication with any outside agent, the electricity was cut off. The Australian Minister, A. R. Cutler, eased the food situation by bringing in supplies, the purchase of which caused angry growls, but soon his delegation too was placed under house guard.

Hardship also faced the employees of the Suez Canal Contractors' Company, whose number had been reduced during the crisis, by extending leave and such means, to around 470. They were rounded up on the Wednesday night, when the bombing first started, some courteously, some rudely, and treated as military prisoners of war. They were put in buses the next day and driven to Cairo, the drivers honking their horns to attract the attention of such louts as cared to hiss and spit. They were then imprisoned in a school, where their guards, like their food, bedding and sanitary arrangements, were of the meanest grade, and exercise was denied them even in the school yard. Not until word of their plight reached that man of mercy, M. Kadler, the Swiss *chargé d'affaires*—fourteen days after their arrest—was there any betterment of their lot.

Meanwhile there were extraordinary scenes on the highways as, with the fighter-bombers swirling overhead, the people demonstrated their confidence in immunity from attack. Air crews, attacking aerodromes or vehicle parks, could see the spectators lined up on the touchline, and on the roads the soldiers stopped their vehicles and bolted for cover at the approach of aircraft, while civilians drove on. It was soon realized that military convoys were safe when entwined with civilian refugees, many of whom were on the move away from the Canal, and of course villages also afforded sanctuary for soldiers. Anti-aircraft gunners, secure in such refuge, achieved an increasing degree of accuracy as the week wore on. All told, the Fleet Air Arm lost four aircraft as a result of enemy action (but only one pilot), the Royal Air Force one, and the French one. Whether they achieved anything positive in this phase of the offensive, other than to give the Egyptians practice in night movement in their withdrawal on Cairo, is doubtful.

For the cafés of Port Said, as for the promenaders, it was business as usual on the Sunday evening. A number of families, especially the richer ones, had gone, but the majority faced the future with typically optimistic complacence, despite Nasser's claim that he would defend the city to the last. British and French residents meanwhile were confined to an anxious state of house arrest, their safety enhanced as excitement rose by the concern of Governor Riad, a dignified figure who had earned the respect and affection of British officers in the days of the occupation. Over Radio Cyprus, repeated every two hours on a frequency approximating to that of Cairo, came an ominous warning: "Citizens of Port Said, evacuate the beach zone to the seafront as far as the rue Tewfik." The cafés still hummed with merry chat.

Shots were fired with gay abandon by the young men of the Liberation Army, recently issued with rifles, as the aircraft circled over the town and, heading seawards to avoid risk of unmilitary damage, made attacks with cannon and rocket on the coastal and anti-aircraft guns sited at the harbour entrance and on the beach.

A battery of Bofors disintegrated with a flurry of swirling barrels and bodies; another, hastily brought in to replace it, did the same. The people watched fascinated, crowding the balconies. It was the best entertainment they had ever had. "It was quite unreal," said an eyewitness. "It was like an hallucination."

More than 250 miles south of Port Said Egyptians were being presented with another apparent hallucination. The Suez road to Sharm-el-Sheikh, from which Egyptian guns controlled entry to the Gulf of Akaba, had already been cut by Israeli troops flown in by Dakota on to a rough air strip. Now Israelis appeared along the seemingly impassable track by the gulf, supplied by hefty landing craft which had been lugged overland from the Mediterranean. They found an island fortress abandoned and now closed on the coastal bastion of Sharm-el-Sheikh itself. The assault began at 3.30 on the Monday morning and six hours later the Israeli brigade of 1,500 had forced as many Egyptians, well supplied and massively fortified, into submission.

As dawn broke to speed the Israelis' deadly work with grenade and sub-machine-gun, away in the Mediterranean it enabled the men in the allied convoys to pick out the outline of two streams of transport aircraft which roared overhead. "A cigarette please, Ken," said Stockwell to his Chief of Staff, Brigadier K. T. Darling. It was his first cigarette for seven years. In half an hour's time his two leading battalions would land within the perimeter of the Port Said defences, violating the accepted rules for an airborne assault. Three fresh battalions, one regular, two National Guard, with tanks, guns, mortars, wire and concrete defences, were waiting to receive them, not to mention the unknown thousands of irregulars and stragglers from Sinai. So much depended on the tanks. There were reports of withdrawal even from Port Said, but certainly some tanks, or self-propelled Russian anti-tank guns, were still in the garrison, and only a few could make themselves very lethal—if handled by men who really knew their business.

CHAPTER TWENTY

The Soldiers' Return

(1956)

A BALL OF fire, blazing out at sea north-west of Port Said as if in reflection of the rising sun, heralded the return of the British on Guy Fawkes' Day, within five months of their departure. It had been dropped by a Canberra bomber to guide the transport planes towards their objective, the coastal airport of Gamil, two miles from the outskirts of Port Said.

The Valettas and Hastings approached in pairs from the west over the narrow strip of land between Lake Manzala and the sea, with the sun, now fully risen, dazzling the pilots. As they drew near the airport Seahawks of the Royal Navy swooped down out of a clear sky and hurled their rockets at pillboxes and other defences around the airfield, setting the control tower ablaze, while R.A.F. fighters strafed anti-aircraft guns nearer Port Said. The lumbering transport planes came on, and out streamed their loads, jerking into apparent stagnation as their parachutes took the strain. Below them rifles and machine-guns crackled from the Egyptian defences, making harsh chorus with the roar of the planes and the bark of the anti-aircraft guns further along the coast. For the honoured men of the 3rd Parachute Battalion, dangling helplessly from their harness, the plunge from mental to physical suspense brought no mental relief, and the ground could not embrace them too quickly.

The falling troops spanned the one-mile length of the airfield, and once down they had a desperate thirty-second struggle to free themselves from their parachutes and containers before rushing into battle at their objectives, to east, west, north, south-east. Most

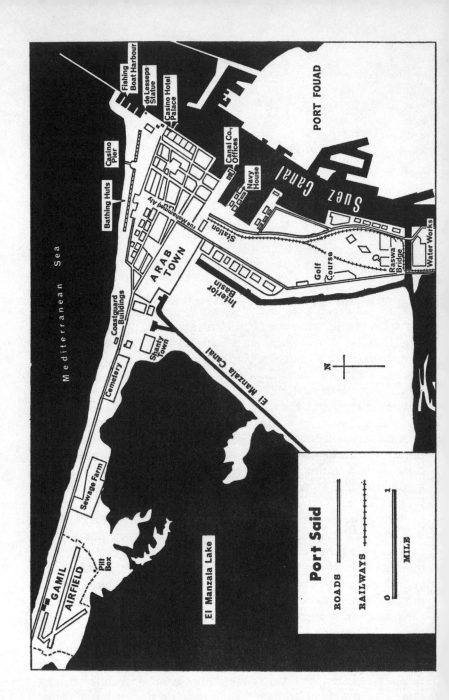

Mediterranean Sea

Fishing Boat Harbour
de Lesseps Statue
Casino Hotel Palace
Casino Pier
Bathing Huts

PORT FOUAD

Canal Co. Offices

Navy House

Suez Canal

Rue Mohamed Aly

ARAB TOWN

Station

Coastguard Buildings

Golf Course

Raswa Bridge

Water Works

Cemetery

Interior Basin

Shanty Town

N

Sewage Farm

El Manzala Canal

GAMIL AIRFIELD

Pill Box

El Manzala Lake

Port Said

ROADS
RAILWAYS

0   1
MILE

of "B" Company, nearest Port Said, landed amid Egyptian entrenchments—there was a cry of, "No, Johnny, no, Johnny, no!" as a paratrooper, sailing down right into a post, hurled his container at it and himself followed, striking out first with boots then with jack-knife, the only weapon immediately available. In half an hour the whole of the airfield was cleansed of its defences, with expert aid from the naval Seahawks, and despite the aerial volleys fired at them and the concentrated mortar fire, from further afield, which greeted their arrival, the battalion had so far had few casualties, thanks partly to the squelchy turf which much reduced the spread of the mortar bombs. The only man killed had been blown towards the beach and landed on a mine; two others landed in the sea but disentangled themselves from their parachutes and safely reached shore. With three of his mortars already in action and six jeep-towed anti-tank guns deployed, Lieutenant-Colonel Paul Crook, the large and calmly determined commander of the 3rd Para, gave orders for the advance on Port Said to begin.

Brigadier Butler meanwhile—a trim figure full of bounce and vitality incongruously saddled with the nickname "Tubby"—had taken possession of the air reception centre, a rather down-at-heel building, the walls of which, flaked with tatty posters of welcome to tourists, were punctured by solid shot from an S.U.100 anti-tank gun (Russian-made but not manned) until its destruction by a Seahawk. As the first of the wounded, Egyptians and paras, were brought in for treatment amid the customs' benches, Butler passed news of his success on to the command ship *Tyne*. This was not so easy. His main rear-link set, and spare parts, had been casualties of the landing, and he was left with an old 19-set which was reliable but lacking in range.

No sooner had the British planes dropped their loads than another double column of aircraft—the French Nord Atlases—flew overhead and circled left-handed over Lake Manzala to approach Port Said from the south. They carried men of the 2nd Colonial Regiment, under command of the colourful Colonel Chateau-Jobert, alias Conan, a small, bald, bearded man, possessed, under a camouflage of bland innocence, of crusading zeal for the glory of France which eventually was to turn him into an outlaw in the cause of *Algérie Française*. With them came some British sappers and a reconnaissance party from the Guards Parachute Company.

Their objectives were of the greatest importance, their task one of great hazard. Just to the south of Port Said there is a short, wide canal connecting the Suez Canal and Lake Manzala. The two bridges over it, one of them a combined road and railway bridge, afford the only means of exit to the south. On the south bank of this canal is the waterworks, supplying the whole of Port Said from the Sweet Water Canal. Bridges and waterworks had obviously to be captured intact, but the area was heavily defended and the only dropping zone available was desperately cramped, a mere strip of land 150yds. wide between the Suez Canal and the lake, south of the bridges.

The planes came under heavy fire as they approached the bridges. They dropped smoke canisters and returned for a second run-in. At a height of 450ft., 100ft. lower than allowed by normal safety regulations, and at minimum speed, they disgorged their cargoes with high professional alacrity. The Frenchmen came down firing their weapons, thanks to a technique not adapted by the British, and every man, though not all their equipment, landed on target amid the folds and craters of baked mud and sand, from which they rapidly winkled out defenders disturbed at their breakfast. There was urgent scuffling to retrieve containers.

As the smoke cleared, shells and mortar bombs whistled in among the Frenchmen, the Egyptian anti-aircraft gunners being quick to switch to the ground target. French fighter-bombers screeched in to attack, and the paras fought their way forward, encouraged over the radio by the voice of General Gilles, the parachute group commander, a tough, one-eyed, hard-swearing character who circled over the battlefield in a Nord Atlas, impervious to its buffeting by anti-aircraft fire. The Egyptians fought hard and many of them were killed—before the French broke through to the lesser of the two bridges, only to see it subside; the demolition party, escaping by launch, were in turn demolished by a mortar bomb. A lively assault was now made on the main twin-bridge. The French rushed in, overrunning gun emplacements, and the British sapper officer, having distinguished himself in the attack, found the bridge bare of detonators (which in fact were still in a hut nearby). The noisy ejection of snipers from the waterworks and its shrubberies completed the task, at a total cost of only some dozen casualties, French and British. The party of guardsmen—one officer and six men—had by now set off down the road to Ismailia. They marched 10 kilometres, found no sign of life or obstruction, and in due course returned to the French position for

the strange reason that a "bombline" restricted movement southwards until mid-morning next day, beyond which allied aircraft
could shoot up any vehicle they saw.

The Egyptians—believed to be at battalion strength—let fly
with all the weapons they could muster as the 3rd Para Battalion
began their advance towards Port Said from Gamil. The small-
arms fire, as of old, achieved far greater volume than effect, but the
gunners demonstrated their traditional superiority and good use
was made of the weapons grouped round the coastguard barracks
and the block of flats that formed the western extremity of Port
Said. The self-propelled anti-tank and the anti-aircraft guns here
had to be switched from positions dug with other targets in mind,
and some multi-barrel, "whining Minnie" mortars also blazed
away, but there was no sign of real tanks, nor in fact were Russians
manning the guns.

The first objective was the sewage farm, approached by an
extensive and thick bed of reeds. It was slow going and when the
men emerged among the sewage troughs they came under attack
by French aircraft which miraculously hit no one. The Egyptians
did not fight at close quarters and the position was cleared at slight
loss. Another company then passed through and at 12.30 (local
time) put in an attack on the combined cemeteries, Moslem, Jewish
and Christian, strong in defences, weird and macabre in aspect.
Seahawks' rockets effectively paved the way and the paras sped
through the tombs and gravestones, flushing the remnant of a
company who left thirty dead on the position, a wide range of
weapons, and a bren carrier. The paras were now within 200yds. of
their final objective, the barracks and flats overlooking the coastline to the west and the native quarter to the east. Little remained
of the barracks after the Fleet Air Arm had assailed them, still
meticulously observing the indemnity on civilian property.

The Royal Navy had meanwhile visited Gamil. The first helicopters came in at 11.30, four hours after the landings, relieved the
hard-pressed medical teams of their non-Egyptian casualties, and
left behind them gifts of cigarettes and beer. Never did sailors give
soldiers such service. Having shepherded them on to their objectives with their rockets, they brought them refreshment and carried
off their wounded to comfort, and the para hearts overflowed with
gratitude.

An hour later a Dakota landed on Gamil's mile-long runway. It

brought a liaison officer from General Gilles who had come merely
to find how things were going and to take off wounded. His arrival
stressed, whether with such thought in mind or not, the chance
that was going begging of flying reinforcements in, either from
Malta, Cyprus, or the carriers of the fleet. All that did arrive, by
parachute at 3.15, was the remainder of Crook's battalion, a
scratch company of 56 men to supplement the 668 who had
landed in the first drop. Three jeeps and some ammunition, of
which only that for the mortars was needed, came with them.

The reinforcements were able to take over protection of the
western approaches and thus free a fresh company for the assault
on the flats and barracks. But it was decided not to put it in. These
buildings were within the arc to be covered by the naval bombardment for the sea assault next morning and there seemed no point
in risking casualties to capture ground that would have to be
evacuated. There seemed as little point in holding on to the
cemetery, overlooked as it was from the flats and vulnerable to
counter attack. Crook, therefore, with consent from Butler,
ordered his leading company back to the sewage-farm, having
first seen them knock out a machine-gun post in the flats with aid
from their captured bren carrier. The soldiers then withdrew, and
insatiable mosquitoes took the place of graveyard ghosts as their
nocturnal companions.

The French also received reinforcement—and in very much
larger numbers. A further 460 men of the 2nd Colonial Regiment
dropped on the other side of the Suez Canal, around the southern
outskirts of Port Fuad, opposite their companions on the twin-
bridge. Many of the Egyptians who potted at them did not live
long to regret it. Les Coloniaux attacked their barracks with great
gusto, piled the corpses high, and sent the Egyptians scuttling out
of doors and windows, some in their underpants, some in galabiyas,
some with their weapons, most without. (This urge by the Egyptian soldier to turn himself into a civilian once the pressure was on
had already been noted by the British paras, and from now on it
was to become all dominant.) In a remarkably short time the fiery
Colonials had taken possession of the whole of Fuad, the attractive
residential district, strongly French in flavour, containing as it did
the homes of the old Canal Company employees. A convoy of
Egyptian vehicles, attempting escape across the ferry, was turned
into a might blaze by the ever alert French aircraft, but the town
itself received very little damage and soon after nightfall the black-

uniformed Egyptian police, retaining their rifles, were patrolling the streets against urchins and ruffians in co-operation with the French.

Around five o'clock, with barely an hour left of daylight, Brigadier Butler climbed into a helicopter at Gamil to visit Chateau-Jobert at the waterworks, and as he did so a message arrived from Chateau-Jobert that the Egyptian commander had made contact with him and asked for a cease-fire. Butler took a second helicopter with him, and it returned with French wounded while he discussed with the little Frenchman the terms they should demand, having first signalled the *Tyne* to ask for a suspension of air activity. They decided, after half an hour's discussion, that the Egyptians must lay down their arms and march to a concentration area at Gamil or the salt-mills of Fuad. They then notified the Egyptian, over the civil telephone system, that they were ready to receive him.

Soon after dark, two large American cars bedecked with white flags, drew up at the waterworks. Four officers stiffly emerged, clad meticulously in service dress, with revolvers dangling from their Sam Browne belts; General El Moguy, the commanding general, had brought with him his chief of police, his fortifications officer and the chief of Special Police, Colonel Hassan Rouchdi, a man with the surly air of defiance apposite to his post. There were no chairs in the ante-room where, after being kept waiting a few minutes, they were received by Butler and Chateau-Jobert. The atmosphere was pregnant with pique from the start.

El Moguy was a typical Egyptian officer, small and plump with a face remarkably like Nasser's. He was of a type with whom the British had had considerable acquaintance, both in Egypt and on courses of instruction in Britain, and could make contact, but Egypt was now a police state and El Moguy did not remain spokesman for long. Scarcely had Butler outlined his terms when Rouchdi intervened. Truculently he admitted that arms were being distributed to the civilian population and declared that the Egyptian people would defend themselves to the death. "Then why do you require a cease-fire?" Butler pertinently enquired. Warning of the bombardment planned for next morning deflated the Egyptians to a certain extent but Butler did not feel too confident when they left to consider their reply, with a provisional cease-fire still in force.

Butler's 19-set wireless found the task of penetration to *Tyne* even harder after dark, and his only channel of personal communication was through General Gilles, again circling tirelessly overhead, to whom he expressed his fears of the outcome in his best schoolboy French. Sure enough, El Moguy rang through shortly before 10.30 to say that he could not accept the terms. So dismal did he sound that Butler felt quite sorry for him. Strained to the limit, the 19-set sent the sad news on to *Tyne* by morse, from which it rapidly reached London, contradicting an earlier report that, by some distortion in transit, had converted the fact of the meeting into acceptance of the terms.

Unfortunately for El Moguy and the inhabitants of Port Said communication with Cairo was still open by underwater cable and along this cable came orders from Nasser that the city must fight to the last, spiced with the stimulating news that the Russians had stepped in to rescue Egypt and were raining atom bombs on London and Paris. Whether or not Nasser believed this might happen, it affords an apt illustration of the Russian art of causing maximum turmoil at minimum risk, and in Port Said they had a most dedicated and industrious practitioner of this art, their consul, Anatoli Tchikov. He had spent the day supervising the distribution of fire-arms—brand-new Czech rifles still in preservative grease—like firewood to the poor, sending lorries into the streets with a broadcast invitation to old and young to come and help themselves, and for devotees to the cult of baksheesh it seemed as if the heavens had opened. Now his broadcast vans toured the streets announcing the destruction of Paris and London and shots of joy rang out as children played delightedly with their new toys. Deep defeatism had descended on the city, according to the reports of Europeans, when the parachute landings had first been made, but the failure to achieve swift exploitation, with no massive reinforcement arriving by air or sea, gave the propagandists the chance to set ablaze the embers of optimism ever smouldering in the people, and it was accepted brilliantly. And as the shots were fired and the loudspeakers cackled, heard weirdly and dimly by French and British sentries outside the town, Europeans jostled outside the Italian Consulate to receive the refuge which the Consul, Count Mareri, had with derided foresight been preparing for them.

Russia entered the arena belatedly but with a bang, partly no doubt to embarrass America, partly to strengthen her position in the Middle East, and partly to divert attention from her atrocities in Hungary, which were the subject of highly indignant but utterly vain protest in the United Nations, in such contrast to the moves to stop Britain and France. Notes from Bulganin reached London and Paris late on the Monday night, but their content had already been broadcast. After referring to the rockets which he could fire at any moment, Bulganin said, "We are filled with determination to use force to crush the aggressors and . . . hope you will show the necessary prudence and will draw from this the appropriate conclusions." The message, as menacing as it could be without exactly amounting to an ultimatum, caused consternation at the United Nations, which was already obsessed with the danger of another world war, and much to the rage and confusion of the Americans the Soviet delegate followed it up with a resolution to the Security Council that the United States and the Soviet Union should together take military action to pull the British and French back. Lashing out at the Soviet's "sombre record of cynicism", Cabot Lodge dismissed the proposal as "an unthinkable suggestion", but no one knew what the Russians might not do on their own.

Eden, it seems, drew fresh resolve from the offensive Russian note. The day had brought another resignation of a junior Minister, that of Sir Edward Boyle, Economic Secretary to the Treasury, the department concerned with the cost; news of Nutting's had leaked out from his absence from the House and it had been announced the previous Saturday. There was exasperation too among friends at the United Nations, where the helpful Canadian initiative was in danger of being swamped beneath an Afro-Asian attempt, led by Krishna Menon of India, to indict Britain and France as aggressors. The pressure was mounting, and the contradictory news from Port Said, following the first jubilant announcement of the cease-fire in the House, added further strain to nerves that had already borne enough to break a fit man, let alone a seriously ill one. Yet Mollet, receiving a 1 a.m. phone call to discuss the Russian note, found that Eden was in no mood to be intimidated.

Even so, both Prime Ministers urgently needed assurance that they could rely on American protection against Russian attack. Eisenhower, entrenched in self-righteousness behind his slogan "One law for all—friends as well as enemies", was not to be drawn to the telephone. He too was under strain which his physique was in no state to resist. The morrow was the day of the Presidential election, and with no Dulles at hand to sustain him, having been rushed to hospital for an emergency operation, the Russian note grimaced at him with frightening menace. The British and French

17

had at all costs to be stopped, not encouraged, and the only assurance they received was a curt one from the State Department that the United States "will respect its obligations under the North Atlantic Treaty arrangements". It was vague, but definite enough to bring realization that American obligations under N.A.T.O. did not extend to the approaches to Port Said.

Fever germs from New York, London and Paris spread to the invasion fleet as it ploughed through a calm sea on the last night of its journey. After a day of endless speculation, spiced with good-natured jeering at the distinction of their airborne rivals—"those Peg-arses" as they called them from their Pegasus badge—in going in first, the men of the Royal Marine Commandos dossed down early, knowing that the assault was to go in at dawn as planned. There was no such certainty, or rest, for the gunners. Hours of meticulous labour had gone into the preparation of the bombard-ment task tables, but now at the eleventh hour instructions arrived calling for the revision of them all. No gun was to be fired of heavier calibre than 4.5 in. (which excluded the cruisers); charges had to be reduced to avoid "skip" (such as had caused so much devastation when Seymour bombarded Alexandria); and the target area had to be reduced both in width and depth. Then came the order "Cancel bombardment", and commanders and their gunners groaned. But something had to be arranged; the men had to have some protection, however important it was not to hurt the enemy. A makeshift fire support programme, carrying none of the sting originally intended, had hastily to be worked out.

It proved adequate for its prime purpose of getting the troops safely ashore. As the holds of the transports were flooded to set afloat the amphibian Buffalos, their occupants—the leading waves of the 40th and 42nd Commandos, driven by men of the Royal Armoured Corps—had glimpse of dense smoke clouds rising from the stretch of beach, just to the west of the harbour entrance, where they were to land. Beach huts were ablaze, forming a much-needed smoke screen, for the sun had risen and the sky was blue. The Buffalos swam shorewards, only their rims showing above the waterline, and as they drew near the beach, jet fighters took over the task of covering fire from the frigates and destroyers, zooming down frighteningly close to the craft, while to their right, about a mile distant, the machine-guns of Crook's paratroops stuttered. Firing south of the town added to the inferno. Egyptian tanks—or rather, self-propelled anti-tank guns—were shelling the French positions around the waterworks as if attempting to fight their way out. In subduing them, allied aircraft set an oil-well ablaze, and the threat from the Russian armour expired in a massive pall of black smoke.

The great square hulks of the Buffalos emerged from the water and roared up the beach at 20 m.p.h., fifteen of them in all, with a half-troop of thirty men tight-packed in each, unprotected by the armour plating with which they should have been, but were not, equipped. They drove through the blazing huts, in which abandoned stocks of ammunition were exploding, and pulled up beyond the seafront, where the men leapt out at commando speed and rapidly forced their entries into a motley assortment of well-to-do buildings, ranging from the Casino Palace Hotel on the left to large blocks of flats further right, most showing mark of the bombardment but none badly battered. Meanwhile a second wave of commandos waded ashore from assault boats, noting all the signs of a hasty retreat around those huts which had escaped burning.

The commandos had arrived practically unscathed and made their foothold from which to expand. But now the trouble began. The town was packed with armed men, some of them soldiers, some auxiliary policemen, some irregulars of the Liberation Army, some children, and all, practically without exception, clothed in nightshirts or galabiyas, under which arms could so easily be concealed. Some were organized defenders of strong points, some free-lance *francs-tireurs*; some were brave, very brave, others were not, but all had only to aim to kill, and once the impact of the initial onslaught had subsided, they made the most of their opportunity, often yelling like drugged or drunken men. The commandos, so few of whom had been in battle before, faced the supreme test of a soldier, a test not only of skill and courage but of patience and restraint. Captain Douglas Clark, an experienced reservist officer who landed with the commandos to direct gunfire from the fleet, marvelled at the humanity they displayed as he watched them clear out building after building. He saw women helped to safety, screaming children soothed, and wounded gangsters given priority for first-aid treatment even though they had been potting at marines engaged on mercy tasks. Fire came from all directions, yet it was only returned at those seen with weapon in hand. It was a proud day for the men in the green berets and their intrepid leader, Brigadier Rex Madoc.

Progress in such circumstances could not be fast, but Centurions of the 6th Royal Tanks had come ashore, in waterproof clothing, on the heels of the commandos, and in conjunction with air strikes on troublesome strong points they helped to accelerate the advance, blazing away with their Browning machine-guns at known centres of opposition and using their smoke canisters to help the marines across roads. 40th Commando, on the left, advanced briskly down the road alongside the Canal entrance, with behind them the massive figure of de Lesseps pointing the way from his plinth with serenity that mocked the image he would have presented if he had been alive to witness the tragedy. They had soon captured the police station, protected across its open approaches by the hulls of their tanks. 42nd Commando were more enclosed by houses but by 9.30 they had broken out to the power station, south of the town, having re-embarked in their Buffalos and charged down the spacious boulevarde, the rue Mohammed Aly. Feverish fire greeted them, some from windows, some from side roads, where the shooters had women and children all round them, but it nearly all went over the heads of the commandos as they blazed back from the rim of their intimidating but very vulnerable vehicles. Even so, they had their losses, both in killed and wounded.

The 45th Commando had by now joined the battle, being taxied in with a mighty roar by their assorted fleet of twenty-two helicopters which varied in their load capacity from three men to seven. They landed on the seafront after a hazardous reconnaissance by their commanding officer, Lieutenant-Colonel N.H. Tailyour, who landed by mistake on a football-field and had a miraculous escape from the fusillade that greeted him. Tailyour was less fortunate when his supporting aircraft, misdirected by control, swept down on his men just as they were beginning their task of clearing houses between the other two commandos. He was one of nineteen casualties incurred.

Many Egyptians, of all ages and both sexes, were now streaming out of the only escape route open to them, the line of the Manzala Canal running south-westwards through the lake. Crook's paratroops from Gamil watched and let them go, not knowing which were soldiers. Earlier they had without loss gained the block of flats and barracks, their final objective of the day before, but in the adjacent shanty town they came up against a strong point. The naval gunfire called down to silence it started a blaze which soon spread through the whole compound of pitiful sheds and shacks.

Mareri, the Italian consul, had meanwhile been making valiant efforts to arrange a cease-fire. He was in touch with Governor Riad who was just as eager to achieve this end. A message was sent to the French in Fuad, and on landing, unopposed, with his commandos, Massu was greeted with the request to negotiate a surrender. "What a beginning for an invasion!" he is alleged to have groaned, raising his great beak to the sky. Nonetheless he tried, but without success, to arrange a meeting. An hour or so later a British tank lumbered past, and almost into, the Italian Consulate, which soon came within the commandos' gains. British officers were welcomed inside. A call was made to the Governor and a rendezvous arranged —eleven o'clock at the Canal Company's palatial office (an objective of 40th Commando not yet secured).

By good fortune for the allies, without which they would have been able to get none but the leading, waterproofed tanks ashore, there was no serious obstruction across the harbour entrance, despite all the wreckage inside, and by some brisk improvisation the other two squadrons of the 6th Royal Tanks had soon begun unloading at the fishing harbour, near the Casino pier. The remainder of the invasion fleet stood well out to sea and well dispersed. Admiral Durnford-Slater was not going to take risks. He had a fear, rather flattering to the Egyptians, of frogmen saboteurs. It was not the only fear. There were reports from Turkey that aircraft had been plotted overhead, flying southwards from Russia, and that Russian ships were entering the Dardanelles. Later a message was to reach Cyprus from the War Office: RUSSIA MAY INTERVENE IN THE MIDDLE EAST WITH FORCE.

If Stockwell and Durnford-Slater had anxieties they did not show them. On hearing of the surrender initiative they set off in the Admiral's launch, taking with them Air Marshal Barnett and Stockwell's administrative chief, Brigadier John Lacey. It was the same Brigadier Lacey who had been the last British soldier to leave Port Said the previous June, and now he was returning with an elaborate surrender document, prepared overnight after urgent consultation with Keightley's headquarters in Cyprus. The launch chugged sedately past the forlorn mastheads that littered the harbour and on towards the shining offices of the Canal Company, with Navy House just beyond it, divided by a berthing basin. Dense clouds of black smoke still rose from the oil-wells, emphasizing the whiteness of these buildings and the cosy smugness of Fuad on the left. Admiral and General looked on the scene impassively, quite unmindful of the fire that was obviously being directed at them. A bullet crashed into the woodwork an inch from Stockwell's ear. Its target did not even sway. "Not quite ready for us," the Admiral observed. Stockwell grunted agreement, and the launch circled round. "Give 'em a squirt, sir?" asked a seaman standing at a machine-gun. The Admiral nodded and bullets streamed from the Royal Navy into the building which had flown the White Ensign so long.

Stockwell brought his party ashore at the Casino Palace quay and was hospitably received by Mareri at the Italian Consulate. But the negotiations could not even be begun. It was an absurd situation. The Governor had urgently asked for a cease-fire, but could not now be traced. The garrison commander had been one of the first prisoners taken by the commandos; he expressed his eagerness to stop the fighting, but claimed to have no power. General El Moguy had also been captured; he got through to Rouchdi, of the secret police, and an hour's truce was agreed for consultation with Cairo. Nothing came of it, no reply arrived. Rouchdi, safely tucked away in the Arab town, held the power, and it seems that the Russian, Tchikov, was at his side, nurturing his defiance. The loudspeakers were still blaring from this quarter, adjacent to the 42nd Commando's line of advance: "Hold firm, people of Port Said! At ten tonight London and Paris will be destroyed by Russian rockets." The instrument of surrender remained unsigned in Lacey's brief case.

40th Commando, on the canalside, found the going stiffer after the pause. They captured the Canal Company's palace, but met stubborn resistance from Navy House and the warehouses around it. The Egyptians were cornered, and as happened before, they fought to the last. The Royal Navy had regretfully to bring up their fighters to strafe their old headquarters, and as the sun began to sink they wheeled into the attack with their usual unfailing accuracy, blasting out posts of weirdly clad soldiers window by window. The defences were silenced, the last big obstacle reduced, but it was not till next morning that the survivors came out to give themselves up. They left thirty dead comrades inside.

The unloading at the fishing harbour of the 6th Royal Tanks' other two squadrons was complete by one o'clock. One of them went to give further aid to the commandos, while the other set off southwards to head the advance down the causeway. This second squadron was forced off the road by an air strike, which fortunately did them no damage but caused them delay, since the tanks foundered in the soft sand of the golf-course and had to be pulled out. Not until four did they at last join up with the Frenchmen, having passed the still burning oil tanks and the wreckage of battle around them, burnt-out self-propelled guns, corpses and forlornly straying animals released from the abattoir. It was of no importance that they were late. It seemed inconceivable to the British military mind, despite the reports that had come in, that the Egyptians would not take advantage of the vast possibilities for obstruction afforded by the causeway, and Stockwell was so keen that the tanks should not be caught unsupported that he would allow them forward only as far as El Tina, ten miles up the road. Having collected some Algerian soldiers to ride on them as escort, a troop set off and duly reached this objective, passing *en route* (though without spotting them) the reconnaissance party of guardsmen who had again eagerly sallied forth and collected an interesting haul of straying Egyptians, some genuine civilian, others bearing sign of military or pseudo-military connections.

For Brigadier Butler, whose brigade was due to lead the advance with the tanks under command, it had been an afternoon of exasperation. His seaborne battalions were scheduled to have started disembarkation at 8.30 that morning, but their intended quay, beyond Navy House, was inaccessible, and so many other frustrations intruded that his troops and vehicles could not begin offloading, from fishing harbour and Casino quay, until nightfall, 6 p.m. It was no aid to the marshalling of the paras' jeeps and trucks that their road was also being used by the vehicles and tanks of the commandos in support of their attack on Navy House and its warehouses, flames from which illuminated the scene of scrimmage and enlivened it with explosions which sometimes were mistaken for enemy fire. Butler's administrative staff officer, Major A. H. Farrar-Hockley, was meanwhile engaged on an important errand in Port Said, impressing every commercial vehicle he could lay his hands on to carry his dismounted paratroops.

At 7 p.m. (5 in London) a strange order reached Keightley's headquarters: a United Nations force would be arriving to take over in Egypt and there would be a cease-fire from midnight (2 a.m. in Egypt, though in fact military watches had been retarded to Greenwich time) and in the meantime all feasible objectives should be attained. Eden had been unable to hold out any longer. He had been told by Hammarskjöld that both Egypt and Israel had accepted an unconditional cease-fire and that Egypt was believed to be willing to admit the United Nations force. Eden had already told the nation that "If the United Nations would take over this police action we should welcome it", and with revolt brewing inside his own party and the loyalty of his Cabinet under heavy strain, he had no alternative but to prove his good faith. The economic pressure was quite as strong as the political. With oil supplies disrupted, Britain's economy was in danger of a crash, and from America had come the blunt message that relief was conditional on the acceptance of an immediate cease-fire. Eisenhower could apply a thumbscrew quite as painful as Bulganin's, and Conservatives prefer to point to his form of torture rather than admit the impact of the Russian menace which certainly scared one Cabinet member, probably most. There seems little doubt that unanimity was rapidly reached.

For Eden, on the verge of physical collapse, the hardest part of this day of anguish was to notify Mollet of the decision his Cabinet had made. The French were aghast, and Pineau in particular favoured carrying on alone, convinced that Nasser's regime could not survive the occupation of the Canal. But the cause of solidarity, for which the French had already sacrificed much, prevailed. Mollet, however, obtained one concession: instead of five, as originally intended, the cease-fire was put back to midnight.

Members of the Commons attended the ceremonial opening of the new Parliament that afternoon, in the strange absence of the Prime Minister. The Queen, with the jewels of her crown glistening, spoke of the pleasure with which she looked forward to the visits she and her husband were to pay to Portugal, France and Denmark, briefly expressed hope of "a prompt and just settlement in the Middle East", and told of a bill that would be introduced, emphasizing the paradox of the Suez venture, to give the Gold Coast independence under the name of Ghana. Just after six that evening Eden entered the House and told Members of the decision his Cabinet had made. He said that pending confirmation of the expectations expressed by the Secretary-General of the United Nations, the Government were ordering a cease-fire that night. Both sides cheered. Both claimed victory.

It was a long time before the news reached the man most closely affected, General Stockwell. The decision was agreed in principle, according to Eden's memoirs, at a Cabinet meeting which began at 9.45. Seven hours were to pass before the order, or warning of it, reached Keightley, and when it was in turn passed on to *Tyne*

Stockwell was nowhere to be found. He had spent the afternoon roving the battlefield, ever indifferent to the bullets that were still flying around from in front and behind—and among the interesting sights he had seen was that of another lieutenant-general. It was Campbell Hardy, Commandant-General of the Royal Marines, who had had himself illicitly smuggled in by helicopter to be with his men in their hour of trial. "Is this a perfidious British plot to supersede me as second-in-command?" asked Beaufre, keeping pace with the tempo of British humour.

Having seen the disembarkation of Butler's paratroops under way and ordered him to advance to the southern end of the causeway as soon as he could, Stockwell went to the waterfront in search of a lift back to *Tyne*, since it was too dark now to go by helicopter, as he had planned, and Durnford-Slater had returned in his launch. "I'll take you, sir," volunteered a marine with all the eagerness of a taxi-driver starved of fares, and Stockwell got in his assault landing craft with Lacey and his G.2, Major R. E. Worsley. They plunged hazardously over the breakwater beyond de Lesseps' statue rather than go the extra mile round it, and in the heavy sea beyond the engine failed. It was pitch dark and they had no wireless. The engine revived with aid from the passengers, but *Tyne*, standing well out to sea, shone no homing light and Stockwell was in the unusual position, for a land force commander, of being lost out at sea. "S.O.S.—G.O.C.," flashed Worsley on an Aldous lamp, straining his knowledge of Morse, and at last, some two hours after they had set out, they found their ship, and Stockwell climbed aboard to be greeted by a most unamused Durnford-Slater brandishing two messages. One told of the danger of Russian intervention, the other of the cease-fire. It was well over an hour since news of the latter had been broadcast to the world.

Stockwell had some four hours left to him. Eschewing spectacular ambition, he chose El Cap railway halt, where there is a bulge in the causeway, as a feasible objective. This was eight miles beyond the tanks at El Tina and five miles short of the end of the causeway at Kantara. Butler was in process of issuing orders at the waterworks for the advance to Kantara, as a first objective, when he was interrupted by the call from *Tyne* notifying this amazing change of plan. He did not take it seriously at first. It seemed past belief that with the fruits of victory at last ripe for the plucking, the harvest should be cut short by some absurd self-denying ordinance conjured up by politicians without advice from the men on the spot. Then came realization that even the limited objective laid down by Stockwell might not be so easy to attain. The men of the 2nd Parachute Battalion were still far from their start line and the only means of speeding them yet available was a shuttle service run by jeep. Officers fussed and fretted, and General Massu, come across from Fuad to assume overall command of the break-out, snorted and fumed. But of course the advance could not begin until sufficient force was assembled to smash any opposition encountered to smithereens.

At last Farrar-Hockley, the brigade D.A.A. & Q.M.G., arrived with his weird assortment of impressed vehicles, buses, lorries, vans, most of them advertising their fares, and the paratroops jumped on board and rode to El Tina, where the tanks were waiting. There were forty minutes left, eight miles to go. The Centurions hummed along at 20 m.p.h., with Algerians still riding on them, one troop on the Canal road, one on the Treaty road, visible to each other in the moonlight. They reached El Cap—just as any of the soldiers who for the last two days had been on the causeway could have done. There was a forlorn conference between the officers of the paratroops and tanks, headed by three impetuous Irishmen, Butler, his battalion commander, Lieutenant-Colonel H. E. N. Bredin, and the one-armed Lieutenant-Colonel T. H. Gibbon of the 6th Royal Tanks. The temptation was great: they could be in Ismailia in another two hours. But the eyes of the world were on Butler, through the medium of the journalists, American, British, French, who had hooked themselves on to the tail of the column, determined to get a good story after all the frustrations of stringent censorship at Cyprus. From Bredin, told to get his men dug in, they obtained a quote that sums up the feeling that had gained increasing hold on the fighting soldier from the earliest days of preparation: "War is really a pretty simple thing. It only becomes complicated when the politicians take a hand."

In Port Said itself the battle came to no clear-cut end. Co-ordinated resistance had been crushed, but desultory firing went on all night, mainly from the Arab quarter, and fires still blazed, causing one frightening explosion. Not until dawn did the paratroops from Gamil link up with the Royal Marine commandos, as Egyptian freedom fighters slunk away from the Arab quarter, through the smoke of the still smouldering shanty town, and off with the refugees by boat along Manzala Canal. The Battle of Port Said was over, exactly two days after it had begun.

It had cost the 3rd Parachute Battalion three killed and thirty-two wounded and the 3rd Commando Brigade eight killed and sixty wounded. The Army lost a further five killed and four wounded either in the battle or during the ensuing occupation, while in the air operations the Royal Navy had one killed and the Royal Air Force four killed and one wounded, making the overall British total twenty-one killed and ninety-seven wounded. The French suffered ten soldiers killed and thirty-three wounded, and one sailor missing.

As for the Egyptian losses, the legal investigator specially appointed by the British Government estimated the figure at 650 dead and nine hundred seriously wounded in Port Said and a further hundred killed in Fuad. The 30:1 ratio of dead, Egyptian to British, was only slightly lower than at Tel-el-Kebir, and for this the combined exertion by the secret policeman and the Russian consul deserves the credit. They were the real victors of the day.

CHAPTER TWENTY-ONE

Military Might-Have-Beens

EDEN HAD ACHIEVED his declared purpose of dividing the contestants and now that the United Nations were taking over the task, as he had said he desired, it looked at the time as if he had scored a dramatic victory. Not until later, when the United Nations showed stronger inclination to humiliate and frustrate, rather than co-operate, did people in Britain, other than left-wingers, begin to share the Frenchman's anger that the troops had been stopped with the job half done. "We should have gone on!" became the oft-heard cry.

Whether so rich a reward would have been reaped from such a policy is open to dispute. Certainly it would have been possible to have started clearance operations earlier, and this would have brought eventual economic advantage. It is also possible that some of the equipment from the plundered base might have been retrieved. Assuming the thrust up the Canal were swift and painless, as it had every chance of being, the humiliation would have weakened Nasser's standing, both at home and in the Arab world, but the French belief that it would have caused his downfall may well have been based, like so many political calculations, on wishful thinking. Nasser held his capital firmly, fortified by the backing of both Russian and American—and though it was said that he had a plane ready to fly him out of the country, this rumour was current long before the operation began. Opinion is divided even between the staffs of the Australian legation and the British Embassy, both of whom were under house guard at the time but have not lacked sources of information since. The Australian view, as expressed by A. R. Cutler, is that Nasser's regime could not have survived the occupation of the Canal, following the absurd claims that had been made over Cairo radio about the annihilation of the invaders. British Embassy officials, however, are not so certain.

The one conclusion that must stand like a rock out of the mist is that the further the allies had advanced the stronger the pressure would have become, political and even more compelling, economic, to make them desist, and that their occupation of the Canal would have been of no use as a lever for dictating terms for its future usage. Their armies would also have been exposed to terrorist activities which can be guaranteed to have lost nothing in venom from the collapse of Nasser's regime if it had been achieved. By stopping where they did the soldiers at least made the inevitable task of extrication easier for themselves.

However, they had been set the task of occupying the full length of the Canal, and their failure to do so caused much remorse, nurturing the national inferiority complex already sown in British and French alike by disillusionment in their influence in the world. Confidence between the armed services and Government was frayed, and many British Army officers who had taken part seethed with frustration at the cramping, nervy interference they had suffered at the hands of the politicians, which shrivelled both the size and impact of the victory they had won. The men did not greatly care. A staff officer who visited the fighting units soon after the cease-fire to sound opinion found that the age-old philosophy of the soldier still held good. It was enough for them that they had carried out the tasks assigned.

There is to this day certain sensitivity in the Army to criticism of the part they played, and it must be remembered that hindsight confers an incalculable advantage not available to the man who had to make the decisions at the time. Any journalist can turn himself into a brilliant general in retrospect, but is apt to disregard the circumstances prevailing. An important feature of the Port Said operation, easily forgotten, is that the politicians were aware of the timetable the military had prepared. They told them to implement their plans at shortest notice, far shorter than promised, and asked for acceleration when the political timetable went astray. General Keightley could not respond to this demand, except by advancing the parachute landing a day. Once his troops were committed, he was given no indication whatever that his time might be cut short.

Ismailia by November 8 and Suez by the 11th were his phased objectives—until he received an order that he had only seven hours left to gain what ground he could. Yet he has himself admitted in his despatch, "My main concern was naturally that of speed", and it is fair to consider whether the military made full use of their opportunities, whether in fact they might have achieved the victory of which they felt themselves robbed, despite the limitations so unexpectedly imposed.

The first failure open to criticism is the inability of the services to strike when political opportunity was at its brightest, immediately following Nasser's provocative seizure of the Canal. It was due to deficiencies, of men, aircraft and landing craft, which stem more from political than military causes. The world was ready to applaud summary punishment of the villain, but Britain had no stick at hand ready in pickle.

It would have stirred the hearts of the old and bold if reprisal could have been exacted by swift *coup de main* methods, such as a commando landing at Port Said and an airborne one at Ismailia to regain the Canal Company's stolen offices. Such measures, however, would scarcely have been militarily practicable, since they would have called for air support on a scale far in excess of normal peacetime resources; nor were they politically desirable, since Eden was bent on rallying world opinion and did not want to precipitate military involvement. It is doubtful, in fact, whether his plans were seriously affected by the delay in assembling the great striking force deemed necessary for full invasion, envisaging as they did the leisurely procedure of consultation and negotiation by the Canal users. Nonetheless, nearly seven weeks went by from the day the Chiefs of Staff were ordered to prepare a plan of action until it was ready for fruition. Wolseley, on the other hand, had committed two divisions to battle and seized the entire length of the Canal within a month of the day of Governmental decision. Such comparison, which admittedly is facile, reflects not so much on the staff work of the twentieth-century planners as on the lack of foresight at Cabinet and Chiefs of Staff level. Wolseley had made all his plans long before the Government required him to act.

A more cramping, and in the event decisive, impediment was imposed by the decision to use Malta, as opposed to Cyprus, as the base for the seaborne assault. Here again there is rebuking contrast with Britain's previous invasion of Egypt, for it will be remembered that Wolseley had a brigade waiting in Cyprus to seize the Canal in a matter of twenty-four hours, and indeed the spearhead of this brigade, re-directed to Alexandria, was in Egypt within two days of receiving orders. The drawbacks of the Cyprus of 1956 have already been explained on page 208 and there is no need to add more than to express the belief that if the will had been there, backed by the experience in improvisation gained from the Normandy campaign, all the commandos and their tanks could have been launched from Cyprus—and even if an extra two days had been required for loading there would still have been a two-day saving on the eight required for embarkation and sailing from Malta. But of course the soldiers were not keen on concentrating for embarkation when there was a danger of bombs from the Ilyushins falling on them. The journey from Malta afforded ample time for the air battle to be won before the ships came within the danger zone, and if the politicians were not pressing for speedier capability of intervention, there is no reason why the soldiers should have created hazards for themselves. Even so, it seems odd that the assault commandos had actually to be moved away from Cyprus to prepare for action, and even odder that a regiment of tanks was kept aboard its transports off the Isle of Wight, while the one much nearer the enemy needed two days' warning (mainly for the task of waterproofing) before it could hope to sail. And when the latter did at last get under way it did the journey in the slowest time on record, even for an elderly L.C.T.

With the seaborne plans rigid, and known and approved by the political chiefs, the airborne afforded the only prospect of flexibility, and it may well be wondered why there was such resistance to the urging of the French commanders, who certainly had the British paratroopers on their side. It can scarcely be denied that operation Omelette would have been successful and that at any rate from Sunday morning the troops could have landed anywhere along the Canal and gone wherever they chose. Yet there were risks which are apt to get obscured in the mist of hindsight. The Egyptians had spent the Thursday and Friday nights bringing their tanks back across the Canal and on the Saturday, when decision was required at latest, they must still have been in considerable strength around Ismailia, and even if there were no Russian-manned tanks among them the spectre of them had not yet been exorcized. The extra fifty miles inland would have reduced the weight of support available to the paratroops from naval and land-based aircraft, and the air offensive in general would be further impeded by the reduction in offensive effort from the paratroops' aerodromes, Nicosia and Tymbou, which were not equipped to bear the dual load. There was also a shortage of transport aircraft, limiting British and French to a single battalion drop, with the alternative of reinforcement or supply on the return journey.

No one should blame a commander for reluctance to commit his men to unnecessary risk. Yet mere concern for their safety may not have been the only factor. From its very conception the planning bears mark of a firm determination on the part of the British, as evinced by the size of the force prepared, to deny Egypt all chance even of a minor success, be it the capture of a patrol, the sinking of a ship, or the shooting down of an aeroplane. Prestige was at stake, and it seems that Eden was as keenly aware of its importance as his soldiers. Yet of course there was political risk, as daily became more apparent, in this eschewing of military risk, and there was risk too to the soldiers' reputation. The Israelis had knowingly broken most of the recognized rules, gambling on an accurate assessment of the calibre of the opposition. Against different troops their tactics would, as Colonel Robert Henriques has pointed out, "have meant not spectacular success, but bloody disasters". Their success presented challenge which went unanswered. Neither the planning nor thinking of the British was flexible enough to convert the setpiece invasion they had prepared into swift exploitation of the victory already won by the Israelis.

As for the assault when at last it came, two unusual features, quite possibly unique, mark its brilliance on the one hand, its failing on the other. The deliberate landing of parachutists on defended and fortified positions was a daring stroke, in such contrast to the general trend, which was executed with high skill and courage. Both landings were completely successful, with three miles of coastline gained. Yet next day another deliberate assault was delivered, under naval bombardment, at a point within a mile of the coastline already held. And the troops on shore had specially halted in order to allow this second assault, with all its gunfire, to go in.

Of course, if it had not been for the mischance of the hidden cable to Cairo, the paratroops would have gained full possession and white flags would have greeted the invasion fleet. But the paratroops relied more on luck than on strength. Since their landing at 7.15 that morning only 56 reinforcements had flown in to join the two battalions west of the Canal. There was nothing more they could do when the Egyptian commander announced at 10.30 that night that he would fight on. The invaders sat fast while the innocents were prepared for the slaughter, roused to a fever-pitch of resolution by the blare of the loud-speaker and its phony, intoxicating news. For the Russian consul it was a night of triumph; for the allies one of squandered opportunity.

It is strange indeed that no real effort was made to gain the Port Said beachline when the main purpose of advancing the date of the parachute landing was to prise open the gates of the town without resort to naval bombardment. Crook's parachute battalion, according to Keightley's despatch, "was to advance into the town and occupy it if resistance was slight but if unable to do so it would wait for the seaborne assault on the following day". The resistance met was stronger than slight but Crook would deny that he was unable to advance any further. He stopped because there was no point in going any further; the coastguard barracks formed the final objective assigned him and he did not occupy them because he would have had to move out next morning to avoid being hit by the guns of the fleet. He has expressed the view that his leading company could have captured the barracks and that a fresh company, freed from protective duties by the arrival of the scratch reinforcements, could then have passed through and seized the docks during the night. All he lacked was the necessary order.

Crook's assessment, made in retrospect, may be optimistic, but there was no reason why his men should have had to battle through the town on their own. Two regiments of French parachutists were champing with envy and impatience in Cyprus. If the British could fly in their planes, as the guardsmen and sappers had done, the French could fly in British ones, especially with the whole of Sunday in which to make arrangements, and instead of the meagre remnant of Crook's battalion, a complete battalion group of dashing Legionnaires could have come into Gamil, either by parachute or on the wheels of their aircraft. Also available—and in fact offered to Stockwell by the carrier group commander, Vice-Admiral M. L. Power—was the 45th Commando, waiting with their helicopters. Resource and imagination had gone into the provision of this highly mobile reserve, and here was an imaginative way of taking advantage of the scope it afforded. Previously, a more daring role had been considered for the helicopters, but in the end they were used merely as an additional wave of landing craft.

It is hard to believe that the Egyptians would have long withstood assault by these three motley units, jealous for the pride both of nation and corps. Indeed, their mere arrival would probably have brought submission before the shock of the initial landing had worn off, and there would have been little chance for the Russian to demonstrate his flair for instigation.

Even if the town were only partially cleared overnight, Stockwell would have been admirably placed at daybreak to effect a speedy break-out, which in the event took second place to the reduction of Port Said but which surely was the more important task, whether time was limited or not. A mobile force was at hand, of fifteen Centurion tanks and fifteen Buffalos, with some 450 commandos on board, ready to dash for Ismailia from the moment they touched the beach. If an obstructing post were encountered on the causeway, the Buffalos could outflank it, either across the lake or along the Sweet Water Canal, but the route in fact was clear and patrols from the French-held position could have established themselves at the end of the causeway if they had not been cramped by the self-imposed restriction of the arbitrary bombline.

The Buffalos were tuned up to cruise at 24 m.p.h. on land and the Centurions could keep with them. They could probably have covered the fifty miles to Ismailia in three hours, and surely in five, that is by eleven o'clock, and their task there would have been to open the route southwards, not to clear the town. The helicopters were available to fly in reserves and supplies, and the road could have been kept open first for a second squadron of Centurions and then for the French AMX tanks. These have a speed of 50 m.p.h. and if further Frenchmen had been dropped around midday in the neighbourhood of Suez—instead of being left to work off their frustration in Cyprus—the *"mécanique rapide"* would have had a 55-mile journey to reach them from Ismailia and some seven hours of daylight left, with a further eight hours available before the cease-fire came into force. They would have been unlikely to have failed. Thus the task could have been achieved within the allotted span, and without any alteration to the dispositions of the allied force assembled for the battle—and at least the soldiers would have been happy and able to claim that the Israelis were not the only troops capable of the spectacular.

Those who were there would not dispute the feasibility of this plan produced by the leisurely application of hindsight. They would merely say, "But how were we to know? No one told us time was that short." They have a point there. At the same time, the need for urgency was acknowledged, the means of acceleration available, and with air supremacy complete there can be no excuse for ignorance of the enemy dispositions. One cannot escape the conclusion that the operation was rigid and over-ponderous. The hammer was raised and the hammer had to fall, and across the path of its heavy deliberation lies not only the spectre of Russian-manned weapons but the shadow of political interference.

Soldiers are the servants of Government and it is up to them to carry out the bidding of their political chiefs in peace and war. In an operation of this nature, half war, half peace, shared by two nations, it was inevitable and right that the politicians should exercise close control over military initiative. Yet the control placed vexing strain on the soldiers. From the moment of its concept in early August, the operation was a saga of change, and even as the troops journeyed towards their objectives, instructions streamed into the headquarters in Cyprus calling for amendment to assault and fire support programmes and for consideration of fresh ideas. In the end a stubborn resistance to change reveals itself through the liquid of plan and counter-plan. Clarity of purpose became the outstanding requirement and plans remained unchanged merely through fear of the confusion which further change might cause. The parachutists would go in a day earlier if they must, but further adjustments to meet the changed situation were eschewed.

It may also be that "ponderosity", as Lord Wavell termed it, had become a habit of the British Army and that the seeds were sown in the sand of Egypt. In the early days of the desert fighting in the Second World War, dash and enterprise brought glorious dividends, but later practitioners were worsted by Rommel in the fluid battle and disillusionment set in. Montgomery restored faith in orthodoxy and crushed the enemy by deliberate and unspectacular methods, bringing the full, co-ordinated weight of his divisions to bear. "Balance" was his watchword, but it was not one to inspire great daring, and military teaching in the post-war years was concerned more with avoiding such a misfortune as the one at Arnhem, the one occasion when Montgomery's troops were caught off balance, than with fighting lightweight wars against lightweight opposition. In the imaginary battles fought at the Staff College the opposition was always formidable, the supporting weapons available to both sides massive. No such frivolous thing as a gallop through Egypt received consideration.

But the history of Egypt shows that speed was never one of Britain's military assets. It did not matter to Napoleon that half his troops might die of thirst in the desert; they had to get to Cairo, and get there they did, with no hanging around for stores to be off-loaded and the ration train to come up. Abercromby would run no such risks. Displaying flair for unflurried deliberation from the very start, British troops devoted their first four days in Egypt to their administrative needs, and in the process lost the chance to enter Alexandria. When at last they set off for Cairo the journey took them more than three times as long as it had done the French. The pattern was set, even if circumstances to a certain extent differed. The next time French troops intervened in the affairs of Egypt was when their tiny detachment turned up at Fashoda, having run risks which astounded the British officers who had been methodically borne to Khartoum by the mighty administrative machine that revealed Kitchener's true genius. It was predictable enough that when the two nations teamed up for the joint attempt on Egypt the French should always be calling "*Allons!*" the British restraining them with "Steady!"

French impetuosity also played its part in the 1882 intervention. It was the French politicians who gave the British the initial shove, and they then backed away, leaving it to Britain to unfold her might and majesty. Thanks to the genius of Wolseley, all details had already been carefully thought out, administrative as much as operational, and the operation was an unqualified success, but Wolseley had many advantages for which Keightley must have pined. The Government, self-consciously unmilitary, were thankful to leave all the details to him, and his terms of reference, as announced to the world, were vague enough to give scope for deception, which, with fortuitous aid from de Lesseps, enabled him to seize the Canal intact. World opinion was complacent and there was no febrile political agitation to disturb the military pulse, even though Arabi had his sympathizers. But the military critics were a constant source of irritation, doing their utmost to cause stampede. Wolseley contemptuously ignored them. In the best traditions of the British Army he was balancing himself to deliver a mighty blow, taking no chances on the shortcomings of the enemy, and was determined not to strike until he had attained equilibrium.

There is affinity between Wolseley's resistance to pressure by the critics and the determination shown by Keightley, Stockwell and

Durnford-Slater to stick to original plans. Wolseley would have sympathized with them and have backed the stand they made; he, too, had dread of impetuosity. But it seems likely that with all his flair for transport improvisation he would have so disposed of his forces as to be able to deliver a heavier blow in shorter time. Wolseley had been governor of Cyprus and fully appreciated its strategic value. He would surely have seen that it packed a stronger punch.

And if the British and French ran true to form, so too did the Egyptians. Slow to react, incapable of effective counter-stroke, and irresolute in open positions, they yet showed that there were some among them prepared to fight to the last for the final positions. Though history repeats itself only in vaguest form, students of the campaigns of 1798, 1801, 1882 and 1898 could well have foreseen developments as battle approached in 1956.

CHAPTER TWENTY-TWO

Farewell Again

(1956)

LITTLE MOVED IN Port Said on the Wednesday morning, November 7, except dogs, English soldiers, flood water from burst mains, and the flicker of flames round the oil installations. It was a city of the dead, with corpses in the streets and both prison and police stations empty. But there was activity enough in the harbour as landing ships came in rotation to the few berths available, and lighters, which luckily had gained immunity from scuttling through the influence of their owners, were impressed into service to unload larger ships. The salvage ships of the Royal Navy had meanwhile begun their mammoth task of clearance, five days of which had to be devoted merely to clearing a lane through to the inner harbour. Further up the Canal the Egyptians just as emergetically carried on with their task of obstruction.

The army also had an urgent task on hand in clearing up the mess they had made. Commandos diligently searched houses and relieved defiant youths of their weapons; fifty-seven 3-ton lorry-loads, made up of widely assorted arms, ammunition and equipment, were removed from the Arab quarter in a single day's haul. Engineers took over the waterworks and power-station, neither of which was damaged, and repaired breaks in distribution with aid from the Egyptian fire-brigade, the one service to remain faithfully on duty. The flow of sewage, impeded as a result of an air strike for the paratroops, presented a more vexing problem and was the lasting cause of stink and anxiety. Army medical teams brought swift succour to the hospitals, two of which had been badly damaged, while the military police got prisoners of war to line up their dead, ready for identification and removal by the Egyptians—or more often than not removal unidentified—in what was to prove a sad and grim proceeding.

Governor Riad was found in the house of the Commandant of Police and brought in a tank to Stockwell's headquarters, now established in the Canal Company's palatial office. He had been under fearful strain, caught between the crossfire of the demand to resist from Cairo and his own earnest concern for the safety of his people, and was in no state to re-establish his administration. However, a Civil Affairs officer, who had landed hard on the heels of the fighting troops, installed him in a temporary office with the Commandant of Police, since the Governorate had been badly hit, and evoked a measure of uneasy, defeatist co-operation. A quarter of the police force—four hundred out of 1,600—had reported for duty by the week-end, wearing expressions as black as their uniform, but no magistrate offered his services and looters risked little more than custody in the redcaps' compound. Greater success, and co-operation, was achieved in the sphere of welfare. With army tents and rations, a relief centre was established for the destitute and homeless, most of them from the burnt out shanty town, and so popular did it become that its inhabitants rose from an immediate six hundred to close on three thousand before the Red Cross took over responsibility for their care. There was no food shortage in Port Said, and the two ships that accompanied the convoy with emergency supplies remained unloaded out at sea, as also did two French wine-tankers filled with water.

Gradually the inhabitants emerged from their hide-outs. There was little wreckage of battle left now, except for the occasional crumpled building, such as Navy House, the Governorate and the coastguard barracks, and the distorted remains of an anti-aircraft gun which Stockwell had ordered to be left outside his headquarters to commemorate the accuracy of the Fleet Air Arm. Shops were ordered to be opened over the week-end, and it was hoped that trade would flow briskly with the aid of the million Egyptian pounds the British had brought with them, for distribution to troops and contractors: a legacy of the hoarding forced on the British Army consequent on the judgement given against it for the destruction of Kafr Abdu. There was some slight relaxation, the occasional smile to be seen here and there, and the Greek or Lebanese trader could truthfully say, after a furtive look round him, how glad he was to see the British back. Swarms of children scampered for sweets chucked at them by Stockwell from the driving seat of his Landrover, and young men flocked round the soldiers' billets with the merchandise for which Port Said is famous.

The holiday was soon over. With the occupation barely a week old, the shops abruptly shut down again and the street-vendors vanished. A general strike had been declared, with murder displayed as the penalty for blacklegs. It was another trick to Rouchdi, of the secret police, and his Russian mentor, Tchikov. Stockwell had had Rouchdi arrested, but had ironically been constrained to release him in the cause of co-operation with the local authorities.

The bulk of the 3rd Division had by now arrived, after dropping the 1st Royal Tanks off at Malta and leaving the Life Guards behind in England—though the officers' mess truck of the latter was one of the first vehicles ashore when the convoy reached Port Said. The first troops to land, on November 10, were the 1st Queen's Own Royal West Kent, a battalion that had accompanied Abercromby's expedition and come again with Wolseley. They were due to relieve the 2nd Para on the El Cap position, and while the commanding officer was making his reconnaissance, two distinguished journalists, the American David Seymour and the Frenchman Jean Roy, drove straight through the position, came under fire from the Egyptians, and met death in the Canal. Although the Egyptian troops did not arrive until two days after Bredin's paratroops, they appeared to believe that they had halted the advance, and indeed with Cairo Radio extolling the heroism even of the airmen in the great battle of "the new Stalingrad" they had no reason to doubt their own. Constant firing during the night of the 10th drew retaliation from the paras, but next morning the Royal West Kent relieved them in daylight and in peace.

It was a bizarre life in the forward positions, for the visitors almost outnumbered the troops on the ground, and the bar of the officers' mess provided the most urgent problem of supply. Confined though they were, the troops here were in a happier position than the men of the 19th Infantry Brigade, which had the task of keeping order in the town, where a six to six curfew had been imposed as a result of the belligerence that attended the general strike. The hardest lot, initially, fell to the 1st Royal Scots, who had to enforce the curfew in the narrow, festering streets of the Arab town which they cleared by jeep patrol, with horns blaring, while myriad eyes watched the bedlam from balconies that almost met across the streets. Firing broke out nightly, and almost as frequently came calls for the regimental medical officer, who, as civilian doctors were unwilling to venture out at night, acted as midwife, physician and casualty officer to them all. Much time was devoted to administering to domestic needs, and among some notable incidents was the single-handed rescue by a sergeant-major of the Royal Military Police of a family of seven trapped in a blazing house. A great crowd of Egyptians cheered.

There was a distinctly cosier atmosphere across the water at Fuad. The French paid less heed to the welfare of the inhabitants and more to their own. Their most important reinforcements consisted of a contingent of "nurses". One of them was General Massu's cook; others had less skilled and more conventional duties to perform. ("But they are not nurses, they are 'ores," explained a French liaison officer when a British one naïvely asked whether they really expected such heavy casualties.)

The advanced party of the United Nations, consisting of ten observers, arrived at Port Said on November 13 and emerged from the massive jaws of a landing ship to face a battery of news-reel cameras. They attracted as much interest as men from Mars, and indeed their Canadian commander, Lieutenant-General E. L. M. Burns, who flew to Cairo from Palestine, where he had command of the U.N. observer team, cut a peculiarly out-of-this-world figure in the sky-blue uniform he had had specially made for the purpose, so that his national, British-style uniform should not give offence. His incongruously rugged features were guarded and stern when he first came to Port Said. His visit was a begging one, to obtain vehicles from the British and blue paint from the French.

Hours of frantic planning had gone into the raising of this first ever United Nations Emergency Force, and in a short time contingents of Norwegians, Danes, Swedes, Finns, Yugo-Slavians, Colombians, Brazilians, Indians and Indonesians were on their way, some making their army's first appearance overseas, and backing them were technical troops from Canada, sent after protests from Nasser which nearly caused Burns to resign. After staging at Naples, where arm-bands were issued and helmets painted sky-blue, the leading elements were flown into Abu Sueir airfield, near Ismailia, on November 20, barely a fortnight after the conception of the force, and next day a company of Norwegians arrived by train at Port Said. Such was the exuberance of the welcome accorded these men—liberators to the Egyptians, Bluebells to the British—that the West Yorkshires had to clear a passage for them through to their camp in the Governorate gardens. Danes, Swedes and Colombians soon followed, either into Said or Fuad. Yugo-Slavs and Indians passed through Port Said. The former were keen to show their contempt for the invaders and were much exasperated at being unable to unload their ships without British aid; the latter seemed determined to show that they did not share the indignation of their political chiefs. "Great to see you again" was their usual welcome for a British officer, and a major was heard to inquire of a former Indian Army colleague, "When do we start fighting the wogs?"

Storm meanwhile was brewing again in the United Nations. Britain and France had accepted the cease-fire "pending confirmation" that the United Nations force should effectively ensure both peace between Israel and Egypt and a settlement of the Suez Canal dispute and that clearance operations should go fast ahead. These requirements had not as yet been met, and now Krishna Menon was preparing another all-out indictment of the invaders, while Nasser arrogantly laid down conditions for the United Nations' entry and continued sinking blockships in the Canal. Cabot Lodge, the American representative, persuaded Menon to water down his resolution to one expressing regret "that intervening forces remain" and urging that they "withdraw forthwith". In the debate on November 24 the American gave it his vote with most of the world, much to the fury of British Tories in particular and the despair of his abstaining N.A.T.O. allies, one of whom, Spaak of Belgium, had proposed an accommodating amendment. Following the cease-fire, Eden had had a friendly chat with Eisenhower and been given to believe that he would welcome an early meeting with him and Mollet. But Selwyn Lloyd, in America for the General Assembly meeting, was given the coldest of cold brush-offs. The Anglo-American relationship had reached freezing point. "The United States Administration," Eden bitterly commented in his memoirs, "seemed to be dominated at this time by one thought only, to harry their allies."

Lloyd sombrely returned to London, having obtained no more than an undertaking from Hammarskjöld that the United Nations force would remain until its task was deemed to be fulfilled. Two days earlier, on November 23, Eden had also crossed the Atlantic, bound, not for Washington, but for Jamaica, where he was to take a rest. He had capitulated to the debility that so drained resistance to the strain of anxiety, and Lloyd was left to announce the Government's capitulation to the House. Financial ruin was the alternative, such was the half-nelson the Americans applied.

He broke the gloomy news on Monday, December 3, allowing himself some meagre room for bargaining by announcing that the British and French Governments had agreed to "withdraw forthwith" without naming any date of completion. He made five claims for the intervention, each of which drew a great outburst of laughter from the Opposition. "We have stopped a local war. (Laughter.) We have prevented it spreading. (Laughter.) The extent of Soviet penetration has been revealed. (Laughter.) We have caused the United Nations to take action . . . (Laughter.) We have alerted the whole world (loud and prolonged laughter) to a situation of great peril." These claims did not all deserve derision, but the cost, as he admitted, was heavy and the wider objects desired by most Tories, "the effective safeguards for our vital interests", were further from attainment than ever. There was rebellious depression on the Government benches, triumphant mockery on those opposite. Next day Harold Macmillan, as Chancellor of the Exchequer, announced an increase of 1/5 in the price of petrol, which had already been rationed, and gave hint of further hardship to come to rectify a £100,000,000 fall in gold and dollar reserves. Support for the Tories, as indicated by opinion polls, plunged dizzily from its apogee of the days of action.

As for the French, they were in no position to hold out on their own, for they had other wars for their troops to fight and had begun to withdraw them even before the General Assembly debate. But the Israelis, typically, were not to be coerced. Having gathered in their bumper crop of captured weapons and documentary evidence of aggressive intent, they held tight to the key features they had captured.

As it became evident that the British were definitely going, guerrilla warfare broke out in Port Said. The first grenades were thrown on November 28, and from then onwards British troops, and often civilians, came daily under attack, sometimes even in their billets by fire from rocket launcher. It was a tense time for the street patrols, who had to move back to back, and the Argylls were kept busy around the shanty town running boat patrols on Lake Manzala, across which stocks of weapons and ammunition—and trained terrorists with them—were being smuggled into the town, as evidenced by the capture of a monster haul. There was already plenty of evidence of an underground organization in Port Said, which had been issuing terrifying posters signed by "the Black Hand" until its printing-press had been captured. It was obvious now that the inspiration came from much further afield, and to encourage the rebellious, Cairo Radio rose to such a fever-pitch of venom that Keightley took the ungentlemanly step of permitting jamming from Cyprus. Stockwell made strong complaint to Burns against the constant violation of the cease-fire. But the United Nations had no means of exerting pressure other than formal protest, nor did they intend to get involved in any fighting, friendly and co-operative though their relationship was with the British command in Port Said.

General Hakim Amer, speaking for Nasser's Government, publicly disclaimed responsibility for the guerrilla campaign and gave assurance that the policy was to allow the re-embarkation to proceed without incident. It was not in his interest, nor of Nasser's, that their authority should be seen to be flouted, and there is trace here of a faltering hold. There had been angry rumblings in Cairo, not far removed from open demonstration, when the first much-publicized Red Cross train arrived from Port Said with its load of wounded and brought a story that so contradicted the arrant boasts made by Cairo Radio. Some wailed for the sufferers, some for Egypt's wounded pride. Fiery spirits, both in military and political ranks, felt the same sense of shame as provided such a spur to the revolutionary movement after the Palestine War. It was as well to find an outlet for their passion, and it was perhaps with such a thought in mind that Rouchdi was despatched to Cairo on a Red Cross train, bandaged beyond recognition, except by the very cute. Thus did the field commander come to the War Office—and who can say what his real motive was?

The British presence dwindled. Within a week of Lloyd's announcement the El Cap position had been handed over to Indians and most of the British and French forces, with most of their five thousand vehicles, and many bereft natationals, British, French and Italian, had gone. The 19th Brigade remained to fight a rearguard action in Port Said, while the French kept two battalions in Fuad. But there was danger now that their departure might be delayed. General R. A. Wheeler, an elderly American, had arrived to take charge of the United Nations salvage operation, dressed in black and exuding self-righteous indignation at the sins of the unrepentant British (who had once honoured him with a knighthood). He announced that he would get the job done without aid from the powerful Anglo-French salvage fleet which had already achieved so much.

He soon had to go back on his word. The Egyptians had now sunk thirty-two ships in the Canal (apart from a further twenty-one in Port Said harbour) and blown up bridges with true Russian flair for destruction, and Wheeler had to admit that the task of clearance was beyond the resources he could obtain without calling on the offending nations. Already there had been maddening delay because the Egyptians refused to allow the work to start until the withdrawal was complete, even though Eden had offered to place his ships under United Nations command. Now Wheeler asked for these ships, but on Nasser's terms—stripped of all weapons, identifying flags and uniforms. British pride demanded a stand, adding briefly to the delay already caused by the other party with most to gain from the clearance, but the only concessions that could be obtained were that the United Nations would provide protective picquets and that the crews retain their personal weapons below decks. It was a hard task for Admiral Durnford-Slater to persuade the men of the eighteen salvage ships (and one French) selected that such alienation was in their country's best interests. However, agreement was reached before the planned, but unannounced, day of departure, December 22.

The terrorists stepped up their activities, as if determined to write their names large across this postscript to the long chapter of British occupation, taxing the nerve and patience of the troops to the utmost. On December 11 they kidnapped a national service officer of the West Yorks, Lieutenant Moorhouse, who after a successful raid the previous evening was apparently tricked into stopping in a crowded street as he drove himself alone (against orders) back to his lines for breakfast. His vehicle was recovered, and a big black car was found abandoned, but despite determined searches no trace of Moorhouse was found. On the night of the 15th the guerrillas made their biggest effort, as if in the exuberance of their success. Grenades crunched, bullets cracked and rockets banged, and in the Arab town a company commander of the Royal Scots was mortally wounded. The tanks were brought in. Their machine-guns chattered their long, grating bursts, and the braves were hurt and chastened.

This show of force brought respite for the long-suffering 19th

Infantry Brigade and they encountered little harassment as they began to pull back to their final bridgehead. Yet one task still remained, and such were the fluctuations over its arrangement that it received the whimsical code-name of Yo-Yo. It was the exchange of prisoners, the 230 captured by the British and French, for the civilian ones impounded in Cairo.

The captive delegations—150 British, four Australians and 150 French (who since October had been without their Ambassador)— had already gone. They went by train to the Libyan frontier some four days after the cease-fire and were welcomed by the 60th Rifles, who manfully took on reception duties at short notice. The 470 "contractors" were also moved, thanks to urging by their Swiss protector. They went to more sophisticated schools, the Victoria College, Maadi, and the English School, Heliopolis, and enjoyed much better conditions, with a grant available for the purchase of a change of underclothes and better food. At last the day of deliverance was announced, December 20—only to bring frustration. The Egyptians had demanded the return of an officer prisoner flown away by the French, and the French, finding it hard to understand the British concern for the return of "*les entrepreneurs*", as the misleading word "contractors" was translated, did not feel inclined to bring this particular prisoner back. However, they relented to British urging, and at 7 a.m. on the 21st the contractors quietly slipped away by train from Cairo, bidden a friendly farewell by their prison commandant, who put on his civilian clothes for the purpose. The exchange took place at Kantara, under Indian and Finnish supervision—and at the tail of the Egyptians came General El Moguy, telling assembled reporters that if it were to begin again he would do the same, "Fight! Fight! Fight!" Soon the contractors were drinking tea served by British soldiers and chaffing them for not having troubled to come to their rescue. It was the end predicted by the Tory rebels to the civilian base experiment.

As the sun went down over Port Said next evening, Saturday, December 22, a solitary burst of automatic fire disturbed the gloom. It was aimed without success at the rearguards of the West Yorks as they withdrew to form a final cordon round the Casino Palace quay. There was the heavy rumble of tank engines and the last Centurions of the 6th Royal Tanks lumbered backwards up the ramp of a landing craft. The Yorkshiremen stood their ground for half an hour or so and then quietly followed them in, section by section. Only the brigade commander, Brigadier E. H. W. Grimshaw, remained on the quay. With him was a United Nations officer who had had Moorhouse pointed out to him in Cairo. He would be returned, it had been melodramatically promised, just as the ship was due to sail. Either it was a cruel game of cat and mouse or a ruse to hasten the British on their way. For Moorhouse was dead—suffocated, it was later claimed, because his captors had to leave him gagged in a cupboard while the British searched the house.

Soon after seven Grimshaw gave up his vigil and boarded his craft. As it sailed out to join the troopships and their naval escort, other craft set out from Fuad with the French rearguards aboard, keeping the alliance cemented to the last. Soon the whole of Port Said exploded in the wildest *feu de joie*. Tracer bullets sped skywards, flares set the night ablaze, and explosions rocked the town, reaching ears far out at sea and rumbling ominously round the galleys of those disguised ships of Her Majesty left behind on clearance duties.

Yet the Union Jack still flew. During the previous night proud and daring officers had scaled de Lesseps' statue and bedraped him with two great flags, the Union Jack and the Tricolour, and behind the statue stood a flagpole, the mast of which was coated with grease by an adventurer as he made his descent after nailing the Union Jack to its head. There was frantic scuffling round the base of these hated symbols as the ships sailed into the night. De Lesseps was successfully denuded and a few days later tipped, with the aid of dynamite, into his Canal. The grease, however, thwarted every frantic endeavour to climb the pole and in the end it had to be sawn down. It was a befitting gesture of farewell, symbolizing the end of an era far more appropriately than the modest affair six months previously.

CHAPTER TWENTY-THREE

Balance Sheet

(1957–67)

Two consequences of the crisis, stressing both its irony and pathos, were enacted early in the new year, 1957. On January 5 President Eisenhower showed that he at any rate was seriously worried about the "extent of Soviet penetration" which Lloyd claimed to have been revealed; he enunciated what became known as his Doctrine, seeking (and eventually obtaining) the permission of Congress to engage the United States forces in the Middle East if any of its countries called for aid "to combat international Communism". He thus took over the role of protector forfeited by Britain, with all its potential for mistrust and ill-will. On January 9 Eden yielded to the assault on his physique, the extent of which even members of the Cabinet had not realized, and placed his resignation before the Queen. A few public murmurs of sympathy and as many muffled snarls of cynicism greeted his retirement just when he might have been due, in other circumstances, to receive the Nobel Peace Prize. Assuming the mantle of "unflappability" to act as the tranquillizer so obviously needed, Harold Macmillan deftly set himself to the task of repairing the damaged economy and alliances.

Much debris, both actual and figurative, still remained to be cleared. With brave and rugged tenacity Israel clung to her gains in the Gaza Strip and the Gulf of Akaba in defiance of shooing by all member states of the United Nations, with the exception of her faithful ally France. She could acquire no formal pledge that the Egyptian power to block and hurt would be stifled, but eventually, on March 4, Ben Gurion ordered the withdrawal of his troops behind their frontier on the strength of "expectations and assumptions" derived from private talks at the United Nations. They were fulfilled. The Egyptians were denied military admittance to the Gaza strip and to the fortress of Sharm-el-Sheikh, both of which were occupied, together with a line on the Israeli side of the 170-mile frontier, by the United Nations Emergency Force. Its size originally was 6,615 all ranks, but so effective did it prove in keeping the peace that it was reduced over the years to some 3,500, consisting of five infantry battalions that occupied fortified observation posts and a large reconnaissance element that provided connecting patrols in white jeeps and armoured cars. Of the seven nations represented, India made the largest contribution, and on the retirement of Burns in 1959 an Indian took command of the force from the maze of single-storeyed cement structures that constituted its headquarters at Gaza. Thus Israel received fair reward for military victory—access to the Red Sea and a defensive screen along her Egyptian frontier, provided at other people's expense—and balm was provided for the nerves of the world that the heirs of the Pharaohs and the children of Israel should be kept apart by nurscrymaids capable of boxing ears if need arose.

Not until Israeli troops had gone did Nasser allow General Wheeler and his clearance team to complete their task in the Suez Canal. It was opened to ships of limited tonnage near the end of March, and on Monday, April 8—exactly twenty-three weeks since the Israeli assault presaged the blocking—the clearance was declared complete, though Britain and France, still hoping to impose their terms for its operation, forbade their ships to use it. Egypt published her terms on April 24, allowing no concession to international control other than recourse to arbitration for the settlement of individual disputes. The Security Council met to discuss the problem but soon adjourned *sine die* without reaching any decision. On May 13 Macmillan conceded victory to Egypt by announcing that the Government could no longer advise shipowners to refrain from using the Canal. France followed suit a little later, after a further abortive reference to the Security Council.

The opening of the spy trials in Cairo, on May 12, rubbed salt into the raw wounds of Britain's pride, but they were fairly conducted and the acquittal of two British subjects, against the imprisonment of two others, showed that justice had not been submerged beneath anger and further eased tension, which had already been relaxed by the freeing by Britain of some of Egypt's frozen assets.

Meanwhile Nasser's expansionist activities continued. In March Jordan not surprisingly terminated her treaty with Britain under the promise of compensating aid from her allies of the Arab League, Egypt, Syria and Saudi Arabia. This did not prevent a young officer revolution, inspired from Egypt, from developing against King Hussein, just as Eden had predicted in a letter to Eisenhower the previous September. Hussein suppressed it by his own staunch resolution. Deed was thereupon applied to the Eisenhower Doctrine, though in too clumsy a fashion to gain the gratitude of its beneficiaries. Hussein received the offer of a loan and a consignment of arms, and marines of the Sixth U.S. Fleet were landed at Beirut, allegedly on leave in the "tourist" manner favoured by dictators. Some three months later, that is in July, a revolt in the primitive Arabian sultanate of Oman, also organized from Cairo, was put down by the intervention of British troops, in old-fashioned style, in honour of treaty obligations.

These were Nasser's first setbacks, but he won the next round in this contest between the "tools" of Communism and Imperialism —as it appeared to outside observers, though not to the tools themselves. In the autumn, Syria, that hotbed of firebrand nationalism, brashly arraigned the United States and Turkey before the United Nations for planning to invade her. This gave Nasser his chance. He persuaded President Shukri El Kuwatly of Syria that military unity was not enough, and on February 1, 1958, the two men stood on the balcony of Abdin Palace and proclaimed the fusion of their countries into a single state, the United Arab Republic, drawing wild applause from their countrymen—but not, significantly enough, from their combined mentor and champion at the United Nations, the Soviet Union. Nasser was elected President, receiving 99.9 per cent of the votes in Egypt and 99.8 per cent in Syria. The kingdoms of Iraq and Jordan at once formed themselves into a rival Arab Federation, with the backing of Saudi Arabia, formerly Egypt's surest ally and financial promoter.

The Arab Federation did not last six months. It was blown to pieces on July 14, when the soldiers seized power in Baghdad, and Nuri es-Said, King Feisal II, and the entire royal family were massacred. It was a tragic day for Britain. Of all countries raised to nationhood from nothing, she had greatest cause for pride in Iraq, and inevitably grief at the fate of her former protégés was tinged with remorse by the thought that the Suez venture had made life perilous for all friends of Britain in the Middle East, however strongly they protested against it. Yet it is probable that Nuri would not have lasted much longer in any case. The man who had fought his way to power as a fiery young nationalist thirty-seven years earlier was now regarded by fiery young nationalists as a fossilized reactionary, and they sought to overthrow him in the only way they knew. The formation of the Arab Federation provided the final impetus, and according to the new dictator, Brigadier Karim Kassem, an order posting his brigade to Jordan spurred him to decision. The British Embassy was burned in the rioting, but British lives and property were not singled out for assault in a day of murder, looting and arson, and care was taken not to molest the oil firms or to disrupt their channels of supply. It was the end of the Baghdad Pact, however, and at the time it looked dangerously like a personal triumph for Nasser.

Fire-brigades were summoned fast to prevent the conflagration from spreading. Subversion in the Lebanon by agents of the United Arab Republic had already been the subject of investigation by a United Nations team, and as soon as Baghdad erupted, the American marines returned in force to Beirut, where they witnessed the establishment of yet another military regime, but by constitutional means. Sensing the knives being unsheathed around him, King Hussein also sent out an urgent call for aid, leaving it to the Americans and British to decide who should supply it. Eisenhower was glad of help in the application of his doctrine, and thus two battalions of the British 16th Parachute Brigade landed at Amman on July 17, as if in fulfilment of a treaty which had been dead for sixteen months. The Jordanians were amazed to discover that most of these men had fought at Port Said; according to their news service they had all been wiped out.

Controversy was in full blaze again. Russia and Egypt hurled their charges against the capitalist-imperialists, and despite the differing circumstances opponents of the Suez policy in Britain made strong protest against the intervention in Jordan, as if thirsty for more royal blood. The dispute duly reached the United Nations where in August an emergency meeting of the General Assembly was held, at which Eisenhower personally stated his case. The meeting came to a strangely peaceful end just when the division seemed implacable. Belying the propaganda that blared, and continued to blare, from their capitals, the Arab delegates emerged united with a resolution, which was unanimously adopted, pledging their respect for each other's system of government and their determination not to interfere. Nasser shed light on the design behind this resolution by having it announced in his newspapers: WE HAVE WON—for combined with the pious pledge by the Arab states was a request for the early withdrawal of the British and American troops.

Nasser was wrong. His aspirations to found a United Arab Empire had reached high tide, and from now on they gradually ebbed. Misadventure in the Sudan, fully independent since January 1, 1956, had already caused a lowering in his prestige, particularly in African eyes. In February 1958 he laid claim to areas of the Sudan, part of which would be flooded if the new Aswan Dam was ever built, and there were clear indications that he planned to gain control of the whole of Egypt's old colony by the established combination of political rising and military invasion. Both moves flopped disastrously. A small force was landed unopposed on the Red Sea coast and put the Egyptian flag up at Abu Ramada, eighty miles inside the Sudan. No screams of welcome went up from Khartoum, and when some Egyptian officials sailed with a small police force upriver towards Wadi Halfa they were ignominiously arrested at the Sudan frontier. Military columns, each of a brigade group, meanwhile set out from Aswan, one attempting an outflanking movement on Wadi Halfa, the other striking across the desert towards Abu Ramada. The first lost its way; the second was marooned by unforeseen problems of supply and many of its men died of thirst. The Sudanese Government made protest to the Security Council, and Nasser withdrew his force from Abu Ramada, brazenly accusing the Sudanese of absurd exaggeration in their complaints of "huge infiltration backed by concentrations of troops". The only success he achieved was in concealing from the world the misfortunes that had befallen Egyptian arms.

The Sudanese elections that closely followed the thwarting of this coup brought increased strength to the Umma Party, the main obstacle to Nasser's ambitions. However, he reached provisional agreement with them that summer over the distribution of the Nile water for the Aswan Dam project, and in October it was announced by Khruschev, at a reception given to Marshal Amer (as he had now become), that a grant of £33,000,000 would be forthcoming for the first stage of the work, for which Russian equipment was to be used. It was the great breakthrough for Nasser at last, even though the aid was no longer on the lavish scale once within his grasp. This was followed, on November 16, by a coup in Khartoum, organized on the pattern set by Nasser and with the same bloodless efficiency, and another military dictatorship was established. It was accompanied by expressions of goodwill to all and the closing-down of all pro-Egyptian papers.

The Arab countries showed over the next two years the same determination to resist the influence of Egypt. Kassem turned from a declared inclination to bring Iraq into the United Arab Republic to open hostility against it, and in the slanging match that developed he had a staunch ally in Khruschev, who nonetheless continued to meet the military needs of Egypt. Hussein meanwhile gained stature daily, having quickly dispensed with the services of the British paratroops, and became ever more assured in his defiance of Nasser.

On September 28, 1961, a blow was struck at Nasser's crumbling ambition, which he himself described as "graver than the aggression in Suez in 1956". Angered by the intrusion of Egyptian officers into their own units, Syrian army officers brought the Arabi-style revolt to full circle, seized control at Damascus, and declared the union with Egypt at an end, having made a prisoner of Marshal Amer, who had hurried to the scene of trouble. "I have ordered the armed forces to move on Damascus," Nasser declared in a broadcast. 120 Egyptian paratroops were dropped and promptly captured. A week later Nasser broadcast again. "Should Arab fight Arab?" he asked. He had decided not and had ordered the paratroops, even as they descended, to surrender. Syria might be in the hands of "a reactionary separatist movement serving the interests of the imperialists", but Arab unity had to come first and it was better that Syria should leave the United Arab Republic rather than wage civil war within it. He declared, however, that Egypt would retain the title of United Arab Republic, without presumably realizing how foolish it now sounded.

Still Nasser refused to accept the limitations which military inefficiency, that endemic ailment of post-war Egypt, must impose on a dictator's ambition. Early in 1962 he gave his soldiers another chance, this time to bring the archaic state of the Yemen within the

United Arab Republic in connivance with internal revolt. Again they were humiliated. Despite their tanks and aeroplanes they could not subdue primitively armed tribesmen, and at last, just as his brigades were becoming due for a second tour of service, he acknowledged defeat, although not in as many words. With great display of brotherhood and humility Nasser met the Royal Yemenis' patron, King Feisal of Saudi Arabia, at Jedda on August 24, 1965, and there signed an agreement providing for the withdrawal of all Egyptian troops within ten months. Shortly afterwards a military spokesman announced that there could be no confrontation with Israel for three or four years.

It looked at last as if Nasser had seen the folly in imperialist adventures and might now concentrate, with the wisdom of a Mohammed Aly, on the home problems that had so often before driven Egypt's rulers from search of solution to diversion: unemployment, food shortages, and the ever rampaging growth of population, cause of all other ills. As the High Dam at Aswan began to rise, results became more important than the publicity it could achieve, and they would always lag far behind promise if the military machine gobbled every piastre the State could raise.

Nowhere were there stronger hopes for the peaceful prosperity of Egypt than in Britain. The Suez intervention acted as a purgative. Treaties and trade agreements were blown sky high, and for three months there were vindictive expulsions and sequestrations, sometimes by order, more often by intimidation. Most of the remaining settlers of the Kitchener school were driven out—Wise Bey among them—and so too were 3,600 British colonials, the majority of them Maltese, many of whom found a new home in Australia. However, agreement was eventually reached under which the Egyptian Government promised to return all sequestered property and to pay compensation to the tune of £27,500,000, a not unreasonable sum for the claims that were made, and in December 1959 a British diplomatic mission returned to Kasr-el-Doubara. With the political relationship healed, but on a more remote and more relaxed basis, Britons found a warmer welcome awaiting them in Egypt than ever before. Experts with knowledge of Egypt's needs were asked over for consultation and were listened to attentively, with none of the suspicion of old: British brains and British equipment have made their contribution to the building of the High Dam, and it has been a larger one than the Egyptian Government would care to admit. Trade made a good recovery, the export figure from Britain reaching that of the pre-Suez years by 1961. Tourists returned in increasing number. Even in Port Said friendship was shown towards Britons such as had never been known in the old days, and officers of the British Army on leave in Cairo were invited by Egyptian officers to play polo with them at the Gezira Club. It was the great achievement of the British airmen and soldiers who attacked Egypt in 1956 that rage against their country so quickly subsided.

Sadly, the sun did not penetrate the clouds for long. Pride demanded that Nasser could not give up his role as self-appointed champion of all Arab people, and the role demanded that revolt must be nurtured in Aden. The ten months passed and the Egyptian troops were still in the Yemen, no longer offensively engaged against the Royalists but ready to march into Aden, on the advertised departure of the British, in support of the organisation that was trying, with raucous backing from Cairo, to gain control of the place by murdering as many people as it could.

Nor was Russia at all keen that Nasser should shirk his responsibilities as crusader-in-chief for the Arab cause, in other words as instigator-in-chief of trouble for the West. Russian arms poured in with such profusion that soon Egypt had over twice the number of tanks and twice the aircraft that she possessed before the destruction of 1956, and much of her equipment was the most modern available, such as Mig-21 fighters, Tupolev-16 bombers, and radar-controlled anti-aircraft missiles. The debt incurred for all these implements of war must far exceed revenue and was made all the more binding by an unfortunate disease that atrophied a cotton crop. And just to emphasise that Nasser's hegemony was not necessarily assured, the Russians also lavishly supplied Egypt's rival-ally, Syria, without revealing to the other the extent.

There was no neutral screen across Israel's frontiers with Syria and Jordan, and shells and murder gangs frequently came across them, drawing occasional reprisal from Israel. Ever the most hysterical in their cries of death to the pirate state of Israel, the soldier rulers of Syria constantly taunted Nasser for cowering behind his United Nations shield instead of renewing the fight against the common enemy. Yet the final, effective goad, according to Randolph and Winston Churchill, came from Russia. It was the Soviet Government that passed to Cairo the completely false information that the Israelis were massing their troops on the Syrian frontier. Nasser had to make some gesture, unless he were prepared to surrender all claim to the leadership of the Arab world. He sent reinforcements streaming into the Sinai desert, and on May 18, 1967, made formal request to the Secretary-General of the United Nations, U Thant:

"The Government of the United Arab Republic has the honour to inform your Excellency that it has decided to terminate the presence of the United Nations Emergency Force from the territory of the United Arab Republic and Gaza Strip. Therefore, I request that the necessary steps be taken for the withdrawal of the force as soon as possible."

When Hammarskjöld was Secretary-General, Britain and Israel had separately been given assurance that the United Nations force would remain until its task was deemed to be fulfilled, and in any case the General Assembly, not Egypt, had brought it into being and had the right to decide whether or not it should be terminated. But U Thant, apparently regarding the prestige of a nation as more important than its safety and perhaps from fear for the safety of his United Nations men—a constant brake on effective police action—took on himself the decision, and the very next day the United Nations flag descended on its pole at Gaza and the most valuable task performed by the organisation since its inception came to a sudden and alarming end. Nasser may well have been as surprised as anyone.

The situation was similar to that in a previous May, of 1948, when the withdrawal of British troops from Palestine compelled Egypt to turn posture into action. But there were differences, and among them was the enormous increase in strength of the Egyptian forces. Whereas scarcely one division could be deployed in 1948, as many as seven were now assembled in the Sinai, of which one belonged to the vaunted Palestine Liberation Army and two were armoured. The infantry divisions also had their own tank battalions, bringing the tank strength of the force to between 900 and 1,000. Its soldiers numbered 100,000, and allegedly a further 140,000 were under arms on the other side of the Canal.

The traditional preliminaries were observed. Announcements of complete preparedness, alertness, and solidarity were made simultaneously in Cairo and Damascus and received with wild delight by milling masses; Jordan, Iraq, and Egypt's former ally and recent enemy, Saudi Arabia, all proclaimed their eagerness to participate; commandos of the Liberation Army were accorded a rapturous send-off from Cairo; reservists were called up; and a

Jihad was declared from the Mosque Al Azhar. On May 22 Nasser declared the Gulf of Akaba closed to all Israeli ships and to ships carrying strategic material. This drew some empty gestures of protest from the United States and Britain for which they were cheekily rebuked by Nasser; having cancelled a consignment of grain, for the familiar reason that Egypt had again become too closely tied to Russia, Johnson's America was now identified as the "main enemy" and Wilson's Britain as her "lackey". The most sinister indication that something more painful than mere bluster was intended came on May 30. King Hussein of Jordan arrived in Cairo, to be kissed on the cheek by his would-be exterminator. He announced the signing of a defence pact, under which he agreed that Jordan's army should come under Egyptian command in the event of war. A similar announcement, made in Amman in October 1956, had goaded Israel to action once before.

Exactly what Nasser and his generals expected to happen is obscure—and perhaps it was to them too. The only offensive action they took was to send some shells, mortar bombs and murder gangs into the Israeli settlements. Their troops in Sinai were deployed in greater depth than in 1956, in better fortified positions, and at a strength of seven divisions as opposed to three. Perhaps they hoped to provoke an attack, or else that their mere passive might would eventually force Israel to her knees, forgetting that she too had been building up her armaments. Either way, the Egyptians displayed sublime complacence, fooled by the simulation of Israeli complacence. The newest fighters and bombers—pride of Russian technology—stood wing-tip to wing-tip on the airfields, almost as if decoys.

The awakening came at a carefully chosen hour, 7.45 on the morning of Monday, June 5. Skimming over the palm trees, Israeli aircraft appeared simultaneously over ten airfields on either side of the Canal and smote their runways and marshalled planes with rockets and bombs, and as one lot departed the next arrived. Slow to react as ever, the Egyptians could do nothing to retaliate, despite all the expensive equipment at their disposal. They were utterly overwhelmed by the sustained ferocity of the attack and in the course of three hours, during which most of the Israeli aircraft made three visits, they are reckoned to have lost more than 300 of their 340 combat aircraft: an estimate supported by the complete air supremacy so speedily gained by Israel. With more planes available and fewer to destroy, Barnett and his men from Cyprus and the Mediterranean had needed two days for the task.

Half an hour after their planes shuddered and lurched beneath the first attack, the Egyptian defences near Rafah came under sudden bombardment. The tanks followed, charging bull-headed for the objective with that most demoralising form of fanaticism that seems to draw inspiration from the destruction of the leading wave. A double-pronged assault was made, and in the afternoon the Israelis were in Rafah, having cut the Gaza strip at its base. All round them columns of black smoke billowed from the wreckages of tanks, and dead Egyptians lay in their hundreds across their battered defences. They had fought bravely, but their tank men in particular, even in the Stalins, had neither the skill nor presence of mind to compete with the dash and accuracy of their opponents. By nightfall the Israelis had bumped the perimeter defences of El Arish. There was no pause. The tanks crashed through and after desperate fighting the whole of El Arish had been captured by dawn.

Meanwhile another Israeli force—each was roughly of divisional strength—had been advancing on Abu Ageila in four columns. Soon after nightfall they completely enveloped this great Egyptian bastion, held by the 2nd Division. Paratroops were then landed by helicopter adjacent to the Egyptian gun lines. As they attacked from the north, a brigade of infantry on their left began to mop up the main defences under cover of a great artillery bombardment, and at the same time an armoured brigade swept in round the paratroopers' right. It was too much for the poor Egyptians. Like El Arish, Abu Ageila had fallen by dawn on this Tuesday morning.

The third Israeli force had the deepest penetration to make and it advanced its first sixty miles almost unopposed by taking a route deemed to be impassable—almost an Israeli habit!—between the two strongholds under assault, El Arish and Abu Ageila. The Tuesday was spent in smashing Egyptian reinforcement columns, and on the Wednesday morning two tank battalions set off on a dramatic dash for the Mitla Pass, fighting their way into position to block it that evening and leaving behind them a trail of their own soft-skinned vehicles, mostly ablaze. At the same time a column from the force at El Arish captured the village of Bir Gifgafa on the ridge north of Mitla astride the Ismailia road. Along the coast road the Israelis had already reached the Suez Canal.

The Egyptian troops that remained in Sinai had their exits

barred, and the skies above them buzzed with Israeli planes. There were some incredible scenes as they attempted escape. Near El Nakel a full brigade's complement of Stalin tanks was found unblemished and untended, the crews having abandoned them by order of their brigadier. Other brigades fought stoutly, and for them the journey usually ended in an inferno of flame, shot, smoke and sandcloud. At Mitla the carnage matched the congestion as vehicles piled up nose to tail, and Bir Gifgafa became a scrapyard for tanks come from east and west, some to counter-attack, some to escape. By the Thursday no Egyptian remained alive in the vehicles strewn so profusely round the two stops, and by that evening the Israelis, defying their exhaustion, had fought their way through to the Canal. Their enemy's losses in Sinai were as near total as any army has suffered, short of being driven into the sea.

Jordan proved a stauncher ally to Egypt than Syria. Her soldiers made attack from Jerusalem on the Monday morning, as soon as news reached them of events in Sinai. It cost them dear and by Wednesday night they had been thrown back beyond the Jordan. Not until the Friday morning, after the general acceptance of a cease-fire, were the Israelis able to deal with the real villains of the piece, the Syrians. They attacked them in their strongly fortified hill positions, from which the kibbutzes had suffered so much shelling over the years, and after a very tough fight drove them out. Evidence of Russian participation was obtained here, and there were reports that two Russian 'advisers' were captured. They might with justification, if not justice, have been publicly whipped as vicarious punishment for their masters in the Kremlin who had rushed to succour the state of Israel in childbirth, when it suited their mischievous purpose, and had then incited her simple, hot-headed neighbours to wage a war of extermination against her, supplying them with most lethal weapons for the purpose.

There were still some left of the 100,000 Egyptians in Sinai uncaptured and not yet dead. They roamed across the sand dunes and past the derelict vehicles, with no boots, no arms, swollen tongues, and despair stark in their eyes. Some were retrieved by the Israelis and shepherded across the Canal, and others collapsed and died with open mouths, a common enough fate for Nasser's soldiers. Most of these men had recently come from the Delta and had set off so jauntily before cheering crowds, duped into believing they would return as conquering heroes, despite all the evidence. Disillusionment had come in the most hideous form imaginable, and meanwhile the man whose vanity had sent them to their death was being reinstated as President by popular acclaim, after accusing the Americans and British of joining the Israelis in their air assault and making a display of penitence for the consequent "grave setback".

As for the Canal, the Israelis remained in occupation of its eastern bank, causing its blockage, and at the time of writing, three months after their arrival, they are still there. Nothing has been done to shift them, partly because the United Nations are disunited on this issue and partly because no one dare take independent action, although Russia and Algeria have been vying with each other in encouraging Egypt to continue the war. Stoically accepting an extra twopence on the price of petrol, the British seem to have forgotten that the Canal was meant to be their lifeline and happily go on driving their cars without restriction.

One result of this ridiculous and tragic course of events is that it is possible to see Eden's intervention in clearer perspective. Although the country made a rapid recovery, both in its economy and prestige, there has certainly been no diminishment in the anger of Eden's critics on left or right. His own former supporters are usually the most bitter. They complain that he took steps for "the protection of our vital interests and property" and achieved the wholesale uprooting of life, property, trade and representation, and this is true enough, although in the long run Britain's "vital interests" would appear to be the more secure the less close her political involvement in the area concerned. But their main charge is based on assumption that his primary purpose was to dislodge Nasser and that on his failure to do so all the tribulations that have since beset Britain in the Middle East and Africa can be laid. Neither assumption can be proved, and both are as easy to oppose as to support.

The words used by Eden himself, defending the ultimatum in the House of Commons, were, "The first and urgent task is to separate the combatants." They were not only separated but kept apart for over ten years, and now that they again have their claws in each other it becomes easier to appreciate that the task was well worth achieving. Cynics may say that its manner of achievement was far different from anything planned by Eden, but he had often expressed the desire to work "within the framework of the United Nations charter" and had in this same speech said, "If the United Nations were then willing to take over the physical task of maintaining peace in that area, no one would be better pleased than we." What is quite obvious is that the member states of the United Nations would never have been driven to the effectual and imaginative measure of raising a force to divide the combatants without the sense of crisis inspired by the intervention of two great outside powers. Any mere verbal initiative would have been smothered by Russia, that goad of Arab belligerence.

Yet the intervention produced only a temporary settlement, which it proved quite beyond the powers of the United Nations to turn into a permanent one. Its clumsy manner must carry some of the blame for this. Egypt could pose as victim of aggression, and as such she could be assured a sympathetic hearing, even if not immediate compliance, when she asked for the force to be removed in later years, while Britain, cast in the role of villain, was in no position to demand that it remain. It seemed to be forgotten that Egypt had started the trouble by conducting a campaign of terror raids, by insisting that she was still at war with Israel, and by flaunting her military might.

Such was the peril facing Israel—and it seemed very real at the time—that there should be no cause for moral indignation that Eden not only secretly acquiesced in her bid for survival but sought to turn it to lasting advantage. The pity was that he had to show such blatant favour to one side. If the Egyptians had been called upon to withdraw to a line ten miles east (instead of west) of the Canal and the Israelis to one thirty miles east of it (which would still have allowed them the entrance to the Mitla Pass) there could have been no complaints of partiality, and if the ultimatum had been accompanied by an invitation to the United Nations to send in a relief force, Nasser would be denied the role of victim and all the influence accruing from it, even if he survived the humiliation. Furthermore the military problem would have been much simplified. It would be necessary merely to ensure air supremacy and then drop a parachute battalion to block each of the three routes through the desert. They could be supplied by air until the United Nations troops arrived.

It seems most unlikely that such a plan was ever even considered, and the reason is that one was already worked out, and awaiting execution, for the seizure of the Canal. By clinging to this plan as a final means of settling a stale dispute, Eden placed himself in a strait-jacket. He ensured that when opportunity of a different nature arose, world opinion was against him, most of all that of the Arab states which he so coveted, his motives were suspect, and the military were committed to a course of action strangely out of alignment with one of their declared aims, separating the combatants, and in laughable contradiction to the other, safeguarding the Suez Canal. By his obsession with regaining the Canal, long after the political peril had become blatantly obvious, Eden deprived both himself and his soldiers of room for manoeuvre. And the cause, quite clearly, is that he allowed himself to become emotionally involved.

Emotion in fact emerges as the key by-product from a study of the years of the British occupation. Britain was cast in the role of possessive parent, Egypt in that of rebellious child, with each equally aggravated by the behaviour of the other, and this was apt to suppress the strong currents of affection running underneath. When at last the child threw off the final vestige of parental restraint, its most obvious reaction was to throw its weight about, cock a snook at the parent, and boss around the other much younger children who had been released from the political nursery while Egypt was still grappling with the unwanted parental embrace. Nasser was the embodiment of this urge for self-assertion, which has brought such tribulation to Egypt and should have long since been worked out of her system if only Britain had been prepared to treat her as an adult when she released her from Turkish rule.

As for the parent, it was intolerable to see the child behave in a petulant, irresponsible and aggressive manner. There was emotion enough at the parting, as evinced by the revolt of the Conservative M.P.s, for whom the sentries on duty on the Canal banks played as essential a part in the destiny of Britain as those outside Buckingham Palace. Most, however, were persuaded to support Eden's "act of faith". Egypt's hostility to the Baghdad Pact, her willing acceptance of Russian patronage, her vituperative propaganda, and its fruits displayed in the crumbling of British influence in Jordan, these aroused in the spurned parent all the passion of faith betrayed and when the final act of defiance was done, Eden vowed to prove to his critics that he was not the man to be wronged with impunity. Pathetically and ironically, he was confident that the world would watch with approving eyes as the punishment was meted out, just as it had done when Britain undertook the task seventy-four years earlier. Gladstone could order his ships to subject Alexandria to cruel bombardment without international protest and with only the faintest stain on his reputation for humane liberalism. Eden went to unprecedented lengths to strike without harming, and the world, so far from applauding, was aghast.

And still the fellah, that eternal footstool, waits stoically for the great tomorrow "when the apricots bloom". He is ruled now by his own countrymen, but he is as much slave to their ambitions as he was to those of the Mamelukes and he must uncomplainingly bear the cost of the military adventures for which the appetite, perversely, becomes the keener as each successive failure sharpens the national inferiority complex. His sons may no longer have to be dragged away to join the army, as were Ibrahim Pasha's conscripts, but they face greater danger when they go on service—and without tasting those brief moments of ecstacy to be derived from the defeat of the enemy. Indeed, their lot has closer similarity to that of Arabi's soldiers, who were the first to endure the shortcomings of the indigenous, town-dwelling officer corps. It makes little difference that Arabi's battle has since been won. Egypt may have her freedom, in theory at any rate, but her soldiers must still have their Tel-el-Kebirs.

APPENDIX

Appendix: Sources

CHAPTER ONE—The Invaders' Prey

13   Details of the departure were kindly provided by Brigadier J. H. S. Lacey, reinforced by newspaper reports.

The history of primeval conquests was drawn from Lieutenant-Colonel P. G. Elgood's *Egypt* (Arrowsmith, 1935), T. A. Doidge's *Alexander* (Houghton Mifflin, 1890), A. J. Butler's full and scholarly book *The Arab Conquest of Egypt* (Oxford, 1902), T. A. Archer and C. L. Kingford's *The Crusades* (Unwin, 1894), H. G. Wells's *The Outline of History* (Waverley Book Company, 1920), John Marlowe's *Anglo-Egyptian Relations, 1800–1953* (Cresset Press, 1954), and Tom Little's *Egypt* (Ernest Benn, 1958). The last two became great stand-bys and formed my main source of information for political and social developments within Egypt up to the time of the Suez crisis, with Marlowe predominating until the start of the Second World War, and Little thereafter.

CHAPTER TWO—The Coming of the French

I have leant heavily on J. Christopher Herold's vivid and excellently documented book *Bonaparte in Egypt* (Hamish Hamilton, 1962) and it is from this that the quotations by Lieutenant Desvernois and Bonaparte himself are drawn.

Also consulted: Alan Moorehead's *The Blue Nile* (Hamish Hamilton, 1962), which makes very good reading, and T. A. Doidge's *Napoleon* (Gay and Bird, 1904).

28   Lacey's experiences with the Turkish Army are vividly related in Lieutenant-Colonel E. W. C. Sandes's *The Royal*

Engineers in Egypt and The Sudan (Institution of Royal Engineers, 1937).

CHAPTER THREE—The Coming of the British

Britain's first victory over Bonaparte produced a crop of semi-official accounts, written by people who were there: Captain Thomas Walsh's *Journal of the late Campaign in Egypt* (London, 1803), Lieutenant Aeneas Anderson's *Journal of the Forces* (London, 1802), George Baldwin's *Political Recollections Relative to Egypt* (London 1801) and Colonel Sir Robert Wilson's *History of the British Expedition to Egypt* (1803). Wilson's is the most interesting of these and is quoted on pages 34-5 and 37.

The best source, however, is Hon. J. W. Fortescue's *History of the British Army*, Volume IV (Macmillan, 1906), which gives a majestic account of the landing and ensuing battles. Carola Oman's *Sir John Moore* (Hodder and Stoughton, 1953) is also of great value.

29-30   Abercromby's words are taken from Fortescue, p. 812.

38   Menou's words are from Herold.

39   Professor Henry Dodwell's *The Founder of Modern Egypt* (Cambridge University Press, 1931) was my principal source for the life of Mohammed Aly, though Marlowe also gives a good account of his rise to power.

40-2   There was no rush (understandably) to write the story of Fraser's campaign. I have relied on Fortescue, Volume VI, Scudamore Jarvis's article in the Army Quarterly, Volume XXIV, 1932, Colonel Hugh Pearse's history of The East Surrey Regiment and G. D. Martineau's of The Royal Sussex Regiment. Moore's views of the campaign, quoted by Carola Oman on pp. 412-3, are significant.

CHAPTER FOUR—Aly's Empire

Apart from Alan Moorehead's description of the Sudan campaign in *The Blue Nile* (see under chapter 2) there is a shortage of material on Mohammed Aly's military achievements. Pierre Crabitès's *Ibrahim of Egypt* (George Routledge, 1935) gives an interesting personal study of his subject but is sketchy on his generalship.

46   Lord Cromer's *Modern Egypt* (Macmillan, 1908)—the

foundation work for the study of the ensuing period—is good on the raising of Egypt's conscript army.

50   Colonel C. Field's *Britain's Sea Soldiers—A History of The Royal Marines* was my principal source for Napier's operations on land.

CHAPTER FIVE—*Mastheads Through The Desert*

Drawn primarily from : Hugh J. Schonfield's *The Suez Canal in World Affairs* (Constellation Books, 1952), from which the account of the inaugural proceedings comes; Sir Arnold Wilson's *The Suez Canal* (Oxford University Press, 1933), which is strong on the political developments and also quotes Sir Ian Malcolm's account of the opening ceremony from *The Quarterly Review*, January 1930; and Ferdinand de Lesseps' *Recollections of Forty Years* (Chapman and Hall, 1887).

57   Disraeli's reactions were drawn from André Maurois's *Disraeli* (The Bodley Head, 1927).

CHAPTER SIX—*Pride and Consequence*

Marlowe and Cromer form the foundation.

58-9   The book quoted is Edwin de Leon's *The Khedive's Egypt* (Sampson Low, Marston, 1879).

60   Mary Rowlatt's *Founders of Modern Egypt* (Asia Publishing House, 1962) tells the stories of El Afghani and Arabi and is full of interest, drawing freely on A. M. Broadley and W. C. Blunt. Desmond Stewart's *Young Egypt* (Allan Wingate, 1958) also ably gives the Egyptian viewpoint, tracing the struggle for liberation from Arabi to Nasser without rancour.

64   Interesting details of the bombardment are contained in Volume I of *Cassell's History of the War in the Soudan* (Cassell, undated), written by James Grant, who accompanied the fleet and reveals the outlook of the bombarders. Mary Rowlatt, whose grandfather was there, throws vivid light on the experiences of those at the receiving end.

64   Beresford is quoted from Rear-Admiral Sir William Jameson's *The Fleet That Jack Built* (Rupert Hart-Davis, 1962), which includes a lively chapter on his career.

65   Gladstone's letter to Granville is quoted from John

Morley's *Life of Gladstone* (Macmillan, 1912), which throws stronger light on Gladstone's reactions than Sir Philip Magnus's *Gladstone* (John Murray, 1954).

CHAPTER SEVEN—*The Subduing of Arabi*

Colonel J. H. Maurice's official *Military History of the Campaign of 1882* formed the backbone of this chapter. Wide use was also made of Joseph Lehman's splendid biography of Wolseley, *All Sir Garnet* (Jonathan Cape, 1964) and Commander Charles Royle's thorough work, *Egyptian Campaigns 1882–85* (Hurst and Blackett, 1900).

68   Wolseley's memo is taken from Maurice.

69   Lord Salisbury's views come from Gordon Waterfield's *Layard of Ninevah* (John Murray, 1963).

70   Rowlatt relates, first-hand, the experiences of the midshipman.

70   For Arabi's proclamation, see James Grant (see under chapter 6).

71   The description of Lieutenant-General Willis comes from Colonel R. H. Vetch's *The Life and Letters of Lieutenant-General Sir Gerald Graham, V.C.* (William Blackwood, 1891), also impressions of Tewfik.

72   Royle describes de Lesseps' anguish but admits the story may have become exaggerated.

79   A good eyewitness account of the fighting appears in John Gordon's *My Six Years With The Black Watch*, 1881–87 (The Fort Hill Press, Boston, Mass., 1929). Lieutenant-Colonel L. B. Oatts's *Proud Heritage: The Story of The Highland Light Infantry* was also used.

80   Sir Archibald Alison's account is as recorded by Grant.

81   For details of telegraphic communication, see Sandes's
1.24 *Royal Engineers in Egypt* (see under chapter 2).

81   Butler's words come from his autobiography, quoted by Lehman.

85   Rowlatt provides the story of Arabi's trial, imprisonment and retirement.

CHAPTER EIGHT—*The Victors Humbled*

Political developments are drawn primarily from Cromer. For a well-balanced picture of Gordon and his relationship

310

with Cromer (then Baring) Alan Moorehead's *The White Nile* (Hamish Hamilton, 1960) is recommended.

87   Rudolf Slatin Pasha's classic *Fire and Sword in The Sudan* (Edward Arnold, 1896) gives a vivid picture of events inside The Sudan, including the disaster which befell Hicks's expedition, and Hicks's quotation is taken from it.

93-7   The military story has been drawn from Royle, Lehman, Vetch (see under chapter 7) and of course from Sir Winston Churchill's *The River War* (edition used, Eyre and Spottiswoode, 1949). Martineau's history of The Royal Sussex Regiment, J. P. Jones's of The South Staffordshire Regiment, and Lieutenant-Colonel H. D. Chaplin's of The Queen's Own Royal West Kent Regiment were also used. John Gordon (see under chapter 7) gives a private soldier's view of El Teb, Tamai, and the Nile expedition.

94   Bordeini Bey's account was obtained by Major F. R. Wingate and recorded in his copious book, *Mahdism and The Egyptian Sudan* (Macmillan, 1891).

97   Kitchener's report is taken from Sir Philip Magnus's
l.31   *Kitchener—Portrait of an Imperialist* (John Murray, 1958).

CHAPTER NINE—Prestige Restored

Sir Winston Churchill is the main support of this chapter with his *The River War*, *My Early Life: A Roving Commission* (Thornton, Butterworth, 1930), and on the political side *A History of the English Speaking People*, Volume IV (Cassell, 1958). Extensive use has also been made of Magnus's *Kitchener* (see under chapter 8), supplemented by Sir Ronald Wingate's life of his father, *Wingate of The Sudan* (John Murray, 1955), who as Kitchener's staff officer accompanied him as far as Fashoda; also of Royle.

108-10   The Battle of Omdurman provided an unparalleled harvest for accompanying journalists. G. S. Steevens' *With Kitchener to Khartoum* (William Blackwood, 1898), a very lively book written in the style of an account of an M.C.C. tour, was published with such speed and profit that the one I consulted had Christmas greetings (1898) written inside it and yet belonged to the 13th edition—all within sixteen weeks of the battle. I also used Bennet Burleigh's *Khartoum Campaign* (Chapman and Hall, 1899), which is interesting for its photographs.

112,l.31   Churchill's quotation is from *The River War*, p. 362.

114   Details of the Denshawi incident were taken from *The Times*.

115   Cromer's address is taken from Tom Little (see under chapter 1).

116   The book referred to is Lord Edward Cecil's *The Leisure
l.38   of an Egyptian Official* (Hodder and Stoughton, 1921).

117   The book quoted is Sydney A. Moseley's *With Kitchener in Cairo* (Cassell, 1917).

CHAPTER TEN—Through Two Wars

For the preliminaries to the outbreak of war with Turkey I consulted Winston Churchill's *The World Crisis*, 1911–14 (Thornton Butterworth, 1923).

Elizabeth Monroe's excellent book *Britain's Moment in The Middle East, 1914–56* (Chatto and Windus, 1963) exerted influence on this and ensuing chapters.

118   The quotation is from Dr. Rohrbach's *Die Bagdadbahn*
l.17   published in 1911.

120   The quotation is from Lieutenant-Colonel P. G. Elgood's *Egypt and The Army* (Oxford University Press, 1924), which formed my main source for events in Egypt during the Great War, including Egyptian losses quoted on p. 122. The official history by Lieutenant-General Sir George Macmunn and Captain Cyril Falls, *Military Operations Egypt and Palestine* (H.M.S.O., 1928) and Colonel A. P. Wavell's *The Palestine Campaign* (Constable, 1928) were also consulted.

123   Wingate (see under chapter 9) throws interesting light on immediate post-war developments.

124   Details of the rebellion were drawn primarily from Sir Valentine Chirol's *The Egyptian Problem* (Macmillan, 1920).

115-8   Lord Wavell's *Allenby—Soldier and Statesman* (Harrap, 1946) predominates.

128   Details of the fighting come from Brigadier R. C. B.

312

Anderson's *History of the Argyll and Sutherland Highlanders* and the regimental magazine of the Leicestershire Regiment.

129   Impressions of Lord Lloyd have been drawn primarily from his own book *Egypt Since Cromer* (Macmillan, 1934), supplemented by Duff Cooper's review of it.

132-3   For the experiences of guardsmen at Kasr-el-Nil I am indebted to Mr. Andrew Forrest, Lieutenant-Colonel G. F. Turner, Mr. C. G. Lovekin, Mr. E. T. Farnworth, Mr. S. G. Greenway and the Editor of the *Household Brigade Magazine*. *Oriental Spotlight* (John Murray) by Rameses (Major C. S. Jarvis) gives a satirized but revealing picture of pre-war Cairo. Other, private, contributors remain anonymous.

133-4   The birth of the Free Officers' movement is as described in Colonel Anwar El Sadat's *Revolt on The Nile* (Allan Wingate, 1957), which I followed over matters in which the author was personally involved. I have also made extensive use of a biography of Nasser, *The Boss* (Arthur Barker, 1960), written by an American, Robert St. John, who drew deeply from Egyptian sources without losing his critical faculty.

134   For the withdrawal of Egyptian battalions, see Winston Churchill's *The Second World War*, Volume II (Cassell, 1949), p. 381. For the announcement of the fall of Sidi Barrani, see John Connell's *Wavell: Scholar and Soldier* (Collins, 1964).

135-6   For help over the Anglo-Egyptian relationship during the war years I am much indebted to Sir Charles Empson.

136-7   Details of the Abdin Palace ultimatum, so often distorted, were kindly related to me by Lieutenant-General R. G. W. H. Stone. *The Memoirs of Lord Chandos* (The Bodley Head, 1962) were also consulted.

137   The exposure of the plot is as related by El Sadat, who was imprisoned for his part.

139   The formation of the Arab League has been drawn primarily from Marlowe (see under chapter 1).

CHAPTER ELEVEN—Withdrawal

Monroe, Little, Marlowe and St. John form the main book

sources, backed by facts kindly provided by the Foreign Office librarian.

143
1.35

Lord Attlee's views come from Francis Williams's *A Prime Minister Remembers* (Heinemann, 1961).

144-6

Brigadier J. H. S. Lacey kindly provided information about the move of G.H.Q. to Fayid, Colonel F. H. Anderson and Major J. W. Barnes of the departure from Kasr-el-Nil.

CHAPTER TWELVE—Defeat

149
last
para

The quotations are from Dov Joseph's *The Faithful City* (Hogarth Press, 1962), p. 31, and from El Sadat (see under chapter 10), p. 90.

152-6

Major Edgar O'Ballance's *The Arab-Israeli 1948* (Faber and Faber, 1956) formed the basis for my account of the fighting and is, I believe, the only unbiased record available. Lieutenant-General Sir John Glubb's *A Soldier With The Arabs* (Hodder and Stoughton, 1957) and Netanel Lorch's *The Edge of The Sword* (Putnam, 1961) give good opposing accounts, while Nasser's thoughts and experiences were drawn partly from St. John, partly from his own *Egypt's Liberation: The Philosophy of The Revolution* (Public Affairs Press, Washington, 1955).

154

Lieutenant-General G. H. A. MacMillan's valedictory message comes from his article *The Evacuation of Palestine* (The Journal of the R.U.S.I., 1948).

CHAPTER THIRTEEN—Explosion

This chapter is drawn mainly from private sources against the background provided by Little, Marlowe and John Connell in his *The Most Important Country* (Cassell, 1957). I am particularly grateful to the late General Sir George Erskine and his former Chief of Staff, Major-General R. F. K. Goldsmith, for extensive help, and also to General Lord Robertson of Oakridge and to Major-General F. R. G. Matthews, who had command of the 1st Division. Their information is tempered by some from an anonymous non-military donor.

167

Major T. P. Shaw, Major J. F. Davis, Major Gaw and Mr. E. Inchbald, all of the Lancashire Fusiliers, very kindly gave eyewitness accounts of the battle for the police stations. *The Times* also contained a good account.

168-71 Little (who was there) and St. John both give very good accounts in their books of the burning of Cairo. Among those who gave private information I am much indebted to Brigadier C. Goulburn, who was the military attaché, to Major Alec Wise Bey for the details described, and to others who were there.

169 The quote is from Sir Anthony Eden's *Full Circle*
l.15 (Cassell, 1960), p. 232.

CHAPTER FOURTEEN—Revolution

This chapter is based primarily on Little, backed by an anonymous source.

176-7 For Farouk's appeals to the United States Ambassador and for the policy directive to the British Embassy, see Eden (as under chapter 13), p. 240.

CHAPTER FIFTEEN—Evacuation

I am very grateful to Lord Robertson, the Rt. Hon. Anthony Nutting and Major-General E. R. Benson for their help over the story of the negotiations.

187 l.12 The quotation is from Glubb (see under chapter 12), p. 377.

192-3 For the meeting between Eden and Nasser, see Eden, p. 221, and St. John, p. 161.

194-5 Glubb is interesting on the visit of Templer.

195 Terence Robertson's *Crisis—The Inside Story of The Suez Conspiracy* (Hutchinson, 1965) is well furnished with information from United Nations sources and gives a good account of Hammarskjöld's visits to Cairo and Tel Aviv.

196 The information on the Suez Contractors was kindly supplied by Major-General G. C. Humphreys and Mr. John Osmon.

CHAPTER SIXTEEN—Outrage

197, l.7 The story about the Syrian tanks is told by Glubb (see under chapter 12), p. 95.

198 I am indebted to Lieutenant-Colonel J. P. Fane, a
last former assistant military attaché, for his help over the
para general opinion on the Egyptian army.

200   The account referred to is from Herman Finer's *Dulles*
l.20   *Over Suez* (Heinemann, 1964).

201, l.5   The quotation is from Eden, p. 421.

201   The information on the seizure of the Domaine Com-
l.36   mune is from a private, fully reliable source.

202   The text of Nasser's speech is contained in the Royal
Institute of International Affairs' *Documents on the Suez Crisis*.

203   Nuri's advice also comes from a private source of high
l.23   reliability, with first-hand information.

CHAPTER SEVENTEEN—Plans Frustrated

My main public sources on the Suez crisis were: Sir Anthony Eden's *Full Circle* (see under chapter 13), supplemented by William Rees-Mogg's (pre-Suez) *Sir Anthony Eden* (Rockliff, 1956) and Randolph Churchill's *The Rise and Fall of Sir Anthony Eden* (MacGibbon and Kee, 1959); Guy Wint and Peter Calvocoressi's *Middle East Crisis* (Penguin Books, 1957), a very sound book, specially in its description of the approach of the crisis and its analogy to a Greek tragedy; Merry and Serge Bromberger's *Secrets of Suez* (Pan Books in association with Sidgwick and Jackson, 1957), a lively book by two French journalists; Paul Johnson's *The Suez War* (MacGibbon and Kee, 1957), which makes complementary reading to John Connell's *The Most Important Country* (see under chapter 13) in presenting the cases of the rival political parties; *The Record on Suez* (Manchester Guardian, 1956); A. C. Watt's *Documents on the Suez Crisis* (Royal Institute of International Affairs, 1957); Lieutenant-Colonel A. J. Barker's *Suez—The Seven Day War* (Faber and Faber, 1964), which gives a detailed account purely on the military side, drawn from many individuals in default of access to official records; and Terence Robertson's *Inside Story of the Suez Conspiracy* (see under chapter 15), which lives up to its title in that it contains revealing statements from the political leaders of France and Israel as well as reaching behind the scenes at the United Nations. Monroe, Little and St. John also provide useful material.

For information and views privately contributed I am grateful to the Rt. Hon. Viscount Tenby, Major Patrick Wall, the Rt. Hon. Anthony Nutting, Mr. Gordon Waterfield, Colonel H. V. Fraser, Major-General J. B. Churcher, Brigadier J. C. de F. Sleeman, and others who prefer to be nameless.

207, l.6   Dulles's words are as quoted by Terence Robertson.

212, l.1   Churchill's description is drawn from his *The Second World War*. Volume I; p. 201

212-3   Eden's reasoning has been derived partly from his memoirs, partly from a source of highest reliability.

213   For the quote on Gaitskell, see Eden, p. 320.

217   For Menzies' impressions on his visit to Cairo, see Eden, pp. 470–73.

218, l.41   For the quote on Dulles, see Eden, p. 484.

CHAPTER EIGHTEEN—*Ultimatum*

I have relied, as indicated, primarily on Robertson for the early part of this chapter.

225-32   Again Major Edgar O'Ballance has provided an unbiased account of the fighting, and I have used his book *The Israeli Campaign in The Sinai 1956* (Faber and Faber, 1959) as standard grist, leavened by Colonel Henriques's *100 Hours To Suez* (Collins, 1957). St. John provides useful information on the Egyptian side, and I am also in debt to private contributors.

228   Nasser's expectation is as revealed to Desmond Young
l.17   in *Young Egypt* (see under chapter 6) on p. 189.

228   Sir Humphrey Trevelyan himself very kindly gave me
l.23   this description of his interview with Nasser.

CHAPTER NINETEEN—*The Agonized Approach*

Robertson, Barker and private sources provide the ingredients to this chapter in about equal proportions, spiced by Captain D. M. J. Clark's *Suez Touchdown* (Peter Davies, 1964), an entertaining eyewitness account from an officer who accompanied the Malta convoy.

235   For the telegrams to Eisenhower, see Eden, p. 525–26.

236-7   For the interception over the Egyptian coast, see Eden, p. 524.

237	Air Chief Marshal Sir Denis Barnett very kindly told me how the air offensive started.
241	The attempts by the French to accelerate the operational timetable are condensed from the Brombergers and confirmed by private sources.
242 1.36 245 1.25	For the request for armoured reinforcements, see *Despatch by General Sir Charles Keightley* (London Gazette, September 10, 1957), also for the notice required for cancellation.
246	For impressions of Cairo I am grateful to Major Wise and Mr. A. R. Cutler, V.C.
246-7	For the imprisonment of the Contractors I am indebted to private accounts by two of them, Mr. J. E. Foden and Mr. John Osmon.
247-8	The scene at Port Said is as related by the Brombergers who arrived there two days later.

CHAPTER TWENTY—The Soldiers' Return

My chief published sources for the Battle of Port Said were Keightley's despatch (see under chapter 19), Barker, Clark, the Brombergers (for operations by the French), Brigadier Bernard Fergusson's *The Watery Maze* (Collins, 1961), C. A. Hogg's *Sound and Fury*, written by a subaltern who dropped with the 3rd Paras, from *The Unquiet Peace* (Allan Wingate, 1957), and *A Jump With The French* (from the Household Brigade Magazine), by Captain M. P. de Klee, who had command of the reconnaissance party of guardsmen.

Among those who kindly gave details privately were Brigadier J. H. S. Lacey and Lieutenant-Colonel J. M. Badcock, who were with Force H.Q., Major-General M. A. H. Butler and Major G. O. Mullins, of the Para Brigade, Captain M. J. Barrett, of the Royal Marines, Lieutenant-Colonel T. H. Gibbon, of the 6th Royal Tanks, and Mr. Peter Berry, who had command of the Buffaloes.

CHAPTER TWENTY-ONE — Military Might-Have-Beens

The criticisms made in this chapter have not been adopted from any outside source, public or private.

272   Henriques's words are to be found on p. 80 of *100*
l.21   *Hours to Suez*.

273   Crook's views come from a report written by himself.

CHAPTER TWENTY-TWO—*Farewell Again*

Barker had been followed in the main, bolstered by private information very kindly supplied by Major-General Sir Robert Hinde, who was chief Civil Affairs officer, Lacey, and others.

279   Sir Edwin Herbert's report Damage and Casualties in
l.29   Port Said (H.M.S.O.) gives details.

280-7   A good account of the activities of the 19th Infantry Brigade is provided by Lieutenant-Colonel Edward Fursdon, former brigade D.A.A. and Q.M.G., in *The Unquiet Peace* (see under chapter 20), under the heading *Musketeer*.

CHAPTER TWENTY-THREE—*Balance Sheet*

289   Information on the United Nations force, comes from the Secretary-General's report, kindly loaned by the United Nations Information Centre.

290-3   Lieutenant-General Sir John Glubb's *Britain and the Arabs* (Hodder and Stoughton, 1959) and Keesing's Contemporary Archives were my main sources for post-Suez developments.

292   The account of Egypt's military failure comes from a highly reliable source, in the know at the time.

295   For information on the British position I am grateful
l.3   to the Board of Trade and to private sources.

295   Details of expulsions were kindly provided by the Foreign Office Librarian.

INDEX

INDEX

Abbas Pasha, 52
Abdin Palace, 61, 84, 136, 171, 195
Abdulla, King, 152, 153, 195
Abdullah, Khalifa, 100–1, 106–10
Abercromby, Lt.-Gen. Sir Ralph, 29–34, 276
Aboukir, battles, 25, 27, 31–2, 71–2
Abu Ageila, battles, 156, 229–31, 298
Abu Hamid, battles, 98, 106–7
Abu Klea, battle, 95
Acre, battles, 26, 48
Aden, possession, 49
Adly Pasha, 126
Agreement, 1956, 186–91
Ahmed Pasha, 26
Al Azhar, Mosque, 25–6, 60, 231
Albanian troops, 34, 39, 41–3
Alexander the Great, 15, 20, 27
Alexandria, entered, 16, 22, 40, 69; expansion, 51; bombarded, 63–4; bombed, 135; objective, 210
Alison, Maj.-Gen. Sir Archibald, 79, 81, 84
Allenby, Fld.-Mrshl. Lord, 125–9, 130, 146
Amer, Maj. Hakim, 175; Maj.-Gen., 179, 184, 224, 227, 284; Mrshl., 293
Amr Ibn El As, 16
Arabi, Col. Ahmed, 60–5, 69–70, 76–85, 140, 146, 172, 185, 205, 240
Arab League, 135, 139, 141, 150, 156, 193, 290
Arab Legion, 151, 157
Arabs, invasion, 16; revolt, 148
Argyll and Sutherland Highlanders, 128, 283
Armoured Division, 10th, 207, 210, 242
Atbara, Battle of, 107–8
Attlee, Clement, 143–6, 149–50, 188–9
Austria, troops from, 50
Australia, troops from, 120, 138, 236, 238, 286
Azzam, Abdul Rahman, 150–1

Baghdad Pact, 192, 194, 291, 302

Baird, Maj.-Gen. David, 36, 38, 91
Baker Pasha, Gen., 90
Balfour, A. J., 113, 123
Balfour Declaration, 122, 135, 148
Bardisi Bey, 39
Baring, Sir Evelyn, 88–9, 91, 97; Lord Cromer, 103, 107, 114–5, 123, 129, 131
Barjot, Vice-Adml. P., 209, 241
Barnett, Air Mrshl. D. H. F., 237, 242, 261, 297
Beatty, Lt. David, 105
Beaufre, Gen. A., 207, 242, 265
Beersheba, battle, 153–6
Belliard, Gen., 37
Bengal Cavalry, 78, 80–3; Infantry, 81
Ben Gurion, 149, 155, 193, 195, 222–225, 228, 289
Benson, Maj.-Gen. E. R., 186, 190
Beresford, Lord Charles, 64, 97
Bernadotte, Count, 154–5
Bevin, Ernest, 142–3, 161
Beybars, Sultan, 18–19
Beylan Pass, Battle of, 48
Biselah, battle, 44
Bismarck, Count, 59
Black Watch, 33, 80, 91
Bonaparte, Gen. Napoleon, 20–7, 33, 37–9, 48, 51, 276
Bourgés-Maunoury, Maurice, 205, 244
Boutros Pasha, 115–16
Boyle, Sir Edmund, 257
Bredin, Lt.-Col. H. E. N., 266
Bright, John, 65
Bromberger, Brothers, 229
Brueys, Admiral, 25
Buffs, The, 165
Bulfin, Lt.-Gen. Sir Edward, 125
Bulganin, Marshal, 237, 257
Burns, Lt.-Gen. E. L. M., 281, 284, 289
Butler, Brig. M. A. H., 242, 251, 254–6, 263
Butler, Col. Sir William, 81

Caisse de la Dette, 103–4, 106, 113
Cairo, founded, 17; entered, 24–5, 28, 83–4; developed, 58; celebrations, 55, 190–1, 197; riots, 124, 168–9; bombed, 230; conditions in, 246
Cambridge, Duke of, 67
Cambyses, King, 14–15
Cameron Highlanders, 80–1, 111
Cameronians, 33
Campbell, Sir Ronald, 143
Capitan Pasha, 34–5, 38, 49
Capitulations, 21, 51, 112, 127, 130
Cecil, Lord Edward, 116–17
Challe, General, 223
Chateau-Jobert, Col., 251, 255
Childers, H. C. E., 67
Chou-en-Lai, 194
Churchill, Randolph, 295
Churchill, Sir Winston, 95, 109, 112, 134, 141–3, 162, 166, 168, 182–3, 188–9, 192, 212, 295
Citadel, The, 37, 43–4, 83–4, 144
Clark, Capt. Douglas, 259
Clemenceau, Georges, 65
Cleopatra, Queen, 15–16
Codrington, Admiral, 47
Coldstream Guards, 32
Connaught, Duke of, 70, 80, 84
Constantinople, conference, 63–5; Convention, 103
Cornut-Gentille, M., 236
Cromer, Lord, *see* Baring
Crook, Lt.-Col. P. C., 251, 254, 273
Crossman, Richard, 218
Curzon, Lord, 123
Cutler, A. R., 246, 269
Cyprus, as base, 68–9, 183, 208
Czecho–Slovakia, 153, 194

Daily Express, 14
Daily Mirror, 213
Damietta, 18, 35, 39
Darling, Brig. K. T., 248
Dayan, Maj.-Gen. Moshe, 222
Dean, Sir Patrick, 225
de Blignières, M., 59
de Freycinet, 62, 65
de Leon, Edwin, 58–9
de Lesseps, Ferdinand, 51, 52–6, 71–72, 260, 276, 287
de Lesseps, senior, 40
Dempsey, Gen. Sir Miles, 144
Denshawi, 114, 191
Desaix, Gen., 24, 26
Desvernois, Lt., 23

Disraeli, Benjamin, 56–7, 61, 68
Dixon, Sir Pierson, 236
Djemal Pasha, 120
Dongola, battle, 105
Doughty, C. M., 54
Dragoon Guards, 4th, 82–3; 7th, 75
Dual Control, 59–62, 88
Dulles, Foster G., 192, 200, 206–7, 214, 217–9, 235, 257
Dundas, Henry, 29, 36
Durnford-Slater, Vice-Adml. D. F., 241–2, 261, 265, 277, 285

Earle, Maj.-Gen., 98
Eden, Sir Anthony, 130–1, 135, 138, 150, 159, 162, 169, 181–2, 186–9, 191–3; Prime Minister, 201, 203–7, 211–25, 235–8, 243–5, 257, 263–4, 282, 285, 288, 300–3
Egypt, geography, 15; religion, 16; population, 113, 199; Protectorate, 119; independence, 127, 130–1
Egyptian Army, conscripted, 46–7; strength, 70, 152, 208; disbanded, 84; re-formed, 100–1; campaigns, 104–10, 152–7, 225–32, 296–300, 301
Egyptian Navy, 47–8, 155, 229
Eisenhower, President, 212, 217, 225, 235, 257, 264, 282, 288, 291
El Afghani, 60
El Arish, battle, 156, 231–2, 298
El Banna, Sheikh Hassan, 140, 142, 157
El Din, Fuad Serag, 163, 165–7, 183
Elfi Bey, 39
Elgood, Lt.-Col. P. G., 120
Elizabeth II, Queen, 204, 264
El Kuwatly, President Shukri, 290
Elliot, H. G., 55
El Maraghy, Mortada, 175
El Moguy, Gen., 255, 262, 286
El Sadat, Col. Anwar, 149, 177, 184
El Teb, battle, 90
Erskine, Lt.-Gen. Sir George, 163–6, 169–70
Essex Regiment, 93
Eugénie, Empress, 55–6

Farida, Queen, 174
Farnbacher, Gen., 211, 225
Farouk, King, 59, 130, 133–7, 139, 144, 150, 154, 160–3, 169–71, 173–177
Farrar-Hockley, Major A. H., 263, 266

Fashoda, 111
Fatima, 17
Fawzi, Dr. Mahmoud, 220
Fayid, 145, 152, 164, 196
Feisal I, King, 123
Feisal II, King, 203, 290–1, 294
Feluja, battle, 154–6
Fertile Crescent, 139
Festing, Lt.-Gen. Sir Francis, 175
Firket, battle, 104–5
France, policy, 21, 38, 49, 59–62, 65, 105–6, 113, 159, 205, 222; troops from, 208, 233, 240–1, 251–2, 254, 267, 287
Fraser, Maj.-Gen. A. Mackenzie, 40–2
Free Society of Officers, 134, 137, 140, 157–8, 174–5
Fuad I, King, 127, 129–30
Fuad II, King, 176, 179

Gaitskell, Hugh, 203, 211, 213, 218, 236, 244–5
Gambetta, L., 62, 65, 205
Gaza, battles, 15, 22, 152–6, 232, 298
George, Lloyd, 125
Germany, 113, 118, 134
Gezira Club, 131–2, 246
Ghuri, Sultan, 19
Gibbon, Lt.-Col. T. H., 266
Gilles, Gen., 252, 256
Ginnis, battle, 100
Gladstone, W. E., 56–7, 61–6, 68, 86–87, 89, 91, 98–9, 102, 303
Gloucestershire Regt., 32, 33
Glubb Pasha, Lt.-Gen. Sir John, 151–2, 187, 195
Gohar, Gen., 17
Gordon, Maj.-Gen. Charles, 89–96, 108, 112
Gordon Highlanders, 33, 80, 84
Gorst, Sir Eldon, 115–6
Goulburn, Brig. C., 177
Graham, Maj.-Gen. Sir Gerald, 75–6, 79–80, 90–1, 98
Grand Vizier, 27–8, 30, 35, 37, 48
Granville, Lord, 56, 62, 65, 86
Great Britain, major decisions, 20, 28–29, 40, 49, 53–7, 59, 65, 88–92, 98–99, 103, 106, 113, 119, 127, 130–1, 149–50, 204, 228, 264, 283
Greece, revolt, 47
Grenadier Guards, 73, 132, 196
Grenfell, Maj.-Gen. Sir Francis, 101
Grenville, Lord, 40
Grimshaw, Brig. E. H. W., 287

Guardian, 213
Guards Brigade, 1st, 71, 80–1, 166
Gulf of Akaba, blocking, 297

Hady, Abdul, 157, 183
Hafir, battle, 105
Haifa, 150–1, 154, 159, 229
Hamilton, Gen. Sir Ian, 94, 176
Hamilton, John, 176
Hamley, Lt.-Gen. Sir Edward, 75, 80
Hammarskjold, Dag, 195, 220, 263, 282, 296
Hankey, Robin, 183
Hardy, Lt.-Gen. Campbell, 265
Hartington, Lord, 92
Hassanein Pasha, 137
Hayes, Major, 39
Head, Antony, 186, 188, 225, 242
Heliopolis, battles, 16, 28
Henriquez, Col. Robert, 272
Hicks Pasha, General, 87, 92
Highland Light Infantry, 80–1
Hilaly, Neguib, 173, 175
Hilmi, Khedive Abbas, 103, 119
Hitler, Adolf, 135, 141, 199, 203
Hoare, Sir Samuel, 130, 132
Homs, battle, 48
Hunter, Maj.-Gen. Archibald, 106
Hussars, 19th, 94
Hussein, Ahmed, 200
Hussein, King, 195, 223, 290–3, 297
Hutchinson, Maj.-Gen. Sir John, 34–37

Ibrahim Bey, 20, 24, 26, 35
Ibrahim Pasha, 44, 47–51, 54–9, 70, 303
India, troops from, 36, 72, 77, 98, 282, 289; route to, 50–1, 56, 104
Infantry Brigade, 19th, 280, 285–6
Infantry Division, 1st, 72, 78, 164; 2nd, 75–8; 3rd, 164, 207, 242, 280
Iraq, 135; at war, 152–6, 296; 192, 290–1
Irish Guards, 132–3
Ismail, son of Aly, 45
Ismail, Khedive, 54–6, 89, 105, 127, 199
Ismalia, seized, 72–3; battle, 166–7
Israel, tribe, 14; state, 151; at war, 152–7, 225–32; 187, 190, 221, 297–300
Italy, 104, 129–30, 133–4

Jaffa, battles, 26, 30
Jengis Khan, 19

Jerusalem, 17–18; Mufti of, 148; 151–153
Johnson, President Lyndon, 297
Jordan, 151–7, 193–5, 221–4, 290, 295–7, 299, 302
Joseph, Dov, 149

Kadler, M., 247
Kafr Abdu, 165
Kamal, Sultan Hussein, 119, 127
Kasr-el-Nil, 61, 84, 132, 145, 170
Kassassin, battle, 74–6
Kassem, Brig. Karim, 291, 293
Keightley, Gen. Sir Charles, 209, 241–242, 245, 264, 269, 273, 276, 284
Keith, Lord Admiral, 28
Khalifa, see Abdullah
Khartoum, 46, 87–97, 112, 128, 293
Khrushchev, Nikita, 237, 293
Killearn, Lord, see Lampson
King's Royal Rifle Corps, (60th), 80, 286
Kitchener, Maj. Herbert, 94, 97; Col. 102; Maj.-Gen. Sir, 104–11; Lord, 112, 116–7, 118–9, 120, 129, 131
Kléber, Gen., 27–8, 30, 37
Konia, battle, 48
Kress von Kressenstein, Col., 121

Lacey, Brig. J. H. S., 13, 261, 265
Lacey, Capt. Thomas, 28
Lampson, Sir Miles, 129, 131, 134, 136–7; Lord Killearn, 139, 142–3, 166
Lancashire Fusiliers, 162, 167–8
Lancashire Regiment (P.W.V.), 32
Lancers, 16/5th, 128; 21st, 108–10
Lebanon, 152, 291
Leicestershire Regiment, 128
Libya, 17, 138, 210, 242
Life Guards, 72, 145, 204, 220, 280
Lincolnshire Regiment, 110
Lloyd, Lord, 129, 146
Lloyd, Selwyn, 195, 219, 224, 235, 282–3, 288
Lodge, Cabot, 235–6, 257, 282
Lorraine, Sir Percy, 129
Louis IX, King, 18
Louis XIV, King, 21
Lowe, Maj.-Gen. Drury, 75–6, 82–4

MacDonald, Lt.-Col. Hector, 109–10
MacDonald, Ramsay, 127
MacMillan, Lt.-Gen. G. H. A., 154

Macmillan, Harold, 194, 283, 288, 289
Macpherson, Maj.-Gen. Sir Herbert, 77, 82
Madoc, Brig. Rex, 259
Mahdi, The, 86, 89, 91, 95–7, 99–100, 181
Maher, Ahmed, 139, 142
Maher, Aly, 134, 136–7, 171, 173, 176–8
Mahmoud, 106–8
Mahroussa, 55, 59, 176
Malta, 21, 30, 69, 209, 233
Mamelukes, 18–20, 23–4, 36–43, 65, 114, 303
Marchand, Major, 111
Mareri, Count, 256, 260
Massu, Gen., 233, 241, 261, 281
Maurice, Col. J. F., 73
Maxwell, Lt.-Gen. Sir John, 119, 121
Meade, Maj.-Gen. Hon. R., 41
Mecca, 17, 44, 49
Menon, Krishna, 257, 282
Menou, Gen., 30–1, 33–4, 36, 38
Menzies, Robert, 214–7
Middle East Command, 138, 142, 144–6, 183, 209
Middle East Supply Centre, 138, 141
Milner, Lord, 126
Missett, Major E., 39–42
Mitla Pass, battle, 226–9, 298
Mohammed Ahmed, see Mahdi
Mohammed Aly, 27, 34, 39–52, 113, 133, 144, 174, 177
Mohammed, Prophet, 16, 17
Mohieddin, Maj. Khaled, 184
Mohieddin, Col. Zakaria, 179
Mollet, Guy, 205, 222–5, 234, 257, 264, 282
Molotov, V., 192
Moltke, Gen. von, 49
Monckton, Sir Walter, 225
Monroe, Elizabeth, 141
Montgomery, Fd.-Mrshl. Lord, 68, 138, 144, 275
Moore, Maj.-Gen. John, 30–1, 33–5, 37
Moorhouse, Lt., 285, 287
Morrison, Herbert, 161, 182, 204
Moseley, Sydney, 117
Moslem Brotherhood, 140, 145, 150, 157, 160, 163, 168, 184, 191
Mounted Infantry, 73, 82–3, 93, 114
Murad Bey, 20, 22, 24, 26–7, 36
Murray, Gen. Sir Archibald, 121–2

Nahas Pasha, Mustapha, 129, 131, 136–7, 161–5, 171, 178
Napier, Commodore, Sir Charles, 50
Napoleon I, Emperor, see Bonaparte
Napoleon III, Emperor, 54, 56
Narriman, Queen, 174, 176
Nasser, Gamal Abdel, Lt., 133; Capt., 137, 140, 155–9; Col., 174–5, 177, 182–7, 191–6; President, 197–204, 211–9, 224, 228–32, 256, 268–9, 281–2, 289–97, 300–1, 302
N.A.T.O., 161, 186–7, 192
Navarino, battle, 47
Nazib, battle, 49
Negev, The, 154–5
Neguib, Gen. Mohammed, 174–9, 181–5, 192, 211
Nehru, President, 194, 201, 213
Nejumi, Wad-al-, 102
Nelson, Adml., 22, 25
Nile, the, importance, 15; Battle of, 25; expeditions up, 23, 34–5, 45, 92–7, 104–11; use of water, 128, 130, 292
Nokrashy Pasha, 143, 146, 157
Nubar Pasha, 59, 89
Nuri-as-Said, 139, 192, 203, 212, 223, 290–1
Nutting, Anthony, 190–1, 236
Nuwar, Aly Abu, 224

O'Ballance, Maj. Edgar, 153
Observer, 244
Omdurman, Battle of, 107–11
Osman Bey, 36
Osman Digna, 90, 92, 98, 102, 107–8, 110
Osman Rizky, 61
Ottoman Empire, see Turkey
Oxfordshire and Buckinghamshire Light Infantry, 67

Paget, R. T., 203
Palestine, 122, 139, 144–6, 148–50
Palmerston, Lord, 49–50, 53–4, 56
Parachute Regiment, 164, 169, 207, 242, 249–54, 266–7, 291
Pelusium, 14, 16
Peres, Shimon, 222
Persia, 14–15, 159, 161
Pineau, Christian, 205–7, 220–4, 234, 244, 264
Port Said, 13, 55; seized, 72; battle, 247–67
Power, Vice-Adml. M. L., 273

Ptolemies, 15, 55
Pyramids, Battle of, 24–5, 210

Queen's Own R.W. Kent Regt., 280
Queen's Royal Surrey Regiment, 41

Rafah, battle, 230
Rahman, Sir Sayed Abdul, 181
Ras-el-Tin Palace, 64–5, 176
Riad, Governor, 247, 261, 279
Riaz Pasha, 61, 85
Robertson, Gen.-Sir Brian, 168, 182–183, 198
Robertson, Terence, 222, 234
Rohrbach, Dr. Paul, 118
Roman Empire, 15–16
Rommel, Gen., 135–7
Rosetta, battle, 40–2
Rothschild, Baron, 57
Rouchdi, Col. Hassan, 255, 262, 280, 284
Roy, Jean, 280
Royal Air Force, 130, 164, 247, 267
Royal Artillery, 90
Royal Engineers, 28, 83, 91, 94, 165
Royal Horse Guards (The Blues), 72
Royal Irish, 80, 94
Royal Irish Fusiliers, 37, 80
Royal Marines, 50, 72–3, 80; Commandos, 207–9, 233, 258–62, 267
Royal Military Police, 281
Royal Navy, 90, 130, 253, 261, 278
Royal Scots, 280
Royal Sussex Regiment, 42, 67, 93, 96, 165
Royal Tank Regiment, 209, 215, 220, 233, 260, 280
Royal Welch Fusiliers, 32, 207
Ruffn, M., 26
Rushdi Pasha, Hussein, 119, 123
Russell, Earl, 54
Russell Pasha, 146
Russia, 38, 47–9, 99, 103, 147, 149, 151, 161, 188, 204, 256–7, 295, 299, 302

Sabry, Capt. Aly, 179
Sabry, Hassan, 134
Said Pasha, 52–3, 56
Saite Pharaohs, 14
Saladin, Sultan, 17–18, 26
Salem, Wing Cmdr., Gamal, 179
Salem, Major Salah, 179, 181, 184, 187
Salisbury, Earl of, 18

Salisbury, 3rd Marquis of, 69, 102–3, 106–7, 113
Salt, Consul-General, 47
Sami, Mahmoud, 62
Sarras, battle, 101
Saud, King, 212
Saudi Arabia, 152, 294, 296
Scots Guards, 33, 71, 84
Seaforth Highlanders, 42, 72, 81
Selim, Sultan, 19
Serapeum, battle, 120
Sève, Col., 46
Seymour, Adml. Sir Beauchamp, 63–64, 68, 70, 72, 84
Seymour, David, 280
Shaiqiyas, 45
Sharett, Moshe, 190
Shea, Maj.-Gen. Sir John, 125
Shepheard's Hotel, 51, 58, 136, 168
Shepilov, Dimitri, 195, 198
Sherif Pasha, 61, 70
Sherine, Col. Ismail, 175
Shirkuh, Gen., 17, 20
Shubra Kit, battle, 23
Sidky Pasha, 143–4, 146
Sinai Penisula, seizure, 298–9
Sirry Pasha, 173, 175
Sirry Pasha, 173, 175
Slatin, Rudolf, 96
Slim, Fd.-Mrshl. Sir William, 182
Smart, Sir Walter, 177
Smith, Sir Sidney, 26–7, 31
South Staffordshire Regiment, 69
Spaak, Paul-Henri, 282
Stack, Maj.-Gen. Sir Lee, 127
Stansgate, Lord, 143
Stephenson, Lt.-Gen. Sir Frederick, 92, 100
Stevenson, Sir Ralph, 170, 177, 183, 186, 190
Stewart, Lt.-Col. Herbert, 83; Maj.-Gen. Sir, 95–7
Stewart, Col. J. D. H., 94
Stewart, Brig.-Gen. William, 41–2
Stockwell, Lt.-Col. C. M., 81
Stockwell, Maj.-Gen. Hugh, 151; Lt.-Gen. Sir, 207, 211, 241–2, 248, 261–5, 273–4, 276, 279–80, 284
Stone, Gen., 70
Stone, Lt.-Gen. R. G. W. H., 136–7
Sudan, The, campaigns, 45–6, 86–99, 104–11; Convention, 112, 127, 130, 144, 181; troops from, 46, 80, 101, 104–11, 128, 155; 292
Suez, 36, 51, 71, 136, 164–5

Suez Canal, early projects, 14, 21, 51; making, 53–6; seizure, 68, 72; Convention, 103, 113, 159, 187, 212; defence of, 120–1, 135, 144, 188; users' conference, 214; pilots, 219; blocking, 239, 285, 300; unblocked, 289
Suez Canal Company, 53, 56–7, 116; seized, 202–3
Suez Canal Contractors' Company, 196, 246–7, 286
Suez Canal Zone, occupation, 145–6; evacuation, 190, 196, 213
Syria, 14–17, 26–7, 48, 135, 152–7, 193, 197, 221, 290, 293, 295, 299

Taha, Col. Sayyid, 155
Tailyour, Lt.-Col. N. H., 260
Talleyrand, 21
Tamai, battle, 90
Tchikov, Anatoli, 256, 262, 280
Tel-el-Kebir, 68, 75; Battle of, 78–82; 166, 172, 190, 196, 303
Templer, Gen. Sir Gerald, 194–242
Tewfik, Khedive, 59–63, 69, 71, 82, 84–6, 103
Thant, U, 296
Times, The, 198
Tippoo Sahib, 21
Tito, Marshal, 192, 201
Tokar, battle, 102
Toski, battle, 102
Treaty, 1936, 130–1, 142, 147, 156, 159; abrogated, 162, 186
Trevelyan, Sir Humphrey, 228
Tripartite Declaration, 159, 191, 199
Tuman, Sultan, 19
Turf Club, 168, 246
Turkey, invades, 19; policy, 26, 39–40, 47–50, 53–4, 63, 103, 118–9, 187–8, 192; troops from, 24, 27, 30, 34–7, 42, 45, 90, 120–1
Tussum, battle, 120
Tussun Pasha, 44
Tyn, H.M.S., 242, 256, 265

United Arab Republic, 290, 293–4
United Nations, 139, 146, 149–50, 153–4, 195, 219, 235–6, 238, 243, 257, 282, 300–1; emergency force, 281, 289, 296, 301
United States of America, 55, 149, 151, 162, 182

Victoria, Queen, 56–7, 71, 81, 84, 98, 112

Wafd, 123, 127, 140, 160, 171, 179, 184
Wahabis, 44
Wakil, Zeinab, 183
Walsh, Capt. Thomas, 36
Waterhouse, Capt. Charles, 189, 196
Watson, Capt., 83
Wauchope, Maj.-Gen. P., 41
Wavell, Lt.-Gen., Sir Archibald, 134–135, 275
West Yorkshire Regiment, 282, 285–6
Wheeler, Gen. R. A., 284–5, 289
William II, Kaiser, 57, 118
Willis, Lt.-Gen. Sir George, 71
Wilson, Prime Minister Harold, 297

Wilson, Rivers, 59
Wilson, Lt.-Col. Sir Robert, 24, 37
Wingate, Col. Reginald, 111; Sir, 123–5
Wise Bey, Major Alec, 170, 246, 294
Wodehouse, Col. Josceline, 102
Wolseley, Lt.-Gen. Sir Garnet, 67–78, 81–84; Lord, 92–4, 97–8, 270, 276
Wood, Maj.-Gen. Sir Evelyn, 100
Worsley, Major R. E., 265

Yemen, the, 49, 293, 295
York and Lancaster Regiment, 74, 80
Yunes, Maj. Mahmoud, 203

Zaghloul Pasha, Saad, 123–9, 131
Zobeir Pasha, 89